WAYLON

WAY

A BIOGRAPHY

by R. Serge Denisoff

THE UNIVERSITY OF TENNESSEE PRESS / KNOXVILLE

Frontispiece: Composite line drawing created by Tom Walker expressly
for presentation in this volume.

Clothbound editions of University of Tennessee Press
books are printed on paper designed for an effective
life of at least 300 years, and binding materials
are chosen for strength and durability.

Library of Congress Cataloging in Publication Data

Denisoff, R. Serge.
  Waylon: a biography.

  Bibliography: p.
  Includes discographies and index.
    1. Jennings, Waylon. 2. Singers—United States—
Biography. I. Title.
ML420.J36D4 1983 784.5'2'00924 [B] 82-24786
ISBN 0-87049-387-6

TO THE "CASUALTIES"

When the flowers bloom
I feel they will never leave.
—GABRIEL R. BATY, 1982

CONTENTS

ILLUSTRATIONS

ACKNOWLEDGMENTS

This book would have literally been impossible without the help of many people who provided information, photographs, and other materials. I especially want to thank Mick Brady, John L. Smith, and Roberta Plunkett for supplying leads and all sorts of esoteric data. In alphabetical order I would like to acknowledge the aid of a vast number of people who allowed interviews or provided written responses. Some wished to remain anonymous. The "on-the-record" folks were:

Richie Albright
Tommy Allsup
Herb Alpert
Chet Atkins
Bob Bare
Paula Bateson
Don Bowman
Mick Brady
Sonny Curtis
Fred Danker
Bill Denny
W.J. ("Hi-Pockets") Duncan
Duane Eddy
Chet Flippo
Kinky Friedman
Chuck Glaser

Tompall Glaser
John Goldrosen
Bob Hilburn
Harlan Howard
Bill Ivey
Felton Jarvis
Tommy Jennings
Frank Jones
Kris Kristofferson
Grelun Landon
Don Larson
Bob Luman
Loretta Lynn
Dan McPhail
Mike McQuade
Bill C. Malone
Jack Miller

Bob Montgomery
Ralph Mooney
Topper Morris
Jerry Moss
Nitty Gritty Dirt Band
Ray Odum
R.A. Peterson
Roberta Plunkett
Floyd Ramsey
Neil Reshen
Billy Ray Reynolds
Virgie Risinger
Gamble Rogers
Mrs. Betty Rood
P.J. Russell
Pat Salvo
Roy Silver

Hazel Smith   Virg Warner   Johnna Yursic
John L. Smith   Peter Yarrow
Tanya Tucker   J.R. Young

Lauretta Lahman and Pat Carpenter aided considerably by transcribing what seemed to be miles of tape. Barbara Asmus, as always, did a splendid job of typing and preparing the final manuscript. Theresa Delorto's and Kathy Hill's help is also appreciated.

R. SERGE DENISOFF

PREFACE

While researching *Solid Gold: The Popular Music Industry,* I was impressed by the differences between Nashville and the rest of the music business. Music City even in the early 1970s was a throwback to the producer-dominated early 1950s in pop music. Nashville was a closed community of omnipotent producers, a handful of session people, a few booking agents, and music publishers. Collectively, they decried faceless corporate executives in New York and Los Angeles. Remarks frequently were passed dealing with the "new" morality or lack of it in the rock scene. Music City seemed to be a fortress designed to preserve something of the old in an ever-changing world. At the same time, I was intrigued by a group of artists who appeared to be challenging the system. Dave Hickey in *Country Music Magazine* labeled them "telecaster outlaws." The renegades were Tompall Glaser, Willie Nelson, and Waylon Jennings. Beginning to look into this area, I quickly found that any one of these gentlemen would make an interesting subject for a book, but Jennings was the one who best epitomized the conflict in Music City. More than Glaser and Nelson, Waylon symbolized the barbarian at the gates of Nashville. His background in music was southwestern— West Texas and Phoenix. He had worked under the middle-of-the-road tuteluge of Herb Alpert in Los Angeles. According to the masters of the "Grand Ole Opry" and other traditionalists, he wasn't "country." He is also a unique individualist whose life alone would make an outstanding movie and perhaps already has in *Pay Day*.[1]

After several years of interviewing and digging through some of the most esoteric magazines and newsletters possible, I was able to assemble the story of an individual and also an organizational structure. As the facts accumulated, it became increasingly difficult to separate the two. It is a saga of the West Texas kid who, after some twenty years in the business, finally makes it big and on his own terms—or so it would seem. The story may have an Horatio Alger flavor. Rags to riches is nothing new to the music business, as any record company publicist will happily proclaim. But there is much more. The invisible forces of the Nashville system are always present. Jennings, by all rights, should have been a superstar years ago. It didn't happen until Waylon, Willie, Neil Reshen, and the Glasers challenged most of the conventional wisdom and sacred cows in Music City.

In writing this book, I have tried to stay out of Waylon's private affairs as much as possible. The "roarin'," as the song says, "you already know." Indeed, Waylon's lifestyle and people's perception of it frequently beclouds the central import of the man and his music.

Waylon once told a journalist, "If I was everything that people make me out to be, I'd be dead long ago." Perhaps his road life at times paralleled that of the late Hank Williams, Hank Jr., and John R. Cash prior to his "born again" phase. Most of the rumors and stories, however, are impossible to substantiate. Many are more lore than fact. Readers of the *Music City News* would be shocked to find that many of their favorite clean-cut country *and* gospel favorites "mess around" while touring: "That's road life." In this book, only those relationships that affected Waylon's career are treated.

Waylon: A Biography is the story of a unique individual and the social forces that influenced his life.

R. SERGE DENISOFF
July 1982

WAYLON

WAYLON

Introduction

GETTING INTO WAYLON JENNINGS

"Overnight sensation" is one of those catch phrases that brings knowing smiles to the faces of people involved in the record business. "Yeah! He's *only* been around for twenty years" comes the sarcastic retort. On June 22, 1974, "This Time" became the top country single on the *Billboard* charts. Three months later, "Ramblin' Man" reached the same position. Subsequent singles followed suit. *Outlaws* became country music's first album selling over a million units. *I've Always Been Crazy* was the first Nashville product to "ship gold," or sell 502,000 copies. "Waylon Jennings became an overnight sensation," or so it was said. Things, it appeared, were finally coming together for the bearded singer with the black and white leather guitar. It took twenty years of recording for Waylon to finally reach the top spot in the country chart. He had yet to crack the sacred soil of Top Forty radio. The nearest thing to a pop hit was his recording of Jimmy Webb's "MacArthur Park," which barely made the ninety-third position for two weeks. "I couldn't go pop with a mouthful of firecrackers" says Waylon, only half-joking. But he obviously has.

Waylon Jennings is an enigma. He is too much an individualist to do things the easy way. But his time has come, although success has not been easy. Nonconformity has its price, especially in country music. Waylon has never fit any neat category. His musical directions frequently have been misunderstood. He has made unorthodox choices: country singers aren't supposed to

record hard rock material like "Honky Tonk Woman." Waylon is
his own man. He doesn't wear sequined cowboy suits or introduce many of his songs while on stage. He doesn't look like a
country artist. He isn't an "Okie from Muskogee." He publicly
admits to having taken "uppers" and has been married four
times. Country singers are not supposed to do things like that.
Understandably, he doesn't like labels. "You kinda get lost like
after a while," he says, "because you lose all identity when you
put a bunch of labels on one thing."[1]

There is something different about the singers that have come
out of southwest Texas: they are neither hillbillies nor pop
crooners. They have the potential to succeed and fail in both
fields. It is no coincidence that the rebels and outlaws of Nashville all seem to have Texas birth certificates. Their careers are as
hard to manage as they are to categorize. Many of Waylon's fans
have grumbled about his management and his recording company. "They're not doing enough for Waylon," complains Roberta Plunkett, who has been a fan since his Phoenix nightclub days.
"They just don't know what to do with him!"[2]

From the very beginning when he was playing with Buddy
Holly, there was never much doubt that Waylon possessed an
extraordinary amount of talent. Presenting and packaging that
talent has always seemed a problem. On his RCA Victor albums,
Waylon was touted as someone who had "it."[3] Some nine years
after his signing with Victor the liner notes were still trying to
explain Waylon to record buyers. One of his most ardent fans
explained, "Waylon is a performer who will make you *listen* to his
music, not just *hear* it."[4]

The trade magazines, *Billboard, Variety, Cashbox,* and some
music critics repeat the same line. *Los Angeles Times* critic, Bob
Hilburn reported, "There can be both a rugged, uncompromis-
ing strength in Jennings' voice and an amazingly delicate sensitiv-
ity. 'He ought to have a Number One record every time,' Phil
Spector, who has produced so many Number One records over
the years, said from a ringside table as Jennings sang 'The Chokin''
Kind.' And I'm tempted to agree. The public has discovered
Kristofferson's music in recent months and hopefully they'll
soon discover Jennings."[5] In fact, nearly every article on Jennings urges people to "get into Waylon Jennings." RCA released a
promotional album with that title.

By 1974 after Waylon had been recording for seventeen years,
people finally were getting the message. Waylon continued to be

the hardcore individualist. His public appearances typically have been uneven, a mix of brilliance and seeming indifference. Bob Hilburn, long a Jennings fan, says: "part of his problem seems to have been attitude. He has proven to be a terribly inconsistent performer. He gave such an indifferent concert at the Shrine Auditorium one night that the audience response wouldn't even have registered on an applause meter. Yet, he came back a few months later to the Palomino Club in North Hollywood and gave one of the best performances I've seen."[6] When writer Jay Elher asked him about the criticisms, Waylon replied, "I've worked on that because of those articles."[7]

Midwest Nashville, now a rock club, was another stop on the country circuit. A converted bowling alley near downtown Toledo, Ohio, the club featured fairly well-known performers like Bob Luman, Tommy Cash, and Waylon Jennings. The club booked Waylon in for two nights in May of 1974.

As with all openings featuring a "name" artist, disc jockeys and a few press people mingled at a table set aside for Waylon's party. WTOD (Toledo's main country station) disc jockeys were visible with their flaming red jackets reserved for such occasions. Slowly the cast began to appear as Johnny and the Hurricanes opened the bill. Johnny Paris is Toledo's rock contribution to the world of popular music. "Red River Rock," the big hit of years ago, resounded in the background. First, guitarist Billy Joe Reynolds, then harmonica wizard Donnie Brooks come upon the scene. They looked more like Austin "street people" than country musicians. The rest of the Waylors were no different. Paul Randall, a tall blond Texan just appointed RCA's Nashville publicity person, greeted a reporter with the usual cop-out, "I tried to call you." Finally, the road manager Johnna Yursic and the headliner appeared. More introductions and "soul shakes," which seem to link the record industry in some invisible but knowing manner.

"I'll be damned. I used to play his records in Lubbock," said Waylon, referring to Paris. Waylon actually was flattered that Johnny Paris was his warm-up act, despite the fact the Hurricanes hadn't had a hit record in over a decade.

There is an aloof air about Waylon Arnold Jennings. He's not the usual run-of-the-mill country or pop music performer. There is a stand-offishness that is reminiscent of a hundred grade-B gunfighter movies: the man in black who both commands respect and stirs a bit of uneasiness. "You don't fool around with a ramblin' man," goes his song. Many writers have commented on

this quality. One critic described Waylon as "a rugged—somewhat renegade—figure who can exhibit traces of tenderness and
understanding."[8] *Newsweek's* Maureen Orth wrote, "Jennings,
dressed all in black, managed to look ornery and sensitive at the
same time." Former *Rolling Stone* contributor John Grissom declared, "Deep down he may even be a cad. Yet the honesty and
the openness is there. He's likable."[9]

While Johnny and the Hurricanes continued to play, members
of the Waylors wandered around the cavernous club stopping to
have an occasional beer. Johnna Yursic protectively monitored
people's access to Waylon.

"I want to do an interview," a reporter told the manager.

"You into his music?" he questioned.

A few obscure Jennings songs were mentioned. Yursic whispered something to Jennings, whose eyes shifted in the writer's
direction.

"He'll see you at five tomorrow . . . at the Holiday Inn," said
Yursic, dismissing the writer.

"Waylon will be up in just a minute," announced Johnny Paris
from the stage.

That was the signal. Waylon politely excused himself and left
to get his custom-made Fender Telecaster already tuned by a
band member. One of the red-coated deejays appeared on stage
to introduce Waylon but not before plugging the station and
current contest. "Be sure to get your own, 'TOD bumper
sticker . . . ."

Waylon opened the first of three sets with "Only Daddy That'll
Walk The Line" and rapidly ran through a mix of his hits and
material from his album *This Time*—it had just been released. A
handful of devotees sat on the dance floor just below the singer.
Waylon has never liked dancing when he's playing, so they were
safe. Rarely does he introduce his songs or talk to the audience.
This night, once, between Willie Nelson songs, he paused and
remarked, "This guitar's been with me through three wives and a
helluva lot of recruits." Laughter. "Pick Up the Tempo" follows.
There was meaning there *if* one knew the song was about
Waylon. More puzzling was that the song was from *This Time* and
yet no reference was made to the album. Country performers are
notorious for plugging everything from slick picture books to
autographed color pictures; albums are their bread and butter.
Even surly rock bands remember to say, "This is from our new
album."

Photograph taken at the Nashville West in Toledo. John Rockwell,
Popular Music and Society, copyright 1974.

Billy Reynolds had laryngitis and missed several choruses. Waylon only laughed. Once, a kickoff was missed, and the Waylors stopped. "My fault," apologized Waylon and resumed the song. (Unlike most performers, Waylon does not have sets planned. He starts, the Waylors follow.)

During the break Waylon returned to the table and signed autographs. He stood up to have his picture taken with various fans. The flashbulbs nearly blinded him, but he was cooperative and gracious. Handing the napkin and pen back, he said "Thank you," returning to his Coke.

"He's great," said the Victor publicist.

The converted nodded. But the audience did not seem convinced. Applauses were polite. It was Friday night and many were more concerned with what would happen after the show than with the performance. The magnetism of the singer was fairly well hidden. Not long before, the *Boston Phoenix* had characterized Waylon's performance as "lacking luster" and "mechanical."[10] In Las Vegas, he had been called "erratic." All performers have off nights. Nevertheless, there was always the unique Jennings sound.

The sorrowful baritone voice that underscored the idea that even outlaws are subject to deeply felt pain was not easy to ignore. Even on an off night Jennings was better than most singers. The reaction of many of the ladies at the club was incredible. Long-haired street girls as well as farmers' wives with their blond beehive wigs were mesmerized. For them, "Ladies Love Outlaws" was more than just a Lee Clayton song; it was a fact of life. There was little doubt about it: Waylon Jennings has charisma, a quality most superstars must have. Peter Yarrow of Peter, Paul, and Mary once said, "To be a star you have to have that magic or charisma. You can't merely be one of the audience."[11] Waylon Jennings has that elusive quality, "it."

The next day, a reporter and photographer arrived at the Holiday Inn. "Waylon's just getting up," explained Yursic. "It will be another fifteen minutes." Performers are never on time for interviews. Johnna thumbed through his schedule book, occasionally pulling out press clippings. Waylon often complains about the press: "they're too demanding." Johnna's customary reply: "It's just friends. It's all on the basis of friendship."

It was apparent on this occasion that there was some invisible means to get to Waylon Jennings. Time passed as the usual industry gossip is exchanged. At 5:25 P.M. the phone rang and the press people were ushered into room 417, which was just another bland Holiday Inn suite: the same two beds, sitting chairs, 17-inch television, and dull reproductions hanging on the wall. Jennings sat on the bed, propped on a pile of rumpled pillows, sleep still in his eyes. Introductions were repeated.

"I can use some coffee! You guys want anything?" asks Waylon.

"You started with the Texas Longhorns . . . ."

"Damn," he exclaimed, "where'd you hear about that?" He seemed genuinely surprised.

"Let me play you something." The opening bars of Waylon's first record, "Jole Blon," filled the room.

"Where the fuck did you get that?"

"Is that the first record?"

"That was it," he laughed. "Goddamn." The whole atmosphere changed. "Jole Blon, Hey, Hey, Hey," he sang several more lines.

The stand-offishness was gone. Even some of the weariness had disappeared from his eyes. The passport to Jennings, what his manager called being "friends," was starting to surface. The key, for Waylon, is being accepted. He demands more from his fans and the press than most artists. "Communication" or "re-latin'," he calls it. Once the communication is established, Jennings is warm and open. At fan fairs, he would stand for hours posing for pictures and signing autographs. He would also give a frank and open interview.

Chain-smoking Winstons, Jennings acknowledged his ten-year struggle with Nashville, taking pills, and whatever else the reporter wanted to know.

"You don't introduce any of your songs?"

"I'll tell you what it is," answered Waylon. "I've seen so many country acts in particular, that will sing themselves right on top and then talk theirselves right into a hole and just bury it . . . . I'm a singer basically and that's what they come to hear is our music . . . we try to give 'em twice as much as anybody else." It became fairly apparent that Waylon did care, but he would not be willing to do just anything to satisfy people and the demands made on him. "The way to get my dander up in a minute is to say I owe them that."

In an angry letter to a fan he once wrote, "All I owe anyone is a good performance as an artist and entertainer. . . . I am thankful for my success. I worked hard for years and no one gave me

"On the Road: Another Holiday Inn" in Toledo. John Rockwell. Courtesy of *Popular Music and Society*, 1974.

anything."[12] Waylon wants to be a superstar and to do it on his terms. He considers glitter rock artists like Alice Cooper and David Bowie as sensationalists, but he refuses to put them down, saying, "It's their thing."

After two hours, the interview was finished.

That night at Midwest Nashville, Waylon Jennings was a different performer. The charisma and magnetism only hinted at the night before now fully on display. Few could have surpassed him that night. "Only Daddy" again opened the show. Willie Nelson songs joined Kris Kristofferson's "The Taker" and "Bobby McGee." Waylon mentioned *This Time* after singing "Pick Up the Tempo." He joked—introducing the band. "Short stroke, the girls in Denver call him," he said, pointing to drummer Richie Albright. "Donnie Brooks lives in New York but don't hold that against him."Sammi Smith came by and helped Waylon through "MacArthur Park."

"He's terrific. He should be a big star," a patron said.

A local review of the concert concluded, "Waylon Jennings is the best male vocalist in all pop music and at Midwest Nashville he showed why." This view was not shared by everyone.

"It is only when talent and desire are nearly balanced does success come," according to Teddy Bart, a Nashville television personality; "the mixture of talent, desire, and perseverance are the ingredients."[13] Talent is a fleeting quality that is defined by the record industry and the public, usually in that order. "You can be a musical genius, but if you can't get it to the right persons, you might as well be zero," acknowledged Johnny Paris. Buddy Holly, Herb Alpert, and Chet Atkins all thought Waylon had talent, as they produced him. Fellow artists and musicians agree. Kris Kristofferson: "The best damn country singer around." One of Tanya Tucker's backup men: "Whew, he's gonna be the next superstar. He's something else."[14]

Waylon has perseverance. He has been in the business for nearly twenty years and has logged millions of miles, playing Kentucky bars with dirt floors and west Texas honky-tonks. He did about 300 dates a year. The road is a hard and demanding mistress. The endless highway miles take their toll. "It's boring," admits Waylon; "the green and yellow sign of the Holiday Inn ain't the most beautiful thing. You have to get up for shows, basically, mentally. You have to get yourself geared to it. It's hard to do that, you know. Just to keep doing it year after year, day after day. When you traveled all that distance. That's where people get on pills and booze and what have you."[15] The road has caused Waylon other problems. Touring killed Buddy Holly when Waylon was traveling with his group. One of the Waylors died on a slick, icy Illinois bridge, an accident that nearly cost Waylon two million dollars. Richie Albright, Waylon's friend and drummer, quit the band after bumping through Crab Orchards (Rowdy country—music night clubs) in a pickup truck. He later came back. Donnie Brooks left for good. Waylon has been playing clubs and traveling since he was fifteen.

Talent and perseverance are easy to define, but desire means many things. some music people see desire as doing *anything* for success. "Artists must give the public what it wants" is a commandment in the boardrooms of Columbia, Capitol, and RCA Victor.

There are limits to what some people will do to achieve stardom. Some artists, including Waylon Jennings, feel that there should be limits to one's effort to please people. When asked to sing "Back In The Saddle Again," Jennings remarked, "Hell, I'm country . . . but I ain't that country." He occasionally refuses to do requests. Many fans like "Green River," which was a big hit for Waylon. "I despise it. I can't stand that song. I can't stand to sing it." He pauses, "I'm sorry, but right or wrong, good or bad, I'm me and they're going to have to take it the way it is." Waylon's individualism goes beyond not doing "Green River" or Gene Autry and Roy Rogers songs. His music, appearance, and lifestyle are a real concern with died-in-the-wool fans and writers. A writer complained in the *Las Vegas Panorama*: "Waylon, ditch your filthy clothes, take a bath, get a shave, act like an entertainer, and come back to the country fold, where your roots are and with the people who gave you your start."[16]

"I could never have been a rock singer," answers Waylon. "I'm a country person, a country boy, whatever you call it, cow person." Although he has recorded songs by the Beatles, the Rolling Stones, and the Allman Brothers, he considers himself a country singer. Doing what *other* people want is a constant problem for any performer. A popular saying in Top Forty radio is, "people know what they like and like what they know." This goes double in country music. Country music fans are loyal, but they don't like changes. There is an irony to this because most country artists long for pop hits. Chet Atkins, director of A & R (or production) at Victor, declared, "There's not a hillbilly in this town who doesn't want those pop hits. So the problem you have, is he goes into the studio and he wants to compete with Andy Williams. He wants to go pop or rock. There's not a chance. The thing he should do is stay with his country audience because they'll stay with you. You can have one hit record in country and live on it the rest of your life." Atkins expanded this argument: "The gas station attendant, the farmer, the trucker, the average blue collar worker is the country music audience. They don't want to analyze lyrics. Just hit 'em in the face with it."[17] Waylon's music does just that, but it also contains lyrics by some of the best songwriters in Nashville. He resents the idea that good lyrics turn off country fans. Waylon told Chet Flippo, "That's one of the big problems of country music. They don't want the country folks to know very much and they don't give 'em credit for knowin' very much. Country fans are as *smart* as anybody and it's an insult to 'em when a program director says, 'Well, that song's too *deep* for our audience.' Bullshit!"[18] Songs by Kris Kristofferson, Mickey Newbury, Lee Clayton, and others do have pop potential, but the more traditional country deejays often do not like them. Waylon Jennings, for years, was caught in this squeeze.

Dan McPhail's bitter comments, quoted above, go beyond Waylon's music. He disapproved of Waylon's shoulder-length hair, his clothing, and his entire lifestyle. In the rock world little would be said, but some country fans who remember Waylon's powder-blue stage costume and 1950s slick down pompadour even prefer that to his "hippie" look. His first famous drug bust caused problems. On June 10, 1969, two of the Waylors, Jimmy Gray and Richie Albright, found themselves in the Niagara Falls jail charged with the possession of marijuana. The amount was small. They were arrested at the Rainbow Bridge connecting the United States and Canada. *Music City News*, then the influential country music paper, warned Waylon, "There is nothing that would turn him [the fan] away, however, nothing he would draw the line at faster than a country singer's using marijuana."[19] Waylon didn't smoke pot, but many of his fans and friends thought he did. "All they do is smoke on that bus," one famous country singer said. "That's not 'relatin'.'"

There are other demands and expectations. Producers have a certain sound in their head when sitting behind the glass in a recording studio. Waylon thinks that a good producer "makes the artist do his thing." He has argued with producers over what goes on tape. Once, he announced, "I want to cut this song today."

"We cut that yesterday."

"We did," he replied, "your way! Today we're gonna do it my way."[20]

Promoters and nightclub owners want the artist to be "up" for a show, even if he or she has traveled 800 miles by bus that day. They also demand to hear the artist do hit songs from many years past. "If people drive fifty miles and pay their money," says agent Roy Silver, "baby, you'd better do the songs they want to hear."[21] Sometimes Waylon will—but on other occasions, he won't. Despite his popularity in the Nevada and Arizona region, numerous clubs in Tucson and Las Vegas refused to book him. Ideally, an artist is on the same wavelength as his fans, management, producers, and disc jockeys. This is not always the case. Many talents, for all kinds of reasons, have chosen to march to a different drummer. Waylon Jennings is one of those people.

He has fought with a series of wives, producers, radio station owners, managers, and even fans in order to chart his own course. Promoters and some disc jockeys even claim Waylon is "spooky" or unreliable. Waylon doesn't think so, he revealed to an anonymous interviewer: "The artist should control what's happening to him. That's career-wise and especially in the recording studio. It's your life that's it. When you're an entertainer, if you have no control over what's happening to you; it can drive you crazy." Waylon believes he should determine the rise and maybe even fall of his career. Waylon Jennings is an individualist. Dismissing him as a "bad ass" or "spooky" is a mistake. Musicians and critics alike see him as having all of the talent it takes for superstardom. However, his entire career has been plagued by cross-currents. Many were his own doing, but others no one could control. "Getting into" Waylon's music is easy, but understanding the man requires a bit more.

1

RHINESTONE SUITS AND BIG SHINY CARS

The night life ain't a good life,
but it's my life . . . .

I've always been crazy
but it's kept me
from goin' insane

. . . the devil made
me do it the first time.
Second time I done it on my own.

Low down freedom, you done cost me
everything I'll ever lose.

Music City is more a state of mind than a reality. Music City, as Nashville's country music section is called, is a mere cluster of eight blocks in a run-down part of the city's south side. Music City Square is a collection of modern recording studios nestled between weather-worn, old, brick, two-story houses. Sixteenth Avenue, South has come a long way. *Time* and *Newsweek* have devoted cover stories to the Nashville Sound. Willie Nelson has made the front of *Newsweek*. Over 1,534 radio stations daily air its product. Nearly 20 percent of record buyers today identify themselves as country music fans. The days of "hillbilly" music are long since dead. Country music is no longer tied to rural regions of the south and Midwest. Frank Mancini, RCA's promotion director, estimates that 51 percent of the singles sold are recorded in Nashville. Country music is now *very* big business.

Country music's going "uptown" hasn't been all that smooth and easy. From the beginning, the simple folk sound of the Kentucky hills was challenged by new musical styles and ideas. Blues, jazz, and rock 'n roll all impacted upon the "Grand Ole Opry" and the studios on Sixteenth Avenue, South. Nashville's traditional way of doing things has been challenged by so-called outlaws and renegades such as Bob Wills, Tompall Glaser, Willie Nelson, and the outspoken Waylon Jennings. The widespread popularity of country music today is partly attributable to the mavericks and rebels of Music City.

Country music is a child of the marriage of southern folk song and commerce. It was sired by balladeers from the hills and hamlets of West Virginia, banjo pickers from Kentucky, traveling patent-medicine hawkers, and the National Life and Accident Insurance Company. This was a unique marriage in which the simple values of fundamentalist religion and hard work were wedded to contradictory and explosive elements of southern life. Songs about hard drinking and violence were sung in the same breath as religious hymns. Both music and the lyrics were a mirror of a region where the bars and stripes remained a forceful symbol. Early country music sharply defended rural values against the big city, the agnostic Clarence Darrow and evolutionist John T. Scopes, and ineffective Prohibition. The famous "Monkey Trial" at Dayton, Tennessee, was applauded in songs such as "Bryan's Last Fight,"Vernon Dalhart's "The John T. Scopes Trial," and Uncle Dave Macon's "The Bible's True": "God made the world and everything that's in it/He made man perfect and the monkey wasn't in it."[1] Moonshining songs like "Green Corn" and "Mountain Dew" weren't in keeping with the national edict:"The call it that good ole' mountain dew/Them that refuse are few."

The basic simplicity of the music had tremendous commercial potential, especially for record makers and those plotting to sell anything from political candidates to life insurance policies. In 1927, National Life sponsored the first "Grand Ole Opry" broadcast on WSM; the show quickly captured the attention of millions of radio listeners on Saturday nights throughout twenty states. Record promoters like Ralph Peer scoured the rolling hills and valleys to find performers like the Carter Family and Fiddlin' John Carson. Sears's mail order catalogs prominantly featured the latest recordings of "hick" performers. The records were billed as "traditional music." From its inception, country music was the voice of a region as well as a product to be bought and sold.

For its fans it was something special, sound untainted by the city slicker (or so it appeared—Vernon Dalhart, the voice on "The Wreck of the Old 97" and "The Scopes Trial," was in fact Texas-born Marion G. Slaughter, a light opera singer from New York).[2] The Carter Family's "No Depression in Heaven" was as much creed as a popular record: "I'll leave this world of toil and trouble,/My home's in heaven, I'm going there." Paul Hemphill, author of several books about the South, recalled in his *Nashville Sound*:

> My old man, who came out of hamlet in East Tennessee when he was thirteen years old and spent his whole life working the coal mines and the railroads and the truck lines out of Birmingham, came closer to understanding Jimmie Rodgers than he did, say, Kate Smith, for God's sake. So he listened to the country stations because they spoke his language and he really couldn't care less if most of the rest of the country *did* call it "hillbilly" music. The music was his music and he liked it, and it did something for him when he heard it and that is what music is supposed to be all about.[3]

From the beginning, the regional and class consciousness of country music was pervasive. It's Li'l Abner aspect gave performers and fans a strong feeling of solidarity. Bass players who doubled as comedians found warm responses to their stories about the foibles of city dwellers. Even the name "Grand Ole Opry" was a comentary on the outside world. It didn't matter that others called it "hillbilly" or "shitkicking" music or that the city fathers of Nashville looked askance at the "Grand Ole Opry" as not being in keeping with their image as the Athens of the South. Fans and performers knew it was reaching as many people as had President Roosevelt's fireside chats in the region.

By the late 1930s no one could doubt the importance of the "Opry" or the loyalty of country music fans. Success provided a formula. "Ole-timey" *was* country music; fiddles, guitars, banjos, mandolins, and autoharps *were* the tools of country pickin'. The "Opry" elaborated strict rules of conduct that covered a wide area. Only certain string instruments could be played on the stage of the Ryman Auditorium, and drinking, smoking, and cussing were not tolerated. Artists were tied to a certain number of appearances at very low pay. Few objected, as WSM's 50,000 watts provided maximum exposure.

As the Bill Monroes, Hank Snows, and Roy Acuffs dominated the Saturday night airwaves, states farther west were evolving a musical sound of their own. Originally, this sound came wrapped in the guise of a singing cowboy. The singing cowboy was a continuation of America's long love affair with the West as well as a response to the talking movie. Motion picture star Ken Maynard was the first popular gunslinging good guy who sang pretty ballads when not catching outlaws. Hollywood producers, seeing the reaction to Maynard, went out to find their own artists who could "ride, rope, shoot, *and* sing."

Gene Autry was one of their first discoveries. A protege of Will Rogers, Autry had billed himself as "Oklahoma's Singing Cowboy." In 1931 he enjoyed great success with "Silver Haired Daddy of Mine." His original influence had been Jimmie Rodgers, the Mississippi "blue yodeler." Rodgers had been a maverick who thought nothing of using a Hawaiian guitar or a jazz great on his recordings.[4] But as Autry saddled up in countless Republic Westerns, his style lost most of the "down homeness" so closely identified with the singing Brakeman. A number of cowpokes followed in Autry's footsteps—Roy Rogers, Jimmy Wakeley, Tex Ritter. Even western heroes who couldn't pick or sing to save their spurs included musical interludes in their movies, with cowboy bands around the campfire. Gene and Roy kept the famous Jimmie Rodgers yodel but little else. "Twilight on the Trail" and "Riding Down the Canyon" were a far cry from Bill Monroe's "Blue Moon of Kentucky" or the Carters' "Can the Circle Be Unbroken?" What was coming to be called "country and western" music was much more western than country.

Unlike Kentucky, Tennessee, and West Virginia, Texas had no single ethnic or religious background. "Anglo, Negro, Chicano, Central European, and Cajun," observes historian Bill Malone, "all contributed to the diversification of music styles in the region."[5] On the hills of West Virginia, the social center was the church, but in Texas it was the saloon, where exhausted oil riggers could get drunk and reach for a fun-loving lady. In the saloons a patron was as likely to hear a "colored" jazz band as a quartet of country pickers. The crowded dusty taverns of the

Lone Star State gave birth to what was to be called "Western Swing".

Since the late 1920s, big bands like Paul Whitman's had enjoyed tremendous popularity in the cities. In the mid-1930s, Benny Goodman, the Dorsey brothers, and Kay Kyser were the rage. Many fundamentalist preachers considered swing to be evidence of big city corruption, "the devil's music."[6] Apparently, rip-roarin' Texans did not share this concern. Swing became part of the sound of many a Texas band.

Bob Wills, a hard-drinking, cigar-smoking fiddle player from Limestone, Texas, popularized western swing. His band, the Texas Playboys, played all over the Southwest, but his appeal did not extend to Nashville. He was contemptuously called "the country Glenn Miller." "His records were never really promoted," recalled singer Willie Nelson, "because they were into a different kind of music altogether in Nashville."[7] As "San Antonio Rose" and "Take Me Back to Tulsa" became familiar tunes, Wills and his Texas Playboys were finally invited to appear on the "Grand Ole Opry." Wills in the early 1940s made only one appearance at the Ryman; restrictions against drums and his ever-present cigar sent him scurrying back to the Southwest. The band leader was the first of a line of Texas boys who did not take kindly to the "Opry" and the values of Music City.

World War II had a profound affect on country music. The war uprooted millions of rural dwellers and scattered them around the country in barracks and defense plants. Radios in factories and at military bases blared out Red Foley's "Smoke on the Water" and Carson Robison's "Have to Slap That Dirty Little Jap" and Elton Britt's "There's a Star Spangled Banner Waving Somewhere." Some city dwellers within earshot moaned, but in time many were converted to Nashville. "Camel Caravan" even broadcast "hillbilly" bands to the boys in uniform. In Okinawa a popular enemy cry was "To hell with Roosevelt! To hell with Babe Ruth! To hell with Roy Acuff!" even the Japanese Imperial army knew about the "Opry" star. During the four years of the war, country music probably reached more people than it had in the previous twenty.

"How you gonna keep 'em down on the farm?" was as true in 1946 as it was following World War I. Many good ole boys did not return to their bib overalls or miner's caps, preferring the industrial plants of Los Angeles, Chicago, and Detroit. "By day I

BOB WILLS

"He's Still the King in Texas" (from a W. Jennings' song).

make the cars—by night I make the bars" ("Detroit City") was a social reality. Sociologist Lewis Killian noted that for many, the tavern became both family and church. It was a meeting place for the single person, an escape from everyday urban life, and an opportunity to be with people from down home. The ever-present jukebox with country music contributed to the atmosphere.[8]

After the war, "honky-tonk" music became *the* style in country. It started in the bars of Texas. The lyrics were a statement of loneliness, searching, and rejection. They suited the transplanted southerner as well as the drifters of the Texas oil fields. Honky-tonk songs were about drinking, despair, adultery, and the rigors of the city, and they had such titles as "Your Cheatin' Heart," "If You've Got the Money, I've Got the Time," "Release Me," and "Honky Tonkin'."[9]

Kitty Wells's classic "It Wasn't God Who Made Honky Tonk Angels" complained, "too many times married men think they're still single—that has caused many a good girl to go wrong." The music itself was also different. In order to compete with the din of clinking glasses and loud talk, Texas bar bands resorted to the use of a deep bass fiddle and the electric guitar. Tavern owners to overcome crowd noise found these additions especially useful for jukebox play.

Ernest Tubb pioneered honky-tonk music, but it was the son of an Alabama tenant farmer who was the king of the hill. Hank Williams had the soul of a Texan. He was raised on fundamentalist hymns and influenced by Black Belt blues. Like Wills, he was somewhat of a rogue. Bob Shelton, then with the *New York Times*, wrote of him: "Hank Williams, an extraordinary poet and musician, died at twenty-nine of too much living, too much sorrow, too much love, too much alcohol and drugs."[9] Williams' voice and his songs had a mournful quality that captured all of his pain and misfortune. Country music fans, both north and south, identified with Luke the Drifter. His biographer, Roger Williams, not related to Hank, wrote: "Opry officials in those days started trembling at the mere mention of alcohol, and Hank's recurring bouts with it left them faint with fear about propriety, the Opry image, and so on. They had tolerated his escapades in the hinterlands, even though these escapades reflected poorly on Mother Opry herself. But when Hank brought his drinking problem right into Ryman Auditorium, something had to be done."[10] It was—he was suspended from the "Opry". In 1953 he died—the result of drinking a mixture of whiskey and chloral hydrate in the back of a Cadillac.

Hank Williams's importance for the promoters and producers of Nashville was immense. Hank's songs had found their way into the song bags of pop crooners. Ex–big band singers like Jo Stafford and Tony Bennett recorded highly successful versions of "Jambalaya" and "Cold, Cold Heart."[11] Williams's music publisher and collaborator Fred Rose observed this trend. Originally he felt that Mitch Miller was taking advantage of Nashville, but as the royalty checks started coming in, Rose reconsidered. In short order he was pitching Hank's compositions to A & R men in New York. Some country artists resented the practice, as pop singers frequently diminished their sales. Nashville music publishers were delighted with their newly found bonanza.

Prior to this, a few hillbilly songs had been restylized and sold to the pop market. The Andrew Sisters' version of "Pistol Packin' Mama" was a big seller. "The Prisoner's Song," as well as Floyd-Tillman's "Slippin' round" and Red Foley's "Chattanooga Shoe Shine Boy," also reached the pop charts. None of these had the impact of Williams or "Tennessee Waltz," the song originally performed by Pee Wee King and Redd Stewart. Two years later, Patti Page recorded it; her version sold over 5 million copies. King and Stewart could only shake their heads in disbelief.

Steve Sholes, a former New York jazz musician in charge of the RCA division in Nashville, was one of the first to see the pop potential for artists. "Music is becoming assimilated," he said. Sholes envisioned Nashville as a major recording center. To this end, he built a studio and hired guitarist Chet Atkins. Atkins, a native Tennessean, could play any kind of music. Together Sholes and Atkins would effect the marriage of the country chart and the Top Forty. This was called "crossing over." Their first candidate was crooner Eddy Arnold, frequently labeled the "country Bing Crosby." Arnold had considerable success in 1948 with "Bouquet of Roses." "Eddy Arnold was one of the few country stars who had made the pop charts," recalls Chet Atkins, "so we focused a lot of attention on him. He like the use of voices and occasionally used strings and horns to give a modernized flair to his ballads. He stayed on the country charts, but more importantly, he moved up on the pop charts . . . ."[12]

RCA's success with Eddy Arnold in the pop market was unusual. Most country singers continued in the Hank Williams mold. Texans George Jones, Webb Pierce, Ray Price all but lived on the country charts. As America passed into the seeming tranquility of the 1950s and the Eisenhower administration, nobody was prepared for the revolution looming in the music industry.

The unlikely figure of Bill Haley fired the first shot. The pudgy ex-polka and western swing band leader brought a strange new sound called "rock 'n' roll." Few outside of the black ghettos were aware of it. "Rock Around the Clock" was the death knell of the musical status quo in pop and country. Executives in Los Angeles, New York, and Nashville at first dismissed Bill Haley's song as a novelty or just another movie theme. But it refused to go away.

"If I could find a white man who had the Negro sound and the Negro feel, I could make a billion dollars," Sam Phillips, the owner of a small Memphis record label, Sun, used to say. Phillips's wish came partly true when a singer with the improbable name of Elvis Presley walked into his studio.[13] Elvis Presley was the first bona fide country singer in decades to become a national sensation. Hank Williams's songs had enjoyed considerable popularity, but Elvis, who had been a regular on the "Louisiana Hayride," was heading toward Number One on country as well as the popular music charts. Other country singers on the Sun label were making it as well. Rock-a-billy was a reality, but the reaction from Nashville was still mixed.

Some traditionalists like Roy Acuff rejected the new sound out of hand: it wasn't country and had questionable moral value. Some conservatives got together to mount a $75,000 fund to fight the spread of the yellow Sun label. A number of country radio stations were approached with appeals that rock-a-billy not be aired. Some Music City people agreed with the White Citizens Councils' view that rock 'n' roll was part of a sinister Negro plot to corrupt white youth. Others ignored it, hoping it would go away.

Nashville's reaction to the early Presley mania clearly outlined a basic dilemma. It was impossible to maintain the Li'l Abner image and still enter the economically lucrative Top Forty and easy listening markets. It was either regional consciousness or more dollars.

On the basis of Elvis's Number One country song "I Forgot To Remember To Forget," RCA signed the hotly disputed singer. Presley's manager, Colonel Tom Parker, approached Steve Sholes and offered him the singer as well as his Sun releases.

Courtesy of NBC-TV, 1957. Elvis Presley, the man who shook Nashville up.

Sholes paid the unheard-of ransom of $35,000. Privately he feared his job was on the line. He later told a writer, "They called me in and wanted me to assure them that they would make their money back in the first year. I gulped a little and said I thought we would. How the heck was I to know?"[14] In several months, "Heartbreak Hotel" was Number One in both country and pop. A few months later, "Don't Be Cruel" accomplished the same feat. Sholes stood vindicated.

Most of Music City continued with its honky-tonk singers like Kitty Wells, Webb Pierce, Ray Price, Carl Smith, and others. They were still selling but had to share the country music charts with Elvis, Gene Vincent, and number of Sun artists. Rock-a-billy was not only taking over Top Forty radio, it was also making strong inroads on the sixty or so full-time country stations, especially in the Southwest.

Columbia was the first to play turnabout with rock music. A bluegrass band, Sid King and the Five Strings, did a bluegrass arrangement of "Blue Suede Shoes." By 1957 the executives at Dot Records were willing to adopt an "if you can't beat them" attitude. Ferlin Husky was rushed into the studio to record "Gone" using a pop vocal group and an arrangement that closely resembled earlier Presley ballads. Although the butt of considerable criticism, Dot enjoyed a smash hit in two markets.

In a matter of weeks Columbia followed "Gone" with Marty Robbins's "A White Sport Coat." Again, Nashville had produced a double hit. Next, Owen Bradley, the Father of Nashville production, recorded pop hits "Dynamite" and "Sweet Nothings" with teenager Brenda Lee. The cracks were beginning to show and the dam was about to burst.

"Elvis changed everything," Chet Atkins told the *New York Times* in 1974. "After he came along—all the country artists wanted to make pop hits. Presley almost killed country music. Every country boy thought, 'I've got to make pop records with those triplets'—those little piano trills that were played behind every rock 'n roll singer then."[15] Outside Nashville the situation was even more serious. Many singers raised on "Grand Ole Opry" sounds were entering the rock-a-billy field. All had sideburns, tight black pants, and the Sun record sound. Charlie Feathers, Roy Orbison, Harold Jenkins (Conway Twitty), Carl Perkins, Jerry Lee Lewis, and Johnny Cash all were rock-a-billies. Once again, Texas came up with something different. In Lubbock, Buddy Holly developed his distinctive hiccup style in

"Peggy Sue." In his "Party Doll," Buddy Knox showed a Tex-Mex influence. Rock 'n' roll was here to stay and a lot of country boys were cashing in on it.

Disaster quickly descended on the rock-a-billies. Auto accidents severely injured Carl Perkins and took the life of Eddie Cochran. Jerry Lee Lewis found himself blacklisted after his controversial marriage to a thirteen-year-old cousin. Elvis, the King, was drafted into the Army. By 1959 the southern rockers had been replaced by handsome young Arrow Collar men from Philadelphia who sold their wares daily on ABC's "American Bandstand."

For Chet Atkins and Steve Sholes the rock-a-billies had further demonstrated that their approach worked. Buddy Holly had pioneered a rock-a-billy sound with strings. Holly's songs were much like Eddy Arnold with an up-tempo rhythm section. The famous hiccup was present. Roy Orbison and Elvis had both enjoyed success with straight ballads accompanied by strings. The formula also worked for the velvet voice of Jim Reeves and the more traditional Don Gibson. Reeves, a former Arizona disc jockey, had none of the nasal twang identified with country music. He would record a song and Chet would "sweeten" it with strings, chorus, and even horns. Lyrically, his songs weren't far removed from the honky-tonk. "Welcome to My World," "Four Walls," and "He'll Have to Go" were typical heart-rending barroom sagas. "I'll tell the man to turn the jukebox way down low—and you can tell your friend, there with you, he'll have to go." It was the arrangements that sold them to pop audiences. Although a product of Shelby, North Carolina, Don Gibson also fit the Atkins model. He was country but not bluegrass. His "I Can't Stop Loving You" sounded more like a pop version of an early Hank Williams song than a honky-tonker. Its flip side, "Oh Lonesome Me," was a pop hit. With it, Gibson proved his ability to cross over.

The early 1960s found country music fragmented into different styles. It was quite possible on a Saturday night at the Ryman to hear ole-timey bluegrass, see a Texan in a sequined cowboy suit do a honky-tonk weeper, and then applaude a Jim Reeves, Ray Price, or Marty Robbins for his latest pop-and-country hit. The pop material was sung minus the brass and violin section on the record.

The music was evolving but the "Grand Ole Opry" show's

stress on fundamentalism, political conservatism, and right living hadn't changed. A few beers at Tootsie's around the corner with the good ole boys was okay, but any outward display of rowdiness was frowned upon. Also, performers who enjoyed the benefit of WSM's 50,000 watts on Saturday nights were required to make frequent appearances—even if it cost them money. National Life thought nothing of suspending Chet Atkins, one of the most prestigious citizens of Music City, for not making the required number of shows.

Appearing on the "Opry" was still the ultimate in country music. Privately, a number of artists were starting to grumble about having to drive hundreds of miles from a Friday night concert in Ohio, Michigan, or Indiana to make the show. The "Opry" pay scale was poor. Moreover, fans wanted to hear their hits—many recorded with horns or drums—which the "Opry" would not allow. During the 1950s, the biggest concession "Opry" manager Jim Denny, would make was to let the Everly Brothers use a snare drum on the Ryman stage. The drum, however, was hidden behind a curtain. Drums smacked too much of rock 'n' roll.

In 1961 there were only eighty-one full-time country stations. Some Nashville artist were aired on stations using block programming, of which half an hour daily was called "The Hillbilly Hour." The "Opry" was important because of WSM's powerful transmitter; still, it had no influence on millions of record buyers in the big city.

"Country music was really dead at that time," said Bob Luman.[16] The Country Music Association (CMA) estimated that its audience in the 1960s as being at a low 6 percent of the record-buying public. Reaching the scattered country audience presented quite a problem. Performers were constantly on the road doing grueling appearances throughout the country. Churches, American Legion halls, high school auditoriums, and bars provided the settings for country music. For many, the grind of the road was all but unbearable. Alcoholism, divorce, and pill popping became prevalent. Music City tolerated drinking and "slippin' around," but the use of drugs was an unmentionable. Hank Williams's morphine habit was only whispered about. Performers using pills posed a considerable problem for producers at RCA, Columbia, MGM, and other labels. Narcotics were condemned in the tones of righteousness usually reserved for fundamentalist ministers. Yet some of the biggest names in country music—Don Gibson, Roger Miller, Johnny Cash—were prime offenders.

While country performers were burning out their station wagons and Cadillacs roaring from town to town, Music City was developing its own standardized sound. The Nashville Sound was the product of certain studio musicians origianally assembled by Chet Atkins and Owen Bradley. Floyd Cramer, Boots Randolph, Buddy Emmons, and Atkins himself made up the core of the RCA label; pretty much everything they played had a familiar ring. The piano of "Last Date" was to be heard on most Victor recordings. Owen Bradley at Decca gathered his own group of "Nashville Cats." When artists came into town, they used a particular studio, producer, and his gang of musicians. In a matter of years a musical Nashville Establishment emerged. "The System," as Waylon Jennings calls it, was not far removed from the omnipotent days of pop impresario Mitch Miller at Columbia. Producers with "hot hands" had almost total control over recording sessions and the choice of songs and musicians. Crossing a Chet Atkins or an Owen Bradley was definitely not the thing to do. At recording sessions nobody talked back to Chet Atkins. Once, country comedian Don Bowman called Chet "superpicker"and shocked disbelief swept the studio.

For a time, the Nashville Sound worked. Floyd Cramer had country and pop hits with "Last Date" and "On the Rebound." Faron Young's "Hello Walls," produced by Bradley, was one of the top records in 1961. Bobby Bare's "Detroit City" once again affirmed the magic of the Atkins touch. Chet would tell artists, "We're gonna make some hits together."

Collegiates' interest in "folk music" aided some Nashville artists. Bluegrass and cowboy music became a staple at festivals and university concerts. Mainstream country performers were not welcomed at Vanderbilt or Columbia, but performers like Bill Monroe and Johnny Cash found a new audience. Nashville producers longed to break into this well-financed youth market. It was too late.

Beatlemania ended the folk revival and Nashville's ability to sneak onto the pop charts. Music City could not cope with the long-haired rockers whose fans agreed they were "more popular than Christ." Chet Atkins recorded an instrumental album of Beatle songs. But Music City Row was worlds apart from Liverpool and even further from San Francisco and its hippie scene.

"The rock revolution," as northern journalists were calling it, effectively returned country music to its loyal fans, fans who disapproved of the new morality, civil rights protests, and drugs. Merle Haggard's two political songs, "Okie from Muskogee' and "Fighting Side of Me," although not written until half a decade later, perfectly captured the revulsion felt by country music audiences. "We don't smoke marijuana in Muskogee . . . ." In the mid-1960s, country music was "getting its wagons in a circle" and discounting pop as having gone the way of Sodom and Gomorrah. Ironically, however, the flower children's philosophy of "doing your own thing" was already invading Music City.

Bobby Bridger, a balding young folk singer, with a guitar strapped to his back went to Nashville like hundreds of others to make his fame and fortune. He was lucky and got a contract, but he also ran into The System. "The whole approach," Bridger said, "is you do what we want you to do first and then you can do what you want to do. So I said okay, and after about three years, I was wearing my hair the way they wanted me to, singing the songs they wanted me to sing, and doing everything they wanted and still going nowhere. So I quit . . . ."[17] But many stayed.

Tompall Glaser and his brothers arrived in Nashville in 1959 to record for Owen Bradley's Decca label. "When I got to Nashville," Glaser told *Billboard* in 1974, "everything was sewed up by a few people and I didn't like that idea . . . what I really resented were those in power not allowing things to be done any way but theirs. Working away from that was and is like any other liberation movement."[18] A liberation movement in Music City? Unheard of! Glaser and his brothers produced their records, took care of bookings, formed a production company, and built a studio. Most people thought he was a bit crazy and, at times, Glaser agreed with them. For one thing, the Glaser Brothers never had the monster hit. In 1967 "Through the Eyes of Love" reached Number 27 on the country charts and later "California Girl" got to Number 11. But most of the Glaser's early songs never passed Number 20 on the all-important charts.

In the 1960s and 1970s, production, choice of musicians and songs, and style became crucial. Steve Sholes and Chet Atkins had made RCA Victor *the* country label. Their system worked smoothly. Chet was in charge of production and gave each artist individual attention. Sholes took care of the mountainous paperwork and played games with the New York office. His untimely death threw a wrench into the system. It was impossible for Chet to continue both producing with forty artists and administering the Nashville branch of RCA Victor. For many Victor artists, his solution wasn't a happy one. Chet hired a number of assistant producers—Danny Davis, Felton Jarvis, Bob Ferguson, Ronny Light, and Jack Clement. Many of his singers felt deserted. Waylon Jennings, Willie Nelson, Skeeter Davis, and Bobby Bare all suffered. Bare finally left RCA. So did Nelson, fleeing both the record company and Nashville. Waylon Jennings stayed. Temperamentally Waylon and Nelson were cut from the same cloth as Wills, Williams, and Glaser. Both hailed from West Texas and had reputations as "roarers." Jennings, especially, was considered a rebel on several counts. His style, both in music and life, sorely tested The System.

Waylon's use of pills did not sit well with straitlaced Atkins. He disagreed too often with Danny Davis and other production people. His association with "pill freak" Johnny Cash and his western background pointed him in musical directions still considered "uncountry." He thought nothing of performing songs by the Beatles or the Rolling Stones and using material by unknowns like Kris Kristofferson.

Jennings symbolized a number of crosscurrents sweeping Nashville during the closing years of the 1960s. John Hartford's "Gentle on My Mind" had returned Nashville's attention to the pop market. "Gentle's" arrangement is considered a turning point in the Nashville Sound. "We needed to get away from the strictly three-chord honky tonk things and Hartford's 'Gentle on My Mind' did that," says Tompall Glaser.[19] Hartford was a shock to Music City as he rambled around in hippie dress. He was a California folkie. His songs, even when sung by Glen Campbell, were more Bob Dylan than Hank Williams. Hartford rekindled the movement toward uptown, but it took an ex-Rhodes scholar and Army helicopter pilot to push futher into the big city.

Kris Kristofferson, the son of an Air Force major general, was hardly country. He had a beard and wore his hair long like a hippie. His songs like "Me and Bobbie McGee" could be sung by rock star Janis Joplin, by folkies Gordon Lightfoot and Jack Elliot, or by the likes of Roger Miller, Johnny Cash, and Waylon Jennings. His original successes had taken place outside Music City, at folk festivals in Newport, Big Sur, and Berkeley. Some of his songs like "Blame It on the Stones" and "The Law is for Protection of the People" didn't fit in a city where Chet Atkins had been alone in openly supporting Hubert Humphrey in the

1968 presidential election. Most country artists favored George Wallace's "law and order" ticket.

Songs like "Help Me Make It Through the Night" and Ray Price's "For the Good Times" graphically spoke of "going to bed." "Lay you head upon my pillow—hold your warm and tender body close to mine." "They thought it (Help Me Make It) was dirty," Kris told *Country Music*, "but now every song you hear has something about a body or touching skin in it."[20] Eyebrows were raised when Sammi Smith recorded "Make It Through the Night." Yet the prestigious CMA voted it the best single of the year.

Even now Music City Row is a house divided, torn between the past and the present. It produces some of the most exciting music imaginable yet only grudgingly tolerates innovation. Past rebels Jimmie Rodgers, Hank Williams, and Bob Wills are in the Country Music Hall of Fame. Tompall Glaser, Willie Nelson, and Waylon Jennings remain a mystery. "There will be more changes," promised Tompall, "and those who were not heroes to the old crowd will be heroes of the new one."[21]

2

IT'S EITHER PICKIN' COTTON OR GUITAR

*A Texan ain't nothing but a human
being way out on a limb. . . .*

—John Wayne in *The Searchers*

The West Texas ground is parched. It's dusty. The first inhabitants were Indians, then Mexicans, and finally the Gringos. The Panhandle was cattle country, as seen in thousands of Westerns. George Washington Littlefield was a cattle baron in the tradition of the Chisholms and the King family. A lord and master over thousands of acres in the flatlands, there was no Shane to topple him.

In 1913, with the end of the frontier, Littlefield created a railroad crossing that grew into a town. Naturally it was named after its illustrious founder. With the passing of time, the open cattle range was eaten up by cotton and grain fields. Littlefield became just another country town serving the cowboys and farmers of Lamb County. After World War I, land prices made cattle grazing too expensive. Cotton became king, the dominant crop. The region's economy dipped with each drought and harvest loss. The climate was unpredictable. Summerlike weather was interrupted by blizzards, dust storms, and bone-chilling winds.

The social makeup of the city was as full of contrasts as the weather. It was a town of haves and have-nots. A few of the landowners and their local support industries had money. But there was the other side of the tracks. Here, blacks, poor whites, "trash," and Chicanos were lumped into one group. They were the laborers who picked the precious cotton for substandard wages. These were the people most greatly affected by the Great Depression.

In the 1930s the little town was hit by dust and economic depression. Farms were lost. A daily concern was food and shelter. During these hard years William Alvin Jennings of Young County married Lorene Shipley, a dark-haired beauty from McKinney, Texas. He was five years her senior. "W.A." was a hard worker and a dreamer. He tried his hand at many occupations. He pulled cotton, drove a truck, and did all the things necessary for survival in West Texas. "He never really succeeded in any type of business," recounts Waylon. "Every time he got into something, it seemed like it went wrong." Hard times and misfortunes plagued him. Lorene scrimped and saved, trying to make ends meet. She, too, picked cotton, and she did housework for the few well-to-do people in Littlefield.

On June 15, 1937, Lorene gave birth to a son. Dr. R.E. Hunt delivered the boy at 10:30 A.M. W.A. insisted that his firstborn carry the same initials. In keeping with the Jennings family tradition, the baby was baptized Wayland Arnold.[1] He was named after a Church of Christ bible college sixty miles away in Plainview, Texas. Where the "d" got lost is a matter of some dispute. One version was told to Johnny Cash: "My grandmother, when she was young, her boyfriend's name was Wade and I was their first grandchild. She wanted to name me Wade, and Mama wanted name me Gaylon, and dad wanted to have W.A. for initials cause it's a traditional thing . . . and now you know why I spell it Waylon. Mama changed that."[2] Lorene took the newborn to their tent on Route 1 situated on the outskirts of the city. Problems occurred almost immediately. Wayland rejected her breast milk. Lorene feared he might starve to death.[3] A makeshift crib was placed upon the oil stove "to keep the rats from eating him." W.A. was pulling cotton to feed the family; Waylon survived; and a year later the marriage produced another son. On August 8, 1938, Lorene gave birth to a boy they named Tommy.

In 1939 W.A. broke his back. After a short hospital stay he

returned to the cotton patch and toiled with a brace on his back.
He needed nine dollars for Christmas presents.[4] Their landlord
gave them a two-room shack to live in. A dust storm blew out one
of the windows and Tommy's hand was severely cut. "I can still
remember that because I still got the glass in there and every time
I look at it—I remember. I guess I kind of carry a grudge against
that period of time from what I've heard. I know my mother
would clean the house for the people that lived up on the hill. She
went up and worked all day cleaning that house and they gave her
a nickel can of hominy. Of course, my dad was working for fifty
cents a day."[5] For his half-dollar, W.A. rose at dawn to milk cows.
He drove a tractor all day. In the evening the farmer's cows
would need attention again. Grandpa Jennings helped the family
with loans. Alfred Shipley contributed produce from his hauling
operation.

Despite the rural poverty, Waylon and Tommy enjoyed a
happy childhood. "We didn't have a pot or nothin'," says Tommy, "but I think we had one of the best childhoods that anybody
could possibly have. . . . we all worshipped Daddy and Mother."
Waylon agrees. "I know that my Dad was the greatest man I'll
ever know."[6]

The boys' upbringing was traditional. Lorene was a Church of
Christ member and a "God fearin' woman." She took the boys to
services regularly and hoped Waylon might someday become a
minister. He recalls:

> I went to church—too much. But look at how they teach religion.
> They tell about a God who says, "Now look here my child, I won't be
> around, but you'd better believe in me and do everything I say. If you
> do, I'll save a place for you in heaven where the streets are paved with
> gold. Have blind faith. Don't ever doubt me and don't ever question
> me. And you must go through great pain, because the Devil's
> around. Now I love you and everything, but if you don't do what I
> say, I'm going to throw you in a pit of fire and burn you so you're in
> pain for eternity."[7]

Cussing was not permitted in the house. "Cuss words were
hung on the door before they ever came into the house."[8] W.A.
and Lorene, though poor, were always proper. Lorene took care
of the discipline. She used to say, "they'd drive a wooden person
crazy." Waylon's guitar playing elicited that comment the most.
But W.A. was the man of the house.

Waylon and Tommy slept in the same bed. As with most
children, they fell asleep reluctantly. They fought and scuffled in

the bed. "I'm coming in there," W.A. would shout, according to Tommy. "So we would get quiet for just a little bit and we would start again." "Boys, I'm coming in there," W.A. would repeat. To emphasize the point, he would drop a foot on the floor. Waylon and Tommy would stop, thinking he really was coming. On occasion, the foot trick didn't work; then he did come into the bedroom. He symbolically spanked the boys. They didn't feel a thing because of the "foot of covers" on the bed.

World War II boosted the Littlefield economy. Produce and fabric were in high demand and things got better. W.A. went to work driving a truck, a vast improvement over work the cotton field. Lorene began to save a little money. They were dreaming of buying a truck and adding a room to their little house on the corner of Austin Street.

"We used to pull the truck up to the window and run the jumper cables in to the battery radio. We heard the Carter Family on Friday night, the Grand Ole Opry on Saturday, and Clint Texas, the rest of the week. And parched peanuts on the pot-bellied stove."[9] Sometimes they went to Grandpa Shipley's house, as he had a wind charger for his radio.

Waylon, Tommy, and cousin Wendell Whitfield, who was a fixture in the Jennings household, played the usual imagining games to pass the long hot dusty days. Cowboys and Indians was a favorite. As with all boys of that era, Lash LaRue, Sunset Carson, and Gene Autry were an important part of their lives. Waylon has a lasting impression of having watched cowboy star Lash LaRue. LaRue appeared in Littlefield and accidentally ripped open the town's movie screen with the whip tricks he used in his films. "I went up to get some popcorn or something after the show was over and he was standing in the lobby there, and he still had his guns and his whip on. And they were telling him that he was going to have to pay for that, I mean the movie screen, and he said 'I'm not going to pay for that; you should have insurance.' And they said 'You are going to pay for it,' and he said 'Well, I got a whip and a gun that says I'm not going to," and I looked around me to see if I was the only one in the world that had ever heard that man, I thought that was the greatest thing, and anytime after that if I played cowboys and Indians or anything I used that line. Somewhere in the place of Gene Autry."[10]

They built forts to keep out imaginary marauding Indians. Not all hiding places were impenetrable. Waylon and Tommy dug a cave right next to an old outhouse. After hours of hard work, they climbed into the hole. Suddenly, a dirt wall gave way and years of refuse began to pour in. "You never seen a bunch of kids get out of a hole as fast as we got out of that." Other attempts at house building were more successful.[11]

Cowboys and Indians Texas style sometimes got rough. In one re-creation of the Old West, Wendell and Waylon were the cowboys and Tommy the feared Apache. Just as in the movies, the ranchers won. Wendell and Waylon tied Tommy up in an old barn with barbed wire. (Tommy claims that it was Waylon who was the victim in this story. His brother insists this is the correct version.) It was around noon and a hot Texas sun hung overhead. "Let's go play football," someone suggested. So they went off to a nearby pasture to choose up sides. Running up and down the field, the boys let the hours slip by quickly. When it was time for supper, Wendell and Waylon went in to wash up and eat. Sitting down at the table, W.A. asked, "Where's Tommy?" Mrs. Jennings warned, "If Tommy don't get hisself in here, he ain't gonna get no supper." "Oh Lord," thought Waylon, "he's still in the barn." Hastily excusing themselves, Waylon and Wendell raced to the barn. Tommy was still there, strapped down with barbed wire. Needless to say, the captured Indian was angry. They freed him. "He kicked on us, he beat us. We was ready to let him do it though, 'cause we felt like we deserved it." Tommy wasn't the only person who beat on the cowboys that night.[12]

The barren plains of southwest Texas have spawned a disproportionate number of singers and pickers. Buddy Holly, Billy Walker, Roy Orbison, Mac Davis, Sonny Curtis, and Waylon Jennings all grew up in the area.[13] Music was a vital part of their lives, one of the few distractions from a hard rural life. On Saturday afternoons, it was the matinee at the local picture show if you had the money. On Saturday nights they would tune in WSM's 50,000 watt signal to hear the "Grand Ole Opry" or some Texas jamboree. Ernest Tubb, Hank Williams, and Bob Wills were household words. They were heroes admired and looked up to as much as any of the cowboy heroes who rode the silver screen.

In West Texas, music was more than just entertainment. It was a vehicle out of the dreary cotton patch. "You'll do anything to get out of West Texas," explains Waylon. "Music always has been big in that area . . . . I'll tell you what it is—either music or pull cotton for the rest of your life . . . . I'll tell you, you'll learn to do something, if you've ever been to a cotton patch."[14]

W.J. Duncan, called "Hi-Pockets" by his friends, started a
number of young singers in the business by using them on the
KSEL "Saturday Jamboree." He was Buddy Holly's first manager.
Duncan agrees with Waylon:"We have a whole lot of kids raised
in a cotton patch out here that wants recognition and to get away
from the cotton patch. I think this is kind of a basic drive for
them. They do have talent out here, I don't think they have any
more talent in the south plains area than they do down in South
Texas or East Texas or in Arizona. I do think they do have a little
bit more desire and maybe that is the push to do something about
that desire."[15]

As far back as Tommy Jennings can remember, Waylon had
that "big desire." "I think the one desire in his main thing was his
guitar. And not records, just the idea of singing." "Ever since I
can remember that's all I wanted to be" says Waylon. His main
inspiration was W.A. W.A. had done some picking and singing in
the West Texas region, but it was mostly a hobby. In the evenings
W.A. would sing and chord his way through cowboy songs on his
store-bought Gene Autry guitar. On its face were paintings of
the Old West. Waylon and Tommy would sit enthralled by the
performance. They wanted him to play all night. Finally, he
would say, "You know, my fingers are gettin' stiff." They wanted
more songs about cowboys in his Jimmie Rodgers style. Tommy
recalls, "He was good. He wasn't a guitar picker. He was, you
know, a good rhythm man. He really could entertain." W.A. had
a desire to be an entertainer, but supporting his family came first.
Any dreams he may have harbored remained just that—unfulfil-
led desires.

When W.A. was out working, Waylon would mess around
with the Gene Autry guitar. He thinks he started as early as four
years old.

Waylon's grandfather owned a cafe. The food store was a
natural place to hang out. Mrs. Jennings worked there and took
Waylon and Tommy along. They were fascinated with the nick-
elodeon or jukebox. Behind the restaurant, Waylon, Tommy
and his uncles Carlos and Elvis would fantasize performing on
the "Grand Ole Opry." "We would get out there and get a box
and stand on top of that box with a broom and part of us would be
audience and Waylon and Carlos would entertain," recalls
Tommy.[16]

Carlos pretended to be Hank Williams or Jack Guthrie.
Waylon was always Ernest Tubb. "I had an old broom stick with

About age fourteen. Virgie Rissenger Collection.

part of the broom still on it and I'd be Ernest Tubb! I always had to be Ernest, because I've always thought he was such a great singer . . . can you imagine a squeeky voice singing 'Walking the Floor Over You'?"[17]

His first guitar was a secondhand, five-dollar Gibson bent like a "bow and arrow." It didn't have much of a top part, but the bottom sounded all right. With his instrument he learned a few chords. "My fingers on my right hand, for a long time, were two inches longer than the ones on my left hand, because of the callouses, bending them trying to hold them strings down."[18] Lorene had worked the arduous cotton field to buy it for him.

When not imitating Ernest Tubb, Waylon joined Tommy and his cousin Wendell Whitfield in hell-raising. Tommy remembers, "We were always into some damn trouble." Once they burned down a government storage grainery. "It was just something to do." A hobo lived in the grainery. The boys decided to steal his Prince Albert tobacco. On a summer day the building was too hot, so they proceeded to play around a truckload of cotton. For some reason they began throwing matches at the cotton. Deciding this was too dangerous, they tried to extinguish the cotton. It continued to burn. As they were doing this, W.A. called the three boys: "We're going to Grandpa's!" While they were gone, the building burned down.

Johnny White, a local troublemaker, told the authorities that the Jennings kids had done it. Because of his reputation for orneriness, the police did not believe White. They were convinced he had committed the evil deed. "He had broken into school houses and stuff like that and he was meaner than sin and they wouldn't believe him, in fact, thy tried to pin it on him" recalls Tommy. Not only did Johnny have to cope with the police, but the Jennings boys stomped him for "ratting on them."[19]

W.A. went to work driving a truck for Ben Borshea. He enjoyed driving more than picking cotton. While working for Borshea, W.A. decided he wanted to go into business for himself, which would require money and a truck. Lorene put money away in an old tobacco sack, and they finally saved enough for a down payment on an old 1941 Ford pickup truck. With his new truck, W.A. and the boys would drive to East Texas. Waylon: "I can remember helping to shovel grain out of the truck. We'd go to what they called 'wheat harvests' and we'd go buy fruit and vegetables, sell them and then, Dad would go buy watermelons from East Texas. I would sit on the depot lot and sell them and I wasn't much bigger than knee high to a grasshopper."[20] Not all of the trips were successful. Once, they hauled back a load of apples. Only two of the bushels sold; the rest had to be sacked up and piled against the house so the truck could be used again. The smell of rotten apples soon permeated the yard and the living quarters.

W.A. went into the produce business. He bought cream and eggs from local farmers. He also sold feed. Lorene Jennings Gilbert wrote a fan: "When he (Waylon) was 11, we ran a produce—buying cream and eggs and selling feed. His job was washing cream cans. We had a bench for our customers, but he made it very hard for the customers to sit on it—because of practicing on his guitar."[21] Tommy was assigned the task of cleaning out chicken pens. Neither Tommy nor Waylon liked his job. W.A. decided to train Waylon to "meet customers." This way he would have more time for his guitar. W.A. played some pranks. Once he sent Waylon out to buy an "oxometer." After school, Waylon spent several days looking for an "oxometer." There was no such object.

As the produce store slowly prospered, so did the Jennings family. They moved from Austin Street to a better part of town. Their house on Sixth Street was nice. Tommy Jennings: "We weren't looked down on or anything like that. When we were young kids we were like gypsies part of the time and just poor people. Then after my dad was making a little money that was kind of a boost for us. We gained more respect, I think if it hadn't been for that we would have possibly been considered trash!"[22]

One Christmas when the produce business was doing fairly well, W.A. bought Waylon a Harmony guitar. Tommy received a mandolin. It was arranged for Waylon to have lessons. The first two sessions were spent teaching him the feel of the instrument at 75 cents a lesson. The teacher didn't show up for the third. Waylon taught himself to play. Tommy never learned to pick the mandolin.

Waylon and Bill Pollard entered the KSEL Jamboree, which was broadcast on Saturday mornings from Lubbock. Hi-Pockets Duncan was the host. Waylon and Bill at the age of twelve, won first prize on the show—a table top radio.

Waylon entered talent shows all over the area. In "Last Movie Show" houses in nearby Brownfield, Levelland, Anton, and other little towns, Waylon and Bill played in contests staged by

About age sixteen. Virgie Rissenger Collection.

Truitt Benson, the manager of Littlefield's theater. According to
Tommy, "Waylon would come out pretty much 'top-dog' on
nearly all of them."[23]

Bill and Waylon played an ode-timey Texas box supper that
was attended by a newspaper man who owned KVOW. "He saw us
and liked us and let us have a 15 minute program on Sunday
mornings."[24] KVOW was a little station with a block programming
format: every quarter of an hour was programmed for a different
type of music. "Hillbilly Hit Parade," "Music from Dixieland,"
"Montavani," all were on the air. Bill and Waylon would do
fifteen minutes of their country music, featuring songs by Hank
Williams, Carl Smith, and, naturally, Ernest Tubb. The first time
they appeared as "Waylon Jennings and the Texas Longhorns,"
Waylon messed up the songs. "One time I was trying to learn two
songs before the show—Webb Pierce's 'That Heart Belongs to
Me' and Carl Smith's, 'Are You Teasing Me'—I got so scared that
I sang the words of one to the melody of the other."[25]

Waylon's first paid stage appearance had not gone well.
Booked sometime in about 1950 on a show with Billy Walker,
Jimmy and Johnny, and Tillman Franks, he began to sing a
popular Faron Young song, "If You Ain't Lovin' Then You Ain't
Livin." Halfway through the number, disaster struck. "I lost my
voice, like choked to death, on top of a nervous bustdown. That
was my first experience on stage and it almost ended the whole
thing."[26] Despite the embarrassment, he continued to perform.

Waylon played anywhere he could. He dressed in a cowboy
shirt with a white Stetson hat. On the face of the dark F-shaped
guitar was inscribed "Texas Longhorns."

At the age of fourteen Waylon had dropped out of the tenth
grade. He did not like high school—he planned on a music career
and Littlefield High did not seem to have any application in that
direction. Reportedly, the football coach was sad to see him
leave. Waylon was a promising place kicker, and as Tommy says,
"folks take their football mighty serious down here." Waylon
wrote his first song, "Big Time Ladies Man" when he was fifteen.
He used the song to pay off a $20. debt some four years later to
one of the disc jockeys at KLLL, "Lord, it never became a hit. It
was the worst damn song I ever heard. I think three lines rhymed
and the rest of it was a mess."[27]

When not working the radio station or playing guitar, Waylon
spent his free time cruising Main Street in the best *American
Graffiti* fashion. "You'd meet the same people comin' and

goin'." "Back in Littlefield Mama could hear me plumb down on Main Street and that was twenty blocks away. She'd say, 'Boy, I heard you down there and I heard the siren too and me walkin' the floor waitin' on you. I heard you go plumb outta town.' "[28] Waylon hung around the local drugstore. "He would get bow-legged from sittin' on the stool," says Tommy.[29] He dated a lot. "Women have been my trouble since I found out they weren't men," the song says.

Waylon constantly refers to Littlefield as "a suburb to a cotton patch." In an interview with Pat Salvo he did elaborate: "The people in Littlefield did one thing that is probably the wildest thing in the whole world. I gotta tell it on them though. You know, for a hundred miles around, there's no lake, water, or anything. Except that 12 miles through the city limits of Little-field, out there, there's a natural canyon that's five to six miles across; and there's two natural springs that feed this man-make lake, and it's about four miles across one way and about three in the other. There's natural rocks, and caves in the sides of the mountains; and the rest of the country all around it is real flat. But Littlefield made that its city dump—the lake. Do you believe that!!" He continued, "Fun in Littlefield? Well, we put taps on our boots you know. That was before the hip-huggers were made, when they fit up snug. And you'd put your collar up high, put on a black cowboy hat, and make sparks with them cowboy boots on Saturday night. Just walk up and down Main Street, 'til you got where you could have a car, then drag Main Street. That was the whole three blocks." Waylon had a 1947 Chevrolet. "We used to drag race that. We played football. I went to the football games. I'd try to swagger around where the girls would look at us and look for a fight. We did really. I guess we did a lot of fightin' in those days, because there wasn't nothing else to do."[30] Most of the fights followed footballs games between Littlefield High and nearby Sudan. An intense rivalry existed between the two schools.

In the course of performing in west Texas shows, Waylon met Maxine Carrol Lawrence at a beauty contest in one of the small communities surrounding Littlefield. "She won it or he won her one way or the other," says Tommy. They started dating. Waylon would take the car and go for rides or to the picture show. There wasn't much to do in Littlefield. One day, Maxine announced she was "in the family way." "If a woman's pregnant, and if it's my child, I gotta marry her," Waylon told a *Photoplay* correspondent.[31] Being under age, Waylon had to have his mother's consent. She drove the couple across the New Mexico border, where they were married. Maxine was not pregnant. "We got married at 3:00 P.M. and at 8:00 we found out she wasn't."[32] Maxine moved in with the Jennings family until she and Waylon could get a place of their own. The arrangement worked well. "She was a nice person," recounts Tommy, "she fit into our family."[33] Maxine was possessive and had a hot temper. As with most newlyweds, Maxine's and Waylon's first years went well. A year after the marriage Terry Vance Jennings was born, on January 21, 1957.

Waylon continued to work at the radio station. His meager earnings were supplemented by part-time jobs. "In his early years," according to Waylon's mother Mrs. Gilbert, "he worked for a grocery store, a men's ready-to-wear dry goods store, and a lumber yard, and delivered freight."[34]

Waylon's unanticipated marital status did not deter him from planning a radio career or performing. It would be hard now, but he persisted. His early marriage was an economic blow, one from which he would not recover for years. "He came from a poor family," remembers Hi-Pockets. "He was kind of on his own when he was a kid. He didn't have a big paying job. He married young and started to raise a family. This is something that should not have happened in the first place. He was always in desperate need of money and I guess that has been the story of his life."[35] Waylon did take his family responsibilities seriously, but music was still his major concern.

The Jennings produce business had done well. They actually saved a thousand dollars. Fate once again stepped in: agribusiness began to move into the area, and smaller farms were eaten up by large conglomerates. W.A.'s volume began to decline. He was forced to get a second job driving a school bus. During this period, Waylon drove a truck. "I used to haul hardwood from east Texas to Littlefield for a lumber company I worked for. I drove a ready-mix truck for awhile."[36] "I also drove a freight line truck for Lange Transit. I didn't really leave a dent in none of them, either way; I didn't have a wreck or I didn't do anything that really impressed them to much." Another account suggests Waylon did roll over the cement truck, dumping its contents on a well-manicured lawn.[37]

In April of 1958, Maxine presented Waylon with a baby girl.

Julie Rae was named after singer and actress Julie London, whose song "Cry Me a River" had been on the 1955 charts.

For Waylon and Tommy, Littlefield is an unpleasant memory. Tommy stops short of criticizing the community because his mother and brothers still live in the city. "Course, the population keeps decreasing for *some* reason so somebody is finding out something, you know," he notes.[38] Waylon, as always, is more candid. He told a fan, "To hell with them. They didn't even know I existed. Now that I am a little someone, now they want to claim me. They gave my family and me absolutely nothing."[39] His bitterness is not without cause. Life in "cotton picker shacks" did not supply happy memories. Nor do their experiences in the cotton fields, which surround the city like a blanket of snow, engender warm thoughts. Waylon obviously disagreed with the Littlefield Chamber of Commerce pamphlet that proclaims: "You can really enjoy life in Littlefield. Relax in the pleasant atmosphere of a small town with friendly people who are interested in you." As Waylon told this writer, "You'll do anything to get out of West Texas." Fans who walk up to Waylon and proclaim they are from Littlefield are in for a very rude surprise.

WAYLON

3

THE LUBBOCK CONNECTION

Lubbock is some eighty miles south of Interstate 66, a highway incorrectly immortalized in song. Approaching Amarillo, tourists are besieged by blue signs urging them to visit the "Hub of the Plains" just a "few miles" on I-87. The city is in the heart of cotton country, surrounded by five million acres of the fiber. The Lubbock Chamber of Commerce boasts that it is "the third largest inland cotton market in the world, producing more than two million bales a year." In addition, the cotton oil mills in the city contribute to the fact that Lubbock is known as "the cotton-seed oil capital of the world." For many residents of the area, Lubbock was *the* big city, although northern urbanites might scoff at the idea. Waylon was duly impressed, "That's the biggest town I'd ever seen in my life."

Lubbock was one of the first cities to have an all-country music radio station. In September 1953, Dave "Pappy" Stone (David Pinkston) and Hi-Pockets Duncan left KSEL and joined musician Ben Hall in establishing KDAV. Despite the fact that KDAV was a country station, in 1955 Stone began broadcasting "Rock 'n' Roll Hit Parade" on the station. The program highlighted the latest efforts of Bill Haley, Carl Perkins, and Elvis Presley. Local teenagers were delighted. The show was a throwback to the KSEL days when rhythm and blues was played for half an hour, followed by a thirty-minute block of rock 'n' roll.

Another transplanted program was the "Sunday Dance Party."

Stone and Duncan had hosted "KSEL Jamboree," a live show on Saturdays with local talent and occasional visiting Nashville celebrities, who were Opry regulars. It was on this show that Waylon had won his radio. At KDAV, the "Jamboree" changed its name and day, becoming the "Sunday Dance Party." A trio doing bluegrass was a favorite on the afternoon show. Bob Montgomery, a member of the trio along with Buddy Holly and Larry Welburn, described the program:

> It wasn't really a Dance Party, it was Dave Stone having a station out there and every Sunday afternoon he would let local groups come in and play. It was all local hand and tool kind of thing. It was Sunday afternoon and it got a pretty good response, why we ended up with a thirty minute show every week—every Sunday. It was really just having the station kind of just open up. He was really responsible, I think, for giving a lot of people a lot of incentive to do something because they could get on the air. It was really a loose kind of thing. I think it got a lot of people having that kind of outlet help spawn a lot of talent.[2]

The "Dance Party" was important because it was the major vehicle for local talent. Waylon Jennings says, "It was about the only exposure you could get." Sonny Curtis, who also appeared on the show, agrees, "Dave Stone did a lot in exposing the town and the growth of it."[3] Sonny impressed people with his playing of "Meet Mr. Callahan."[4] In the music world, that was akin to being the fastest gun in town.

In the mid-1950s, Buddy Holly, Bob Montgomery, Sonny Curtis, and Waylon Jennings all used KDAV to polish their musical skills. Waylon went down to Lubbock, hoping that he could repeat his previous successes on talent shows. He knew Hi-Pockets from KSEL; he had also met Sonny Curtis, who had been dating his cousin, Anita Shipley. Arriving at the KDAV studios, he came across Buddy Holly for the first time. "I met him in Lubbock in 1954 on a radio show. He had a three peice group . . . we worked a lot of shows together, them as one act and me as another."[5] Waylon does not seem to have been particularly charismatic in 1954. One performer said, "Evidently he didn't make too good of an impression on me and I didn't make one on him."[6] "I don't remember Waylon ever being on there," observed Hi-Pockets Duncan. "He was such a kid that I really didn't remember him hardly at that time."[7]

The "Dance Party" did provide Waylon with new contacts. Because of the shows, he and other performers could play var-

Sonny Curtis as a solo performer in the pre-outlaw period. Courtesy of Sonny Curtis.

ious movie houses, car lots, and similar places for $10 to $20. "We played for however much we could get," recalls one of the "Dance Party" musicians, "which was very low fees. We would play at a dance for about $10—which would be a very good night. Ten dollars a piece was real good. Sometimes we would only get $.50 or $.75. It was a means of earning extra money."

Through the "Dance Party," Waylon met other young musicians who could talk and dream about musical success. In Lubbock, anyone who could sing and pick was immediately accepted. Sonny Curtis: "Anybody who sings is in the group."[8] The KDAV crowd and aspiring musicians from other parts of West Texas hung out together. Waylon recalled, "I remember, one time we all were together; me, Buddy Holly, Roy Orbison, and Weldon Myrick, who was a great steel guitar player in Nashville, and Sonny Curtis, who everybody knows, and at the bus station in Lubbock, Texas, and we had a quarter and Sonny put it in the juke box and played Chet Atkins, and that's about all we had was a quarter and we snuck into a Sonny James, Jim Reeves Show. That's a bit of history for you."[9] Buddy Holly would shortly be recording rock music history.

On January 5, 1955, Elvis Presley—billed as the "Hillbilly Cat"—appeared at the Cotton Club in Lubbock for the grand sum of $25. KDAV had sponsored the show. Buddy flipped. Buddy and Bob became a duo, performing "western bop," In almost no time, Buddy converted his group to a trio. He recruited Sonny Curtis, and then Don Guess. Sonny recalls: "We had an Elvis type group and I played like Scotty Moore and Don Guess played like Bill Black and Holly played guitar. So we worked several shows and dances like that because it was just like Elvis."[10]

In the meantime, Elvis added a drummer. Buddy immediately followed suit. "Of course, we had to have one too." Jerry Allison, a Bob Wills fan, became the fourth member of the group. On October 23, 1956, the *Lubbock Evening Journal* announced: "Lubbock now has its own answer to Elvis Presley." The paper went on:

> Holly, who had a "three-piece orchestra just like Presley's" has reverted to playing and singing rock 'n' roll exclusively. He plays an electric standard guitar and wears "fancy" sports coats for his singing engagements, but the resemblance to the widely known entertainer ends there. Holly refuses to wear one of the bright sport coats on the street, even for publicity.[11]

SONNY CURTIS

Post-outlaw period, while Sonny was touring with W. Jennings. Courtesy of Elektra Records.

In 1956, singers who resembled Elvis were in high demand. Eddie Crandall, Marty Robbins's manager, saw Holly and offered to get him a recording contract. Returning to Nashville, Crandall approached a number of labels but with little success. finally, he spoke with Jim Denny, who was leaving the "Opry" to devote his full time to his booking and publishing interests. The "Opry" had asked Denny to divest himself of his outside activities which he refused to do.[12] Music City gossip has it that Denny was using his "Opry" position to further his own publishing and booking interests.[13] Crandall's enlistment of Denny was a turnabout; the agent had told Elvis Presley, following his only "Opry" audition, that the Hillbilly Cat should go back to driving a truck. Denny agreed to help Holly, but only after he had called Dave Stone to check out the singer's personal habits and physical appearance. Satisfied with what he heard, Denny talked with Paul Cohen, Decca's A & R man in Nashville.

Cohen, along with many residents of Sixteenth South, was somewhat baffled by the rock-a-billy trend. It wasn't country, but it did sell. although Elvis was condemned, his sales figures were envied. Cohen, like his counterpart at RCA Victor, Steve Sholes, wanted to reach the pop market without offending those who felt rock-a-billy was the death knell of country music. The bespectacled Buddy Holly seemed a safe bet, and so Cohen signed the Lubbock singer. Nashville pioneer Owen Bradley was assigned to produce Holly.

Buddy and his band left for Music City only to run into The System. John Goldrosen, Holly's biographer, describes the problems:

> When the Texans arrived at the Decca studio in Nashville, Holly found that although Decca was willing to let him use Curtis and Guess on the session, they did not want Holly to play his own rhythm guitar—they argued that the instrument would feed into the vocal microphone and interfere with the quality of the recording. Nor did they think that a rock 'n' roll style of drumming was necessary on the session.
>
> . . . Nashville was a closely knit society and teenage rock-a-billy musicians from West Texas were not part of it. Decca personnel were not deliberately unfriendly—after all, Holly was under contract to them and any success he gained would have been to their profit. But Holly and his friends could easily sense what was the unspoken attitude: That they were inexperienced "hick" musicians with nothing special to offer a large, old, sophisticated record company.[14]

Despite the lack of communication, Buddy did cut a number of songs in Music City. Buddy was Decca's country hope to reach the pop market. His first single, "Love Me" backed by Ben Hall's "Blue Days and Black Nights," was a "stiff." It sold 19,000 copies and was a commercial disappointment. Finally, Cohen told Buddy he did not have the voice to be a singer. Buddy returned to Lubbock disillusioned but not totally discouraged. Using a home recorder, he continued to experiment with rock-a-billy songs. He sang many Presley songs, some Chuck Berry material, Fats Domino's "Blue Monday," and his own songs.

In 1957 Holly formed the Crickets with Jerry Allison, Nicki Sullivan, and Joe B. Mauldin and began working with Clovis producer Norman Petty. Petty was best known to middle-of-the road audiences as the leader of the Petty Trio, which placed "Mood Indigo" on the charts. Petty had recently signed several Texas rock-a-billy acts, Buddy Knox and Jimmy Bowen, which met with some success. "Party Doll' was a big hit. Norman had some difficulty selling the Crickets, but Bob Thiele at Brunswick finally signed the quartet. The Crickets' first Brunswick release, "That'll Be the Day", quickly became the Number 3 song nationally. "Peggy Sue" on Coral also reached the same spot. By the winter of 1957 Buddy Holly was an established rock-a-billy star. Buddy's success further ignited the Lubbock scene. If one local boy could make good, there were possibilities for the others.

Unlike stations in the Appalachian states and parts of the deep South, where rock-a-billy was frequently equated with measles, chicken pox, or some other juvenile disease, Lubbock's radio stations programmed the genre as a vital form of country music. Ray Odum said that Dave Stone recalled: "We thought of rock-a-billy as just being another kind of country music—so we always played it."[16] Another deejay said, "Rock-a-billy was more popular than bluegrass. This has always been true out here." Lubbock, like most parts of the Lone Star state, was more influenced by Bob Wills, Ray Price, and Elvis Presley than many of the favorites on the "Grand Ole Opry." Consequently, Buddy Holly was considered to be in the local musical mainstream. Buddy, Sonny, and the other Lubbock artists were about to be caught up in a ratings war between KDAV and KLLL.

KDAV was one of the most respected country music stations in Texas. Pappy Stone was considered by many broadcasters to be the Todd Storz (the father of Top Forty radio) of country music.

A number of stations patterned their playlists (songs to be aired) after KDAV, which was the top-rated station in the area. A challenge however, was on the horizon.

In 1958, the Corbin brothers acquired KLLL, located high atop the Great Plains Life Building, which towered over downtown Lubbock. Ray Corbin, called Slim, was an easygoing musician who doubled as a disc jockey. His brother Sky was the opposite, a nervous and demanding station manager. Slim as was his nature, left most of the administrative details to his older brother. Hi-Pockets Duncan was employed for a daily thirty-minute program. Shortly after that, he became sales manager and continued to do his disc jockey show in the morning. The Corbins also hired Waylon Jennings away from KVOW. By now, he had at least five years of broadcasting experience. Hi-Pockets remembered him from KSEL. Slim had watched him perform and liked him. Waylon received $75 per week for two shows a day. KLLL took on KDAV with a staff of four.

For its time, KLLL was a "progressive" country station. It featured rock-a-billy and the latest efforts of Jim Reeves, Don Gibson, Johnny Cash, and Sonny James. The station did broadcast some more traditional material—especially by Texas boys like Lefty Frizell and Ernest Tubb. The main emphasis was on what would later be called the "Nashville Sound." Bob Wills got some air time. The station also featured remote broadcasts from Moore's Fruits and Vegetables and other local businesses; Waylon and Hi-Pockets usually did these. Waylon would sing current hits and Duncan took care of the commercials. Occasionally Duncan, who was also a local bandleader, would join in. Jennings did not always appreciate the help. Duncan would "sing bass to his bass." Waylon usually got angry when this happened. Despite the duets, the remotes went fairly smoothly and were quite popular.

KLLL stressed personality radio. Announcers for the most part did their own thing. Record introductions were ad libbed, but commercials and news reports were to be read straight. Waylon did not always appreciate the difference. Until the arrival of Don Bowman, Waylon was the madcap personality on the station. Listeners and station people offer various descriptions: "He was devil-may-care." "He'd always get his foot in his mouth." "He was a good ole boy on the air." Sky Corbin did not always respond to this approach casually, but his sales manager thought otherwise. "He was Waylon Jennings and he would boo-boo and

Buddy Holly and the Crickets, 1958. Courtesy of Buddy Holly Memorial Society, used by permission.

make all kinds of fluffs and turn around and say, 'what did I say?' But he was strictly an individual personality and did a fine job."[17]

Waylon's ad libs were generally accepted by the listeners, according to the mail and phone calls the station received, but Sky was dubious until the ratings came in. Female listeners especially liked the show. Housewives between the ages of twenty and forty-five made up the bulk of his afternoon audience. Slowly, KLLL was beginning to cut into KDAV's ratings and becoming a central hangout for Lubbock's musicians.

Pickers from the old "Dance Party" days used to stop by the twentieth floor studios or hang out in the coffee shop one floor below. Buddy Holly, when not on the road, spent a good deal of time at KLLL visiting Hi-Pockets and Waylon. Sonny Curtis also stopped in. "I'd go over to the radio station and sit in the coffee shop until Waylon had to go on the air and talk about the music business and drink coffee. He'd go on the air—I'd sit in the control room with him. He'd talk to me on the air. The show was a free-for-all. He was kinda crazy."[18] Buddy Holly stopped by with tapes of his new songs. Tommy Allsup, Jerry Allison, and some of the Clovis studio musicians came by. The Great Plains Building coffee shop became the "in" spot for the rock-a-billies and hillbillies of Lubbock. One participant recalled, "There was a lot of people hanging around . . . everybody was hanging around. Then they'd go up to the station and watch a number of young ladies who hung around, too." "Girls came up to see the swing-ingest guy around," according to Allsup. Don Bowman, who later joined the staff, quipped, "All I got out of the coffee shop was a divorce from the secretary on the sixth floor . . . . God I spent a lot of time in the coffee shop. I should have spent more time at home."[19]

The owners of the building were not happy either with KLLL or the musicians in the coffee shop. "So hayseeds moved into society as far as that building was concerned," says Waylon, "but they really didn't like it. Country music was being played in the tallest building in West Texas, but there should have been a sophisticated radio station there. Pretty soon it became Number 1, anyway. We had a pretty good thing going there."[20]

The coffee shop scene began to pay off. Buddy taped some spots for the station using "Peggy Sue" and "Everyday." The songs always ended with "country clout of KLLL." Sonny Curtis did another spot for KLLL. Dave Stone, watching his ratings slip to the newcomers, became increasingly angry with Holly and Curtis. "I went through hell with him," says Sonny, "but Pappy didn't own me. . . ."[21]

During the coffee shop bull sessions, Duncan began to pitch Waylon to Buddy. He reintroduced the two. Waylon had been playing Holly's records, and Holly was grateful. Buddy and Waylon resumed their relationship from the "Dance Party" days. Their bond is easy to understand. They were remarkably similar men. Both were highly cautious around people; some called them "shy." They shared a desire to succeed in the music business. Waylon, perhaps, was more flamboyant, but there were enough other similarities to cement a close friendship. Buddy liked Waylon and decided to teach the newcomer the lessons he had learned on the road. Duncan recalls: "Buddy liked Waylon; he liked him well enough that he took him over to the barbershop and had his hair cut the way he thought it should be cut. He took him to a clothing store and dressed him the way he thought. . . . Back in those days, Waylon was a little bit sloppy in the way he dressed because he just didn't have enough time to pay attention."[22] Duncan might have added that Waylon was nearly always broke and could not afford a decent wardrobe. He was constantly borrowing money at KLLL. In order to pay off one debt of $20 he gave a co-worker the rights to "Big Time Ladies Man."

Supporting a family was a burden. Maxine stayed at their Fifth Street home taking care of the kids, reading movie magazines, and drinking large amounts of Coca-Cola.

KLLL also served as an informal booking agency. Because of the remotes, Waylon and Slim frequently got $10 to $20 jobs, and gradually an informal band formed. Waylon, Slim, and George Atwood, a local studio musician played various social gatherings. One time, Hi-Pockets took them down to Spur, Texas, to play for the town's golden anniversary. The show consisted of Ray Price, June Carter, the Crickets and Sonny Curtis. That night, Waylon sat in as Price's bass guitar player. It was the first time he had played the instrument.

In October 1958, Buddy had arranged for New York studio musician King Curtis to fly down and record with him. (Holly had met the saxophonist several years earlier at an Alan Freed show in New York). Curtis was best known for his work with the Coasters. He was considered the father of the yackety sax, a style Boots Randolph would later popularize in country music.

Buddy called the King in New York. "I want you to come down to do the session," he said.

"Well, that'll be $500 and plane fare."

"Ain't that a little high?" replied Holly.

"Well,you're making yours all the time and I gotta make mine. You send the money up to New York."

"No, if I was to send you $500 and the plane crashed, I'd lose my money and my sax player."

"Mr. Holly, just send the mony and don't talk like that." He sent the money.[23] King was paid $600.

Buddy also decided to record Waylon. They picked Harry Choates's "Jole Blon," a Cajun standard. Buddy had been considering the song for himself but decided to try it with Waylon. Jennings, who remained more country than rock, seemed better suited for the French hillbilly waltz. "He cut the record on Waylon because he liked his style," recalls Sonny Curtis.[24] Neither Buddy nor Waylon understood the Cajun dialect. They listened to the Choates record for several days and wrote down the words as best they could. "When Sin Stops (Love Begins)" gave them less trouble. The song, written by Bob Vanable, a Lubbock songwriter, was an upbeat honky-tonker.

A recording session with King Curtis was, in the words of Sonny Curtis, "an event." One evening most of the Lubbock crowd drove to Clovis for the session. Buddy, Sonny Curtis, Bob Montgomery, Jerry Allison, George Atwood,Tommy Jennings, and Waylon all went. In the studio they were joined by King Curtis, Tommy Allsup, Bo Turner, and the vocal group known as the 4 Roses, who appeared on numerous Holly recordings. The 4 Roses startled Tommy Jennings. "They had these four funny fellas . . . it was the first time I'd seen a fag in my life. I didn't know what they were."[25] Tommy spent the night getting coffee for the musicians and the "funny fellas."

"Jole Blon" was a unique arrangement. It was a country song with a rock 'n' roll beat aimed at the pop market. John Goldrosen described it best: "A rhythm and blues saxophonist, a national rock 'n' roll star, and an aspiring country & western singer combined forces to record a Cajun waltz with a West Texas rock-a-billy beat and lyrics which were meaningless in any language."[26] Waylon was visibly nervous. This was his first recording session. It was also Buddy's original attempt at producing. "I wasn't near ready to start recording then, but the record itself didn't come out too bad," argues Waylon. "Hell, scared as I was—it was a lot of fun."[27]

"Jole Blon" was a showcase for the King. The saxophonist kicks off the song and plays the entire two minutes. Waylon adds the nearly unintelligible versus. Only the chorus, "Hey, hey, hey . . . ," is understandable.

Having set the French language back hundreds of years, Buddy and Waylon turned to "When Sin Stops." While "Jole Bon" was dominated by King Curtis, the Vanable song was pure Buddy Holly. Once again, the King opened with the first bars but the background—familiar to Holly fans—of the Roses and the Crickets chimed in. The chorus, "Don't stop . . . baby, please don't stop," is also unmistakable. Even some of the phrasing is Buddy Holly. Waylon liked "Jole Blon" but he didn't care for this one. "It was the worse song I ever heard."[28] (Waylon has said the same about other tunes, especially "Big Time Ladies Man.") The song leaves little doubt that Waylon Jennings was definitely Buddy Holly's protege.

After cutting the two songs, Waylon watched as Buddy did "Reminiscing" with Curtis. Buddy wasn't too happy with the outcome. Then they turned to "Come Back Baby," a song written with Norman Petty. Buddy did not really want to cut the song but his producer kept insisting. "I don't think he was into that tune at all," recalls Jerry Allison. Buddy did the song but, as Bob Montgomery suggests, "it didn't really come off as well as the Jennings songs."[29]

Following the "Jole Blon" session, Buddy returned to New York to work with another young singer, Lou Giordane. In December he wrote "Stay Close to Me" and had Lou record it for Brunswick. Buddy was also talking with Irving Feld about a tour.

Feld was one of the prime packagers of national pop music tours. He was the president of Super Enterprises, which put together the "Biggest Show of Stars." Souvenir books published for the tours boasted: "the show that brings you more top stars than any other tour package. And, we at Super Enterprises, Inc. intend to maintain the 'Biggest Show of Stars,' the biggest entertainment value on the road." Buddy had appeared on several of these, sharing the bill with Chuck Berry, Fats Domino, Paul Anka, Eddie Cochran, Buddy Knox, and the Everly Brothers.

In October 1958, Feld joined with Buddy Howe and Tim Gale of General Artists Corporation to cosponsor "live" shows with deejays across the country. A series of 75 to 200 artists were scheduled to go out on the road for ten months, with a layoff during July and August. The first such tour was to be the Winter Dance Party, beginning in mid-January. Feld approached Buddy with a proposition that he headline the first tour. At first Buddy rejected the offer, but finances were becoming an increasing problem.

Buddy returned to Lubbock for Christmas with a GAC offer in his pocket. One back in Lubbock, he returned to writing and producing. Buddy spent hours in the KLLL studios. during Hi-Pockets' morning show, Buddy, Slim, and Waylon decided to write a song. Buddy threw out, "You're the one that's a-causing my blues . . . ." Waylon and Slim added, "You're the one I don't wanna lose." Then someone contributed, "You're the one that I'd always choose." In less than fifteen minutes the song was finished. Borrowing a guitar, Buddy sang the lyrics into a KLLL tape recorder. Waylon and Slim provided a choppy rhythm by clapping their hands. "You're the One" was ninety seconds long and sounded a bit like "Maybe Baby."

If Buddy Holly were to go on tour, he would need a band. Relations between Buddy and Clovis were strained, so he discounted using the original Crickets. Buddy approached Tommy Allsup and asked him to form a band. Tommy knew Charlie Bunch, a Texas drummer who had worked with Oribson. He agreed to join the band. Then Buddy asked Waylon if he wanted to play bass on the Winter Dance Party tour.

WAYLON

4

THE DAY THE MUSIC DIED

When I read about his widowed bride,
Something touched me deep inside
The day the music died.

—Don McLean, "American Pie," BMI

As Christmas neared, Waylon filled with anticipation and excitement, approached his boss at KLLL. Glenn "Sky" Corbin was not anxious to have him leave. Despite the studio antics and the now familiar "Why did I say that?", Waylon was one of the most popular jocks at the station. One poll showed his afternoon show having a 60 percent share of the audience. He was unpredictable, but he got the job done. Corbin had little choice but to agree to a "leave of absence."

The situation at home was not so simple. Maxine did not like Waylon's going "at all." She was pregnant, again. But he was resolved to go. Brother Tommy, who was left in charge of things, put it this way: "When he left and went with Buddy Holly on the road she was pretty tore up. . . . I used to go over and look after her and she would get awful disgusted. She didn't like the idea of him being gone all the time." The argument over the Holly tour would be one of many. The battleground was always career versus marriage. "An artist will give up more. They will give up everything for that shot," cautions Tommy, "it's not that they walk off and leave you, but they want you to understand them . . . be there when they get back."[1]

Ever since Buddy's invitation, Waylon had been practicing the electric bass. He had played the instrument once before, when Ray Price needed a pickup band and Waylon found himself pounding the unfamiliar four-stringed box. It was not as easy as Buddy had promised:

"Here's this bass—you learn it. . . . "You can play it. . . . "Now, here're my albums. . . . You learn 'em and you got a week-and-a-half to do it."

Tommy Allsup showed Waylon some of the notes and chord positions. Waylon just memorized the notes. It would take another month before he could say, "I realized what I was doing and what was happening—why, when you hit that note, it made that sound."

The bone-chilling winds that swept the Panhandle were a foretaste of the winter of Gotham and the frigid cold of the northern Midwest, where the tour was scheduled. Blizzard conditions prevailed. The Littlefield paper announced, "Waylon Jennings leaves for New York Monday." It was typical of the short notices of arrivals and departures that dot every small town paper. Another later notice read: "Waylon Jennings, 21, of Littlefield—left for New York Monday to become a member of 'Buddy Holly and the Crickets' of 'Peggy Sue' and 'What'll [sic] Be the Day' fame."[2]

Finally Monday arrived. Waylon was packed and ready to go. Bidding the family good-bye, Buddy's new bass player climbed into the old Plymouth for the two-hour drive to the Amarillo airport.

The TWA flight destined for Wichita left on time. This was Waylon's first commercial flight and he was nervous. The uneasiness was mixed with excitement. He was headed for the big time. On the plane, Charlie, Tommy, and Waylon laughed and talked of the good things that awaited them in the Big City. In Wichita, they boarded another plane for Chicago's Midway Airport. On Tuesday, Waylon's anxiety over flying was heightened. A TWA flight from Chicago to New York had just crashed into the Mississippi River. With considerable apprehension, the three musicians boarded the next flight to New York.

New York, for Waylon, was an overwhelming experience. "I

was looking for the Empire State Building . . . standing right under it . . . not knowing it."[3] There was little time for sight-seeing. Buddy insisted on long hours of rehearsals and did some recording. On his own home tape recorder, Buddy cut two songs with Tommy Allsup on the bass. Waylon had not yet mastered the instrument.

Despite Jerry Allison's "ownership of the name," General Artists Corporation (GAC) decided to label his new backup group "The Crickets." Buddy's reasons for accepting this billing are not totally clear. This may have been a move to slight Norman Petty or to pressure Jerry and Joe B. to rejoin him. The relationship between the Clovis producer and Holly had gotten much worse. Norman, according to Waylon, had Buddy's funds completely tied up. Buddy did not have enough money to pay his rent, despite a Clovis bank account containing an estimated $50,000. Petty was the only person authorized to draw on the account. The account clearly was a tool to force Buddy back into line. Jerry Allison had declared that "Norman wanted Buddy to come back . . . I think that's probably why he wanted us to stay. . . . I don't think he thought he had any great talent in me and Joe B. . . . I only found out after Buddy's death that Norman had been telling Buddy and his lawyer that Buddy owed us a bunch of money from tours, and that we'd have to get that all straight before Buddy got his money." Buddy was furious. "I'm going to Clovis and break everything in sight," he threatened, "including Nor-man's back."[4] Buddy's economic situation was the major factor for his going on the ill-fated tour.

Irving Feld, the GAC promoter who was to be Buddy's agent, urged him to join the Winter Dance Party. Friendship and a $2,500 advance convinced the singer that the freezing cold cli-mates of Minnesota in February might not be a bad idea. Buddy's widow, Maria, told biographer John Goldrosen, "the money was a reason for going . . . my aunt had been lending us money to fix up our apartment and all."[5]

Waylon and Tommy stayed at Buddy's part furnished Fifth Avenue apartment, which Buddy and Maria were remodeling. Between rehearsals they discussed plans for a studio in Lubbock where Buddy would produce Waylon. Snuff Garrett, then a deejay, said, "Buddy was going to have a record company and a publishing company of his own and name it after the color of his Cadillac—Toth. He was looking around for artists for Toth Records."[6] Others claim Buddy was going to Champion Prism

Records. Another version is that Dick Jacobs of Coral had offered him $500 per master. None of the people around Buddy have made sense out of this situation. Many hours were spent figuring out expenses for the masters and Texas studio. Occasionally, Buddy mentioned the possibility of Waylon's moving into the New York apartment. "He actually wanted Waylon to come and move in with us, to live with us," says Maria. "Because he felt like that way, he could really come to know Waylon and his feelings and write songs that matched him." There was no doubt that Waylon Jennings was the protégé of Buddy Holly. Waylon's career was now closely tied to Holly's. The night before starting the tour, "Peggy Sue Got Married" and "That Makes It Tough" were cut on Buddy's home recorder.

Their last night together, Buddy and Maria had unusual dreams. Buddy saw a small plane that kept landing and flying off. Maria had a vision of a big ball of fire falling to the ground in a desolate region.

On January 23 the tour began. Buddy and Waylon were joined by Richie Valens, Frankie Sardo, J.P. Richardson (called "Bopper"), and Dion and the Belmonts. Most were coming off or enjoying big hit records. Valens, not yet old enough to buy liquor, had "LaBamba" close to the top of the pop charts and on every Top Forty radio station. Bopper was famous for "Chantilly Lace" ("Hello Baby"), Dion and his Belmonts, named after a street in Bronx, had been on "American Bandstand" with "I Wonder Why," "No One Knows," and "Don't Pity Me." Buddy's "It Doesn't Matter Anymore" was climbing the charts. Only Sardo was hitless. Part of the duo "Frankie and Johnny," Frankie was a hopeful willing to open the star-studded show.

The GAC Dance Party was little more than a traveling jukebox or Top Forty show. A number of name artists were assembled to go out on the road and do their hits. Usually the performer would not have to do more than two or three songs. A local disc jockey would be employed to introduce the acts. The Winter Dance Party was put together the same way. Sardo would open the show with currently popular songs that were not his own. Dion and the Belmonts would follow, doing their three big hits, and they would be followed by Richie Valens with "Donna," "LaBamba," and several rock-a-billy songs. Bopper then did his famous song (phone and all) and some comedy routines. The Crickets opened their set with "Gotta Travel On," the Billy Grammer hit. Waylon and Buddy would then sing "Salty Dog Blues," a traditional

W.J., Tommy Allsup, and Buddy Holly on the "last tour." Courtesy of Don Larson, used by permission.

country song, and then run through the famous Holly hits. Buddy rarely said much on stage between songs, just a polite "thank you."

Midwest audiences were a natural for this type of package. Living in isolation and usually tied to one local radio station or a clear-channel 50,000 watt giant hundreds of miles away, teenagers welcomed the opportunity finally to see the stars sing their favorite songs.

The tour began in Milwaukee. It was 25 degrees below zero. Going from the hotel to the taxi, Tommy Allsup found it hard to breathe. In the cab they wondered if anyone would go out in the freezing cold. As the taxi approached George Devine's Ballroom, they were amazed to see lines of teenagers, seemingly stretching for blocks, outside waiting for the Winter Dance Party to begin.

That night, Waylon and the rest of the band appeared in black coats and grey trousers with yellow ascots. Buddy opened with "Travel On" and closed with "Peggy Sue." Waylon's bass playing was adequate; he did turn the volume down somewhat. The audience loved the show.

Leaving Milwaukee for Kenosha, the Dance Party quickly discovered that the bus provided by GAC would not keep them warm. The heater in the bus could not keep out the Wisconsin winter. After the Eau Claire concert the Crickets were faced with yet another problem. "Goose" had lost his stage clothes. This left the band with only their matching brown pants and checkered coats. Only Buddy could now wear the black and grey combination.

On the bus, keeping warm became the main concern. Passengers were huddled on the seats wrapped in all the clothing they could find. Alcohol seemed to ease the chill—but not much. "It was really cold up there," says one of Holly's musicians. "The first twelve days we were out we had like seven or eight different buses. One would freeze up just going down the highway. I don't know where GAC was getting them, but I think they were coming right from the salvage organization . . . they just didn't have any heaters in them that would work good. Man, it was really miserable."[7]

Waylon and the Bopper quickly became friends. The Texans enjoyed going out after a show and drinking beer or vodka. Bopper and Waylon decided to write a song on the bus designed for their mutual hero, George Jones. The song was "Move Over

Blues." The lyrics to it have been lost. Waylon Jennings says, "I
don't know if it was any good or not—it seemed like it was . . . it
was a real country thing."[8]

On January 31 the bus froze up. On a hill somewhere between
Duluth, Minnesota, and Green Bay, Wisconsin, the engine simply stopped. Huddled in coats, the troupe lit newspapers to keep
warm. Finally, a truck appeared that took several people to a
nearby town. The local sheriff arranged transportation for the
other freezing members on the bus. Buddy's drummer suffered
frostbite on his feet and remained in the hospital for several days.
Dion replaced him during the closing Holly set.

The troupe boarded a train to get to Green Bay. On February
1, the Bopper stopped and purchased a sleeping bag. After the
successful Green Bay concert, the converted school bus headed
for Clear Lake, Iowa. Again, the group ran into engine troubles.
At 6:00 P.M., after a 350-mile trip, they arrived. It had been
nearly six days since the troupe had been in a hotel. "Our clothes
were all dirty and we were tired," says Waylon.[9] They were
scheduled to do a four-hour show that night in the resort community and then continue another 430 miles to Moorhead, Minnesota, for two shows the next night.

In Clear Lake, Buddy decided to charter a plane. He, Waylon,
and Tommy would fly ahead, get some much-needed rest, and
also do the laundry for the Moorhead appearances. Their one set
of checkered costumes were filled with the road dirt. Rod Lucier,
the road manager, encouraged the flight, hoping that Buddy
would take care of any business problems that might arise.
Waylon and Tommy Allsup agreed to share the $108 cost of the
flight. That night at the Surf Ballroom in Clear Lake, Buddy
asked the club manager, Carroll Anderson, to charter a plane.
Anderson called Dwyer's Flying Service. The owner of the charter service was unvailable, but Roger Peterson, a young inexperi-
enced assistant, agreed to the flight. It was to be his day off. He
would fly the three musicians to Fargo, North Dakota, a few
miles from Moorhead.

Hearing about the flight, Bopper came to Waylon, asking to
take his place. "Those bus seats bug me." Throughout the trip,
Bopper had been complaining that a big man could not get
comfortable on a bus. Also, he was suffering from a severe cold,
which made his discomfort even greater.

"It's alright with me, if it's alright with Buddy. You go ask
him!" replied Waylon. Buddy agreed to change.[10]

DION

Holly's replacement drummer on the "last tour," 1959.

At 8:00 P.M. some 1,500 teenagers crowded into the Surf Club to see the Winter Dance Party. Unlike previous nights, Buddy started the closing set alone, singing the Billy Grammer hit "Gotta Travel On." The band then joined him for "Rave On," "Peggy Sue," and most of his big hits. On stage, Waylon and Buddy had a minor disagreement—their first. Waylon's bass was too loud. Buddy kept trying to get Waylon's attention, but with little success. "I couldn't hear him because my bass was too loud. Finally, Buddy shouted through the microphone, 'Turn that damn thing down.' That just crushed me," Waylon told a Phoenix deejay.[11]

Richie Valens learned of the midnight flight. Valens approached Tommy Allsup, a six-foot, three-inch Oklahoman, and asked him, "let me go instead." "I've never been in a little plane before." Valens continued to pester Tommy. As the bus was being loaded, the "LaBamba" star was signing autographs. As Tommy returned from the bus to check on his gear, Richie repeated his request. "Come on—let's flip. Heads I go, tails you go."

"If I lose I get Bopper's sleeping bag?" insisted Tommy. The Bopper had no objections, as he had already scored a seat on the plane. The coin was flipped. It showed "heads."[12]

After the show, Buddy called Maria. He complained about the dirt and cold plus the poor transportation. "Things just weren't as had been promised," she told a writer. "Everybody on the tour was really disgusted with the whole thing."[13]

Shortly after the call, Carroll Anderson, the club owner, drove the three entertainers to the Mason City, Iowa, airport. Forty minutes after midnight they were greeted by Peterson and Jerry Dwyer. Peterson promised that weather conditions were adequate for the flight. Some winds were blowing and light snow was falling to the ground, but a takeoff was still possible.

The airport, however, did not tell the young pilot of several adversaries that had just been announced by the U.S. Weather Bureau. The warnings indicated that instrument flying would be necessary. Peterson had flunked his first instrument flight check because he could not maintain a proper altitude. At 1:00 A.M. the single-engine plane took off.

Jerry Dwyer heard nothing from his pilot. He checked with other airports and grew worried. Hours passed—still no word. In desperation, he decided to retrace Peterson's course. "I was only eight miles northwest of the field when I spotted the wreckage,"

Waylon and Tommy Allsup, "last tour." Courtesy of Don Larson, used by permission.

he told the Civil Aeronautics Board. "I believe the time was approximately 9:35 A.M.."

Police found the plane in a cornfield. There were no survivors. Originally, there was considerable confusion as to the identities of the victims. A black wallet was found near the plane. The driver's license was Tommy Douglas Allsup's, and another item in the billfold was a business card for Prism Records. The officers of the organization were Buddy Holly, listed as president, Ray Rush (promotion), and Norman Petty (sales manager). On the other side of the card was a hastily written name and address, "Wayland Jennings, KLLL—PO 31911, Lubbock Texas. 11 5th Avenue, Littlefield, TX 486-R."

Tommy had given the wallet to Buddy for identification so a registered letter could be picked up. A Mason City radio station put out the information that Tommy had been killed. The identification of Holly and Allsup suggested that Waylon had also been on the plane. In the Texas Panhandle, communication lines were garbled up even further by a storm; telegraph lines were down and radio communications spotty.

Hi-Pockets Duncan was doing his usual remote from Moore's Fruits and Vegetables. Slim Corbin was sitting in for Waylon on the broadcast. The live broadcast was interrupted with "a special bulletin from KLLL News . . . Buddy Holly and his band have been killed."

Tommy Jennings was working on a tractor in a repair shop in Littlefield. KVOW announced that "Buddy Holly and the Crickets were killed in an airplane crash." "I went crazy . . . I just took off and went home." His mother was in hysterics; the entire family was in shock. Several hours later the correction was made. "I say for about two or three hours before they got that correction there—boy, it was a tore up place."[14]

The Bob Montgomerys were driving to Lubbock. "Really be careful because I got a really weird feeling that something bad is fixin' to happen," he told his wife, who was behind the wheel.[15]

At 12:30 the school bus carrying the rest of the touring group arrived in Fargo. Waylon, Tommy Allsup, and the pudgy road manager, Rod Lucier, got off the bus and went into register the troupe. Everyone else was asleep. As Tommy entered the lobby he saw the Bopper's picture on the TV screen. The sound was turned very low, and did not hear the words. "An advertisement for the show," he thought.

"Are you guys with the show?" asked the desk clerk. "Then you haven't heard about the accident?"

"No!"

"They were all killed this morning."

Shaken, Tommy brought the news to the bus. Waylon was in a state of shock. Finally, they decided to call home. Tommy called his mother in Oklahoma. She had thought he was dead. Waylon phoned Littlefield.

Mrs. Jennings and Maxine had also believed, for a time, that Waylon was on the plane. Waylon wanted to quit the tour and accompany Buddy's body back to the windswept plains of West Texas. GAC had other ideas.

No sooner had Tommy and Waylon gotten back to their rooms than the phone rang. The booking agents insisted that the show go on, but their argument was not a convincing one. Then they promised Waylon, Tommy, and the others a paid flight to Buddy's funeral if the tour continued. GAC also assured Waylon and Tommy that they would get Buddy's share for the remaining sixteen shows. This should be around $4,000—not bad for two and a half weeks. At the time, Tommy was drawing $300 a week. Most of the money was being spent on food, lodging, and alcohol. Waylon got $200. Both needed the money and so agreed to continue. To fill out the bill, local promoters needed another act.

Bob Velline was an average sophomore at Central High School in Fargo, North Dakota.[16] Like many of his classmates, he was a rock music fan and dressed like his idol, Buddy Holly. His modified ducktail haircut was more in keeping with Fabian than Buddy. He also knew most of Buddy's songs—note for note. For him, "That'll Be the Day" was "the most original, fresh, unique record I ever heard." Bob's fascination with Holly grew into imitation. In January, almost to the day the GAC tour began, he formed a band. The heart of the unit was Jim Stillman, a rotund bass player nicknamed Moby Dick, and Velline's older brother. The band eagerly awaited the appearance of their idol in Fargo. This was to be the first big time rock show to visit the semi-Arctic city.

Coming home for lunch Bobby heard the tragic news. Buddy Holly was Dead! A few hours later KFGO, Fargo's only Top Forty station, headlined by Bobby Dale, announced auditions for the evening performance. Moby Dick volunteered the band's services. Unexpectedly, they were accepted. The offer may have well been premature. The band had been together only two weeks. They did not have a name or stage clothes. Quickly they rushed out and bought matching white 25-cent ties and angora sweaters. With considerable nervousness, the "no name band" approached the concert.

Backstage the scene was grim. The shock of the past few hours and fatigue hung on. Empty stares, tears, and idle talk—the atmosphere of a disaster prevailed. Confusion was another element. The crash had destroyed the normal pecking order of who went on when. "Who's on first?" was asked repeatedly. Finally, Frankie Sardo was chosen. Bobby's group would follow. A name had to be picked quickly. The band was to be called the "Shadows." For the first time, the Shadows would appear before an audience.

Frankie Sardo opened with a few words and sang Richie Valens's "Donna." Handkerchiefs and moist eyes greeted the tune. The Shadows followed with "Bye, Bye Love" and "Long Tall Sally." Then Dion and the Belmonts and finally The Crickets appeared, minus Buddy Holly. They sang "Rave On," "That'll Be the Day," and "Peggy Sue"—people openly cried. One interesting thing did happen. Waylon's vocal on "Rave On" received screams previously reserved for Buddy. "At first, I thought the cheers were for Buddy," says Tommy Allsup, "but then I realized they were for Waylon."[17]

After the show, the local promoters tried to pay the band less because Buddy Holly was not with them. They tried to pay even less because the Bopper and Valens were dead. Waylon was getting a very quick introduction to the strange ways of booking agents. "After the show, the promoters were all uptight. They tried to dock us for how much Buddy and the Big Bopper and Richie Valens had made. This—after beggin' us to play. We just wanted to go home . . . but we played for them anyway. Real 'nice' people. . . . There was a lotta that crap that I just wasn't ready for and I'd never really experienced."[18]

GAC continued to make promises and the tour went on. They would feed Waylon his meals and repeat, "We'll fly you to the funeral."

The troupe continued on February 3, 1959, to Sioux City, Iowa. Frankie Avalon and Jimmy Clanton came to substitute for the fallen stars. Ronnie Smith, an Oklahoma rock-a-billy, joined the Crickets and shared the lead vocals with Waylon. Mechanically—as if in a hypnotic trance—the band played the songs.

Waylon again received the fervent reaction. The applause matched Frankie Avalon's, the teen scream idol.

Two days later, Buddy Holly returned home for the last time. On February 7, a service was held. He was buried at Lubbock City Cemetary a few feet from the road. The pallbearers were Jerry Allison, Joe B. Mauldin, Bob Montgomery, Sonny Curtis, Niki Sullivan, and Phil Everly.

The promoters did not fly the touring Crickets to the funeral, who instead played the Val Air Ballroom in Des Moines. The free meals stopped. Waylon and the rest of the group stayed on in hopes of collecting the money promised them. They survived by drawing against their salaries. A week after the plane crash, Tim Gale, who helped Feld in developing the dance party idea, told Ron Gavatt of *Billboard*, "Tour would be continued to its conclusion." He also said, "We always fought against the idea of any of them chartering their own planes."[19] Gale did not mention the poorly heated old buses plagued with engine trouble.

The reaction of the booking agency and Buddy's record label was curious. None of the customary memorial pages were taken out in the trades. Only Mercury Records bought a full-page ad to honor the Bopper. There was a definite business-as-usual attitude surrounding the entire tragedy. *Billboard* did announce, "Coral is rushing out an album of Buddy's biggest hits under the title, The Buddy Holly Story." On March 9, when the album was released, the trade magazine applauded the cover of The Buddy Holly Story. "It's a shot that's certain to stir his many fans and draw extra sales."[20]

On February 15 the tour finally ended. Springfield, Illinois, was the final stop on the tour. The show was introduced by a local deejay with an attractive wife. Debbie got considerable attention from the troupe. Waylon and Ronny continued to divide the singing chores. Once again, Waylon's performance got screams and shrieks. After the show, the Crickets climbed on the bus for the last time. They made reservations for a 7:00 A.M. train to New York. On the bus, Waylon resumed drinking vodka and Seven-Up—a vodka bottle in one hand, Seven-Up in the other. He would drink a little pop and then pour the clear Russian liquor into the bottle. As the sips, miles, and time passed, Waylon resumed his comments about Ronny's white pills. When Ronny Smith joined the troupe, he brought some amphetamines with him. He had gotten the "crosses" in a little Mexican border town. Waylon strongly disapproved.

"Those things are gonna kill ya," he would say. "I wouldn't take one of those damn pills for nothing."

After several weeks of remarks like this, both Allsup and Smith had decided something needed to be done. That night, exchanging knowing looks, Tommy and Ronny ignored Waylon's comments. After a while Tommy said, "Waylon, let me have a drink of your Seven-Up." Waylon, distracted by a passenger, did not see Tommy crush a handful of white pills and drop them into the green pop bottle.

At midnight the bus arrived at the Chicago train depot. Getting their tickets and baggage, Tommy and Carl scattered to find chairs for the seven-hour wait. They quickly fell asleep in the worn terminal chairs. Waylon just paced around the depot, back and forth, back and forth. At seven, the trio boarded their New York train. All but one was quickly asleep.

"About every thiry minutes to an hour, somebody would come along and shove me in the arm," says Tommy. "It's Waylon and he's just walking that damn train from one end to another." For two straight days Waylon walked the train as it went up to Canada and down into New York. "He probably walked the length of that train 1,000 times from Chicago to New York."[21] After three and a half days, walking a train for 3,000 miles, strolling around Forty-Second Street and Seventh and Eighth avenues all day, at 5:00 A.M., February 20, Waylon finally fell asleep. This was Waylon's first experience with uppers. In later years he told friends, "after the first one, the second one came easy."[22]

The tour was over but the GAC situation had not been settled. First, there was the matter of the $4,000 promised to the Winter Dance Party Crickets. "At first, they wouldn't even talk to us," recalls Allsup. "Then they refused to pay us." "We gave it all to Buddy's wife," GAC told Waylon and Tommy.[23] After several heated discussions, the booking agency did give them $240 train fare, an amount guaranteed in the original contract. None of the verbal promises made after Buddy's death were kept.

GAC was planning another Crickets tour to capitalize on Buddy's death. However, there were problems. Norman Petty had filed an injunction against the agency for using the Crickets name. He, Jerry Allison, Joe B. Mauldin, Earl Sinks, and Sonny Curtis were in New York. So were the "current" Crickets. An agreement was reached. Tommy, Jerry, Joe B., and Earl Sinks were to be the "new" GAC Crickets. Waylon, "Goose," Ronny, and Sonny would return to Texas. Waylon left the Fender Precision Bass and amplifier in a locker in New York. The four drove back in Jerry Allison's new 1958 Chevrolet; the engine burned out in Missouri.

"Buddy was a real good friend and I thought his loss was all for nothing. It was a mental—I felt like I had lost a brother."[24] Waylon returned to Texas embittered and dejected. He had lost a friend as well as a teacher. All of the plans and dreams he and Buddy had shared together were over. "His mind was in a turmoil," remembers Hi-Pockets Duncan. "What am I doing to do? Which way do I go? It wasn't a matter of not going. It was which way to go without Buddy. This was his first tour with Buddy and this could have been a long drawn-out thing. I am sure they had some plans made. In fact, I know they had some plans to extend this into some more tours. Waylon was set up as the man who did the vocals when Buddy wasn't on stage. The whole thing was working great and I'm sure they had looked into the future and planned it. Then all of the sudden all this stops and you know how a person would feel. Waylon was young and I'm sure he was completely torn up and at wits end as to which way to go."[25]

"It affected me in a lot of ways," says Waylon. "I was completely mixed up."

Waylon's view of the music industry had changed. "Flesh peddlers—that's what they are."[26] He believed GAC had conned him. He blamed Norman Petty for Buddy's death. Waylon felt Norman cheated Buddy and by withholding the money had forced him on the fatal tour. The day after the crash, Petty told Wichita Falls deejay Snuff Garrett: "sometimes things happen like this and there's nothing we can do to control them. We may question *why* things like this happen, of course, but there's always bound to be a reason somewhere."

Waylon had lost more than just a friend. He thought his opportunity for fame and fortune had gone down with the plane. Fate had cruelly postponed his plans for musical stardom. It's a long way back from the glamor of New York to Littlefield. On occasion, especially when drinking, Waylon threatened to quit the music business. But it was an idle threat—Waylon still wanted to be an artist, but now he had to pick up the tempo alone.

WAY LON

5

PICKING UP THE TEMPO

The loss of Buddy Holly deeply affected Waylon. He returned to Littlefield and Lubbock a confused and disillusioned individual. The guitar was stored in his mother's back room and he went back to KLLL. Being a disc jockey didn't seem very interesting. The applause of the tour changed it all. He became even more casual on the air, taking a devil-may-care attitude. He told *Music City News*, "I became irresponsible as far as my work was concerned. I was completely mixed up. I couldn't have cared less about being a disc jockey. Everything got progressively worse."[1]

In March 1959 Brunswick released the "Jole Blon" record. The unique arrangement did garner some airplay. The trade charts did not reflect any action. Why the record was released remains a mystery. Some people believe it was an attempt to capitalize on Buddy's death. Lou Giordane's single "Stay Close To Me" appeared at the same time. Buddy had written the song. The record was a stiff and is now a collector's item.

Things really got crazy when Don Bowman and Waylon were united. Bowman, a native of Lubbock and a graduate of the New Mexico Military Institute, was a short, sandy-haired announcer who was a natural cut-up. Chet Atkins described him as "One of the few people who can walk into a room—walk across the room and sit down and in that space of time he'll either say or do something that'll make you laugh."[2] Prior to joining KLLL, Don had been with a Lubbock rock station, KDUB, for four years.

In March 1959 KDUB hired a female program director. Don "didn't want any part of that" and went over to KLLL, rode up the elevator twenty floors, and asked Sky Corbin for a job. He was quickly hired, being the highest rated deejay in the area.

Don and Waylon quickly became allies. They went to Western movies and bowled together *while on the air.* "Remember those Navy recruiting things. They used to send 'em out on a disc. We'd just roll one up, flop it over on a turntable and go bowling. They do a 45 minute show—so we'd put one of those on and go bowling." One day, the recruiting disc stuck and Sky Corbin caught the errant deejays. Don quips, "Sky has got no sense of humor at all."[3]

"He turned gray headed within about eight to ten weeks after Don and I went to work there," recalls Waylon. "And finally, you know, Don and I would get on the radio together and holy mackerel, you know. So finally, they had this piece of paper up on the wall in the control room that gives you rules, regulations and format and everything. And the Number One rule was: DON BOWMAN AND WAYLON JENNINGS NOT TO BE IN THE CONTROL ROOM AT THE SAME TIME WHILE ON THE AIR."[4]

The notice went up after a newcast. Waylon was doing the news—"Due to the bread strike in Houston, all women who want to get flesh, no—all the women who want to get fresh bread will have to go by the bakery." Bowman was in the control booth. "I fell . . . just fell on the floor. Waylon was already into the next story before he realized what he said." In the middle of the story, "Oh-oh," said Waylon. "Mmm-huh," came the reply over the air. Both announcers broke up. Waylon laughed all the way through the rest of the newcast, even when announcing a plane crash. "All ladies a reachin' to get bread will have to go by the bakery. Ok Waylon," Bowman kept repeating and laughing in the background. At this point, Sky decided to separate the two. Bowman was given the morning seven-to-nine shift and Waylon drew the afternoon three-to-seven time slot. However, this ploy was a failure.

Waylon and Don began to tamper with the taped commercials and air checks. At first, they would take commercials and start them in the middle. An unsuspecting Slim Corbin would put the tape on and find that it made no sense. This was not all. Don would reword commercials; during the tape, a voice would say, "Hi, this is Waylon Jennings. What's going on here?" Don closed

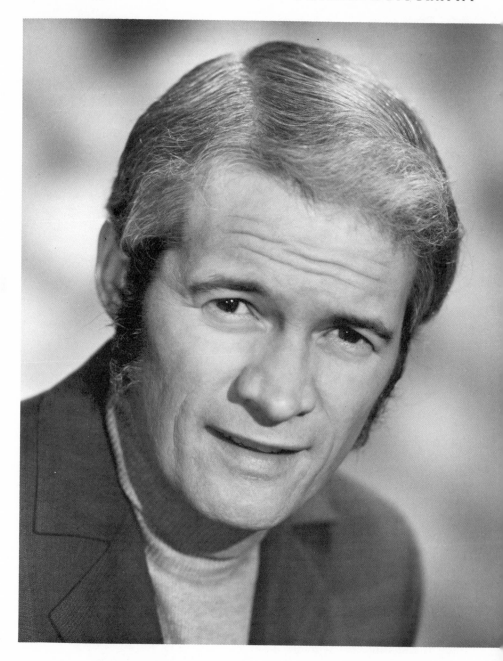

"Waylon's radio partner in crime." Courtesy of Don Bowman, 1975.

the weather forecast with "Fair and warmer and his orchestra."
Even the station identification was fair game. "This is k something or other, serving the Portland-Vancouver area." Tourists
tuned in to kLLL no doubt checked their maps. What Don should
have said was, "This is kLLL from high atop the Great Plains
Tower in beautiful Lubbock."

Sky had a special problem with Bowmen: getting him to sign
logs. Disc jockeys are required by FCC regulations to check in and
out when on the air. The information is found on the control
room panels. Four days in a row Don forgot to sign the log. One
evening, Bowman's phone rang.

"I want you to get in your car and drive all the way back down
here and sign off this log like you're supposed to and you won't
forget anymore!"

"Okay," said Bowman.

The next day, Sky stormed up to Don, "I told you last night to
come down here and sign that log 'cause you forgot it."

"I know—I was gonna come back and do it, but I forgot that
too."

Corbin was furious. It was a wonder that neither man was fired.
"Listen," answers Bowman, "for the money we was working for
he couldn't afford to fire us. He couldn't find anybody else dumb
enough to work for that much bread." There is probably considerable truth to the statement. Sky and Don and Waylon doing
everything except sweeping out the station for $75 a week.
When not on the air or making commercials, each had to serve as
bill collector for kLLL.

Hi-Pockets Duncan offers another explanation. "I've never
heard any complaints about Waylon's programming on the air
(except from Sky Corbin) 'cause everybody took it for granted—
that was Waylon Jennings. We didn't expect anything else. We
expected the unexpected. He was a whole lot like Don Bowman.
Don was a unique character, too. We were all pretty wild disc
jockeys back in those days. . . .that was our job."[5]

While in Lubbock, Waylon took another shot at recording.
Wendal Bagwell, the owner of a fledgling local record company,
offered the singer/disc jockey a percentage of Trend 61 for some
songs.[6] A number of journalists have indicated that Waylon
bought into the company and his records were of the "vanity"
genre. This is simply incorrect. Bagwell merely hoped to capitalize on Jennings's local popularity and the Holly connection. He
was listed as Waylon's manager. Waylon recorded "Never

Don Bowman promoting his syndicated radio show, 1974. Courtesy of Don Bowman, 1974.

Trend, '61 Records, 1961.

Again," "Another Blue Day," "My Baby Walks All Over Me," and "The Stage" with a backup band called the Beavers. (This was before CB jargon.) "Another Blue Day" was immediately released and somewhat popular in the West Texas area.

Waylon left KLLL and ran through a series of odd jobs around the Littlefield area. Waylon worked for a time as a mechanic's helper in Tommy's shop. He quit that job, too. Tommy could not understand his brother's behavior. Waylon had a family to support and he was quitting all these jobs. "Waylon," he said one day, "why don't you go down to Hall's grocery store or down to some other place and go to work?" "Tommy, music is my life and if I was to do anything to my hands it would destroy me."[7] He finally got a job driving the local school bus.

On March 21, 1961, Maxine gave birth to a son. He was named Buddy Dean after Waylon's mentor and the film idol of the 1950s, James Dean. Waylon had yet another mouth to feed on his lowly salary.

Don remained at the station for six months. "That was about all they could take." Don's reason for staying that long was to get the final decree in his divorce from the secretary on the sixth floor. Once that was over, he moved to KELP in El Paso.

Waylon decided to leave Texas. He felt that local creditors were closing in. Maxine had relatives in Coolidge, Arizona. While the arid city wasn't utopia, it did seem an improvement over the windswept regions of the Panhandle. Coolidge is in the middle of nowhere. It is almost an hour south of Phoenix near the sweltering Casa Grande Ruins. Its population is almost 5,000, if all of the rattle snakes and gila monsters are included in the census. Coolidge is in the heart of cattle country and is one of the places to go on Saturday night if a trip to Phoenix, Mesa, or Tucson is not possible. There were a number of popular night spots in town. One, the Palm Tavern, featured a pinball machine. *The* Saturday night place was the Sage and Sand, which Duane Eddy describes as "a dump." "You didn't go in there unless you were armed on a Saturday night. It was dance and fight to the music of. . . ."[8]

Earl Perrin owned several small radio stations in the area. KGLU in Stafford and KCKY in Coolidge were his two major stations. Perrin offered Waylon the afternoon show on KCKY. He could also do some singing on the station as well as the usual "rip and read" chores. The on-the-air singing led to jobs in the area at the Goose and at the Sage and Sand.

Waylon, when not on the air or refereeing the Saturday night barroom brawl at the club, spent much of his time playing pinball with his brother-in-law. Waylon remained restless and broke.

Mae Boren Axton, a sometime publicist in the region, recalled her first meeting with Waylon: "I remember the tiny broadcasting studio . . . and the darkly handsome young man with deep brown eyes and a beautifully crooked grin. I noticed the dark western-cut clothes he wore. In subsequent brief visits, I noted the same suit, and with just a little checking and inquiry, I realized that Waylon was not being paid enough to meet all his obligations and have an adequate wardrobe, too." Mrs. Axton asked Perrin to give his disc jockey a raise, which he did.[9] Asked what happened in Coolidge, Waylon replies, "nothin'."

Sometime during this period Waylon formed a road band. The group played various night spots in the Northwest. The band got as far as Salt Lake City before it broke up. Waylon recalled, "I found out, you don't do this if they don't know who you are." It was on this tour apparently he met Lynne Jones.

During the frontier days Phoenix was cattle country just like Littlefield. The two world wars both diversified and contributed to the city's growth. World War I greatly increased the area's produce and cattle production, not to mention the boost it gave cotton. During the "Great War to Make the World Safe for Democracy," the population of Phoenix doubled to 30,000. World War II increased this figure to 160,000. As the Chamber of Commerce is happy to add, "After World War II, Phoenix mushroomed until by 1955 there were over 350,000 people in the metropolitan area. In this brief time span, manufacturing became Phoenix's number one industry." Phoenix was a mix of Texas and Los Angeles. A land of cowboys, migrants, factory workers, Chicanos, Native Americans, and, of course, tourists. In many respects, it was an instant city lacking tradition.

In the area of music, Phoenix was a mix of a crazy quilt of rock 'n' roll, middle-of-the-road crooners, and country music. Guitarist Duane Eddy explains, "It's a little different thinking than the rest of the country, because we had people coming in from all over the country. From the South, Texas, North and East. It is quite a conglomeration of people."[10] These people didn't especially care for "Grand Ole Opry" regulars. Ray Price, one of the first country singers to use a full orchestra on a record, was a favorite. Native Marty Robbins joined Johnny Cash as a top seller. Ray Odom, a local radio personality, recalled, "You take your more middle-of-the-road artists like Johnny Cash, Marty Robbins, Jimmy Dean, Ray Price—these people have sellouts every time they come to town." Commenting on more tradition- al performers, he continues, "God love 'em. I've played all for so many years and they're good friends, but they don't have the appeal in Phoenix the other artists do."[11]

Phoenix was proud of Buck Owens, a product of Mesa, who dominated the country charts in 1961 with "Fooling Around," "High as the Mountain," and "Under the Influence of Love." Wynn Stewart's "Big Big Love" was *the* country song in Phoenix. Texans Ray Price and Webb Pierce got a lot of jukebox play with "Soft Rain" and "Sweet Lips." Musically, Phoenix seemed per- fect for an artist like Waylon Jennings, who was influenced by Ernest Tubb and Buddy Holly. It was a good place to revive his career from the ashes of the plane crash. Employment for coun- try performers was somewhat limited. Frankie's and Wild Bill's featured live country entertainment six nights a week. Local dances and occasional concerts with name artists provided some opportunities. Phoenix also had two recording studios, Audio Recorders owned by Floyd Ramsey and Arizona Recorder.

In Phoenix, Waylon found a gig at Frankie's Cocktail Lounge. He and his left-handed bass player, Ed Metzendorf, received $35 per night plus tips. Occasionally, they split this with a lanky high school student who sat in as a drummer. For the job, they had borrowed a small tinny amplifier from a record shop on McDowell Road. They told Augie, the owner, that a trial was necessary before they could buy it This was stretching the truth just a bit—they were broke.

Frankie's was a small club that would find itself in violation of the fire code if more than 80 people crowded into the smoke- filled semidarkness. Frankie's, for Waylon, was strictly dues- paying—of the sort all musicians go through: Play the same songs night after night with the crowd barely paying attention. Ed Metzendorf helped him through the current hits of John Cash, Johnny Horton, and Wynn Stewart. "Big Big Love" was a must. Frankie's was like a thousand other country and western clubs, and Waylon Jennings started as just another human jukebox.

Things did improve at Frankie's. "We had about five people on Friday and five more on Saturday. But things got better and finally, we almost got to where we had a full house almost every night."[12] Frankie's did not advertise, so the increased business was strictly word-of-mouth. People also started to listen to the music. In time, the noise died down. Only the occasional drunk or fight interrupted. Waylon added a rhythm guitar player, Jerry Gropp, Ed's port-sided cousin. After several years, Waylon moved up to Wild Bill's, a steak house and saloon in Scottsdale, which seated 250 patrons.

Wild Bill's was a bit like those dude ranches one remembers from the movies of the 1950s. There was sawdust on the floor—easier to sweep up the blood—checkered red and white tablecloths, and a mural on one wall of Camelback Mountain. Lights, partly painted black, were to create the affect of stars on the ceiling. Despite the decor, Wild Bill's was just another "skull orchard" nightclub "where they sweep up the teeth, hair and eyeballs after a Saturday night."[13] The club was the "in" place, but Wild Bill and his wife were not popular with the customers. Their constant bickering and fighting turned many people off. (One night, Bill got angry and knocked out his wife's front tooth. She threatened to kill him. The next day they were "lovebirds" again.) The alcoholic cook was another source of difficulty. He frequently left orders on the grill and went off to get drunk. Despite the management, "it was a small club and everybody was friends," according to the bartender.

Another source of bewilderment for the patrons was a new barmaid from Pocatello, Idaho. An attractive brunette in her late twenties, Lynne Gladys Jones was a character out of Doc Holiday era. Her language was that of a ranch hand or a madam. She literally could out-cuss any man, and the many customers believed she packed a pistol in the best Annie Oakley tradition.

Waylon and the flamboyant barmaid "had a thing going." Waylon had met Lynne on his Utah-Idaho trip just as his marriage to Maxine was becoming increasingly strained, before the actual break-up. "It was during the seventh year that I met my second wife. I did, uh . . . a little sneaky . . . what you call closet," he told John Grissom.[14] Waylon's relationship with Lynne was stormy. Lynne was eight years older than the singer and terribly jealous. She resented the attention Waylon got from the female patrons at the club. On occasion, she would flirt with customers just to get Waylon's attention. Verbal donnybrooks would ensue. One day, Lynne announced she was pregnant.

On December 10, 1962, Waylon and Lynne drove to Las Vegas to be married. Jerry Gropp and his wife Ann accompanied them. A local justice of the peace, Myron E. Leaviltt, performed the ceremony.

Later he would repeat, "If a woman's pregnant and if it's my child, I gotta marry her . . . . I don't think there's too many ole' cowboys running around that could do it any different. I did the best I could at the time."[15] Returning from Las Vegas, they rented an apartment in Scottsdale. Shortly afterward, Lynne suffered a miscarriage.

At Wild Bill's, Waylon continued to use Ed and Jerry. Some people found them a very odd mix: two left-handers and a right-handed lead singer and guitarist. Bob Sesbrough's addition would reverse the balance; Jerry would be odd man out. In the beginning, Waylon's stage presence at Bill's was reminiscent of Buddy Holly's. One customer said, "He didn't have the stage presence as he does now. He didn't talk to the crowd—he just did his job and that was all. He said very little to the audience. In fact, I don't remember him talking to them at all." (Waylon has again reverted to these old stage mannerisms.) Gaining confidence, Waylon did start to open up. He would throw in little comments between songs. The response was good and he continued to try new things.

On his twenty-seventh birthday the band gave Waylon a used Fender Telecaster guitar. They had the bartender at Wild Bill's, Howard Turner, cover the face with black and white leather. "It was kinda ratty lookin'," says Turner. "Had to do something with it." He did. He got a pattern from a leather-working friend, Bob Sterling, "drew a design on cardboard and did the work over a weekend." Waylon's birthday was the next Tuesday. The leather work, very much like that on Buddy Holly's acoustic guitar, cost a grand total of $25.[16] Waylon has played the instrument ever since. "It's been through three wives and a helluva lot of re-cruits."

Even after their marriage, jealousy dominated Lynne's and Waylon's relationship. Patrons recall, "they didn't trust each other." Howard Turner says, "Lynne was proud of Waylon—but jealous." She demanded that Waylon return straight to their apartment following each show. Because of a kidney condition, she could not have children. She insisted they adopt one. Lynne temporarily enjoyed caring for Waylon's children and felt having their own would strengthen the marriage and increase her hold on him.

While at Wild Bill's, Waylon met Phoenix music impresario Ray Odom. Odom was a native of Coleman, Texas, who had gotten into broadcasting after World War II. In 1951 he moved to Phoenix as a sportscaster. In time he began to do live country music shows like the "Arizona Hayride." In 1956 he put KHEP on the air, and it immediately became the Number One station. "Elvis had his big hit record in the same year of 1956 and Jerry Lee Lewis' hit, 'Whole Lot of Shaking Going On' and we really jumped on both of those records. The top rocker in Phoenix at that time was country and as a result, we enjoyed a phenomenal rating." Several years later, Odom sold his station and bought KHAT, a formatted country station.

KHAT was modeled after Dave Stone's Lubbock station. It was basically a country and western Top Forty station with a stress on such local favorites as Johnny Horton, Jim Reeves, John Cash, Wynn Stewart, Marty Robbins, and Buck Owens. "We like to have the station be the personality and then the jock to be the personality with the station . . . within the framework of our type of format."

In 1963 Odom approached Waylon with an offer: would he like to work at KHAT? "He was at one of the clubs," recalls the dapper owner, "and he was hired, to the best of my recollection, as a part-time jock that would work around his evening playing hours. He was a very knowledgeable guy and being a personality was one of the reasons that we wanted to use him."[17]

Waylon did an afternoon show on the station. On the air, his style was subdued in contrast to the KLLL days—but he still managed to put his foot into his mouth. Odom and his account manager had been attempting for some time to lure Arnold's Pickles into buying airtime. After considerable wining and dining, the vegetable company finally bought a campaign on the station. The first commercial was scheduled for Waylon's show. "Now from the land of milk and honey . . . we bring you Arnold's Pickles . . . ." Waylon laughed and said, on the air, "That's the craziest thing I've ever heard." Needless to say, KHAT lost the account. "I think Waylon could have used a little more discretion at times, but who can fault honesty," recalls the station owner. "He said that if he had run around the room a half a dozen times and had a chance to think it out, he wouldn't have said what he said. But he flew by the seat of his pants as some people refer to it. I think that Waylon has made mistakes as we all have."

Floyd Ramsey is the president of Audio Recorders of Phoenix, Arizona. He is an easygoing man with brown hair and glasses—one who might be mistaken for a college geology teacher or a game warden. He started working for his father's radio and television shop after World War II. As a hobby, he built a 12' by 6' studio. Even as an adult, he was curious as to "how sound came off a phonograph record." As the Phoenix economy grew, Ramsey found himself increasingly involved with doing commercials for local radio stations and occasional demo records for bands wishing to break into the world of rock 'n' roll. In 1957 Ramsey built a larger studio behind a North Seventh Street barbershop. He proudly installed the newest two-track available. Here, Skip and Flip did their one big hit. Stanford Clark cut the "The Fool" in Ramsey's studio. Lee Hazlewood recorded a young guitarist, Duane Eddy, at Audio Recorders. Ramsey's only competition in Phoenix was Ray Bolly's Arizona Recording. All of Waylon's Trend sessions were done at Arizona Recording. In 1964 Roy Dunann, previously with Capitol, left Arizona Recording and went to work for Floyd Ramsey. It was Dunann who told Ramsey about Waylon. "One voice (at Arizona Recording) that has hit sound." On the basis of that recommendation, Ramco bought the Trend masters. One Trend master, "The Stage," was to be destroyed. The engineer made several changes in the pacing of the song. They sped up the track to make Waylon's baritone voice sound as if he were fourteen. Waylon shrugs the song off: "It was one of my first attempts."[18] Ramsey replaced "The Stage" with "My World" and later reissued the material.

On April 27, 1963, Ramsey released a single some three years after it was recorded. Trend 106 contained "My Baby Walks All Over Me" and "The Stage." The A-side was a weeper but with an up-tempo rock-a-billy arrangement somewhat in the Johnny Cash vein when Jack Clement was producing him at Sun Records. A heavy bass was mixed to a number of fast rock-a-billy guitar breaks played by Waylon. The lyrics may have been somewhat autobiographical:

> She loves me long, she loves me wrong,
> She rules me and I like it. Well, I guess
> That's a part of nature's plan. . . .

"The Stage" was Waylon's second tribute to Buddy Holly. Originally titled "Stars in Heaven," it was a narrative accompanied by a military drum roll and an "angelic sounding" girl vocalist. The song was very much in the "Three Stars" style dedicated to Patsy Cline and Cowboy Copas, who died in a fiery plane crash. "The Stage" was a tribute to Eddie Cochran, Richie Valens, the Big Bopper, and Buddy Holly. It was a "Hillbilly Heaven" type of thing.

THE STAGE

In a vision I can see stars that
meant the world to me.
And in the vision it's the same as
long ago.
I see a stage beyond compare
and all the stars are assembled there.
They sing the songs of yesterday
We all loved so.

As the curtain open wide
He makes his entrance from the side.
A mighty cheer brings Eddie
Cochran on.
"Summertime Blues" brings a
happy roar. The crowd cheers
loud as they call for more.
It seems he just gets
started and he's gone.

The curtain swirls, a guitar rings.
This brings forth the "LaBamba" King
Young Richie Valens in a happy
Spanish Style. And as he
sings so true and clear,
His young voice rings for all to
hear as he sings "Donna."
We can all see his happy
smile.

The curtain opens wide again.
He stands in the center with
a phone in his hands.
"Hello Baby . . . this is the
Big Bopper speaking"
We hear him say.
Ah, he talks awhile and
then he'll sing a note.
He laughs and jumps in
His leopard skin coat.
The crowd laughs and cheers
As we watch the Bopper
Walk away.

The crowd is finally settled
Back, they know it's time

Now for the final act.
There stands Buddy Holly
Smiling standing tall
His voice is clear. His guitar
Rings. The angels stand in
Silence as Buddy sings.
He sings, "Oh Boy", "Peggy Sue"
In the happiest style of all
We've had the final curtain
Call. And if you've seen any
of my vision at all
Then you've truly seen
The greatest show of all.

In 1964 Ramsey built his three-stage studio on North Seventh, across the street from the barbershop. Waylon used the new studios to record some of the A & M material as well as an "in-house" album for J.D.'s nightclub. the owners of J.D.'s did the twelve-song album in the yellow-and-white studio B with a four-track machine. Mr. Musil, Sr., owner of J.D.'s, stood and watched the clock the entire time. The total cost of the album was less than $100.

In time, Ramsey began to release records on his own label. Local artists like Donnie Owens, Buddy Long, Sanford Clark, a young school teacher named Donna Fargo, and Waylon Jennings found their material in some Arizona record stores. Having a hit with Ramco was difficult, as Floyd had a very small distribution set up. By his own estimates, he printed 100 disc jockey samples per release and dealt with twelve to eighteen national subdistributors owned by Dot Records.

In the middle of July 1967, Ramco appeared with "Never Again" and "My Baby Walks All Over Me." Six months later "My World" and "Another Blue Day" were released two days before Christmas. There is little doubt that these late releases were partly designed to capitalize on Waylon's growing national popularity and also his appearances in the area. Waylon understandably was rather unhappy, as he had "no formal agreement on Ramco" according to its owner. In future years, the ownership of various tapes in Ramsey's storerooms would be the center of much controversy and bitterness.

Besides working Mr. Musil's night spot, Waylon was getting considerable local exposure on Ray Odom's Saturday afternoon television on channel 12. The half-hour program ran for twenty-six weeks. Odom, in his cowboy suit and white hat, did the commercials while Waylon and the band performed their J.D.'s material. The most notable event of the show was the introduction of Tammy Lynne on the air. "Waylon's become the father of a baby girl," announced Odom. The adopted infant made her television debut at the age of five days.

6

JUST TO SATISFY YOU: THE A & M TRIP

Waylon had lost track of Don Bowman, who had endured enough of Sky Corbin and moved to El Paso. After El Paso, Don got into the heady world of big-time broadcasting. He was offered a job with a Top Forty station in a major market. KFWB, "Color Radio," a highly rated station in the San Francisco Bay area, hired Don as its afternoon man. A year later, Bowman was a program director for KDEL San Diego. When not occupied with picking next week's hits and fighting off over-aggressive record company representatives, Bowman started writing songs. He had always had a way with words. He possessed a natural wit with a touch of irreverence. Paul Hemphill described him as a "wise-cracking little guy whose departure from the usual corn of hayseed country comedians keeps him in hot water with fans."[1] He was not a musical wizard. In his own words, he was a "three-chord wonder."

Through the broadcast grapevine, Don learned that his old partner in crime at KLLL was working for Ray Odom at KHAT and appearing at Frankie's and that Waylon could "pick."

One day Waylon picked up the phone. He immediately recognized the voice. "Hey, we ought to be writing some songs together."[2] It didn't seem to be a bad idea. Waylon had been doing some work for people around Audio Recorders. In recent months he had composed "Ten Years Ago," a country weeper for Long John Roller. Roller was a local personality and promoter best known for his flagpole-sitting feats. He and Donnie Owens wrote "My World" for Jimmie Gray. (Gray would later become a Waylor.)

"I had a courtesy card from Bonanza Airlines so I could fly anywhere Bonanza went—free. So, I'd fly to Phoenix about every third week and we'd just lock ourselves in a motel room." Frequently the writing sessions lasted eighteen hours. The collaborations were as wild as the antics in the KLLL control booth. "They'll never forget us," Bowman chuckles. "We knew not what we was doing!" There was a touch of madness in the writing. Don would throw out one-liners, "tastes like a mint, works like a miracle." "All the things we did last summer, we worry about all fall. Push, pull, click, click, change girls real quick." Or, "They can make it illegal, but not unpopular." One night Waylon and Don collected a pile of scratch sheets with leftover lines. "We had about fifty lines . . . so we put 'em all in one song. Didn't make one bit of sense." The tune they used was "Jole Blon." They also managed to write "straight" ballads like "Just To Satisfy You" and "Anita You're Dreaming."[3]

One day Jerry Moss, a co-partner of a small, new record company, walked through the front door of KDEL.[4] His job was to get airplay for his Carnival artists. All promotion men try to get next to program directors, but the personable Jerry Moss was more successful than most. He and Bowman grew to be friends. On weekends when he was not in Phoenix, Don would fly up to Los Angeles and stay with Moss. At Moss's house he met Herb Alpert—the other half of what was to become A & M Records.

Jerry Moss is an impressive man. A tall, energetic New Yorker with a warm friendly smile, Moss started with Coed Records, a small company geared to the needs of "American Bandstand." With the label he spent weeks taking "Sixteen Candles" from one pop radio station to the next. In 1960 he left and moved to Los Angeles. He began producing "closet" or custom records costing $200 to $300. At the same time, Herb Alpert was signed to RCA as "Dore" Alpert. Prior to signing with RCA, Herb had worked with Jan and Dean. The antithesis to Jerry, Herb was a shy native Californian. He had a way with a horn. Jerry Moss produced Herb's only single for Victor. After his experience with Victor, Alpert decided to put aside his trumpet and pursue an acting career. In 1962 Herb returned to the world of records and cut "Tell It to the Birds." Simultaneously, Jerry was coproducing "Love Is Back in Style." A merger was agreed upon and the

Carnival label was born; Jerry would promote and Herb would produce. "Birds" was their first single. What put Alpert and Moss on the map was "The Lonely Bull"; the Spanish-sounding instrumental sold 700,000 copies. Carnival became A & M.

"Lonely Bull" established the company philosophy. "I don't like labels," insists Herb. Jerry agrees. "I have always felt that an artist should have full programming. It's a certain act that appeals to a whole range of people." Prior to "Lonely Bull" the idea that mariachi music could possibly appeal to anyone besides Chicanos was unthinkable. "There was no market for Herb Alpert when he first broke," according to Bob Garcia of A & M. "He created his own market. There's never been a waiting market for any act that we've put out." The philosophy that *good music will appeal to anyone regardless of its roots* proved true again with George McCurn, a black spiritual singer who was with the Pilgrim Travelers, the group that once featured Sam Cooke. McCurn's song was A & M's first big studio production with strings. They recorded "I'm Just a Country Boy," and the song reached the vaunted national Top Forty. With two successes under their belts, which violated the rules of the AM radio game, Herb and Jerry went out to recruit a mixed bag of singers. Soul singer Sonny Knight joined poet Rod McKuen and the folk-singing Canadian Sweethearts on the label. Waylon Jennings would be next.[5]

In the summer of 1963, Don Bowman brought Jerry Moss a demo tape of several songs. The songs were mostly the Trend 61 records. "He [Moss] was honest with me and told me that dubs sounded better than that in Nashville." Herb flipped: "I just fell in love with his whole feeling . . . not too schooled yet it was musical . . . very primitive—earthy." Jerry Moss shared this feeling: "I just loved the sound of Waylon's voice." Herb and Jerry flew to Phoenix to see Waylon at Wild Bill's.[6] After some negotiating, a contract for a single was signed on July 9, 1963. Irving Music, A & M's publishing arm, got part of the rights to "Love Denied." The flip side of the record was "Rave On," a song Waylon had sung on the "last tour." As with previous A & M efforts, Number 722 had a distinct style. (The Holly song was pure rock-a-billy until Herb added a Tijuana Brass close to it.) "Love Denied" was very much in the then popular semi-operatic Roy Orbison mode. Satisfied with the single, A & M signed Waylon to a three-year contract on April 16, 1964. He received a standard 5 percent contract with 2½ percent foreign royalties.[7]

After the signing, the single was released. The record did poorly; 1964 was the year of the English invasion in popular music.

In Phoenix, Herb and Jerry recorded Waylon's most successful A & M cut, "Just to Satisfy You," backed by the Ian Tyson composition "Four Strong Winds." "Just to Satisfy You" was one of the songs written in the motel room. "I got off a plane one day," explained Don Bowman. "I had four lines—'someone's goin' to get hurt before you're through / someone's goin' to pay for the things you do / Just to satisfy you, just to satisfy you.' Then we went to the motel and Waylon put that weird bloody melody to it which knocked me out." "Just to Satisfy You" was definitely a country song. Originally there was a whistle in it by Herb Alpert, but on the record there was a harpsichord.[8]

"Four Strong Winds" was a standard on the folkie coffee house circuit. Canadian singers Ian and Sylvia had recorded it on the Vanguard label. It never reached the Top Forty stations. Waylon heard Dolan Ellis do the song the day before his session with Herb Alpert in Los Angeles. Waylon asked Dolan to teach it to him. Waylon learned the lyrics but forgot the melody. "I didn't have it just right. So I just did it the way I felt it."[9] "Four Strong Winds" was a milestone. This was Waylon's first arrangement with his interpretation of somebody else's material. This was to become his trademark. A popular statement at J.D.'s was to be, "he makes other people's hits his own."

Herb liked the song. He may have been familiar with it because of the Canadian Sweethearts. The song had pop potential because of the folk music revival, which still enjoyed great support on college campuses. So they cut the song. Herb mixed it. The result was an easy-listening record prominently featuring Herb Alpert's trumpet. It was too middle-of-the-road to be folk or country. In August 1964 the single was released. The record got a "nice reception. A lot of airplay," according to Jerry Moss, "a few sales, but we really liked the record."[10] It did not reach many of the charts; only in Phoenix was it a smash. At this time, Waylon was beginning to have doubts about Herb's concept of him as an artist. He was particularly unhappy about "Four Winds." "Herb and I were really good friends outside the studio but we were strangers inside. There was no communication. I was thinking Hank Williams and he was thinking I could be another Al Martino," adding, "they were trying too hard."[11] There was a definite communications problem. "I wanted to get him closer to the pop market," Herb says. "Waylon felt he didn't

Trend, '61 Records, 1961.

Herb Alpert

Rogers, Cowan & Brenner, Inc.
Public Relations
250 North Canon Drive
Beverly Hills, California 90210
(213) 275-4581

BNB ASSOCIATES LTD.
NINETY FOUR FIFTY FOUR WILSHIRE BLVD.
BEVERLY HILLS, CALIFORNIA 90212
(213) 273-7020   CABLE: SHERMACE

PRINTED IN U.S.A.

"The man who tried to make Waylon a crooner." Herb Alpert. Courtesy of A&M Records.

want to turn his back on his country friends. He was more than just a country singer." Herb's belief in Waylon's potential and in his own producing ability kept the studio relationship alive until Bobby Bare and Don Bowman entered the picture.[12]

Bobby Bare in 1963 was RCA Victor's hottest new act. His recording of "Detroit City" stayed on the pop charts for twelve weeks and on the country and western list for eighteen weeks. Chet Atkins had signed him a year before, after discovering he was the performer of "All American Boy," a talking blues about Elvis's induction into the army. It was a big pop record. "I'm gonna cut some hit records with you," promised Chet. "Well, I'm gonna cut a lot of hits," replied Bobby Bare. "I could probably do it as well with you as with anybody."[13] His first single, "Shame on Me," sold almost a million. While promoting the record, Bobby Bare had met Don Bowman, still a deejay at KFWB in Oakland. Their relationship resumed when Don moved to southern California and began writing for RCA Victor.

In 1963 Chet Atkins began receiving dozens of songs from a guy in San Diego. Chet thought the songs funny, but the accompanying letters amused and baffled him. Speaking with Steve Sholes one day, Chet said: "I've been gettin' some songs from a guy out there that are funny songs. But the letters are funnier than the songs. I don't know if he's right off the farm or if he's funny or if he's crazy or what!" Finally, his curiosity got the better of him. Chet called the writer of those "crazy letters."

"Chet Atkins is on the phone," Don was told.

"Hello, this is Queen Elizabeth," Don answered. "Who is this?"

"Chet Atkins . . ."

"No shit! Now come on, who is this?"

"THIS IS Chet Atkins!"

After a long pause, "Yes SIR!"

"Don, God you play bad!"

"Well now Chet, that's a helluva way to start off with. How'd you like it if somebody called you and said, 'Chet you pick bad.' I thought I had them three chords down pretty good. That's why all my songs go G-C-D 'cause I can't go from G to D and back. I gotta go in order or I lose my place."

"You want to make an album? I got 130 songs in my desk and Homer and Jethro couldn't cut all of these if they recorded every night."

"Chet, you gonna make me a star?"

"Well, I'll try."[14]

BOBBY BARE
Exclusively on RCA

RC/I Records and Tapes

Bob Bare got Waylon and Chet Atkins together, several years later he
left RCA and then came back and departed again. RCA promo.

Thus began the association between Don Bowman and RCA. His first big hit was "Chet Atkins Make Me a Star."

In 1963 Bob Bare stopped by KDEL to pick up some of Don's tapes for Atkins. While at the station, Bowman began telling him about this "good ole boy" in Arizona. "Now you be sure to call him when you're in Phoenix." From Don's description, Bare thought, "Waylon Jennings was sixty years old and right off a cotton patch." Bare did not realize it at the time, but Bowman was already hyping Waylon to Chet Atkins as well. Bare forgot about the conversation until Jack Webb, "Sergeant Friday"-turned-Hollywood producer, got him into Arizona mountains to make a second-rate Warner Brothers western. "You do a good job in the movie and I'll consider you for 'No Time For Sergeants'," a television series Webb was putting together. On location, Bobby quickly decided that he couldn't act and didn't care to. Since *Distant Trumpet* was being filmed in Flagstaff and Bob was bored, he remembered the "good ole boy in Phoenix." A "good ole boy" would be a welcome relief. He phoned—no answer. While in Phoenix, Bare heard "Four Strong Winds" on his car radio. He believed in material heard on the radio; that's how he found "Detroit City." "I picked up a copy and took it back to Chet to record." Returning to Phoenix, Bare finally met Waylon. They made a date for dinner. At the time, Waylon was opening at J.D.'s.

Richard Guimont and James David Musil, Sr., originally were partners in a small cowboy bar with a dance floor, Magoo's, in Tempe. In 1963 Guimont and Musil decided to expand to a two-level nightclub and restaurant. The club was to be called J.D.'s, after Musil. A site on North Scottsdale Road was selected and plans were drawn up. The blueprints called for a main level that would comfortably seat 600 patrons. The cellar was to be reserved for rock 'n' roll acts. It was less spacious, with a capacity of 250 people. Musil hoped to open the club with Waylon Jennings headlining the upstairs area. Jennings seemed the surest bet in the Phoenix market. One night Musil approached him and offered him a job at the proposed club. "You come over and plan the bandstand just the way you want it." There was nothing else left in Phoenix, so "why not." Waylon: "Like I told the boys in the band, 'we, if we blow it, we can always come back to work here [Cross Keys]; but if we make it, we can write our own ticket.' " Musil later told a customer that he never would have built the club if he could not have gotten Waylon to play there.[15]

J.D.'s was a gamble. It opened in July of 1964 just as words like "mod," "long hair," "mop-top," and other symbols of social change were beginning to threaten the American consciousness. Arizona, which was then supporting its favorite son Senator Barry Goldwater for president, did not appreciate many of the cultural changes taking place. What Musil and his partner planned to do was to bring together under one roof long-haired college students, executives and Arizona cowboys, a dangerous experiment in 1964.

J.D.'s original appeal was to the cowboys. "It was more or less a cowboy place where everybody danced with their hat on." Waylon, in his tuxedo jacket and black ascot, continued to do his thing. A bartender at Wild Bill's estimated that a good 50 percent of his customers followed Waylon over to Scottsdale Road. With the opening of the Arizona State University campus that fall, J.D.'s became "the *in* place in Phoenix and drew a tremendous number of college kids," according to Ray Odom. "He had that great youth appeal."[16] But, "they weren't accepting long hair at the time," remembers Richie Albright. "There were fights . . . a lot of fights . . . they'd get drunk together in one room."[17] The popularity of the club continued to grow despite the unlikely mix of patrons. The *Phoenix Local Guide,* an entertainment directory, advertised: "WAYLON JENNINGS, recording star, and his WAYLORS[18] are top Valley attraction for Country & Western music. They are one of the reasons J.D.'s, 707 North Scottsdale Road (1 mile south of McDowell) is about the liveliest KEY spot in town." Another ad promised:

You'll Always Have More Fun At J.D.'s!
featuring
WAYLON JENNINGS
AND THE WAYLORS
See Our 7 New Go-Go Girls
Phil and the Frantics playing
continuous music in the
Riverbottom Room[19]

J.D.'s was a country and western nightclub but it also featured the go-go craze, then sweeping Los Angeles and the nation. Johnny Rivers, best known for his theme to "Secret Agent," was appearing nightly to standing-room-only audiences at the Whiskey on Sunset Boulevard. Television host Johnny Carson had called Rivers "the Pied Piper of the Watusi Set," while Jan (of the singing duo with Dean) remarked, "Johnny turns Sunset Boulevard into an adult Dick Clark Show."[20] The go-go format was quite simple. One or two singers, usually playing guitars backed by a bass and drums, would run through current and older pop hits. Rivers specialized in old Chuck Berry songs such as "Brown Eyed Handsome Man," "Memphis," and "Maybelline." Trini Lopez used the same style but applied it more to up-tempo folk songs usually borrowed from Peter, Paul, and Mary. Lopez did everything from Tex-Mex rockers to Peter, Paul, and Mary tunes like "The Hammer Song" and "Lemon Tree." College students and young executives liked to drink and dance to this form of music. The downstairs act, Phil and the Frantics, was an obvious attempt to capitalize on the success of the Beatles. All that can be remembered about the group was that they were loud. A J.D.'s regular said, "It was nothing on a Friday night to see the young executive crowd out there."

J.D.'s seemed to have all the magic of the Peppermint Lounge and the Whiskey. Waylon Jennings was the country Rivers and Lopez of Phoenix. Waylon did sing oldies, "Rave On" and Roy Orbison's "Cryin'," and during "After Hours" he would do the Ray Charles song "What'd I Say," but he basically stuck to up-tempo country and western material with an occasional folk song tossed in.

The apparent success of J.D.'s and its unique audience greatly influenced Waylon's approach to music.

> "The cross-section that we drew was unbelievable. We drew, that was in the days when the first long-haired people came in, the college students, doctors, lawyers, *and all* the cowboys. It was really a cross-section of people because of the music that we did play. We were predominantly country and yet what I started doing was to take pop tunes or tunes that I felt that I could relate to as a country person. . . . If I could relate to it, then anyone could relate to it as far as country fans and what have you. We did them in our own way. Another thing, is that you get flat bored doin' things the way other people do them—so I started changing things around and doing them my own way and thought that it was easier.[21]

It was at J.D.'s that Waylon evolved his musical style. He had always had the sound; the style was much more. It involved choosing the right songs that would appeal to just about anybody in Phoenix. The style focused on his ability to interpret or translate a song to an audience—any audience.

At J.D.'s, Waylon learned to work an audience. He developed some gags between songs. "First show is dirty, the second obscene, and the third is in my motel room." He discovered the knack of controlling drunks—at least most of the time. "Longer you talk, the longer I'm gonna stand here and look ignorant," he would tell the audience. "It's all women. Hush . . . Hush." It worked—even regulars and performers were gently put in their places. "Shut up Spike, I'm talkin'."[22] The madcap Don Bowman, doing a guest shot, was told not to stand so close to the microphone. Considering the mix of people, J.D.'s was a fairly peaceful place, although Waylon did have a few nasty discussions with jealous boyfriends and husbands. A few were armed.

Don Bowman feels that J.D.'s prepared Waylon for Nashville. "The J.D.'s thing was the best thing that ever happened to Waylon. He worked that club for three years [sic—it was eighteen months]. He'd do that every night—six nights a week—for three years. 'Cause if you can work clubs, you can work anything."[23] Don hadn't heard of Crab Orchard, Kentucky, yet.

The structure of J.D.'s was fairly typical for a dance club. It was spacious and housed a long ninety-foot bar. A large seating area surrounded the stage on three sides. Originally the dance floor was for dancing; however, as Waylon's following grew, it became increasingly difficult to dance except during intermissions. "I've never seen that happen in a dance hall," says Richie Albright. "We'd be into the third set before people would get up and dance. They'd just sit and listen . . . it was one of those mystic things about that club. You couldn't get in there sideways on a Saturday night or on a Friday. It was just packed."[24] Tommy Jennings: "A man knows when he is standing on stage in front of all those people that lots of times the governor would trade places with you."[25] One patron told me, "On the weekends, you couldn't get into the place even if you were the Governor of Arizona."[26] One of the best descriptions of J.D.'s is provided by Roberta Plunkett, one of Waylon's most loyal fans:

> They had a huge picture behind the bar. He was just king. From the little girls to bartenders to the bouncers, it was all Waylon. I mean, he was their star and it was that way. They had such a wonderful lighting arrangement for him. They had a spotlight they put on him right on his face and made the room pitch dark and then just show this one spotlight on Waylon's face right at the microphone. I have seen Waylon stand up there and sing and you could hear a pin drop. So much feeling—you could hear a pin drop. He could really bring the place alive . . . .
>
> When people found out how great Waylon was—he drew all kinds

Roberta Plunkett and W.J., 1971. Courtesy of Roberta Plunkett.

of people. You would often see elderly women sitting, watching him with their shawls on. People were just fascinated by his music. He always put on just a great, great show.[27]

This is by no means a minority opinion. Mrs. Betty Rood, another fan, put it this way: "Those two years [at J.D.'s] were the highlight of our lives."[28] Top "Topper" Morris, another regular, observed, "You could hear a pin drop when he was singing it was so quiet. People sat on the dance floor and stood around —anywhere they could."

Howard Turner, who made Waylon's leather guitar cover, described J.D.'s as "Waylon's living room." There was a warmth and security in the Phoenix clubs that Waylon would later sorely miss. One night singer George Jones walked into the place, did a set, and introduced Waylon. As the first song blared through the speakers, applause greeted the tune. George grinned and said, "I'm gonna kill 'em. I'm gonna kill 'em."

Despite the acclaim, J.D.'s was a taxing gig. It was six nights a week with Monday off. The band did three or four 45-minute sets each night and "After Hours" on weekends. "After Hours" was billed as "1:00 A.M. til ????!" It was the "in" show. "That's when all the drunks are gone," explains Roberta Plunkett. "All the people who came to dance are gone. Then Waylon knew that the people who are there are there because of him. This is the finest show of the evening." She continues, "People who want to hear Waylon always stayed because that was when he was really next to the crowd. It became so quiet . . . he talked to people. He knew everybody that was still there, he knew who they were. Maybe 200–300 people, but he knew they were there to hear him."[29]

"After Hours" was a combination of up-tempo songs and the J.D.'s favorites. On many an occasion, "After Hours" was more a living-room rap session than musical entertainment. Richie remembers that many times Waylon did not do more than three songs during a show, spending most of the time joking with Spike Wilson and other regulars. When he did play, most of the material was familiar. The favorites were "What'd I Say," "Big Mamou," "Donna on My Mind," "Sally Was a Good Ole' Girl," and "Cryin'." "Cryin'," the Roy Orbison hit, was one of his most requested tunes, but Waylon didn't like to do it. The last high note caused him headaches.

On November 15, 1964, Bobby Bare returned to Phoenix. The next day, he planned to visit J.D.'s and see the Sunday night

show. After the performance he decided that RCA should sign
Waylon Jennings. "It was really great. I mean, really tore my head
up . . . I mean, not just good but great." Monday, Bare was going
to Las Vegas for a nightclub gig. En route, he called Chet Atkins.

"Chet, you gotta record this boy 'cause he's really great."

"Really."

"Really! Yep, he really is. He's fantastic, he's so good he
deserves to be on a major label. I know Waylon is going to be
recording the same type of stuff, but not the same kind of records
that I do and it will probably hurt my record sales in the
end . . . ."

"Well, ok. Whatever you say," replied Atkins.

"Here's his phone number."[30]

Atkins was not convinced. Bowman had told him about
Waylon many times. Chet liked the A & M version of "Four
Strong Winds." He thought Bare's natural enthusiasm, however,
might be carrying him away. Chet had a limited roster; somebody
would have to be dropped to make room for Waylon Jennings.
Chet did not like administrative decisions like that.

Duane Eddy, known as Mr. Twangy Guitar because of his
unique style, had signed with RCA in 1962. Duane was a native of
Coolidge, Arizona. He, too, was a veteran of the Sage and Sand.
His "Rebel Rouser" was a smash. He was an instant teen idol.
"Ramrod" followed. RCA signed him, hoping history would re-
peat itself. It didn't.

Several weeks after Bare's call to Atkins, Duane was in
Phoenix visiting friends and relatives. He tuned in KHAT, Ray
Odum's station, and heard "Just to Satisfy You." "I was knocked
out with him . . . that's great . . . fantastic." Eddy wondered who
the singer was. "That was Waylon Jennings," the announcer said.
Driving down Scottsdale Boulevard, the guitarist and his wife
Mirriam spied the marquee at J.D.'s with Waylon's name on it.

Several weeks later Eddy returned to Los Angeles for a recording session. Chet Atkins was the producer.

"There's a guy in Phoenix that's fantastic," said Duane. "I saw
him when I was there . . . you really ought to go check him out. I
think he'd really be a great artist for RCA Victor. His name is
Waylon Jennings. Here's his phone number."

"That sounds sort of familiar. I do believe I've heard that name
before. Bobby Bare told me about that. But Bobby's always
bringin' in people. They weren't too great. So I kinda quit paying

attention to him . . . he's really that good, huh? Well, let's go over there and we'll see 'em." Duane nodded a "Fantastic! We'll go over there on Thursday night."

At 9:00 A.M. Thursday morning, Chet called—apologizing—explaining that he had to return immediately to Nashville.

"What do you want to do about Waylon?" asked Eddy.

"Well, if this guy's as good as you think he is . . . *If* he really is good and you really believe that . . . have him call me, *but* only if he's *really* that good."

Duane promised Chet a call from Waylon.[31]

As Waylon's popularity in Phoenix grew, Lynne became more insecure. She wanted to know where Waylon was every minute. "I was a good husband, very straight," Waylon told an interviewer.[32] Despite his denials, Lynne's suspicions continued. Waylon's writing sessions with Don Bowman generated arguments. "Whew, she stayed mad at us," explains Don. "She never believed we were just writing songs." One song especially aroused her ire, "Anita You're Dreaming." "Who is Anita?" she kept asking. Neither Waylon or Don knew anybody called Anita. What Lynne didn't realize was that she *was* the girl: "Anita you're dreaming of a world that can never exist. Anita, it's over—there's nothing that's now left to say . . . that each time you're with me, my conscience reminds me of someone that's waiting alone."

They also wrote another song about Lynne. After writing fourteen serious ballads,[33] Don and Waylon decided to do a humorous song. "Let's write a funny song," said Bowman. "I'm tired of all this love and divorce and b.s." The result was "Poor Ole Ugly Gladys Jones." The title at first contained Lynne's first name, but Waylon decided it should be changed to Gladys. "What if they play it on the radio and she hears it?" With Lynne's maiden name in the title, it would not take her long to figure out who Gladys was. The song was not flattering.

> There's a girl that lives down the block,
> Face would stop an eight day clock.
> Ugliest kid I've ever seen, more like a nightmare than a dream . . . .

Four years later Don Bowman and Waylon recorded the song. Waylon's very identifiable baritone voice comes in with the chorus, "Poor ole ugly Gladys Jones . . . ." Waylon and Don also convinced Bobby Bare and Willie Nelson to overdub a line. Bob chimed in with "Her parents finally moved away from home," with Willie adding "Her body's been declared a disaster zone." The record, when released in April of 1969, did not identify the singers; it merely read, "Don Bowman and Friends.

After Bobby Bare's visit, Lynne became concerned about Waylon's signing with Chet Atkins. When Duane Eddy came by the apartment and told her about Waylon's potential, she objected: "I just don't know, I just don't like it. I'll lose him. I don't want him to be a giant because I'll lose him. I really don't like the idea—I'd rather he stay like he is. [Pausing] I don't like it. I don't want any part of that. *I don't want him to be a star!*" At the time Duane thought, "with an attitude like that, she *is* going to lose him."[34] Duane didn't know she already had.

Returning to Nashville, Chet was exposed even more to Waylon Jennings. Don Bowman continued pitching Waylon and Bob Bare also resumed his campaign. Bare called his manager, Charlie Williams. "We're ganging up on Chet to get Waylon on RCA Victor. Will you call Chet and tell him that you were in Phoenix and this guy's a real world warper?" As Williams recalls, "I didn't know Waylon Jennings from Trigger."[35] But he did call Chet and "gave him the snow job of the earth and didn't have any idea who I was talking about." Bobby also enlisted Harlan Howard in the drive. Harlan was a friend of Bare's from the California days. His publishing company, Wilderness, handled Bare and Bowman songs.

One argument difficult for Chet to ignore was the success of "Four Strong Winds." It reached Number Three on the country and western charts and remained there for nineteen weeks. More importantly, Bare's "cover" of Waylon's arrangement spent seven weeks on the *Billboard* "Hot One Hundred." This fact impressed Chet and Waylon—but in different ways.

"Four Strong Winds" had accomplished what few Nashville produced records could in the height of Beatlemania. It had gone pop—it had reached the folk audience. The folk music revival of the early 1960s provided Nashville with the opportunity to exploit its heritage. Columbia especially concentrated on songs of the Old West—Johnny Horton's "Battle of New Orleans" and "North to Alaska," Marty Robbins's "El Paso" and "Hangin' Tree," Johnny Cash's "Don't Take Your Guns to Town" were designed for the folk market. Jimmy Dean's "Big Bad John" and "PT 109," about President John F. Kennedy in the Navy, did well for Columbia. Country music stars Johnny Cash and Faron Young appeared in folk exploitation films like *Hootennany Hoot.*

The folk music revival primarily helped the forgotten singers of the 1920s and 1930s. Traditional bluegrass bands found eager young audiences at colleges and universities. Bill Monroe, Flatt and Scruggs, and the Stanley Brothers played Columbia, Harvard, and Vanderbilt. CBS and Victor reissued Carter Family records. Mother Maybelle Carter reassembled her daughters into a new version of the old Carter Family.

Mingling with college students at the Berkeley and Newport folk festivals, traditional country artists were both awed and troubled by what they saw. Artists like Bill Monroe welcomed a new audience. College dates were a vast improvement over small high school auditoriums and gymnasiums. But ole-timey country musicians didn't feel all that comfortable with those sophisticated northern students in their work shirts and carefully faded jeans. With the exception of John Cash, few country artists really benefited from the folk revival. Cash found an audience that cared little about his pill problem. Cash, for them, was an authentic folk singer. In this milieu he found new material by some of the "new" writers and subsequently recorded songs like Bob Dylan's "It Ain't Me Babe" and Pete LaFarge's bitter "Ballad of Ira Hayes." Not everybody in Nashville appreciated these songs, but they did sell.

In the college folk audience, Chet Atkins saw an answer to the gloom that prevailed on Sixteenth Avenue, South. "Country music was really dead at that time," recalled singer Bob Luman. "That's when the Beatles came in. It was really hard to get a country record played [on pop stations]. If you had a country record that sold 25,000—30,000 you had a Number One country record."[36] Producer Bob Montgomery echoes this feeling. "A Top Ten country record did 25,000—that's all."[37] Beatlemania and the following "rock revolution" was much more than just a style change. Music City Row and its fans were worlds apart from Liverpool and even further from San Francisco and its hippie scene. The Haight-Ashbury stood for the new morality, civil rights protests, drugs, and nearly everything the Bible opposed. The rock revolution also appeared to end Nashville's ability to sneak onto the pop charts.

Chet Atkins still was not convinced. Remembering Bob Bare's successes with "Detroit City" and "Four Strong Winds" as well as George Hamilton IV's "Abilene," Chet toyed with the idea of a group of singers who, while country, would have a "folk" (pop) appeal. Skeeter Davis, Bob Bare, and George Hamilton IV, all with pop hits, might fit the category. With this scheme in the back of his mind, Chet Atkins called Waylon several days before Christmas in 1964.[38]

"This is Chet Atkins. You like to record with RCA?"

"Yes."

"You tied up?"

"I'm with A & M, but I can get loose."[39]

After the call, Chet Atkins was still not sure he had made the right decision. "What if he's ugly—or 60 years old?" For Waylon, a phone call from Chet was a "nervous bustdown." "I don't think I could have had a bigger compliment than to have Chet Atkins ask me to sign with RCA Victor." He was aware of the campaign to get him on the label, but actually to get a call was another matter. According to Herb Alpert, "It's like a wet dream for a country artist to get a call from Chet Atkins."[40] In the excitement of the moment, Waylon had all but forgotten that he had two and a half years left on his contract.

While Bare and company were working away on Chet, Waylon had become increasingly discontent. Privately, he was unhappy about "Four Strong Winds." No artist feels a copy of his song— no matter how successful—is better. Maybe it was a compliment to have Bob Bare record the song, but why wasn't his own version a hit? After all, it was a smash in Phoenix. Don Bowman provided an answer. " 'Cause they had no distribution as far as country. They didn't have any knowledge of country. Jerry is from New York and Herbie from Los Angeles. They don't know anything about country."[41] Bowman's argument made sense. Neither Jerry nor Herb knew much about the mechanics of a country market. It was a tough nut to crack, especially by a new company headquartered in Los Angeles. A country jock would listen to a new artist on the RCA label doing a Harlan Howard song produced by Chet Atkins, but A & M was another thing.

Herb's sense of music direction with Waylon, at the time, may also have been wrong; 1964 was not just another year in the record business. The British invasion just took over Top Forty charts and made inroads into the easy-listening markets as well. Country stations were locked into triplets, strings, weepers, along with jokes about the Beatles.

On October 24, 1964, A & M had released another Waylon Jennings single, "Sing the Girls a Song, Bill," backed by the Buck Owens hit "The Race Is On." Of the A & M recordings to date, "The Race Is On," a J.D.'s favorite, was the only untampered-with arrangement. Needless to say, it too did not sell outside of the Phoenix area.

With each passing record the disappointment in Phoenix increased. Floyd Ramsey, owner of Audio Recorders, came up with a slogan: "Record one track in Phoenix, sweetened in Los Angeles. Hell of a stereo sound if you're living in Blythe." Because original tracks were done in Phoenix and then shipped for "overdubbing" (the adding of additional tracks), the Los Angeles producer could do just about anything he wanted with the song. One Phoenix musician complained, "I really can't understand why they had to do this . . . all those were in the can, and they were good things." The adding and subtracting of whistles, trumpet solos, bass lines, and other changes only further irritated Waylon and his friends. Waylon felt he was not getting the sound he wanted. "Four Strong Winds" was a case in point, but he was fairly powerless at A & M. Artists without a long string of hits do not get to argue much with producers. After Chet's call, Waylon wanted out. He phoned A & M.

"I got the call every country boy dreams of getting!"

"What's that?" asked Jerry.

"I just got a call from Chet Atkins. He's like to have me with RCA. I told him I was signed to you and I'd talk to you about it."

"Okay, we can talk about it!"

"You guys have been just great to me. You've run up a lot of expenses. I'll stay with you as long as you want me to stay with you. I think you've been real good and . . . on the other hand, I am a country person and Chet Atkins is a legend and I look forward to working with him sometime, too."

"I'll talk to Herbie," said Jerry. Then he hung up.[42]

Despite their musical disagreements, Waylon and Herb liked each other. Herb was convinced he could make Waylon a star! "My instincts told me Waylon was more than just a country singer. At that point in my life, at least, I felt country music could go further than it had. I thought Waylon was being a little bit narrow because of his scope. It was much wider than he would think."[43] Time would prove Herb Alpert correct—but this was 1964.

Hanging up the phone, Waylon thought that his original fears about A & M seemed correct. Jerry Moss had been noncommital. Herb would probably oppose the termination. Herb was Waylon's major supporter at the company. Things did not look bright for a quick release. Waylon had judged Herb Alpert's

Willie Nelson during his RCA period in the late 1960s. Courtesy of RCA.

position correctly; Herb did not want to let him go. In 1964 Herb Alpert was not yet the Tijuana Brass star and primarily considered himself as a record producer. As a producer, he saw Waylon as a hot property—a potential star. In a discussion with Don Bowman, Herb expressed these feelings. "Well, maybe," snorted the comedian, "but he ain't gonna be no pop star with all them Tijuana Brass horns in the middle of them songs."[44] The reference was to "Four Strong Winds" and "Rave On."

Finally, Alpert and Moss met to decide the fate of their country singer. Jerry, always the pragmatist, argued that Waylon could be let out of his contract. "Look, we're getting success with the Tijuana Brass. We're getting some success with other things. We can produce his records for a year or two and if we don't get hit records from Waylon, it's going to put pressure on you." Jerry did not want Waylon's career interfering with the rise of the Tijuana Brass and A & M's other projects. Jerry's basic attitude was, "If he wants out—let him go." "I think you should let him go," continued Moss. "Let me go to Phoenix and cut six more sides with him so we have an album." Jerry reminded Herb that an amiable solution would preserve the publishing agreement they had with Waylon. "We're goin' live to regret it," said Herb in resignation.[45]

Jerry Moss was concerned. He doubted A & M could squeeze six more decent cuts out of Waylon. He traveled to Phoenix and rented Audio Recorders studios for six songs. Jack Miller, the engineer, recalled Moss's repeated pleas for "six more good songs. That's all."[46] Jerry had cause to worry. Richie Albright: "We rushed into the studio and just did 'em." He added, "they weren't too good."[47] The songs were a mix of folk and easy-listening things, including two Dylan songs, "Don't Think Twice" and "I Don't Believe You." The conflict over musical direction is obvious to the listener of "The Twelfth of Never," "Unchained Melody," and the Weaver's "Kisses Sweeter Than Wine." One also gets the impression that Waylon thought, "If they want pop sounding stuff—they'll get it."

Lynne was opposed to the move. She found support for her view from an unlikely source. Willie Nelson, who had just joined RCA, told Waylon to remain in Phoenix. He had a good deal where he was and why quit something that is doing good and go to something that you are not sure of? I told him to stay where the fuck he was. Don't move nowhere—stay."[48] Waylon disagreed; he was set on going to Nashville.

In the first week of December, "between contracts," Waylon recorded a promotional album for James Musil, Sr., co-owner of J.D.'s. The custom album was titled *Waylon Jennings at J.D.'s*. It was to be sold only to patrons at the club. The entire twelve-song album was recorded in some three hours in Audio Recorders Studio B on a four-track Ampex. Musil, who paid $65 for the session, stood and watched the band and the clock. Studio time was $25 an hour. Waylon used his nightclub band. He sang on nine songs, leaving "Money" to Jerry Gropp and two slower numbers, "Lorena" and "Abilene," to bass player Paul Foster. "Crying," the Roy Orbison hit, and "It's So Easy," another Buddy Holly song, were pure rock-a-billy songs. The country material could not be mistaken for easy listening. "White Lightnin'," a J.P. Richardson composition, "Big Mamou," and "Sally Was a Good Ole' Girl," three of the most requested songs at the club, were pure country. Still, the album was a mixed bag; it was certainly more countryish than the Herb Alpert productions but still unique enough in places to defy easy classification.

For the moment, Waylon's recording problems appeared to be solved. He would no longer have to deal with indifferent Los Angeles session musicians and a producer with an eye on the pop market. He was now in the capable production hands of Chester Atkins.

He had molded and shaped a band that reflected his musical directions and ideas. Waylon thought he was ready for Nashville.

7

HEY CHET ATKINS MAKE ME A STAR

Guiding his dusty white Cadillac onto the Broadway Street exit, Waylon encountered a study in contrasts. On one side of the freeway, going south toward Vanderbilt University, are used-car lots nestled between supply houses, run-down restaurants, and industrial parks. Across the freeway is the Ryman, home of the "Grand Ole Opry." Two blocks lined with dingy shops live off the venerable institution. Various enterprises thrive to serve the tourist. Souvenir shops with pennants, bumper stickers, and T-shirts; music shops with recognizable owners like Ernest Tubb; guitar stores; more greasy spoon eating parlors; and of course, on the corner of Sixth Avenue, Tootsie's—the famed watering hole for a generation of "Opry" pickers. Driving down Broadway, one senses a feeling of age and decay.

Music City Row in 1965 was merely a line of buildings beginning at Division Street and stretching several blocks south down Sixteenth and Seventeenth avenues. The founders are closer to Division Street than the late arrivals. The hub is Sixteenth and Hawkins, where Owen Bradley originally built Nashville's first major recording studio. Today, a large beige building stands there with the famous Columbia logo. RCA is a stone's throw away on Seventeenth Avenue. Musicians, song pitchers, bookers, and agents do not have to walk far to make their living off the Nashville Sound. To service the sound of country music, old two-story brick houses have been purchased and converted into offices with dark curtains—as if to keep the external dinginess from entering the smartly redecorated rooms. Outside, the Row shows all the signs of urban blight. The RCA building sticks out like the Empire State Building in the midst of old family-sized dwellings. Most of the former residents have moved to the suburbs. Nashville's southside is not a "nice place to live." Paul Hemphill's impression is probably correct: "Everybody on Music Row is too busy making money to worry about the neighborhood."[1] "It's not safe here after dark," says disc jockey Captain Midnite.[2]

Waylon did not need to go far on Seventeenth Avenue. RCA's studios were there; Harlan Howard's Wilderness Music Publishing Company, a block away, was in a renovated old wooden building with an approach in need of repair. So this was Music City, U.S.A.

Waylon was in for other surprises. Looking back, he says, "I was pretty naive, you know, like a lotta ways."[3] What Waylon did not know about was the Nashville session system and the hierarchy of Music City. From the minute he and the Waylors pulled into Nashville, Waylon unknowingly began violating the norms of the business. He brought his own band with him. This was unheard of. New artists always placed themselves in the experienced hands of a seasoned producer and his session musicians.

Waylon's first recording session was set for March 16 at 6:00 P.M. Three songs were chosen for the occasion. "I Wonder Just Where I Went Wrong" was written in the infamous Phoenix motel room with Don Bowman. "Now Everybody Knows" Waylon composed under his *nom de plume,* Jackson King. Waylon used the pseudonym because of his publishing contract with A & M. The last song was a Harlan Howard composition, "Another Bridge to Burn." This was to be the first of some seventy Howard tunes that Waylon would record. Waylon was in awe of the legendary songwriter.

Waylon, Jerry, Richie, and Paul drifted into the massive Seventeenth Avenue studio. There they found session man Herman Wade and the much sought-after blind pianist Hargus "Pig" Robbins. A vocal trio was also assembled. Don Bowman looked on. At the control panel sat a stern-faced Chet Atkins. Behind the glass, Chet resembled a disapproving parent or preacher who rarely displayed any emotion. One Victor artist described him: "I

Harlan Howard—the man who writes the songs, especially for Waylon during the mid 1960s. Courtesy of RCA.

First RCA promo photo. Courtesy of RCA.

1966 RCA - Moeller promo.

mean, a chuckle from Chet is like somebody being driven through a plate glass window laughin'." After running through "I Wonder Just Where I Went Wrong" several times, the local musicians wrote down the numbers for the chord changes, as is the Nashville custom. Waylon strolled up to the microphone holding his Gibson twelve-string. Chet's voice boomed from the control booth.

"You wanna come back and overdub the guitar? You can't do both at once, can you?"

Puzzled, Waylon answered, "Yeah."

The Nashville people exchanged knowing looks; Pig Robbins smiled to himself. This was not the way it was done. Worse yet, the twelve-string guitar was considered a hippie folk instrument of little value. Waylon, of course, didn't realize this, and he had always recorded while picking his own guitar.[4]

"So he played the twelve-string guitar and sang the song," says Don Bowman, "all at the same time—[the session people] was goin' 'Oh Lordy.' "[5] Waylon had ironically repeated the same mistake that Buddy Holly made at his first session with Owen Bradley some nine years earlier.

In two days Waylon and the band returned to Studio B. Pig Robbins had been replaced by Chet's favorite piano player, Floyd Cramer. Other RCA regulars, Fred Carter and the Anita Kerr Singers, joined the Waylors. Five songs were cut, including Waylon's first big country hit, "Stop the World (And Let Me Off)."

At 6:00 P.M. the next day, four more songs were on tape. "That's the Chance I'll Have to Take" created some technical problems and was overdubbed several times. Chet was still not satisfied. A month later, Murry Harman was brought in to add more drums to the song. Finishing the sessions, Waylon and his band headed back to the safety of J.D.'s.

The March sessions would be the last time for nearly ten years that Waylon Jennings would be allowed to use his entire band in an RCA studio. Very few artists were permitted to record with their own bands. The Waylors remained at the Parkway Motel while he cut most of the songs. "You see, that's something that they really don't like to do, was to let a guy use his own group, 'cause they have all those musicians who stay right in town and do all those sessions, and they've probably done three or four of them before they've gotten to yours that day," sighs Waylon.[6]

"Chet Atkins is kind of finicky about lettin' a road musician in a studio," complained a Waylor; "he just didn't go for it." At RCA, Chet Atkins nearly always hired his old pickin' buddies from the Carousel Club days. Chet played a number of sessions himself. "These dudes were *it* in those days," recalls one excluded guitar picker. Chuck Glaser: "Chet Atkins, Floyd Cramer, Grady Martin, Marvin Hughes, Buddy Harmon, Bob Moore . . . Hank Lockwood, and Harold Bradley. That was just about it. That *was* the Nashville Sound."[7] In 1965 the exclusive circle was expanded to include Jerry Reed, Norman Putnam, Jerry Carrigan, David Briggs, and several others.

The session system worked well for Owen Bradley and Chet Atkins. It was convenient; A & R men did not have to go through the hassle of rehearsing untested musicians. When a recording artist would come into town, off the road, he could walk into the studio and the "Nashville Cats" would be ready to play. The musicians welcomed the steady employment. "An old joke," says Jerry Reed incorrectly, "was that session men drive Cadillacs and artists Volkswagons."[8] In 1965 only a small number of players did all of the sessions in Nashville. A regular told John Grissom, "in 1964 and at the time there were only two Columbia studios, two RCA studios and the old Foster Monument Studio at the top of the hill—that was it. Owen Bradley was building his barn out in Mount Juliett. And out of the three hundred guys whose names were on the union books, there were maybe only twenty or thirty guys who regularly worked all the sessions."[9] For the insiders, the money was good. Regular session people earned in the neighborhood of $40,000 to $50,000 a year. It was a far better life than spending days staring out of a Cadillac limousine with a trailer packed with instruments going from one skull orchard to another for $30 a performance.

Nashville recording sessions begin at 10:00 A.M. and continue all day. Each session is a three-hour gig. Many studio musicians work three or four sessions a day. Ten, two, six and ten are the usual starting times. Carrying their precious instruments in nondescript cars, a handful of men travel from RCA to MCA and CBS. When they set up, a singer or songwriter plays the song for them. They take notes on the chord progression, scribbling on little pieces of white paper. These bits of paper are the musical charts to be used during the session. Chet Atkins calls these "head sessions." "The musicians listen to a demo record and scribble out a bunch of numbers; for example, 1 1–5 5–1 1–4 4. What they're saying is this. If the song is in the chord of C, it is 1; if it remains in C for two bars, you write two 1's. Then if it goes to F, that would be 4 (C, D, E, F); if it stays in F for two bars, it would be two 4's. Together it would be 1 1–4 4. Thus, after hearing the record a couple of times, they can sit down and play it. If the singer should say, 'Well, I don't want that in the Key of C; I want it in B-Flat,' they don't have to transpose. They call B-Flat 1 and E-Flat would be 4."[10] For Waylon, "the numbers" were a far cry from Herb Alpert's arranged sessions or his own method of recording, which involved hours of rehearsing prior to his entering a studio.

In July, Waylon returned to Nashville to record seven more songs. This time only his left-handed guitarist, Jerry Gropp, was included in the two sessions, which lasted from 6:00 P.M. until 1:00 in the morning. These tapings produced "Anita, You're Dreaming," "What Makes a Man Wander," and Waylon's favorite song for many years, "Look into My Teardrops."

On May 4, 1965, RCA released its first Waylon Jennings single, "That's the Chance I'll Have to Take" with "I Wonder Just Where I Went Wrong" as the B-side. Four months later, "That's the Chance" was Number 49 on the *Billboard* country chart. It may have been second from the bottom but it was Waylon's first charted song. A month later Waylon had a major country hit with "Stop the World (And Let Me Off)." It reached the Sixteenth spot on the *Billboard* listing and remained on the chart for thirteen weeks. His next two singles, "Anita You're Dreaming" and "Time to Bum Again," were played extensively on country music stations.

In March of 1966, RCA released *Folk-Country*, Waylon's first album for Victor. Folk-Country was Chet Atkin's concept. He told Chuck Glaser, "That's a label that I created and we are creating a whole package of artists that are going to be labeled folk-country."[11] The artists to be designated "folk" were writer-singer John D. Loudermilk, George Hamilton IV, Bobby Bare, John Hartford, and Waylon Jennings. All of the artists had some experience in the pop field. "He was trying to work some sort of crossover," explains Chuck Glaser, Hartford's producer, "not between country and rock but between country and folk." At the time of the album's release, Chet's assistant producer Felton Jarvis told a reporter a similar story. "Usually we record a new

The "country Bing Crosby" and one of the first examples of the Nashville Sound. Courtesy of RCA.

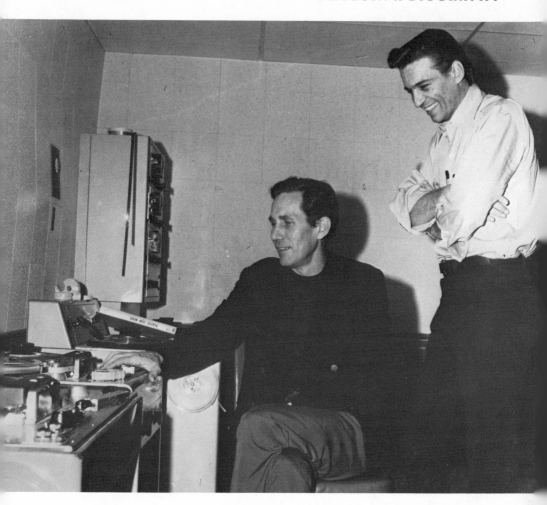

Chet Atkins and Waylon in the late 1960s. Courtesy of Country Music
Foundation, used by permission.

artist on single discs, see how those sell and eventually put the artist on an album. But Chet felt so sure that Waylon would become one of the biggest stars and biggest talents in *the* country—the biggest discovery since Johnny Cash—that he didn't fool around putting the kid on singles."[12] At the time, the major consumers of albums were not visitors to the Ryman Auditorium. Album buyers were found among fans of the folk/pop idiom. By putting the label on the album, Atkins hoped record store owners would put the LP into their pop as well as their country bins.

The inspiration for the concept was "Four Strong Winds," a song that enjoyed considerable commercial appeal. Chet felt that this was one avenue country performers might use to reach the pop market. Waylon Jennings was an obvious candidate for this approach, since Chet was greatly impressed with his version of the Ian Tyson folk-styled ballad. Chet was also much aware of the success of Waylon's roommate, Johnny Cash, with the folk audience. Cash's version of "The Ballad of Ira Hayes," which alienated some country fans, was a smash with protest-oriented young people. His re-recording or "cover" of Bob Dylan's "It Ain't Me Babe" climbed the pop and country charts.

Folk-Country presented Waylon on the jacket holding a twelve-string guitar, an instrument identified with folkies since Leadbelly, and leaning against a pile of stacked lumber. The liner notes written by madcap Don Bowman read, "He can sing a country song or a folk song. You might say he brought country to folk, folk to country and 'country-folk' to all folks!" In fact, the album was completely country despite Waylon's version of "I'm a Man of Constant Sorrow," which had been previously recorded by Bob Dylan. The folk-country concept was doomed, as Bob Dylan and the Byrds had successfully led the collegiate folkies into the world of rock. "The Kingston Trio was dead," recalls Chuck Glaser; "the Limelighters were dead. Everybody in the folk idiom, so to speak, was gone. And I saw no reason for trying to cross over the two."[13] Glaser was right, as the declining folk fans either stuck with the remaining favorites like Tom Paxton and Pete Seeger or joined the esoteric ranks of bluegrass freaks. *Sing Out!* and *Little Sandy Review,* the major folk music magazines, completely ignored Chet's attempts to reach their readers. Listeners to country stations were the main buyers of *Folk-Country.* Today, Chet Atkins disavows the concept, arguing, "I signed Waylon as a country artist and wasn't thinking about any other idiom at that time."[14]

By the middle of 1965 Waylon's relationship with Lynne had reached a breaking point. Another woman had entered Waylon's life. Barbara Rood was the youngest of three children, the first girl in the family. Prior to her fourth birthday the Roods separated. Their father went on to become the inventor of a highly successful mechanical cotton picker; reportedly, Garland Steel Company bought the patent for $16 million. Barbara, according to her mother, Betty, was a beautiful girl with normal tastes, a good student and a pom-pom girl in high school. She was a campus belle but never settled on any one boy. Underneath, she was "kind of shy," but a flurry of activities and anxious males disguised this fact. She never let anybody get that close. Her main interests were dancing—with many partners—various sports, and animals. Betty Rood recalls, "Barbara *just* loved animals."[15] Her horse won some ribbons and trophies. Waterskiing occupied much of her time.

Her preference in males followed the same lines. Her suitors were a baseball player and Jerry Hans, an Arizona State University basketball star. In time, she dropped both of them. Barbara, pretty as a picturebook princess, was not the kind to be the loser—even in the game of love.

Barbara's tall, dark-haired brother, Bill, was a country music fan. Barbara, too, liked Marty Robbins and the other Phoenix favorites. One night at the White Elephant, Bill noted, "There's a guy you ought to listen to."

"Who's that?"

"Waylon Jennings."

Barbara had seen Waylon before. She went back—a face in the crowd. But she was to be much more, as those Hollywood "love at first sight" things happened. Waylon, of course, was still married, and Lynne was even more jealous and insecure. The eight years' difference between them was looming larger by the moment. Lynne came to many of Waylon's shows. Occasionally, Waylon and Barbara talked and talked at J.D.'s, usually in a dark corner during intermissions. Richie Albright served as the decoy, since the rest of the band was married or engaged. Generally after a show, Waylon went straight home to Scottsdale; if he was late there was hell to pay. Lynne erroneously thought Waylon was sleeping all over town.

As the new relationship grew intense, jealousy became a problem. Waylon ordered Barbara to stop dating, threatening if she didn't, "go to another club!" He didn't really mean it. When she did, Waylon frantically called their friends, asking, "Where's Barbara?" A married man with an adopted baby daughter, however, couldn't very well be too self-righteous. Barbara's steady date was bewildered, confused. She put him off. But why? Obviously the triangle situation had to be kept quiet. Barbara's friend was named Danny. "Danny Boy," the Conway Twitty hit, was quickly dropped from Waylon's songbag. Audience requests for the song were met with cold, icy stares from the stage. For Barbara, this was an unusual situation. She was not used to a secondary role. But capturing *the* country performer of Phoenix would more than make up for it.

Leaving Phoenix and the security of J.D.'s was an important move for Waylon. Paul Foster, the bass player, flatly refused to go on the road; he was quite content to play bass in Phoenix and have a good time. One Waylor described him "as disinterested in music . . . never really had the desire." Besides, Paul was planning on getting married, and going on the road was not in the cards. (Several years later, Paul finally went to work for Western Electric.) His departure from the band left Waylon without a bass player.

Waylon and Tommy Jennings had lost communication with each other after Waylon's move to Phoenix. Tommy had gone into the Army, and he rarely heard from his older brother. One day, he got a rare letter, inviting him to come to Phoenix after his discharge. But Tommy decided to return to Littlefield and open a service station. He found that working in a West Texas gas station wasn't at all exciting. "After I shoveled dirt off the front of that service station for about six months, I decided that Phoenix might not be such a bad idea." Waylon's appearance in Littlefield with a new white Cadillac made the appeal of Phoenix even greater. Still, Tommy was not convinced. Waylon kept asking.

"So, I went out there," says Tommy. "Lord I thought I was goin' to burn up. I had an old Ford coupe with no air conditioner in it and I come off them hills down in that valley and my head's a different color . . . two different shades of tan: brown from the sun." Tommy got a job unloading boxcars full of flour in Phoenix's blistering heat. The temperature climbed to above 100 degrees. He worked at that for three days, then quit and moved on to working on electrical machines for AMF. One day Waylon suggested that Tommy might play bass for him. Tommy declined. "Waylon, I'm no bass player. I can't play a bass." The subject was dropped.

In a matter of months, Waylon called. "I've gotta have a bass player and you're gonna play bass for me."

Tommy still was not sure. "I don't know about that."

Waylon explained that Paul Foster was leaving the group and he needed a bass man. "Well, you think it over, but I want you to." Tommy agreed. Waylon was on his way to Nashville, but he'd be back in Phoenix in a week from Monday. "Go get Jerry to teach you how to play bass."

Tommy gave notice at AMF and went looking for Jerry Gropp. "Can you show me how to play bass?"

Gropp, a rhythm guitarist, looked strangely at Tommy. "I don't know how to play bass!"

Upon his return, Waylon wanted a progress report. "How are you doing?"

"I don't know how to play bass."

Pointing to the stage, Waylon ordered, "Well, get up there."

"So that's what started it. I got up on the bandstand and every time I heard something that would sound like what I should hit to sound right, well then I would hit it." Waylon's reasons for having Tommy come and play bass are not clear. The dialogue between the brothers sounds very much like Buddy Holly's with Waylon, when he wanted him to come along as his bass player. Waylon could have been repeating the good deed, or he may simply have been anxious to replace Foster.

Tommy was very concerned about his new role as bass player. "I got self-conscious of hunting for any notes in the bass and guys standing there watching me and I got a bad complex." Tommy brought as many records, mostly soul, as he could find with lots of heavy bass and would go home to practice. One Saturday night, Tommy decided that he had mastered the instrument and that he was going to exhibit his newly found dexterity at J.D.'s.

All that could be heard the first set was Tommy hitting that bass. "I was really honkin' it. All those guitar and bass players from all them other clubs was down there. Saturday Night at J.D.'s."

After the set, Waylon called out, "Tommy come here! Let me see that bass." Waylon then did a number of run, fillers, riffs,

chords, and generally picked "the livin' hell out of it." Tommy
was rapidly getting the point.

"Tommy, if I wanted that kind of bass playing, I would pick it
myself. I know what's wrong with you—them guys down there
were watching you and you got a complex about it. But you're
doin' what I want you to do. I want you to continue to do that
because if they were that good, they would be out somewhere
working on a Saturday night instead of sittin' here watchin' me."

"Ok, boss!"

Tommy picked up the bass and remained a Waylor for several
years. Hiring Tommy did not entirely change the reluctance of
the Waylors to leave Phoenix. Even Tommy got to liking the
scene. "I kinda hated leaving Phoenix. Course, it was a lazy-man
thing out there. All you had to do was go out and pull a gig and
enjoy the heck out of it because he could run for Governor in
Phoenix." Neither Jerry nor Richie were anxious to go. Jerry, as
always, was involved with a girl. Richie, who had joined the band
several months earlier, felt the band needed more work. "I still
think we left a little early. We could have stayed there another
year and really been great. I hated to leave it." Philosophically,
"but I guess it was time to leave if we did." Barbara Rood
accompanied the band to Nashville.[16]

Waylon had met a dissipated Johnny Cash two weeks before
moving to Nashville, when "John R." was doing a date in
Phoenix. At the time of their meeting, John Cash was a troubled
man. Biographer Chris Wren wrote, "Pressed by too many com-
mitments, Cash used amphetamines to carve out enough time to
work on his songs. Moreover, he had domestic problems; his
heavy traveling imposed a strain on his marriage with Vivian,
who could not cope with such a frantic life. But the root cause was
a depression that had lingered with him since Jack's [his brother]
death. Having risen to the top of country music with thousands of
shows and millions of records behind him, he found himself no
more at peace than before."[17] To ease the pain, John turned to
dexedrine. The white pill with red and black particles called "the
great speckled bird" by truckers and country musicians originally
seemed to help. He also discovered "Old Yellers" (uppers). By
1965 John was a frail 140 pounds, losing a wife and missing
bookings. Promoters and disc jockeys considered John R.
"squirrelly." "He was crazy," one booker commented. His country bookings began to fall off as John R. stories circulated

John Cash. "There Ain't No Good on a Gang" or in Madison. Courtesy
of CBS Records, 1977.

throughout the close-knit industry. Owen Bradley, for example, refused to allow the Glasers to do Cash shows or tour with him. Many resented Cash's "hippie protest" songs like "Ira Hayes." In June 1965 John accidentally started a grass fire in Los Padres National Forest while on a camping trip. The blaze swept some 508 acres and required nearly 500 men to extinguish the fire. John again made headlines when he was caught on his return from Mexico with 688 dexedrine pills along wih 475 "downs"; he spent the night in the El Paso jail. Critical articles began to appear in the usually flattering country music magazines. One even suggested that John resign from the Country Music Association. By 1965 John Cash had replaced Hank Williams as Nashville's "bad boy."

To get away from it all, John rented a one-bedroom place at the Fountain Bleu apartments in suburban Madison, Tennessee. The following day, Waylon and Cash resumed their brief relationship.

"If you're looking for an apartment," said the Nashville outcast, "why don't you move out there with me? I'll get them to put up another bed."

Waylon didn't have a place and decided to look the situation over. "Man, you're the worst housekeeper I ever saw. What have you been doing in the kitchen—fighting?"

"I cooked breakfast, biscuits and gravy," replied Cash.

"Do me a favor and don't ever cook me any," stated a somewhat startled Jennings.[18]

Waylon did move in. The two singers divided the $150 monthly rent. Barbara Rood rented the apartment directly below them. Both singers were heavily into pills and going through souring marriages.

"I was on dope," says Waylon. "John and I were big dummies. We were going through a time when we felt uncommonly sorry for ourselves in the process of trying to get rid of one wife while trying to hang on to another woman and neither one of them understood us."

Cash doesn't recall much of that period. He did tell one writer, "I was doing a lot of trashy living . . . maybe I was afraid to face reality then. I wasn't very happy then."[19]

While Waylon was cutting records and living in Madison, the Waylors sat around the Parkway Motel. They were living on $10 a day for the three of them. Those were the "cheese and baloney" days. The motel manager constantly demanded her back rent, threatening, "If you want your meal you will have to pay your rent." Jerry, Richie, and Tommy started to get restless. Nashville was very different from Phoenix. The money was not as good. Waylon was earning only $250 to $350 for a night's work. Session money was scarce. Chet did let Jerry and Richie work several of Waylon's recordings, but these $60-per-session jobs were rarities. "We knew that we were guineas," says Tommy Jennings. "We weren't in the Nashville clique . . . we kind of resented it. Because we knew Buck Owens was going in with the Buckeroos. We knew the Strangers were playing with Merle Haggard . . . another thing, too, we wanted $60 a session time." At one point, they all decided to return to Phoenix. Waylon learned of their plan. "You all are not going back, cause if you do, I'm going with you." They decided to stick it out so Waylon's career would not be hurt.[20]

John did not spend much time at the apartment; instead, he was at Mother Maybelle Carter's house most of the time. "Maybelle used to argue like hell if I wanted to go out there and spend the night." June Carter considered Waylon a bad influence. When John did go, things "got crazy." In his zombie-like condition he was a menace to himself and others.

"They stayed wired. You couldn't talk to either one of 'em," said a frequent visitor to the apartment. Waylon and John originally came to an agreement not to interfere in the other's situation. "We both got some hang-ups. What's yours is yours. If I can help you get off them I will," offered Waylon, "but I won't help you keep them up and don't do it with me either." They concealed pills from one another. "You know both of us would lie to each other and say we weren't takin' any pills. We'd swear we were off 'em and four days later, we'd still be takin'."[21]

John hid his cache so carefully, in fact, that he frequently forgot where he put them. Other times, June Carter would search his room and throw the "uppers" away. When John ran out of pills, things got hectic. He would ransack the apartment desperately looking for the precious white pills. Locked drawers would be pried open, bolted closets kicked in, air conditioners torn apart. One time, Waylon found his Cadillac a mess: "someone ripped open the glove compartment—just tore the panel right off its hinges. And I knew John had done it. I knew right then that he'd run out of pills and gotten desperate." Waylon confronted his roommate, and John denied being in the expensive car. Later he approached Waylon: "You know I did it, don't you? I couldn't keep it from you. I saw your eyes looking right into my soul."[22]

"There was a carpenter who we kept working a lot," recalls Waylon. "Putting the hinges back on our door because we was always locking each other out. Kicking doors in was a common practice." Waylon and John either bolted the front door or lost the key. After four days of pills, John would crash into a comotose sleep. As Luther Perkins once told Gene Ferguson, CBS sales manager, "He'll sleep twenty-four hours. If he awakes— he's alive. If he doesn't—he's dead."[23] When he was unable to raise Cash, Waylon kicked in the door.

Cash had another reason for bolting doors. He believed the Ku Klux Klan was after him. *Thunderbolt*, a racist magazine published by the National States Rights Party, charged that John was married to a "Negress," and the Klan reprinted the false article. Threats were made that Cash would be killed if he appeared in the Deep South. John was in constant fear. Sometimes he hid at producer Don Law's apartment. He armed himself with a pistol, a borrowed shotgun, and a tear gas pencil. Gradually the Klan turned its attention to other "racial outrages," but John's apprehension continued. He constantly believed a car was following him. One day Waylon was in John's car. "Somebody's followin' me! Somebody's followin' me! It's the Ku Klux Klan!" Trying to calm John, Waylon replied: "Did you ever stop to think that maybe there ain't nobody give a goddamn about you?"[24]

John's condition concerned all of those around him. Friends were picking him up in Nashville beer joints and trying to get some food into him. Braxton Dixon was one of the people trying to save Cash from himself. Braxton and his wife, Anna, gave John a bed and fed him spaghetti or beans which he, when "especially hungry" according to Chris Wren, "would scoop up with his hands. Then he would go back to bed."[25]

John's long sleeping bouts greatly concerned people. The Dixons almost phoned a doctor when John was out for thirty hours. "He'd stay down for, like, three days. Then he'd wake up coughing—really almost choking to death," says Waylon. "And I'd have to take him to water or he *would* choke."

Waylon's association with John R. was not completely a matter

"Jennings the Nashville Sound." 1968. Courtesy of RCA.

of "roarin'." He and the Waylors worked many of the Cash road shows for an eight-month period in 1966. Waylon played guitar for several of John's albums, and John recorded one of Waylon's songs. Waylon wrote "Step Aside, You're Standing in My Way" for Cash, who did not use it. Waylon decided to use the song on one of his albums, but Chet Atkins vetoed the idea. "The only song I guess that Chet Atkins ever turned down and said I shouldn't do is a song that I wrote called 'Step Aside, You're Standing in My Way,' which I did write for Johnny Cash." At Lee Hazlewood's urging, Nancy Sinatra finally recorded the song. John asked Waylon to write some things for his *Everybody Loves a Nut* album. Waylon did two songs. John used "Singing Star's Queen." "Jackson King" (Waylon) had written another song, which used Jennings's name in the line "Waylon is a singer, a record selling star." Waylon was somewhat embarrassed about it. "I took my name off of it because I thought it'd look pretty egotistical for a guy to write a song about himself. But actually, I wrote the song and said, 'Johnny is a singer, he's a record selling star,' you know, but John changed it and said 'Waylon.' "

One night while working on some songs, Waylon suggested John move out. "You can afford a mansion!"

"I guess I'd feel guilty," countered John R., "with my girls in California."

"Get yourself a nice house and maybe their mother will let them come visit you."

Cash took Waylon's advice to heart. In the spring of 1967 John bought an unfinished $150,000 house from Braxton Dixon and left the Fountain Bleu apartments.

Most press accounts dealing with Waylon Jennings have stressed his eighteen-month stay in Madison, but that hectic period is not very important, at least not for Waylon Jennings. Christopher Wren, the ex-*Look* editor who wrote Cash's biography, mentions him only once: "He [Cash] shared it with Waylon Jennings—another country singer."[26] Waylon and John R. spent very little time together in that apartment. They were either on the road or elsewhere. John was at June Carter's or Maybelle's place most of the time. The song John did not use on *Everybody Loves a Nut*, written by Bill Mack and Waylon, was "John's Back in Town." The theme of the song was that "When John is out croonin', I'm out with his queen passing his money around." The song ended with the plea, "Buy one of his records or go see his show, help me keep ole' John out of town."

More important for Waylon at this time was his relationship with Barbara, the Lucky Moeller skull orchard tours, and a movie, *Nashville Rebel*.

8

NASHVILLE REBEL

Waylon's first year in Nashville found him spending most of his working time in the RCA studios and touring with the Johnny Cash show. In 1966 he started to branch out when he signed with veteran talent agent W.E. "Lucky" Moeller. Moeller, formerly Jim Denny's assistant, was a major booking agent in Nashville. From his "Opry" days he had developed contacts with nightclub owners and promoters throughout the country. He did not elicit affection, but he did have power. One artist described Moeller as "a hillbilly with a knife." He generated bookings even if they were scattered all over the country. "Routing" was not a word in his vocabulary. His artists frequently had to log thousands of miles a week racing from one show to another. Waylon would soon be on this treadmill, but in the meantime, there was a movie.

Nashville Rebel was yet another grade-B remake of the "young rebel making his way to stardom" theme; half of the film is devoted to name singers doing their hit records. Click Weston, a Chicago writer, merely changed the plot from rock 'n' roll to country music. Weston was not particularly a country music fan. Frank Niles Productions and Show Biz, Inc. picked up the story and commissioned Ira Kerns to do a screenplay. Jay J. Sheridan was hired to direct as well as to help Kerns with the script. He composed the instrumentals for the soundtrack. American International, best known for its inexpensive drive-in horror movies like *I Was a Teenage Werewolf* and cheap rock musicals, agreed to distribute the film.

Kerns and Sheridan probably used an old Elvis Presley script, *Jailhouse Rock*, for the plot. The story line is familiar: Arlin Grove is an ex-serviceman who walks (in the best Woody Guthrie fashion) into a sleepy Tennessee hamlet, Morgan's Corner, with a guitar on his back. Local good ole boys beat up on him. A local girl, Molly Morgan, takes pity upon the roaming guitar-picker and nurses him back to health. Molly's uncle hires Arlin to work in the local general store and pump gas outside. What Arlin does not know is that his benefactor is plotting to get the girl married and he is now the prime candidate. Naturally, Arlin and Molly fall in love. As is to be expected, a traveling music show comes to town and Arlin gets up and dazzles the professionals and the local residents with a version of "Silver Ribbons." Elated with his success, Arlin tries for another conquest. They rush to Molly's bedroom, where they are discovered by her uncle, shotgun in hand. A hastily arranged marriage takes place. Arlin is beckoned by the call of fame and fortune. He joins the hootenanny unit for $75 a week. The villain of the piece is the group's manager, Wesley Lang. Lang takes Arlin and his new bride to Nashville. Here, Arlin meets Lang's lusty girlfriend, Margo. Margo finds the shy country boy interesting and the plot thickens. Arlin takes Nashville by storm and brings down the house at the Black Poodle Club with "Nashville Bum," a song written by Waylon and Slim Corbin. Success and Margo come between the singer and Molly. The slighted Molly goes home to Morgan's Corner, much to Margo's delight.

Between songs and guest appearances by Sonny James, Loretta Lynn, Tex Ritter, and Faron Young, the plot continues. Finally, Arlin gets his chance on the "Grand Ole Opry" and the "Porter Wagoner Show." He has made it. However, the story cannot end here, with Molly in Morgan's Corner. Lang and Arlin fight over Margo, and the country boy wins. Lang plots revenge and books the singer into a swank Chicago nightclub where country music is not appreciated. His career seemingly destroyed, Arlin retreats into a bottle. Margo finds out about Lang's evil-doing and, with the aid of Tex Ritter, rehabilitates the singer and returns him to the bosom of country music. Finally, Molly returns. Arlin discovers she is pregnant and about to give birth. He rushes to Morgan's Corner, where she hands him a baby.

Arlin is now a country star with a perfect marriage and a male heir, and they all live happily ever after.

With this story, Sheridan went out to cast the film. Finding "Grand Ole Opry" people to do cameo performances was not hard. Mary Frann, an aspiring young actress, never heard from again, was signed to play Molly. Veteran character actor Gordon Oas-Heim would portray the scheming lawyer and agent. Finding a lead was a bit more difficult. The script called for an actor who could sing country music. Hollywood casting lists were of little help. Chet Atkins recommended Waylon Jennings. Waylon seemed ideal—a young, good-looking Texan who could sing "folk-country." Also, he had some television experience with Ray Odom. "I didn't have anything to do that morning, so they asked me to come down and audition, just to see what it was like. I did it and they liked me."[1]

Waylon would make *Nashville Rebel* between April 11 and July 25, 1966, when not on the road for Lucky Moeller. Most of the shooting was to be done in Chicago and Nashville during June. This meant hours of driving from bookings. Waylon had no acting experience. Sheridan told him not to worry, the director would show him all the ropes. "When I got through, I didn't realize what I had done because I had such a great director," he told several magazines shortly after its release. However, Waylon did not like movie making. "Sitting and waiting drove me nuts."[2] He was so tired and bored that he fell asleep while practicing a love scene with his leading lady. Mary Frann was furious and would not speak to her co-star for the rest of the filming. Waylon also did not think much of the technical details. "I rewrote it as we went along," he told *Melody Maker*, "'cuz there was a buncha shit in there."[3] Tommy Jennings wasn't very happy either. His bass had to be painted black for the film to eliminate glare from the bright lights.

On February 9, 1967, *Nashville Rebel* opened in Littlefield, Texas, at the Palace Theatre. The very same day hundreds of small movie houses throughout the South and the Midwest and drive-ins all over the country booked the film. Waylon may have passed his screen image as the Waylors were driving from Phoenix to a club in Cloudcraft, New Mexico.

Prior to the Moeller tour, Waylon did his first national news magazine interview. He went down to the Nashville offices of Faron Young's *Music City News*, then the bible of country music.

The *Music City News* was the print equivalent to the "Grand Ole
Opry," as it was the only magazine addressed to country music.
Music City News was basically a fan magazine promoting Nashville artists. "And never is heard a critical word" could well be its
motto. Surprisingly, Waylon did one of the best interviews of his
career. Perhaps he wasn't tired of the questions at the time. The
article, "Nashville Welcomes Waylon Jennings," ran through his
Littlefield days, the Holly tour in detail, and finally his future
plans. Even then, some of the seeds of discontent were planted.
Waylon handled them well. On recording a Beatles song:

> The other side of my new record is a song from England, by the
> Beatles. Chet was playing it on the guitar one day, and asked me had I
> heard it, and I told him "you bet. I bought their album just to hear
> that one song." "Do you like it?" Chester asked. "Yes," I told him.
> "Why don't you record it," he asked, and we both laughed. Well, I
> said I would, and I did it . . . did it country too! There are several
> Rolling Stone, Beatle and Donovon songs that can be done country,
> and I figure that turn-a-bout's fair play. If they can do "Act Natural-
> ly", then we can do some of theirs, country.

When did you start working on the road?" the reporter asked.
"I start Friday," he answered. "You see, I stayed in Phoenix until
I came to Nashville when Mr. Moeller said he'd book me. This is
real wonderful of him because my not having worked the road
before, all he had to go on is my records." Waylon no doubt
surprised the writer by adding, "I'll be using my own band."
Newcomers generally employed "pickup" bands who regularly
played the nightclubs in which they were appearing. Records
would be sent ahead for them to learn. A new artist with his own
band was virtually unheard-of. "It's hard," he explained, "to carry
a band but they were with me in the bad times, so I'm goin' to try
to keep them with me on through the good. They are a part of
me." He concluded with an understatement:

> I'm really looking forward to working the road . . . it isn't an easy life,
> but I don't expect it to be. I'm looking forward to meeting the
> people. People are really all an entertainer has, and I intend to make
> time for the folks who have helped me so much. I can remember
> when I was trying to get back stage to see the stars and I think the
> biggest thrill in my life was when Billy Walker was real nice to me . . .
> Country fans are the most loyal in the world, . . . which isn't true in
> the pop field. Pop artists have to have a hit every time to remain
> popular, but if a country artist comes out with one which doesn't hit,
> the country fans are smart enough to remember the other records,
> and they know he is good and will have another big one.

"The greatest people," he concluded "are the country people and the greatest business is the Country Music industry. I want very much to become a part of it."[4]

In several days, Waylon, Jerry, Tommy, and Richie would climb into his Cadillac with a U-Haul trailer and head for Minneapolis to begin the Moeller tour. Lucky was booking him at $600 or less, not a large sum for a singer with a road band.

Tommy was given the unattractive task of keeping books for the group. He, in effect, was the road manager as well as being the bass player. He did not particularly like his role, but it did provide training in music management. In a short time he would become the Nashville operative for Baron (Barbara and Waylon) Publishing.

Moeller booked Waylon into the Golden Nuggett in Las Vegas for a ten-day engagement. He had always done well in that club. The house band was headed by Ralph Mooney and Red Nichols. "Moon" was one of the most respected steel guitar players in country music. He had formerly been with Buck Owens and Merle Haggard. He was also well known for writing "Crazy Arms," a country classic. Moon and Red opened the show and were followed by the Waylors. The Waylors were scheduled to play four hours, with twenty-minute breaks thrown in. Waylon did his chart material, Johnny Horton's, "Springtime in Alaska," some Hank Williams songs, and, again, Wynn Stewart's "Big, Big Love."[5] Waylon enjoyed Las Vegas because it provided him with an opportunity to gamble, although Lady Luck was not always kind to him.

At the Golden Nuggett, Waylon met the Kimberleys, a quartet of two married couples. Harold, Carl, Verna, and Vera got their start on the "Louisiana Hayride" in the late fifties and had done vocal backgrounds for Johnny Horton prior to his death. They recorded a single for Columbia, Roger Miller's "You Can't Roller Skate in a Buffalo Herd." Their success in country music was minimal, and they retreated for the safety of well-paying Nevada lounges. Waylon was impressed with the group, especially Verna Gay's vocals.

At the conclusion of the engagement the band drove to Flagstaff, Arizona, for a two-night stand. Lucky had them appearing two days later at the Horseshoe Lounge in Ontario, Canada. They left Flagstaff on a Sunday morning headed for Toronto. Waylon's white Cadillac exceeded all the posted speed limits, travel trailer and all. One Waylor recalls, "Well, we was runnin' 100 miles per hour to 110 all the way." Jerry Gropp did most of the driving. Tommy Jennings says, "That boy, he's crazy when it comes to drivin'." Arriving in Detroit, they couldn't get across the border. All musicians playing in foreign countries must get work permits, and Moeller had not arranged for Canadian working papers. "So," says Tommy, "we had to spend all night in a little rat-hole there in a hotel until the next morning till we got Jack Starr, owner of the Lounge."[6] After five days in Canada, the Cadillac was back on the road heading for Milwaukee, Wisconsin.

The road was rapidly taking its toll. Driving long distances, facing the all-too-familiar motel rooms, and performing the same songs over and over again is both physically and mentally taxing. Like many country musicians, Waylon and his group frequently used uppers to stay awake. They also consumed them to get "up for a show." Waylon has been quite candid about this subject. "Nashville created that and the people condemned the people who did it. Like the agencies . . . . They put them on the road and you had to stay on the road to even survive. Some of your bookings were 800 miles apart. You're in a station wagon, or a trailer, packed in there. I'll tell you what, you'll take something, man, if it's a button."[7] He told another writer, "As far as things like pep pills, uppers and downers—no, a cotton puller ain't got no use for a benny, but a singer . . . I was on the road for three hundred days . . . . Now where do you get your energy? Travelin' anywhere from six to eight hundred miles a day in between shows." "You have to get up for shows, basically mentally, you have to get yourself geared to it. It's hard to do that, you know. Just to keep doing it year after year and day after day. When you traveled all that distance. That's where people get on pills and booze and what have you."[8] In Waylon's case it was not just the traveling, or the grind of the road. "You know," he said, "you're takin' country boys, who are just guys, who 90 percent of 'em, are not used to money, and are basically country people or Southern people are *shy* and it's not really easy, to begin with, to get up on a stage in front of people and travel . . . ."[9] This last statement is perhaps more revealing than his comments about the demands of the 300-day Moeller tour.

Because of the film, people came up to the stage with notes asking for "Green River." Waylon hated the tune. "I despise it. I can't stand that song and I can't stand to sing it."[10] He also refused to do "Cryin' " because the ending hurt his voice, especially when he was tired, which was most of the time.

Waylon's honeymoon with RCA was shortlived. Victor's approach annoyed him. Impersonal "Dear Artist" letters were more than irritating. He objected to the manner in which his singles were being released. His first major complaint was that "Look into My Teardrops" was the B-side for "Anita You're Dreaming." "Look into My Teardrops" was a favorite song, but the powers at RCA didn't share that view. "I think that song was there, I think the record was there, but I couldn't get everybody else believing in it. So it wound up on the back side."[11] This was just the beginning. For years Waylon would bemoan Victor's release policies and his string of "two-sided hits." Chet Atkins also disapproved of a beer commercial Waylon wanted to do. He could have used the money the Black Label people offered.

The year 1966 was not a total loss. *Record World*, a major trade paper, chose him as the "Most Promising Male Vocalist" in country music.

ANITA YOU'RE DREAMING

Ever since "Anita You're Dreaming" Waylon had wanted a divorce. Lynne was not agreeable. She made a series of demands: "You pay for my kidney operation, then we'll talk about it." Then she requested part of Waylon's future royalties. Barbara and others felt these were merely the stalling tactics of a woman scorned. During Waylon's Christmas visit to Phoenix, Lynne modified her approach and agreed to a divorce. Reportedly, she was becoming involved with another man, so divorce was to her advantage.

On January 11, 1967, she sued for divorce. The suit alleged Waylon was guilty of "excesses, outrages and cruelty to her." She wanted "reasonable alimony" and "equitable distribution of community property." She further asked for permanent custody of Tammi Lynne and the payment of some $6,000 in lawyer's fees. Waylon did not contest the suit. Lynne got everything she wanted and $1,800 per month support. The cost seemed worth it. (This amount was cut in half when she repetitioned the court several years later.) With Lynne legally out of the way, Waylon was free to marry Barbara.

In October 1967 Waylon and Barbara Rood were married at her millionaire father's home in Scottsdale. The union quickly was faced with the realities of Waylon's career as a country music

Mrs. Barbara Rood Jennings and Waylon. *Arizona Republic*, copyright 1967.

artist. A newlywed has no desire to stay at home while her husband is out "on the road." Barbara felt that Waylon needed a woman every night and that if she were not there, somebody else would be. Barbara, as her mother suggests, was possessive. A striking beauty with many admirers, Barbara was not about to become another "Nashville wife sittin' at home" blocking out the realities of touring. Many Nashville wives are country girls who have followed their husbands to the top. They enjoy big houses, swimming pools, their kids, and the companionship of their counterparts. They rarely think about the snow queens and the lonely bar girls who prance before the husbands, openly advertising their availability. The few that do must weigh the comforts of their existence against the moral issue of "slippin' around."

Determined not to join their ranks, Barbara went on the road. Her existence was not what she expected. She was no longer the queen of the ball. She was just another member of the troupe, resented by some of the Waylors who saw traveling as a chance to party—and wives didn't go to those kinds of parties. Barbara was possessive but realized that Waylon's appeal was primarily to women, so she stayed back at the motel. The Holiday Inn rooms only generated loneliness and visions of other women. Only Basil MacDavid, the road comedian, seemed to understand the dilemma of the girl and the guitar picker.

Barbara played cards and enjoyed the band, but there was always the crowd, the promoters, the musicians, and the demands. Standing behind autograph seekers, disc jockeys, and hangers-on, she grew to feel neglected. Lucky Moeller did not approve of her presence. Once, Lucky ordered Waylon to Las Vegas. Waylon protested, "We have our worst fights there." "Get her home," the veteran promoter suggested. Barbara didn't like Moeller. Waylon shared some of her feelings but felt obliged to the promoter. Some of their most heated discussions were about the Nashville booking agent.

Barbara quickly realized that Waylon's devotion to the road was caused by a need for money; and so she designed several plans to free him. One scheme was to take over the finances of the band. She distrusted Dal Perkins and other people who collected the cash before a show. Some accountability was necessary. The more money Waylon earned, the sooner she and her husband could stay in Nashville or Phoenix. Lucky Moeller underlined this desire, promising Waylon a pot of gold if he continued playing small clubs—getting exposure. Waylon usually believed Moeller; Barbara did not.

Conditions grew worse as the grind of the road heightened. Some band members resented Barbara's interference in business affairs. Worse yet, Waylon's retirement after a show to be with his wife affected their night life. Invitations to "party" frequently were tied to Waylon's availability. Some objected to having any wife join them for a late-hour snack. The road was a male institution. (Traditional southern values closely governed the behaviors of females, even on the road. The double standard was dominant.)

Barbara, the belle of Scottsdale, who at nineteen had been named "Miss Softball," was becoming a Nashville wife on the road. She did not feel significant in the scheme of things. It was the business, but Barbara was new to the country music grind. Quickly, the problems were personalized. Lucky was the bad guy. Her millionaire father attempted to buy Waylon's contract for $50,000. Lucky just laughed. Failing that, Barbara resorted to her ultimate weapon—desirability. When ignored, she would come to shows. An unescorted girl in any bar is a target, and she knew it. Waylon did not like it when she was dancing with another man to his music. When things got too bad, flirting could be a valuable tool. Under these pressures, their relationship was growing stormy. Barbara desired all of the *Good Housekeeping* dreams that previous suitors had promised. The road, pills, Lucky Moeller, all prevented the perfect union. Waylon found her demands unreasonable.

Slowly, the reality of the road impressed itself on Barbara; frustration set in, and animosities grew. Several Waylors were openly contemptuous of her. Barbara's desire to control the money implied wrong-doing on the part of the band. Also, Barbara interrupted the normally adventurous style of the road. Privately, some of the Waylors desired Barbara's departure. "They were jealous of one another," says her mother. Road conditions only made it worse. In Las Vegas, when Waylon appeared at the Golden Nugget, the first of many breakups occurred. Barbara, feeling completely helpless and ignored, decided to leave and did. She boarded the next outgoing flight to Phoenix.

Waylon was depressed. He still cared for Barbara. She did not understand the demands placed upon a performer. Her life as his wife was a long way from the Saturday night hops in Scottsdale.

She found it hard to decline from being "one of the most sought after belles" to being a Holiday Inn live-in. Waylon just was not hers. Barbara's attempt to transform Waylon into a college admirer had failed. Waylon was not convinced by friends' arguments that Barbara just didn't fit into the Grand Plan. The couple had many reconciliations and breakups. Neither apparently could come to terms with the bottom line, life on the road.

As time passed the situation got worse. Together they fought, apart they suffered. Dal Perkins, after a verbal battle, told Waylon he was "happy to see her go." Strangely, her step-father was standing two feet away from the musician. Barbara's attempt at marriage was doomed from the start. Waylon was career-oriented; his mind only occasionally wandered to visions of hearth and home. He was still addicted to Lucky Moeller's formula of "exposure anywhere." The fact that the grind was inhuman crossed his mind, but Lucky knew best. (In a while the pain *should* cease. Lucky said so.) Waylon trusted the agent. Besides, the pills eased the pain.

Barbara didn't accept this analysis. In some respects she had a better feel for the situation. She knew that Waylon's business sense was that of "a five-year-old at a candy counter."[12] His gambling in the Las Vegas casinos and trust in others didn't seem right. However, Barbara's feelings were influenced by her possessiveness. In reality Waylon's mistress was his career, and not even the blonde beauty from Phoenix could compete with that.

After much pain, Barbara became a friend. For Waylon, the breakup took on monumental proportions. The separation was one more rejection. After several years, the one-night stands were becoming increasingly tedious. Motels were more like prisons than places to stay. The situation at Victor was worse.

ONLY DADDY THAT'LL WALK THE LINE

In two years, Waylon's relationship with Chet Atkins had soured; pills were the alleged issue. The producer had gone through two painful experiences with artists who had had severe amphetamine problems. The last thing he wanted was a repetition of the past. A person close to both men at the time explained: "Chet just went through hell with Don Gibson on pills, and he loved Don to death. Chet went through that for years. When he was at a motel, Gibson would call Chet, totally out of it.

Chet went through all of that ... then he ended up turning around and going through it all with Roger Miller. You even say the word 'pill' in front of Chet, and he just goes crazy. And then here comes Waylon ...." Waylon, in an interview with John Grissom, confirmed this view: "Chet Atkins thinks it's a sin to even look at one."[13]

Atkins sincerely cared about his wayward singer. As Harlan Howard indicates, however, Chet's concerns may have been greater than necessary: "Chet thought Waylon was high all the time. But actually that's not true. 'Cause Waylon might be straight for three months and then he would get stoned one day and go into Chet's office and Chet thinks that he is livin' like that ... that's where you get these false impressions. Chet hates pills, drugs of any kind, because Chet has always had himself under control. Some people aren't as strong as Chet. I don't blame him because when you love somebody—you hate to see their talent just being destroyed by anything."[14]

The "pill thing" was compounded by internal problems within RCA's Nashville office. Steve Sholes, the man who brought Chet to RCA, passed away in 1968. He was "Chet's daddy-type figure," according to Harlan Howard. More significantly, Sholes had served as buffer between Nashville and the hated New York office. Sholes had been able, in some cases, to calm the waters between the two camps. In his executive capacity, Sholes had allowed Atkins to have free rein in the studio and front office. But when Sholes died, the responsibility of dealing with New York fell to Atkins. As administrative burdens increased, Chet began to cut his production role. Artists suddenly found themselves in a Victor studio with a strange producer.

Bob Bare, then with the label, recalls: "I was caught up in this production maze. I knew what Chet's plans were and I knew he didn't have the time to spend all the time that it takes to find good songs and cut good material. One time I came in and Felton would record me and the next time Danny Davis, and Jack Clement would cut some stuff on me ... it was confusing me so bad I didn't know what to put out." If Chet produced, he appeared cold and distant. Don Bowman recalls, "He'd get in there with a soldering iron and a C.B. radio torn all to pieces. He's sitting there soldering wires while Waylon's recording."[15]

A majority of entertainers then with Victor have confirmed these accounts. In a letter, Chet Atkins noted that he and Waylon "would probably still be working together but for the fact I kind

Bob Bare (right) and author. Courtesy of John Rockwell, 1974.

of went out in another direction and quit producing so many records, mostly for health reasons."[16] In his autobiography, *Country Gentleman*, Chet hardly mentions this period in RCA's history.

Waylon clearly felt abandoned by his record company. Chet had turned Waylon over to a gaggle of producers, none of whom he felt had any notion of his musical direction. Worse, his recordings were packaged in bizarre ways. He had more two-sided hits than anyone in the industry. This cut down on his income drastically.

Country Music Round-Up asked Waylon in 1966, "What do you look forward to in your career?" His answer was, "Well, to have a Number One record and to be a regular member of the Grand Ole Opry."[17] Waylon would have to wait until 1974 to achieve his first goal, but appearing on the "Opry" was not far away. On January 27, 1967, Waylon got his wish. It was an honor to be booked on the show he had listened to in Littlefield. It's a long way from hearing a faint signal in Littlefield powered by a truck battery to appearing on the stage of the Ryman in the dazzle of the television lights. Once again, Waylon was in for some surprises. The "Opry" was not what he had bargained for. What he found was a live radio show cut up into half-hour segments hosted by well-known country performers. Artists were hustled on and off to do a couple songs and then brought back for another segment. There wasn't much to do except hang around backstage or go across the alley to Tootsie's beer parlor. Waylon earned less than a hundred dollars for his appearance. Most of Moeller's skull orchards paid more than that. Richie's drums were barred from the Ryman stage. Worse yet, some of the "Opry" people suggested Waylon wasn't country enough.

Naturally, Waylon was one of the first country artists to publicly criticize the "Opry." "Who wants to make National Life and Accident Insurance Company richer? If they'd give the money to charity, that would be something else. They're ashamed of country music anyway . . . in the old days it was the only exposure you could get. Now they don't even play country music on WSM except for three or four hours . . . WSM has nothin' to do with country music anymore. The biggest acts in country music didn't make it there."[18] On another occasion he said, "The Grand Ole Opry? I've played there as a special guest star, but I'm not a member or anything. I respect the Opry for the shrine that it is, but that's all that it is. Who needs it?"[19] Waylon's remarks to *Zoo*

World on the surface sound careless, but there is a rationale to his statement that is not merely the opinion of one man. Publicly but more often privately, many Music City artists support this feeling. Bill Ivey, the executive director of the Country Music Foundation, which operates the Hall of Fame, describes the "Opry" as "a historical repertory company, a living museum." Much of the blame for the show's becoming a "shrine" rather than remaining a vital part of contemporary country music lies with its association with the National Life and Accident Insurance Company.

In 1925 National Life and Accident purchased WSM ("We Shield Millions") as a "southern community product." The mammoth insurance company reluctantly entered the broadcasting field. Most of the National Life management opposed the acquisition. Edwin Craig insisted upon the move. Craig, the founder's son, got his station. As sociologist Richard Peterson of Vanderbilt suggests, WSM was to be a "mechanism of selling industrial insurance."[20] One of Craig's first moves was to hire George D. Hay away from the "National Barn Dance" on WLS in Chicago. Hay had been voted the top radio announcer the previous year. Hay introduced the WSM "Barn Dance" on November 18, 1925. He would later rename it "The Grand Ole Opry." Hay and Craig had common ideas about the purpose of the radio show. Hay, according to historian Bill Malone, saw the program as "preserving what was best, while utilizing the new technology."[21] The "Opry" was designed to return people to the "good ole country spirit." Because of this, the musicians and the songs had to be "down to earth." Hoedown bands were featured, as well as black-face "Here Come the Judge" comedians. Groups with the very country names of the Fruit Jar Drinkers, Gully Jumpers, and Possum Hunters appeared. Hay would tolerate any kind of string instrument but no horns or drums. As country music began to change, his policy would create problems. Craig supported the "Grand Ole Opry" concept because it was a cheap and flexible way of selling insurance. Agents approached country folks with the greeting, "I'm from *the* Grand Ole Opry Insurance Company." National Life even published a booklet, *Fiddles and Life Insurance*, containing pictures of "Opry" favorites; it was given to farmers who would enroll in various weekly plans under which they would pay five or ten-cent premiums for life insurance. The "Opry" was designed to keep National Life in the public eye.

National Life was primarily concerned with selling policies, not the music. The company turned down many opportunities to become involved in publishing, recording, or booking. "WSM actively resisted involvement in outside activities," observes Bill Ivey, but "they were image conscious and not comfortable with country music. Actually, the people who ran the company hated country music."[22] From a corporate viewpoint the "Opry" would best serve its purpose if it were "inoffensive and inexpensive." The philosophy was to maintain the company image and keep costs down. Richard Peterson said: "It was a tradeoff. We'll give you the Opry label, you give us a performance cheap."[23] It was because of this policy that the legendary Jimmie Rodgers, already an established artist, refused to appear on the show.

Over the years other performers did not have this choice. They would trade their talents for $30 to get the 50,000 clear-channel exposure. In the 1930s many established artists did not appear on the "Opry," preferring the more lucrative Sears-sponsored "National Barn Dance." In fact, some country music historians feel that WLS ("World's Largest Store") show, featuring Gene Autry and Red Foley, was better than the "Opry." However, the "Opry," with National Life's funds, outlived all of its competitors to become *the* country music showcase.

Tied to the philosophy of Hay and Craig, the "Opry" remained static while country music and the industry changed. "Opry hasn't kept pace with changes in life style and record industry," observed Ivey.[24] Bob Wills was badly treated at the Ryman because of his drums and the ever-present cigar. Cigars were taboo on the Ryman stage. Hank Williams's lifestyle, even at the peak of his career, caused his suspension. When Ernest Tubb shot up the WSM lobby one night, his "Opry" days were jeopardized. Chet Atkins was dropped because he did not make the "proper" number of appearances. In the 1950s, as Nashville turned to "country crooners" and toyed with rock-a-billy, the "Opry" continued to stress its "Air Castle of the South" image.

For many performers the "Opry" became merely a live radio show that did not pay much money. Worse yet, the National Life people seemed to have lost any sense of where country music was going. Many attributed the problems to the selection of Bud Wendell as manager of the "Opry." Wendell had been personnel manager at National Life; his appointment to the show was based on his "ability to handle people."

Waylon Jennings told one interviewer, "They don't pay well. If they want to give the money to charity, I'll play but when it makes WSM that much richer . . . they're many times millionaires, why give them the money."[25] One veteran performer added, "One night they had at least a $50,000 bill up there and it cost National Life about $1,800." Merle Haggard is adamant on the "Opry," calling it "that sacred cow devoted to filling the pockets of a bunch of anonymous bastards who don't know doodleshit about country music or what it means to those of us who love it."[26] Artists make much more for Saturday night bookings elsewhere, and many have refused to appear. In 1978 Tanya Tucker, then a teen star, said "I'd lose $40,000 doing that and it's not worth it. You might sell more records while you're at the Opry, but you don't make money selling records. You make your money when you make appearances."[27]

"Opry" rules regarding content also have turned performers away. Wesley Rose, one of the most powerful song publishers in Nashville, felt rock-a-billy and other less traditional artists could appear if they left their drum sets behind. A snare drum, frequently behind a curtain, is the only concession the "Opry" management would make.

Artists like Waylon Jennings who do not subscribe to the "ole-time" aspect of country and western music invariably have trouble with the management. "Yeah, I played on the Grand Ole Opry, and they've asked me to join it, but we could never get together. A full set of drums is almost unheard of and what have you . . . there's a lot of resistance. They didn't understand, like I've had them ask me, 'when you gonna cut a country record?' "[28] Despite the facts and the feelings of many other artists, Waylon's criticisms were badly received by many in Nashville, who saw his remarks as just another example of his "instability."

The grind of the Moeller tour was also affecting Waylon's writing. Doing an interview with discographer John Smith, he talked about his writer's block.

> You know what? I'll tell you this, for over a year, right at a year I think [1967–1968], I wrote one song or something by myself, because you know, people, artists, and I do, you know, I mean I try to be an artist in what I'm doing but people that are in this business, well some of them are superstitious. I'm not so superstitious or anything like that but I don't know really how to explain it. I actually thought I couldn't write with Bowman, see. And it's frustrating

because, you know, Bowman has had his own career to follow, I have mine and I work from 260 to 280 to 300 days a year sometimes, you know.[29]

Waylon later admitted that another reason for the writing block was the pills.[30] The "uppers" went hand-in-glove with the tours.

9

LOW-DOWN FREEDOM

Ten years after the Holly tragedy, on February 9, 1969, Waylon once again encountered death on the snow-covered plains of the Midwest.

The Cadillac and a 1969 blue Dodge truck camper sped northwest on Illinois I-150, heading toward Peoria. Bloomington was the next city on the ice-covered highway. Winter darkness had fallen early. The illuminated panel clock read 6:45 P.M. Richie was dozing in the front seat. Jimmy Gray was driving. Walter "Chuck"Allen Conway was asleep on a bunk bed over the cab of the camper. The half-ton truck sped on to the frozen Kickapoo Creek bridge. A tire hit a rut and started to slide—left—out of control. The camper section caught on the steel girders of the low bridge. The railing tore open the camper like an aluminum beer can. Chuck was struck in the head and he fell into the icy waters below. Richie and Stew "Allen" (Punsky) were shaken and hurt. Band members dove into the freezing creek water and pulled Conway out. Dragging him up on the road, they found his skull was crushed, face distorted. He was rushed to St. Joseph's hospital and pronounced dead two hours later, at 8:45 P.M. Jimmy was cited by a state trooper for "driving too fast for conditions."[1] Richie was treated and released. Stew remained in the hospital in fair condition. The rest of the group piled into the mud-covered Cadillac and arrived in Peoria in time for the show. "We went ahead and played that day," according to Richie, "Waylon, Jimmy

Waylon on tour, 1968–69. Courtesy of Virgie Rissenger.

and I. We used a couple of other guys and did two shows." They needed the money.

The next day, February 10, the remains of Walter Allen Conway were transferred to Phoenix. The diminished group headed south to play in the warmer climate of Oklahoma. A McLean County coroner's jury decided that death was caused because of bad road conditions, a verdict that contradicted trooper James Alexander's citation. A lawsuit would soon be filed against Waylon and Jimmy Gray, thus adding to the singer's amounting economic difficulties.[2]

On March 5, Waylon taped his first national talk show. It was an experience that soured him on the medium for years. He was scheduled to do the "Joey Bishop Show." On the ABC program were Buddy Hackett, character actor Victor Buono, singer Barbara McNair, comedian Andy Griffith, and Waylon. When he arrived at the studios, he was told where to stand and that one song would be enough. As it turned out, Waylon was let out of the tense "green room" during the last five minutes of the show, broadcast at 12:55 A.M. To this day he recalls that episode: "They snap you on and snap you off. 'Get the cowboy singer on and then get him off, before he opens his mouth and cusses in front of everybody.' . . . Joey Bishop and his big baloney about how he loved country music . . . I played his show and I tried to get him to take my part off 'cause I stood there singing madder than a son of a bitch." After the taping, Waylon approached the talk show host:

"Hey, you're playing a good game called 'fuck the cowboy singer.' "[3]

Bishop protested, but Waylon ignored him, saying: "If you're goin' to present country music, present it right. Don't come on like a big bullshitter. You don't like country music, don't try to put that on me . . . if you like country music you wouldn't have tried to record that album with that damned mandolin."

Waylon's short segment stayed in.

THE LOVE OF THE COMMON PEOPLE

"Chokin' Kind" on August 19, 1967, reached the Country Top Ten. It stayed on the charts for seventeen weeks. The B-side was "Love of the Common People." That song never went past Number 67 in the *Billboard* country and western sweepstakes and languished there for a mere five weeks. However, in the record industry, there are "regional breakouts." This was to be Waylon's biggest breakout.

Gallup, New Mexico, for most people, is a road stop on Route 66 dotted with tourist attractions featuring Native American goods, especially jewelry. For Native Americans, Gallup is the hub of numerous reservations. Reservation dwellers drift in and out of the city selling their handmade goods, drinking, or just hanging out. Father Dunstan Schmidlin is a Roman Catholic priest who has spent over half of his twenty-six years as an ordained priest working with Indians.[4] Father Dunstan started holding dances for the reservation kids in the basement of the Catholic Indian Center in Gallup, in the beginning using local rock bands. In time, Indians formed their own bands, and the priest booked them. He formed Cathedral Productions. On occasion, he would get a major group into the Cathedral High School gym. Mike McQuade, a local deejay, recalls, "We had people early, such as George Jones . . . but the Indian bands, the Wingate Valley Boys and the Fenders were his bread and butter."[5]

Father Dunstan brought in Fats Domino, the Coasters, and other name rock artists. He encountered difficulties, as many major acts didn't care to appear in the Gallup area. The priest grew discouraged. He planned to get out of the promotion business and stick to booking Indian acts. His assistant, Johnna Yursic, called Lucky Moeller and booked Waylon for several appearances in the Arizona and western New Mexico area.

Yursic, a soft-spoken 220-pounder, was one of Father Dunstan's "finds." As a teenager, Johnna was a hell-raiser. "There was nothing else to do," he recalls.[6] Cruisin' Main Street was his favorite pastime, as it had once been Waylon's. He ran liquor to the reservations selling eighty-cent bottles of wine for five dollars. He also worked in his father's restaurant for as many as eighteen hours per day. Father Dunstan got Johnna to help him with the Indian Center and put him into the booking end of the operation.

Johnna brought Waylon into Flagstaff. Following this concert, he was to play Gallup on March 22, 1969. In promoting the Gallup concert, Johnna approached Mike McQuade, a lifelong friend who was working for KGAK. Johnna wanted a big push on Waylon. McQuade dutifully found Jennings's current album, *Jewels,* and played several cuts from it on the hour. "Mental

Revenge," the Mel Tillis hit, was *the* song on the album. McQuade hated it. He rummaged around trying to find something of Waylon's besides "Sweet Mental Revenge" and found the B-side of "Chokin' Kind." The reaction to "Love of the Common People" was amazing. McQuade:

> After about a week, the phone starts crawling off the wall for Waylon's B-side. Like, Indian kids are paying ninety cents to call me from places two hundred miles away and request this song. What monster have I wrought? Then I sat down and really listened to the words. . . . "Living on dreams ain't easy . . ." etc., etc. Like hey man, I found the Navajo national anthem! I'm playing the thing three or four times a night until I'm positively tired of the song! One night, I played it six times in a row and said, "Here people, get it out of your system so I can play something else." No sooner have I played it for the sixth time in a row, when the phone rings and a voice says, "Will you play 'Love of the Common People,' again?" Talk about a study in futility![7]

On the day Waylon was scheduled to arrive, Johnna drove to Flagstaff in the afternoon. He met with Sonny Ray and Richie Albright. Waylon and the rest of the group were to come later. The promoters set up at the Armory, which housed 1,400 people. The time passed and at quarter of nine only Ray and the drummer were present. Johnna received an emergency call. Waylon had chartered a plane from Phoenix. Yursic drove to the airport, which was five miles from the Armory. When the two men met, communications immediately broke down.

"Where's Mr. Yursic?" asked Waylon.

"In Gallup, New Mexico," replied Johnna, who thought Waylon was asking about his father.

"The guy that's doin' the show."

"Well, that's me," said Johnna.

"Where is my limousine?"

Johnna was getting angry. "Boy have I got one," he thought. He had borrowed his father's Oldsmobile. It was washed and cleaned. "Well, I don't have a limousine."

Waylon repeated, "Where in the hell is my limo."

"I don't have a limousine, this is going to have to do."

Johnna's quick temper was getting hotter. He sped back to the Armory on Flagstaff's ice-covered roads, cussing under his breath.

"Don't talk like that around these ladies." Waylon had brought Jessi Colter and a friend along.

"Got a little hot with me," Johnna says, "I was already aggravated because he wanted his limousine. I thought, well that cocky son-of-a-bitch."

Waylon asked where the rest of the band was. "Two people: drummer and the bass player."

"What's the matter kid, are you worried? Afraid it's not gonna come off? I'll really give you something to worry about—my left wrist is broken."

Johnna glanced at the singer sitting in the front seat. His left arm was taped from the elbow down.

"Don't worry," Waylon said, "these people paid to see Waylon Jennings and they'll see him." The show was a success.

After the gig, Johnna and Waylon talked.[8] It turned out that the singer was not concerned about the Oldsmobile but, rather, his own Cadillac, which was being driven from Phoenix.

Several days later, Waylon arrived in Gallup to play at Father Dunstan's Cathedral gym. The auditorium was packed. "There were more Indians than at Custer's Last Stand," says Johnna.[9] Waylon was surprised by the crowd's reaction. After the first set, Waylon asked Father Dunstan, "I'm dying—they don't dig me. They won't clap or applaud or nothin'." The priest explained that that was a sign of respect. "They were deathly quiet," says Mike McQuade, "and just staring at the cowboy in awe. He did 'Love of the Common People' on every set and what little noise there was, ceased. It was so still you wouldn't believe it. That many people in one building—standing absolutely quiet with tears in their eyes. Those of us who put it together were standing there wondering what we had created. Well, after about the second set, Waylon has put it together and he is moved by what's happening. He is right in on the crowd's frequency. The static electricity in the place would light up the city of Gallup. You could feel it in your hair."

Waylon was firmly established with the Indian community. McQuade: "So we immediately booked Waylon back as soon as possible. He comes in and plays another one nighter and the place is jammed and history repeats itself. Pretty soon, all the civic centers on the Navajo reservation are screaming for Waylon. He's playing three dates on each trip in places booking agents in Nashville couldn't spell or find on a road map. The reaction is just the same everywhere he goes on the reservation. The Indians took Waylon to heart—he was the new folk hero."[10]

In time, RCA would use his popularity with Native Americans

to sell records. Chet Flippo's award-winning liner notes to *Lonesome On'ry and Mean* chronicled the relationship.

Returning to Nashville, Waylon began work on a record that would earn him a much-coveted Grammy. "MacArthur Park" was a hit single for British actor Richard Harris. The song was written by Jimmy Webb, a very hot writer at the time, having provided Glen Campbell with a series of hits. For the Kimberlys', a Las Vegas lounge act, album Waylon decided to cover the song. "It was an album cut," he recalls, "and they thought I was crazy when I first told them I wanted to do it. Then when I cut it, everybody wanted to put it out as a single, and I wasn't into putting it out as a single because it had already been a big hit by Richard Harris. His record is a classic of all time. I think that's one of the greatest records ever cut 'cause he can't sing, but he can read. . . ."[11] Despite Waylon's reservations, RCA released the tune as a single in late July. A month later, *Country Folk* was issued. The album was essentially a showcase of the Las Vegas quartet and not Jennings, although "MacArthur Park" was the strongest cut on the LP. Waylon did perform a few of the songs produced by Danny Davis, but the material sounded more like the folk-oriented Seekers than anything appropriate to Waylon featured with a number of pop/folk covers. Along with the Jimmy Webb tune were compositions by Joe South, Donovan, the Seekers, First Edition member Mike Settle, and Jackie De-Shannon. The song bag was more Vegas night spot than country and western. Waylon disputes the pop label that was applied to the album, especially in regard to "MacArthur Park." "There ain't nothing more country than a yellow cotton dress or old men in the park playin' dominoes or checkers." The reason for the *Country Folk* title is difficult to ascertain. Co-producer Chet Atkins strongly insisted, "I'd rather see Waylon be a great country artist and let him 'spillover' into the pop market."[12] By 1969 standards, *Country Folk* was fundamentally middle of the road. The Kimberlys were about as country as Peter, Paul, and Mary, or Dean Martin. Recalling the song, Waylon told *Country Side*, "We got a Grammy for the song but, like I say, neither field accepted it. No field really accepted it as one of their songs."

The premise to the album, "A Famous Star Performing with Stars of the Future," was curious. The Kimberlys, despite their work with Johnny Horton, were virtually unknown outside of Nevada lounge circuits. The suggestion that they would rise to stardom on Waylon's shoulders was somewhat unrealistic. A country artist propelling a pop act—at the time, not even Bob Dylan could revive John R. Cash's flagging career.

Another reason given for the album is provided by some of Waylon's confidants in Phoenix. Some claim Waylon and Verna Gay were briefly romantically linked, until she made demands of the singer. Chronologically, this interpretation is questionable, but it is a popular one. "MacArthur Park" reached Number 93 on the *Billboard* "Hot 100 Charts" and was Number 23 on the country and western listing. The record was not a smash. *Country Folk* did not sell well either.

Moeller scheduled a busy June for Waylon and his band. They would open in Columbus, Ohio, and then zip up I-75 for a six-day tour in Toronto's Horseshoe Lounge, then play a Sunday date in Barrie, Ontario, returning to the States on Monday, June 9. That was the schedule, at least on paper. The road-worn Cadillac followed by the Dodge truck camper, with a new shell, crossed into Canada from Detroit. Driving through Windsor, the performers headed north toward Toronto. Unlike several years earlier, the work permits were ready, and there was no need for a layover in the Motor City. On Monday they arrived at Jack Steppe's Horseshoe Lounge. The first nights were uneventful. On Thursday, a fight broke out. "I walked in with long hair," says Richie, "and this dude took a poke at me." The discussion continued in the alley. Richie swung at his tormenter. During the fight, a Waylor hit a Canadian policeman who had just arrived at the scene. Albright found himself in the Toronto jail along with Curtis Buck and Sonny Ray.[13]

Richie experienced considerable difficulty because of his Beatle hairstyle. "In the South, the people made some nasty comments. Like, 'Baby, do you want to dance?'" Country music fan magazines ran pictures of Waylon about to cut Richie's hair. Waylon would kid about his "hippie" drummer. Waylon did respond to critics: "Hair and appearance never put a sound on a record . . . how they wear their hair is their own business . . . besides we've never said anything to anyone else about how they look."[14] What the Waylors did not know was that many Canadians were quite concerned about the hippie menace on their southern border. Signs dotted Canadian highways reading "Keep Canada Clean! Get a Haircut." Many of Jack Steppe's customers took "Okie From Muskogee" quite seriously. The result was that the Waylors were locked up for a fight they didn't even start.

In light of these events, the Waylors were delighted to leave

Canada. Numerous epithets, especially about the Queen, were heard as their two-vehicle convoy headed south to Nashville to overdub "It's All Over Now." The Cadillac approached the United States border. Bass guitarist Sunny Ray was driving. He had a choice of two routes. One would have taken him directly into Buffalo. Sunny spotted a sign reading "New York" and found himself on the Rainbow Bridge coming to a brightly lit border station. Approaching the gate, Richie cussed and said, "Oh no!" The Dodge pickup followed the limo into the inspection station. The border patrol was suspicious. "Freaks in a big long limo," they thought. The patrolman requested driver's licenses. They looked in the Cadillac and found nothing. Inspecting the camper shell, they discovered Jimmy Gray's bag of marijuana. Gray and Albright were arrested for illegal possession. In a matter of several days Richie was behind bars twice. Judge Nunzio Rizzo set the bail at $500 cash. He would accept a bond of $1,000 if the cash were not immediately available. The two Waylors were to be arraigned on July 11.[14]

It took Waylon nearly a day to locate an attorney, Benjamin Gold, and to spring Gray and Albright out of the Niagara Falls slammer. Waylon was angry. He had warned members of the band about carrying pot, especially across the border. He cautioned that the next one who was caught smoking or carrying it on them was going to get fired. Waylon, according to Billy Ray Reynolds, "is real paranoid about crossing that border."[15]

After their release, Jimmy Gray either resigned or was fired. One account has Jimmy telling the furious singer, "I'll tell you—I can't lie. I'll give you my resignation now." Waylon in a *Music City News* interview claimed he fired Gray. Whichever story is correct, Jimmy Gray was no longer a Waylor. Albright, because of his long-time friendship, remained.[16]

The incident was picked up by the wire services and teletyped nationally. The lead read, "Musicians Face Trial For Pot." Rock fans, accustomed to such happenings in the lives of their musical favorites, would think little of such an incident, but country music fans remembered the Haggard line, "We don't smoke marijuana in Muskogee." *Music City News* stated: "Despite the modernizing changes in country music, the country singer's image remains largely one of hard drinking (in a great many cases), high living, and fast spending. The country music fan usually looks on this with tolerance and even a certain amount of intrigue. There is nothing that would turn him away, however, nothing he would draw the line at faster than a country singer's using marijuana."[17] In *the* country and western magazine, Waylon apologized but added, "If we make any mistakes, we'll pay for them *ourselves*." The defendants were fined and charges dropped.

During all this turmoil, Waylon learned that Jim Musil, Jr., had offered the masters from *Waylon Jennings at JD's* to Decca Records. He contacted Floyd Ramsey and protested. Ramsey explained his hands were tied as there was no contract and the senior Musil had paid for the sessions. "He paid for it. I got to give it, the masters, to him."[18] Waylon was furious. He felt "ripped off." Worse yet, Decca was to use ten cuts from the promotional album on their budget label Vocalion. A $1.99 record would now be competing with his RCA material, an album from which he would receive no royalties. In July, Vocalion released the LP.

Artists on their way up the ladder frequently make tremendous mistakes in judgment, selling songs for nearly nothing. Willie Nelson's "Family Bible" was given away for a mere $50. Waylon sold "Big Time Ladies Man" for half that amount. In Waylon's case, the song didn't become a gospel classic. Recordings for small labels such as BAT follow the same pattern. These recordings are inexpensive to make. The investor, not the performer, usually owns the copyright and the master tape. Should the artist become a star, the masters can be sold to the highest bidder. The performer usually gets nothing from his older recordings. Cut-outs pose a similar problem, as they compete with the performer's current and usually more expensive product.

RCA was butchering the "Delia" promotion. Victor refused to promote "Delia" outside of the traditional country market. Tommy Jennings ordered a large quantity of the single and personally sent it to major pop stations. CKLW in Detroit gave it heavy airplay over its 50,000-watt transmitter. Stations in Chicago and New York were showing interest, although some objected to the lyrics. Victor refused to jump on the bandwagon and a potential pop hit was lost.

Six months after the Vocalion release, right after Waylon's Grammy award for "MacArthur Park," A & M combined all of the Jennings songs in their vaults into an album. Waylon, in this case, was protected by his old contract. He consented to pose for the cover photos. Waylon owed Jerry Moss for letting him out of his contract.

On the basis of "MacArthur Park's" critical success, some media people were starting to compare Waylon to John R., Buck Owens and Glen Campbell as a potential television host. As one fan magazine puzzled, "Did he have that special who-knows-what that turns audiences on? Could he hold pop as well as country viewers for (say) an hour? Could he handle guest stars? Could he . . .?"[19]

The writer went on to cite "The Love of the Common People," the Metro Media production, as proof that Waylon was destined for video stardom. The program was taped in July and broadcast in October. This was Waylon's fourth national television show. In May he had taped a "Hee Haw" segment and an appearance on the "Glen Campbell Show"; prior to those shows he had appeared on "Anatomy of Pop" and the "Bishop Show." In Los Angeles, "Common People" was aired during prime time on October 5 and three weeks later it was repeated.

The title of the show was taken from Waylon's B-side of several years back. The format was described as "country-music with the exciting 'now' sound." Waylon would not have to talk much, as Joe Nixon introduced most of the songs off camera. Guest performers were the Kimberlys, Lorrie and Larry Collins, and Charlie Pride. Perhaps coincidently, Lorrie Collins was married to producer Stew Carnall.

The top of the show featured the title song. It then segued into Waylon doing "Only Daddy" and "Sand and Shovels." The Collins Kids, as they were once billed, and the Kimberlys followed with pop-oriented ballads. Charlie Pride did "Louisiana Man." Several more songs were performed. Midway through the hour-long show, Waylon was joined by the Kimberlys on "MacArthur Park." A tribute to Roger Miller was next. The remainder of the telecast was trendy, closing with the Beatles' "Hey Jude." Waylon sang "Silver Ribbons" from *Nashville Rebel* and "Just to Satisfy You."

The trade reviews were fairly positive. *Variety* described it as "fresh and appealing." The *Hollywood Reporter* praised the program. The paper contrasted Waylon to John R.: "Jennings doesn't have the visual excitement which Cash possesses and does his tunes in a straight forward manner which makes for easy listening and ability to concentrate on the story line . . . but a more visual approach is needed for extended television viewing."[20] Despite such lukewarm comments, the show was well received.

I'M NOT LISA: JESSI COLTER

Mirriam Johnson was the sixth of seven children. Her father, Clyde Johnson, was a mining engineer who dabbled with cars in his free time—when he was not working in the mines of Mesa. Mrs. Johnson worked in the cosmetics business and ran a hotel until the age of twenty-seven, when she was "born again" and became Sister Helen, an ordained Pentecostal minister.

It was in Sister Helen's church that Mirriam received her musical training. "I actually became the church pianist at the age of 11," she told one interviewer. "From that time on, I would travel to various churches for revivals my mother held. And, later on Mother got her own tent and would hold revivals."[21] Jessi also played the accordian at revivals. The Johnson family encountered problems in Mesa because of their religious convictions. The predominantly Morman community did not approve of those who "spoke in tongues." Consequently, Mirriam spent most of her time in her mother's church and was "pretty much a loner." The piano became her constant companion.

At the age of fifteen she entered various talent shows and sang for high school assemblies. She finally auditioned for a children's talent contest on Phoenix television and was accepted. For Lou King and the Rangers she sang "St. Louis Blues" and lost. King liked Mirriam's material but not her band. She occasionally performed with a western band, but there was a problem. The group played in Phoenix bars, better termed as "joints." Sister Helen would never approve of such an environment. Mirriam had to sneak out at night to make the gigs.

Mirriam's big break came at the age of sixteen when her older sister Sharon, now married to Jack Clement, told her of an audition for a rock band led by guitarist Duane Eddy. Unfortunately, the tryout was being held in a bar. Mirriam crept off again.

Duane Eddy was a Phoenix legend. He started picking guitar at the age of five. In ten years he was playing most of the dances and joints in the Phoenix area. In 1957 a local disc jockey and producer, Lee Hazlewood, took an interest. Lee wanted to cut some instrumentals and felt Duane would be a natural. A year later Duane formed a group called the Rebels. They cut a demo, "Movin' and Groovin'," which was sent to Harry Finfer of Jamie Records. They got a record contract. "They put out 'Movin',"" recalls Eddy, "and it did fairly well . . . went halfway up the charts. Enough to encourage us to do another one. So we did 'Rebel

Rouser,' which was the first big million seller." "Rebel Rouser" established Duane as a pop star. He appeared on *American Bandstand* and once hosted the afternoon show when Dick Clark was away. "Ramrod" was another success for the guitarist. On the basis of these hits, Duane decided to put together a tour band with a female vocalist.

Mirriam went to the audition. "She sang so great, she knocked me out," said Duane.[22] Eddy decided to produce her as a recording artist. The first two songs, "Young and Innocent" and Gene Austin's "Lonesome Road," were lost in the maze of popular records released at the time. So they tried a Kitty Wells hit, "Making Believe." The song was Number One in Cincinnati but did little outside of the Ohio River city. Following the Eddy tour, Mirriam Johnson became Mrs. Eddy, a Los Angeles housewife. Duane and Mirriam had a daughter, Jennifer.

Mirriam frequently traveled with Duane, but not as an artist. During these tours she met Harlan Howard in Nashville and Waylon Jennings in Phoenix. Mirriam's first professional encounter with Waylon took place at a recording session. Duane was trying to pitch several songs to Waylon, and Mirriam came along. At the session she sang a duet with Waylon—standing on a box in order to reach the microphone. The song was her composition of "Living Proof."

After that session, both went their separate ways. Mirriam returned to the role of Mrs. Duane Eddy, but she did start thinking increasingly of a career in the music industry. She resumed writing songs. It was "an expression of frustration or unhappiness or whatever."[23] Duane encouraged her. He sent some of her songs to Chet Atkins. He liked them and took four of the tunes for RCA performers. Don Gibson recorded several. Dottie West enjoyed a hit with "No Sign of Living." Duane wanted her to record. Mirriam resisted country music; instead, she wanted to do pop material. This presented a dilemma. Chet Atkins considered her a country artist. Since RCA and Mirriam could not agree on direction, the company passed her on. Duane approached Jimmy Bowen, an ex-rock-a-billy Norman Petty recorded turned Los Angeles producer. Bowen at the time was doing some of Dean Martin's "country" music. Bowen listened and turned Mirriam down because "she sounded *too* country."

Over the years Duane's career had waned. He tried the movies. In one film, *A Thunder of Drums*, he died in Richard Boone's arms. His film career never got past that scene. In Los

Angeles he worked as a session man and did some producing. The Eddys began to drift apart. Duane recalls: "It was just that we had different interests—some of the same interests. But it was just one of those things. We became good friends and we decided that good friends don't get it as far as being married."[24] After seven years of marriage, Mirriam left for Phoenix with Jennifer.

In 1968 Waylon returned to J.D.'s for the Christmas holidays. He was exhausted and depressed. He told friends, "By God, I'm gonna change record companies." His two-sided hits were a major source of concern. He thought "Chokin' Kind" and "Love of the Common People" should have been released separately.

Waylon was equally upset about his breakup with Barbara. "That woman darn near ruined me," he said.[25] He was fatigued and pale. His weight was down to 138 pounds on his six-foot, one-inch frame. His voice was rough. "He looked hurt and tired," said his former mother-in-law. The year 1968 had not been a good one: Barbara had left; W.A. had died from a sudden heart attack, and, to compound matters, Jimmy Gray's brother Paul, the bass player, had been killed in Atlanta.

The week of Martin Luther King's assassination Waylon had been playing a club in Georgia's capital. After the show the Waylors were invited to a birthday party. Richie decided against going, but the rest of the band attended. After a while things started to become rowdy. Birthday cake was thrown around the room, one guest starting squirting champagne, and other guests were throwing a knife around, nearly hitting several bystanders. Things were getting out of hand, so the Waylors started to leave. A disturbance developed in the hallway and several shots rang out. Paul Nelson Gray dropped to the floor with two bullet wounds. He was pronounced dead at Grady Hospital.[26]

John Charles Anderson was charged with the killing. One Waylor commented, "This guy whips out a gun and started firing and why he fired at Paul—I don't know. I really don't know."[27] Waylon had to find another musician. He chose Chuck Allen Conway, a Phoenix resident. His tenure with the group proved to be a short one; less than a year later, he would die in the camper accident on the icy bridge.

The day after Christmas, rookie patrolman Duane Coker and his partner V.E. Jones answered a call at J.D.'s. J.D. Musil had summoned the police after a frenzied Leo Rohr came into the club during closing time and forced members of the Waylors to lie on the floor. He ranted and raved about killing Waylon

Jennings. The police car frightened the would-be assassin, and he fled. The officers cornered him in the back of the club. Rohr opened fire; the policemen returned his shots. As Rohr attempted to escape over a chain-link fence, Jones hit the man in the back with a round. "That was a helluva an experience," commented a Waylor.[28]

During this hectic week, Waylon saw Mirriam Eddy, soon to be called Jessi Colter, a name taken from her great-great-great uncle, who had reportedly been a member of the infamous Jesse James gang. In light of her religious upbringing, Jessi was leery of the singer and his penchant for "roarin'." In fact, she was "scared to death."

"Waylon had a reputation for being a wild outlaw, so when he first asked me out, I wouldn't go anywhere with him. He kept after me and one night he said, 'Would it make any difference if I told you I studied for the ministry once?' It was just so funny that I went with him." The doubts still lingered. "I felt like I was taking a chance seeing him . . . but I would."[29]

During the relationship, Jessi signed with RCA. Chet Atkins described her as "a hell of an artist . . . great singer . . . fine pianist . . . damn fine writer." In mid-1969, Jessi started work on *A Country Star Is Born.* Chet produced some of the album with help from Danny Davis and Waylon Jennings. Waylon sang harmony on several album cuts: "I Ain't the One" and "Why You Been Gone So Long." *Rolling Stone* writer John Grissom, who attended some of the Colter sessions, characterized the album: "It may turn out to be urban blues rather than country funk."[30] The latter was perhaps the best description. After an eleven-month courtship, Mirriam Johnson Eddy became Mrs. Waylon Jennings. They were married October 26, 1969, in her mother's church.

After a brief honeymoon, Waylon went to Nashville to record and then on to Georgia for some concert appearances. Just as things looked brighter, Waylon was charged as a co-defendant in a $2.75 million lawsuit filed in the Phoenix federal court. Jimmy Gray was the other defendant.[31] They were charged with the "wrongful death" of Walter "Chuck" A. Conway, Jr., and also the injuries to Stewart A. Punsky (also known as Stew Allen). Gray was accused of causing the death of Chuck Allen Conway. Waylon was cited as the employer of Gray and owner of the vehicle. The suit sought $2.5 million for Conway's widow, Laura, and her six children. Punsky asked for $75,000 in damages for his injuries and $4,000 in lost wages. The case was assigned to

JESSI COLTER

Mirriam Johnson A/K/A Jessi Colter, 1976. Courtesy of Capitol Records.

United States District Judge Carl A. Meucke. In 1969 it appeared that Waylon was spending as much time in courtrooms as in recording studios.

SINGER OF SAD SONGS

Several days after receiving his $2.75 million summons, Waylon traveled to Los Angeles to record. This action would serve only to compound his troubles with the Nashville folks. Lee Hazlewood would produce. Lee was responsible for Nancy Sinatra's "These Boots Are Made for Walkin," a song he had offered Waylon. In addition, he had produced Gram Parson's first album, *Safe at Home,* for his LHI label. Hazelwood had a reputation of being Attila the Hun in a studio. One of his artists said, "He's a son-of-a-bitch. He picks on musicians and yells at everybody." Waylon recorded most of the *Singer of Sad Songs* album at the RCA studios on Sunset Boulevard. Most of the session people were Los Angeles regulars, including Randy Meisner, soon to be a member of the Eagles. Former Cricket Sunny Curtis worked three of the sessions. Waylon wasn't happy with either Hazlewood or his own performances. "We rushed it too much. We worked eighteen hours one session without stopping because we were behind."[32] Waylon also had a bad case of laryngitis.

On *Singer of Sad Songs,* Waylon included the Rolling Stones hit "Honky Tonk Woman," the first contemporary rock song he had recorded since Chuck Berry's "Brown Eyed Handsome Man." He claimed, however, that the lyrics were country, at least "most of 'em." *Singer of Sad Songs* does not appear to have been an attempt to cross over into the pop field. It was probably more of a reaction to the internal politics of RCA's Nashville operation. Waylon and several other performers like Bobby Bare and Willie Nelson were complaining about the army of different producers they had to cope with. Bare grumbled about the "maze." Waylon's open break with Chet and the system was still several years away. The Los Angeles sessions were just another symptom of Waylon's growing discontent with Music City and the way his career was going. On *Singer of Sad Songs* he still did not get the sound he wanted.

Singer of Sad Songs was well received. It did garner some press coverage, but most of it was confined to the usual avenues of

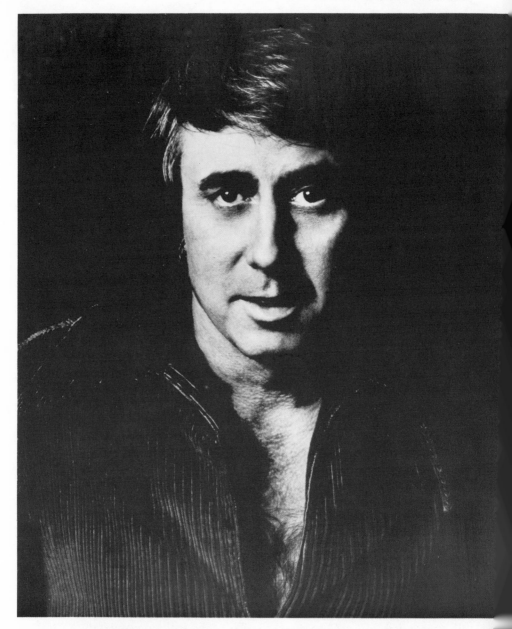

LEE HAZLEWOOD

W.J.'s Phoenix associate and producer.

Courtesy of RCA, 1972.

exposure. *Music City News* gave it one if its standard praise-filled reviews. One writer did have some reservations about the album. He didn't like country artists doing Rolling Stones songs. He wrote: "Jennings' attempt at doing the Rolling Stones' 'Honky Tonk Woman' doesn't quite make it, though. Many rockers can be done in country style successfully, but 'Honky Tonk Woman' isn't one of them." He didn't like some of the production, either. "An otherwise successful version of 'Rock Salt and Nails' is ruined by an obtrusive snore during one of the verses. The snore, apparently, was an attempt by Jennings or one of his producers to be cute. It isn't."[33]

In the music business "recognition" is the name of the game. Any artist can have talent, but recognition of that quality is essential if success is to be achieved. Recognition is bestowed in strange and frequently in unanticipated ways. So it was with Waylon Jennings.

On March 11, 1970, the National Academy of the Recording Arts and Sciences bestowed its Grammy awards in Los Angeles. Surprisingly, "MacArthur Park" was cited as the "Best Country Performance by Duo or Group." Songs that ranked as low as this one had—93rd in *Billboard*—rarely win anything. Afterward, Waylon said it was "particularly pleasing since my [sic] drummer once told me I couldn't go pop if they put a firecracker in my mouth."[34]

The 1970 Grammy awards were curious. This was the year of the "Midnight Cowboy." Joe South's "Games People Play" was voted the song of the year. John Cash received a Grammy for the liner notes to Dylan's *Nashville Skyline*. Waylon Jennings became the first country music artist in history to win a Grammy for what was essentially a middle-of-the-road ballad.

While touring in Texas, Waylon picked up a steel guitar player, Ralph Mooney. "Moon" was an unlikely Waylor. His curly hair is cut short. On stage he wears loafers, slacks, and short-sleeved Hawaiian or polo shirts. He's considerably older than the other band members. Waylon introduces him as "greatest steel player in the world." "Basically, I'm not crazy about steel guitar music. I'm crazy about Ralph Mooney's music though. He's been one of my heroes for years."[35] Moon's credentials were impressive. He had worked with Buck Owens and Merle Haggard, and he had recorded "Big, Big Love" with Wynn Stewart. He had written "Crazy Arms," a country classic, when "Miss Moon" briefly left him. He had cut an instrumental album with super session man

James Burton for Capitol. But in 1970 Moon was in a bind. Wynn Stewart, whose career was on the wane, had not paid him for two months. He was home in the Kennedale-Mansfield area, outside of Fort Worth, weighing his prospects.

Waylon and Moon had met at the Golden Nuggett several years earlier. "So I went down to Waylon's motel and talked to him," says Moon. "He didn't say a thing about a job, but he went on to a date in Austin and then called me from there and offered me a job." "Heck, yeah," he replied. Ralph invited Waylon to return to Fort Worth to rehearse. Waylon accepted. Waylon later told Bo Powel, "I didn't have nerve enough to ask him and he didn't say anything and it took us about three or four hours before we finally got together and me asking him. . . ."[36] Moon has been with the Waylors since November of 1970. Only Richie Albright had been with the group longer.

Waylon's recognition in the rock music world occurred on a fifteen-acre farm in Oregon owned by a long-haired academic dropout named J.R. Young. Young, a rock critic for the *Rolling Stone,* had a master of fine arts degree and two years of university teaching under his belt. The halls of ivy turned him off, so he and his wife moved to a farm in the Northwest. His critical career consisted mainly of idealizing the likes of Alvin Lee and the Grateful Dead. As with all contributors to the *Stone,* J.R. began to receive boxes of free records in the mail from record companies anxious to get exposure in America's most important music paper. Piles of albums began to grow in the farmhouse living room. When you're an established critic, record companies would send just about anything, even if you didn't want it. "Country music was something we never listened to," explains Young, "but it came in every month from RCA."

One crisp fall evening Young put an RCA offering on the turntable and went off to the dining room. Sitting at the table with a friend, J.R. was captivated by a strange new sound filtering into the room. "Wait a minute," he said, "let's go in and listen to this!" The two men rose and entered the living room and stood glued to the speakers. "It was one of those strange moments in your life where you realize there has been something going on that you are totally unaware of but as soon as you hear it, you know all about it." They replayed cuts from *Singer of Sad Songs* for the rest of the evening.

The next day, J.R. phoned Grelun Landon, West Coast publicity director for RCA. Landon is the most respected publicist in the music business. He's honest and, more important, he does not jive or hype writers.

"Grelun! Who is Waylon Jennings?"

Landon, who had written two books on country music, laughed "Well, he's a country singer."

"Why don't you send me every album he has ever made?"

In a week and a half, a special order of fifteen albums arrived at the Oregon farmhouse. For two months J.R. listened to the albums but always returned to the more rock-oriented material. When *Cedartown Georgia* was released, he was "somewhat disappointed." "It was very much pop country rather than rock."

Rolling Stone ran a page-long piece entitled "The Monster Voice of Waylon Jennings." The article began:

> Word is that if Waylon Jennings isn't already a country superstar, he soon will be. And once that occurs, he'll even move beyond the country tag. He'll be a super stylist. So, again, if your ears are tired, depressed, and generally down, let this dude get inside your mind and re-align your senses. Listen to what a song can really be. You'll get more than you ever bargained for, and you too, will wonder where in the hell you've been since '66, because Waylon's been over in the Country & Western rack all along.[37]

Waylon Jennings had made the *Rolling Stone*. Not the cover, but at that time few if any non-rock artists received space in the rock-oriented pages of the magazine. The article did not turn rock fans away from the ever-increasing number of English glitter bands or the likes of James Taylor, but country-rock fans became curious. More important, other rock music publications began to send writers out to cover the doings of the "singer of sad songs." Within weeks of the Young article, reviews of *Cedartown* began to appear. *Door* published a two-page interview conducted by Jay Elher.[38] Although not a household name in the counter-culture, Jennings was beginning to penetrate the lucrative rock market.

It is doubtful that Waylon was aware of the significance of the *Rolling Stone* article. Young was finally introduced to the singer by Grelun Landon. "This is J.R. Young who wrote the original review in *Rolling Stone*." Politely, Jennings shook the writer's hand and said, "Oh yeah, that was good. I appreciate that very much." As Young recalls, "Very simple—that was it."[39]

Waylon had a loyal supporter in the person of *Los Angeles Times* music critic and columnist Robert Hilburn. Hilburn's reviews and articles matched in importance those in the trades. His

Honky Tonk Heroes, 1973. Courtesy of RCA.

opinions appeared every other day in the self-proclaimed capital of the record industry. Bob stumbled on Waylon during the Hank Williams, Jr., concert in Long Beach—"Iowa By the Sea." "It was about 1966, I think," he says. "in fact I interrupted an interview with Hank to hear him do 'Norwegian Wood.' "[40] Hilburn has generally been very supportive of country-sounding music. He was an early advocate of the Byrds and later Gram Parsons and the Flying Burrito Brothers. In January 1969 Hilburn reviewed a three-act concert at the Shrine Auditorium. Buck Owens was the headliner, preceded by Charlie Pride and Waylon Jennings. Part of the review stated: "Jennings is one of the most exciting and distinctive new country talents in years. On stage he has a certain Johnny Cash starkness and electricity about him. But he wasn't wholly successful with the audience. Despite large talent, he seemed distant at times. He doesn't seem to project well enough."[41]

"Waylon's problem is attitude. He's inconsistent," Hilburn remarks. Despite his reservations, the *Times* writer continued to plug Waylon. December 1, 1970, he announced, "Waylon Jennings Will Open Stand." After labeling the singer as "One Of The Best," "Charismatic," and citing the Grammy Award, Hilburn cautioned: "He has proven to be a terribly inconsistent performer. He gave such an indifferent concert at the Shrine Auditorium one night that the audience response wouldn't even register on the applause meter. Yet, he came back a few months later to the Palamino Club in North Hollywood and gave one of the best performances I've seen."[42] Waylon was not unaffected by Hilburn's reviews. He told an interviewer, "I've worked on that because of those articles . . . sometimes my mind is somewhere else. I'm tired of those songs that I've sung for five years. I can't stand 'Green River.' I hate that song with a passion."[43]

The Hilburn columns and the *Rolling Stone* review did not go unnoticed by RCA executives in Los Angeles. Recognition in California did not have much validity in Nashville. After all, Los Angeles was the home of freaked-out cosmic cowboys. Even Buck Owens and Merle Haggard were viewed with some scorn because of their Bakersfield operations. But Buck and Merle had demonstrated that urban dwellers can be motivated to buy country records.

Cashbox, a trade magazine, listed "The Taker" as the Number One country song in its October 17, 1974, edition. This was Waylon's first top-ranked song. Certainly *Cashbox* was not as prestigious as *Billboard*, "the Bible of the industry," but the ranking was a satisfying achievement.

Despite his recognition in the rock press, Waylon was growing more and more disillusioned with Nashville and his career. "I had gotten to the point where I thought, what's the use," he told Bob Hilburn. "I felt I was on a merry-go-round, and I wanted off. I thought about going back to disc jockeying or maybe learning to play guitar better so I could do some session work."

Richie Albright, who had returned to the Waylors on April 11, 1972, encouraged Waylon to continue. "Let's give it one more run," the drummer urged. "Richie told me he'd come back with me and if it didn't work this time, we'd both go back to Phoenix or somewhere and get a sit-down job and take it easy."[44]

"He was going through the motions," recalls Richie, "he wasn't that happy about cutting records and things like that. He just wasn't into it. We got to talking a lot when I came back and talked some things out, you know."[45]

10

WAYMORE'S BLUES

In the opening months of 1972 Waylon was growing weary. The Crab Orchards were taking their toll. The Black Maria was becoming increasingly unreliable. "It seemed it broke down every fifty miles," recalled Harley, the driver. Promoters frequently were asked for front money to pay for gas and repairs. To complicate matters further, Waylon contacted infectious hepatitis in Gallup. He was again playing for Father Dunstan. During his three-day stay, Waylon reportedly drank some of the reservation water and was leveled by the liver disease. Doctors forbade drugs—even beer. He returned to convalesce in a Nashville hospital.

Waylon's illness of hepatitis was compounded by drug abuse. One person involved in the reservation concerts said, "All the rest of us were drinking the water too. Half the damn town was drinking it and nobody got sick." Maureen Orth in *Newsweek* wrote, "Finally, two years ago, Jennings wound up in the hospital—his pill habit was killing him."[1] Sammi Smith, who had previously toured with Waylon, took the band and the black bus to fulfill the missed concert dates.[2]

During the long dull hours in a hospital room, Waylon thought about his state of affairs. "When he got sick and everything," recalls Johnna Yursic, "he had time to really look at the RCA situation and Chet Atkins."[3] His reaction was, "Now wait a minute . . . ." Lying in a hospital bed, Waylon realized that after

"Pre-outlaw period." Courtesy of RCA, 1972.

seven years on the road, eleven charted country albums, and good audience response, he was $250,000 in the hole.[4] Something had to be done.

The "something" was to shake up a number of people. Waylon hired a personal manager, Neil. C. Reshen, who sarcastically described himself as *the* ideal country fan—"A New York Jew with a black wife." Reshen was a prototypical New York music manager in the Albert Grossman tradition who got into the music business after he failed his bar examination. He had worked for Famous Artists and CBS and then expanded into management and the auditing of entertainment companies. If a company short-changed an artist, Reshen's firm, Media Consulting, could be hired to do an audit. Neil purchased a wooded Connecticut home designed by Frank Lloyd Wright with the proceeds from one such financial check. "The house bought by 'What Now My Love.'" His roster of artists at times included some of *the* "oddball acts" in the music industry—Miles Davis, Captain Beefheart, and Frank Zappa.

Neil had originally attempted to sign Waylon in the 1960s after *Nashville Rebel*. Waylon was dedicated to Lucky Moeller. "I don't need a manager," he told Reshen, "*and* I really don't think I need a New York Jewish manager."[5] In 1972 Waylon did not feel quite the same way. He was desperate. "Everybody had a piece of him eighteen different ways," Neil told Terry Guerin, "There were states [Arizona] he could not go into—alimony suits by three ex-wives saw to that. He owed one agent [Lucky Moeller] $50,000. He owed another $45,000 to RCA—the label he'd been enriching for seven years. He was playing 300 dates a year, $1,000 a gig and coming off the road further in debt."[6] George Lappe, manager of Goose Creek Symphony, told Neil about Waylon's troubles. Lappe was a friend of Waylor drummer Richie Albright. Neil flew to Nashville for a two-day stay. He still wanted to sign Waylon. Albright told Waylon, "there's someone I want you to meet."

Neil had picked the right time, as Waylon was ready to take anybody. Still, he had to be persuaded. "He had nothing to lose because he had nothing to start with anyway." Neil agreed that "if I can do 5 percent of what I think I can do, it'll be 100 percent more than anyone else ever did for you." Neil went on to say that perhaps someone outside the Nashville circle would be better for Waylon. "We had no other artist. We had no one to trade off."

The agreement appealed to Waylon. He was desperate. One

Jennings aide said, "Neil was the one who wrote the three-page book on Jewish business ethics—unabridged edition—but if you're gonna fight in the desert, you better have a camel." Waylon called Neil "his mean ole' dog."[7] After a day of discussion, Neil became Waylon's manager. With Waylon sipping a Coke, Neil had a drink with Willie Nelson at the crowded Nashville airport. At that meeting, Neil agreed to sign another country artist. The local reaction to Waylon's new manager was quick and hostile. Waylon's friends told him it was "the biggest mistake of his life." Waylon had violated one of Nashville's basic codes in hiring a Yankee outsider as his manager.

Waylon told Bob Campbell, "Neil is a genius. Me and Willie . . . we were through, you know. We were just up against a brick wall. Neil took us in and fed us and loaned us money and he didn't know if he was ever gonna get it back. But he had faith in us and it was hard to find any place to put faith."[8]

On the plane to New York, Neil began to plan strategies to deal with RCA Victor and the Moeller Talent Agency. Neil's immediate task was to generate some money for his beleaguered client. RCA was willing to advance $10,000 to $15,000. This amount was enough to put Waylon on his feet temporarily. In the process of getting this payment, Neil noticed a strange thing: RCA had not picked up Waylon's option in 1972. Each year, according to all artists' contracts, a record company must exercise its option to either drop or keep a performer. Artists do not enjoy the same privilege. Upon discovering this curious legal oversight, Reshen went to the record company. RCA protested that they did not have an address on Waylon and that the option pick-up had been sent to him in care of Chet Atkins. "With that information," Reshen recounts, "we immediately sent RCA a letter that they had blown the option pick-up and that Waylon was no longer under contract to them."[9] RCA responded saying this was a mere technicality and that Waylon was indeed still with the label.

RCA's position had some merit. Between the time of the renewal date and Reshen's discovery of the option mistake, Waylon had accepted the advance and had recorded in RCA's studios, which could be viewed as tacit renewal. Waylon's new manager approached numerous attorneys and got conflicting interpretations. "We had certain legal opinions saying we could get out, certain legal opinions saying we could not . . . so we took the position that we were out and we started to negotiate with other companies."

While haggling with RCA, Neil approached several other companies. He took Waylon to see Clive Davis at his Nashville hotel suite. Clive was in town for a CBS Records convention. Waylon told the flamboyant record company president, "I want off RCA and to be with your company." Davis admitted he was interested, "but Waylon didn't come back. We didn't discuss money or anything like that."[10] Neil contacted his friends at Atlantic, who were delighted with their acquisition of Willie Nelson and were then establishing a Nashville branch. "Sure, we'd love to have Waylon." The RCA brass was furious. They sent out letters to their competitors ordering them to "cease and desist" tampering with "their" artist. The action only prompted greater interest in the singer. Neil: "Mercury and Capitol, who had not even been talked to . . . found out about it and called up to see if Waylon was available."[11]

Waylon and Jessi were very nervous about the entire confrontation. Neil received many late-night calls. Jessi, especially, was apprehensive. "Neil, sure you're doing the right thing? Do you think that . . .?" Jessi was afraid Neil was alienating everybody and ruining Waylon's future in Nashville. Despite recurring doubts, Jessi strongly supported Waylon in his fight with the giants on Music City Row.

During the dispute, Waylon avoided the RCA studios. May 16, 1973, was his last full recording session. In July and August there were three overdub sessions for the *Ladies Love Outlaws* album. It does not appear that Waylon had anything to do with these sessions. *Ladies Love Outlaws*, he says, was "not really a good album because I didn't get to finish a lot of songs because I was sick and in the hospital when they had to release that album, so we had to release it as it was."[12] Waylon got out of a sickbed just to pose for the album cover with his niece. *Ladies Love Outlaws* is not an album he cares for: "the only good thing about that album is the cover," he told Chet Flippo; "that's my little niece and she always looks at me like that. They wanted me to have a bunch of women around me but I said, hell no. The rest of that album— they picked it out of the cans while I was sick."[13] It symbolized many of his problems with the label. Waylon did not like Ronny Light's production ideas. He felt the album was not finished— especially Hoyt Axton's "Never Been to Spain."

Waylon's avoidance of the RCA building was tactical. Chet Atkins repeatedly tried to have a meeting. "Why don't you come in and talk. We can straighten it out!" Waylon would reply,

"What you call straightened out is not what I call straightened out. What I want to straighten out is exactly what Neil wants and you might as well talk to Neil." All the attempts to go around Reshen failed. Jerry Bradley and Chet Atkins came to the conclusion that they would have to deal with the outsider from New York.

"After a long-term negotiation we had a final meeting where I gave RCA five days," notes Reshen, "to come up with an alternate proposal or we were going to sign with another company."[14] In mid-October the five days ran out. A gossip columnist in the influential *Hollywood Reporter* published an item designed to instill nervousness in Victor executives: "ATLANTIC RECORDS IS HOT ON THE HEELS OF WAYLON JENNINGS. It seems that Ahmet and gang would like to have the gentleman sign some paper and do some songs for their new Nashville-based country operation."[15] The item was significant, as Willie Nelson, amidst considerable fanfare, had already defected to the soul/blues label.

RCA was having some second thoughts about Nelson. His Atlantic recording session received considerable press coverage, particularly in the *Rolling Stone*.[16] His first album garnered rave reviews. Worse yet, Reshen had managed to negotiate away from Victor an entire album (later released on Atlantic as *Phases and Stages*).

Waylon, reported Jan Reid, used Shotgun Willie as an example of his worth to the label. Pointing to a large wall photo of Nelson in an RCA executive's office, Jennings reportedly commented, "Hoss, you already made a mistake with that one."[17]

The showdown came in Chet Atkins's appropriately darkened office. Nashville executives insist on heavily draped offices with the proper wood paneling. Chet Atkins was joined by young Jerry Bradley, promotion head Frank Manceni, and a New York company attorney. Waylon and Neil made their demands. Neil opened. He outlined his desire to end the old controversial contract. He wanted a new one with WGJ (Waylon "Goddamn" Jennings) Productions. Waylon would be allowed to produce his own records. WGJ would also have control over advertising budgets, promotion budgets, and of course they wanted "a very good advance." "And then we got down to a few stumbling blocks," says Neil "like how long that would be—what the advances would be." He requested that Waylon be allowed to delete six or eight old sides that the singer hated. "Green River" naturally was one of them. The list of requirements continued.

Neil Reshen's first 'outlaw.' Willie Nelson, 1973. Courtesy of Atlantic Records.

Neil wanted graphics control over both the album cover and the liner notes. They desired approval of the mix-down and the master. As the stipulations continued, Chet interrupted. "Neil, I don't have those things in *my* contract!" The RCA people refused to give in. Neil said, "Okay, then we won't budge—let's end it here and let's leave." There was what novelists call a "painful pause." "They stopped and nobody would say anything 'cause the first one to say anything was going to lose," according to Waylon. After several minutes, Waylon broke the uneasy silence. Pointing to a bowl of peanuts, he said, "Chet, what kind of peanuts are these?" Neil glared at his client, thinking "please keep quiet"— or words to that affect. The Victor negotiating crew asked for a time out. Waylon and Neil left the office. In the hallway Waylon apologized, "I didn't mean to talk . . . but that was the hardest moment I ever had in my life . . . much harder than going on stage. That silence lasted forever and it was the meanest silence I ever saw in my life." The duo returned to hear RCA's counterproposal. Neil: "It was far better than I thought . . . it was a proposal we were ready to accept." A smile started to form on Waylon's face. Neil stopped it.

"We'll have to go out and discuss it," said Neil. This time, Waylon cooperated. They came back saying, "it's not quite what we want."

This time the RCA crew trooped out. They countered again, with a higher offer. Neil and Waylon agreed. Waylon Jennings had finally gotten artistic control and a $75,000 advance toward a Silver Eagle bus. After the formal meeting, Chet, Neil, and Waylon chatted. Waylon explained, "It wasn't you, Chet, it was the company." It turned out that Waylon now had a better contract then the Father of the Nashville Sound.[18]

On November 27, 1972, Chet Atkins announced in a press release, "Everyone in the music industry recognizes Waylon's incredible talent and limitless future. The heavy bidding that took place at the expiration of his contract [sic] makes it particularly gratifying that he chose to remain with RCA Records." The press release went on to say that "the company is currently in the midst of mapping an intensive national campaign to coincide with a projected personal appearance tour."

The press handout reveals that RCA was not anxious to expose the circumstances of the dispute or the terms of the contract. Waylon did receive artistic control. Within a matter of months,

Waylors—besides Richie Albright—began to appear at the RCA studios.

On February 21, 1973, four members of the road band joined two session people to record "Ride Me Down Easy" and two lesser known songs. It would not be until a year after the signing of the new contract that Waylon would abandon the engineers and studio layout at the beige RCA building for the confines of the Glasers' upstairs recording facilities. It took even longer for RCA to cut out his early albums and to change the graphics on the remaining titles in the catalogue. The album covers for *Good Hearted Woman, The Taker-Tulsa, Singer of Sad Songs,* and *The Best of* were not reshot until the middle of 1978. Self-production was several years down the road for Waylon.

As with most recording company contracts, the actual economic terms in Waylon's contract are difficult to discover. Corporate secrecy, artists' egos, and other factors all serve to keep these details out of the public domain. Certainly, in 1972 Waylon did better than the original 4 percent he received in 1965.

Having temporarily solved the RCA situation, Neil turned his attention to Lucky Moeller. In some respects, Lucky was more powerful even than Chester Atkins. RCA was the leading country music label, but there were others. Victor did not have a lock on the market, and so leaving RCA would not necessarily destroy an artist. But country music booking was another matter. A handful of booking agents like Lucky Moeller controlled "live," the circuit ranging from cheap redneck bars to lucrative state fairs. One Nashville talent agent recalled, "When I got in this business, managers [and bookers] in town were happy to put their cowboy boots up on the desk and be almost belligerent when the phone rang." Moeller had a specific edge over his competitors, as Lucky was one of the first major Nashville booking agents. Unlike their counterparts in popular music, many Music City agents also acted as an artist's personal manager. This had been true in Waylon's case. Waylon in 1965 had signed a booking and management contract with Moeller. According to Neil Reshen, Lucky got 15 percent of everything Waylon earned.[19]

This type of arrangement has been widely criticized. Joe Sullivan, a Nashville manager, notes, "Booking an artist is a fulltime job *and* managing an artist is a fulltime job. To try and do both would be a bit overwhelming." Dan Beck adds, "No longer can a booking agency handle all aspects of an artist's career because the field has gotten so broad."[20] In 1972, statements like these were only privately voiced.

Part of the problem with Lucky Moeller and his competitors was their "Grand Ole Opry" mentality. "They were all short-sighted," notes Reshen. "Their idea of Nevada was the Nuggett—their idea of Los Angeles was the Palamino—their idea of New York was to play somewhere in New Jersey, but never go into New York . . . they had no idea of routing and tours. Commercials were limited to tractors, and you could never do a major commercial and television was 'Hee Haw' and those syndicated 'Porter Wagoner' and 'Wilburn Brothers Shows.'"[21] Nashville agents rarely considered any avenues of exposure outside of the tried-and-tested clubs, fairs, and television shows. Neil desired to change all this—but first Moeller would have to be eased out of the picture.

Waylon thought Lucky was cheating him and wanted an audit. Neil, experienced in this area, argued otherwise. "Waylon would get a statement every month and each month the balance would go higher . . . either Lucky would not take his commissions or he would advance Waylon money or sent the statements to be advanced money . . . Waylon never ordered these statements and I don't think there's anything wrong with the honesty of the statements. I do think there are a lot of mistakes in them. Dates where Waylon may not have played and he got charged a commission or so. Which were honest mistakes on Lucky's part, but nobody on the other side ever checked them out. And at this point, they're too ancient to ever check out."[22] What Neil might have added was that checking out statements is the responsibility of a personal manager.

Waylon also felt that Lucky was using him as a loss-leader. A loss-leader in the music business is a headliner who is paid less in exchange for the promoter's taking another act from the same booking agency. Reshen also qualified this criticism: "That really is the function of a booking agency . . . you use your major acts to get your minor acts established. Whatever Lucky did to Waylon, Lucky also did years before with Kitty Wells and Hank Snow to get Waylon on a show that he might not have deserved to be on. So I view that not as a malicious thing or as anything that you should ever be mad about. It's an evolutionary thing in Waylon's career."[23] Neil's understanding of the situation notwithstanding,

Waylon's ties to Lucky needed to be cut. For one thing, Waylon's distrust was too great to overcome. As one aide said, "once he's down on you, that's it.!"

Waylon owed Moeller nearly $50,000. Lucky's security on that amount came in the form of an assignment on Waylon's RCA contract. Of the singer's royalties, Lucky would take 50 percent toward the debt. The debt never seemed to be reduced, as Lucky's 15 percent commissions continued to drain the singer. Lucky kept booking Waylon for less than $1,750 a night. Neil went to see the veteran agent. At that dramatic meeting, Lucky's response was one of hurt and anger. He had "always done Waylon right." Moeller likened Waylon to his own son. Neil insisted that Moeller's exclusive contract with Waylon be terminated in six months and his booking commission be reduced to 10 percent. Moeller at first refused. Reshen told him that Waylon's contract with RCA was altered. The new version was between the record company and WGJ Productions; consequently, "that great assignment he had that was going to protect him was now no longer a valid piece of paper. No more money would ever be paid to Waylon Jennings as an individual and consequently, no more money would be paid to Moeller." Neil insisted that Lucky only be paid his commission for those jobs he got Waylon. Moreover, Waylon had to approve and sign each booking contract. Previously, Lucky had just told Waylon where to play. Reluctantly, Lucky Moeller consented to this new arrangement.

Moeller disliked the addition of Johnna to Waylon's staff because Yursic had seen the other side of the operation as a talent buyer. "He treated me like a long-lost son," recalls Yursic, "until he realized what was happening." Johnna had always been at the other end of the phone with Moeller.

In a matter of three years, by 1975, Waylon's indebtedness to Moeller was ended. During this period he continued to book Waylon—at a higher price. However, Magna Productions, a New York agency, was coming into the picture and by June 1974 Chuck Glaser's Nova Productions was doing nearly all of Waylon's concert and nightclub appearances.

By the end of 1972 Waylon's career problems were lessened—but far from solved. He had gained some artistic control over his music, although he was still tied to the RCA studios. His popularity was growing in the lucrative youth-oriented urban markets. Perhaps he would stop playing the Crab Orchards of rural America. The Moeller situation seemed resolved. Little did he know that *Ladies Love Outlaws* and his appearance at the Dripping Springs Reunion would be a portent of things to come.

Lee Clayton, the composer of "Ladies Love Outlaws" and "If You Can Touch Her At All," told a journalist, "country music from its inception, has been outlaw music. It's always been."[24] Many students of country music would strongly disagree. They might contend that country music has been a blend of traditionalism, fundamentalism in religion, and racism, with a populist economic strain thrown in. The notion of outlaws in country music, however, is not new. Johnny Cash and Marty Robbins found themselves in black gunfighter attire on CBS record jackets in the early 1960s. The ploy was an obvious attempt to capitalize on the spate of Westerns then dominating the prime viewing hours on American television. The folk music revival found country artists like Cash and Jennings doing the Woody Guthrie "on the road" bit on their album covers. *Ladies Love Outlaws* was a throwback to the turbulent 1960s. It featured Waylon in a black outfit—six-gun and belt—facing a little girl. Some people have pointed to this record as being the turning point in Waylon's career. Historically, it was. But it was not the album that brought Neil Reshen into the picture, nor did it alter Waylon's view of RCA or Chet Atkins. Rather, the album was one of many indicents that further soured the singer on RCA. The "Dear Artist" form letters probably took a greater toll than *Ladies Love Outlaws*.

The origin of Waylon as outlaw is difficult to determine. "Ladies Love Outlaws" was originally recorded January 11, 1972. The album was released some eight months later. The singers mentioned in the song were Lee Clayton, "Waymore, (Waylon's nickname given him by Ray Corbin), and Billy Joe Shaver. After this historical fact, all becomes a maze. Many people take credit for the so-called outlaw phenomenon. Mike Bane, in his book *Outlaws,* applauds Hazel Smith and Dave Hickey for generating the concept. Don Light contends this as a management move on the part of Reshen and RCA. Neil Reshen suggests he urged Waylon to regrow a beard that sprouted during his bout with hepatitis. All versions are partly correct.

In the creation of any successful new idea in the music industry, there are more parents than there are children. Lee Clayton's song did instill the word "outlaw" in the Nashville consciousness. Waylon's new northern urban manager and contract did make him more "uncountry" than ever. RCA however, did not instantly jump on this concept. *Ruby, Don't Take Your Love to Town* was a budget Camden release, and it showed no sign of the new bandit image. In 1973, despite Waylon's famous "I can't go pop with a mouthful of firecrackers," the telecaster cowboy campaign was planned. Neil Reshen explains: "from the point of view of anybody other than Waylon Jennings, I was totally instrumental in it. We laughed a lot because after we got the whole publicity thing done and that whole campaign—we shipped the promotion booklets—Waylon called me up and told me he shaved his beard and mustache off. But fortunately, he grew it back. *Waylon wanted to appeal to a bigger audience*." He continues, "Willie also grew his beard and we've been very successful with the image."[25]

Johnna credits Willie Nelson with beginning the outlaw movement. "Willie started the Austin cult. Neil merely put a name on it. They were people trying to improve the industry." Johnna says, "literally hundreds of people then added on to it. Hazel Smith, Tompall, Dave Hickey, and many others. But Waylon and Willie got all the attention."[26]

Lonesome, On'ry and Mean was the first album to feature the new look. Musically, the album was not a great leap in any direction. It contained some material by new Nashville writers but also had a fair share of typical "lost woman" songs. Perhaps the greatest deviation was the liner notes by Austin-based *Rolling Stone* editor Chet Flippo. He concluded his paid $125 review saying, "There's nothing faddish or contrived or artificial about him. If he sings it—you believe it. Hank Williams had that rare gift and so does Waylon Jennings." Hank's greatest gift was that *his* material was the greatest crossover in country music history, outstripping even that of Eddy Arnold and Jim Reeves.

Flippo's endorsement was not insignificant, for he was viewed as a major proponent of the Austin scene. Six months before the release of *Lonesome* he wrote that a new music industry was developing in Austin. He announced the coming together of "long-hairs" and cowboys in a new scene—cosmic cowboys and girls.

During the heat of Waylon's October 1972 parleys with RCA, Chet Flippo informed *Rolling Stone* readers of the Armadillo World Headquarters, peopled by individuals with shoulder-length hair, beards, floppy Stetsons, embroidered cowboy shirts, faded jeans, and dusty boots. The reporter went on to say that this curious integration in Austin, Texas, was being fueled by artists from New York and Nashville. He quoted proprietor

Eddie Wilson as bragging: "There's all kinds of musical talent here and more moving in. Willie Nelson just moved from Nashville and lives right down the street. Michael Murphy moved here and so did Jerry Jeff Walker. And we've finally got a 16-track studio here. People are movin' in—in droves. That scares a lotta people here who're concerned about keepin' decent livin' conditions."[27] The people of Austin were not the only ones concerned about their living conditions. Music City Row, already beseiged by the Los Angeles country rockers, was not happy.

The relationship of Texas and Nashville has always been volatile. The Lone Star State did not mirror the mores or values of the old Confederacy. Nearly all of the crossover and rock-a-billy artists had come from the Southwest or had made their reputation in these parts. The idea of an "alternative Nashville" did not sit well with producers, session men, or union engineers in Music City. Nor did they appreciate Chet Flippo for advertising these events. One Country Music Association official said, *"Rolling Stone* should stick to them hippie bands. They don't know shit about country music."[28] Many Music City inhabitants echoed songwriter Harlan Howard: "Now Willie can talk all he wants to about moving Music City to Austin . . . you can put a recording studio any place you want to, but you're not going to move Music City U.S.A.! We have a central location—the Opry attracted all these musicians and singers and so forth and it's an ideal place for an artist to take off for any part of the country . . . most of them are going to live here."[29]

Texas, however, was a natural market for Willie Nelson. Neil Reshen reasoned that what was good for Willie should also work for Waylon. In many respects, the atmosphere at the Armadillo was not unlike the atmosphere at J.D.'s in Phoenix when Phil and the Frantics, a rock band, worked Waylon's club. Waylon would be thrust into the Austin milieu at Willie's first Dripping Springs Reunion in 1972. He was beardless then.

Some Nashville insiders took solace from the Dripping Springs Reunion of 1972.[30] The festival, outside of Nashville, staged by Willie Nelson was characterized by the press as "doomed," "ill-fated," and a "financial flop." It was a strange mixture of "drunks, hippies, and cowboys." One writer did note, "It was the first large scale mix of the opposing Austin cultures." But it didn't make any money. Jan Reid provides a bit of the flavor:

Aspiring, dope-smoking, gate-crashers were taken aback by the sight of uniformed security guards toting shotguns, and a Veteran of Foreign Wars trinket vender was equally taken aback by a young man who flipped his frisbee in the air and remarked, "If we'd quit having wars, we wouldn't have any veterans."

The uneasiness had extended on stage. Tex Ritter sang awhile then emceed awhile too long, cracking lame Black Panther jokes and trying to bar Tom T. Hall from the microphone though the crowd was bellowing for an encore. Roy Acuff declared that *he* was the by-God King of country music, then crowed in triumph when an emcee announced Merle Haggard was in a state of collapse and wouldn't make his scheduled appearance.[31]

Kris Kristofferson told the audience to "jack off" and stomped off the stage, refusing to do an encore. A frightened Lee Clayton, making his major debut, almost forgot the words to "Ladies Love Outlaws."

Waylon's set went well. He was even paid before the cash ran out. Gate-crashing had taken its toll, and there was not enough money to pay everyone on the star-studded roster. One of the better know artists, hearing of this situation, refused to appear on stage or to come out of his expensive bus. "No pay—no play."

Waylon reached into his pocket and handed the promoter a fistful of bills. "Here you go—give the old fart his mony. I got no reason not to trust you." The promoter was dumbfounded. Waylon pushed him in the direction of the bus with the closed door. "Hey, you just go pay his highness. . . ."

Waylon returned to the stage and did another set. he made no money. The financial failure of his festival proved to many on the Row that Austin would never challenge the supremacy of Nashville.

All of these events contributed to the outlaw ethos. Tompall Glaser's aid-de-camp and columnist, Hazel Smith, was the first to push a promotional campaign stressing outlaws. A disc jockey from an Ashboro, North Carolina, radio station called Hazel to tell her that he planned a program highlighting four artists—Glaser, Jennings, Kristofferson, and Nelson. He needed a title for the show. "Call it Outlaw Music," she said. The WCSE Sunday afternoon broadcast was a success. Soon, according to Mike Bane, it became *the* "outlaw station" for collegiates in the area.

Dave Hickey, a *Country Music* magazine correspondent and a friend of Hazel's, reinforced the concept in the publication. "In Defense of the Telecaster Cowboy Outlaws" was the first of many magazine articles contrasting the lifestyles of Waylon,

Willie, and others to that of the Nashville Establishment.[32] Hickey noted that there was little in the way of "outlaw music"; rather, "the only thing most of these guys have in common is that they were born country on the west side of the Mississippi and often forget to go watery in the knees at the mention of Jeff Davis." The rest of the article compared the chic parties of the upper crust to the long-haired concert Reshen staged at the Nashville Sheraton Hotel in 1974 featuring the outlaws. Waylon credits Hickey's piece as the beginning. In a song he wrote, "someone called us outlaws in some ole' magazine . . . what started out to be a joke . . . ." Lee Clayton concurs: "When I wrote, 'Ladies Love Outlaws' I wrote it tongue-in-cheek, then I saw it all get out of hand. It started off as being fun and it ended up as seeing who could stab each other."[33] By the middle of 1973, outlaw stories were springing up in all kinds of journals. Journalists are terrible copycats. Nonetheless, Tompall Glaser took the thing quite seriously, sending out "Outlaw Membership Certificates."

WAYLON

11

CONSUMERS BUY OUTLAWS

Following his Grammy Award in 1970, Waylon began telling writers, "I couldn't go pop with a mouthful of firecrackers!" Waylon echoed the statement frequently to reaffirm his allegiance to country music but *not* to the Nashville Sound. The comment was nearly always modified with, "We're entitled to a big beat if it complements our songs. Or if we want to use a kazoo played through a sewer pipe, that's all right too. Why should we lock ourselves in?" Waylon was very fond of the kazoo illustration, using it repeatedly in press interviews.

Despite the disavowals, Waylon's career was being steered out of the traditional country mold. Neil's strategy was to place Waylon in a higher caliber of clubs and even in concerts. The first thing Reshen did was to raise the singer's asking price to $2,500. Lucky never demanded more than $1,750 a night. Moeller and his assistant, Jack Andrews, protested the increase. For a month's period, they appeared to be correct. No bookings came through at the new asking price. Neil then began to book Waylon through Magna Artists Corporation, a New York–based talent agency. Magna clients included Kris Kristofferson and country rockers like Asleep at the Wheel, Commander Cody, the New Riders of Purple Sage, and ex-Byrd, Roger McGuinn.

Neil also did some job hunting through his offices. In a matter of weeks, Waylon was playing dates at the new price and higher.

He was performing in big cities and New York, which was not, as Merle Haggard would say, "hippie-free."

The conflict between Reshen and Moeller during this period continued. Lucky booked Waylon for two nights at the old price. Neil refused to take the bid. Instead, Reshen telephoned the talent buyer. "We can't work for less than $2,500. a night," he stated. The voice at the other end said, "You got it." Neil was surprised, "What do you mean?" he asked, "why did you make the offer at $1,750?" The promoter explained, "Well, I found out—I do business with all the Nashville agencies the same way. I call 'em after 6:00 and I get their answering service and I put my offer in on their answering service and then two days later I get a contract in the mail and no one *ever* calls me back to raise the price. I've been willing to pay Waylon more for two years but you're the first guy who ever called me to ask for a raise. I'll be glad to pay Waylon $2,500."[1]

One of Neil's first promotional moves was to introduce his client to New York audiences (Waylon had played New York City in the past but strictly in country and western clubs such as the Nashville Room in June 1968). That was no simple task. Country headliners, even on star-studded shows, did not do well in the metropolis. In New York, music fans preferred either the classics, Broadway musicals, or the city's own unique rock music scene. The rock community was notorious for championing loud, kinky cult groups and artists such as Lou Reed and the then seemingly outrageous New York Dolls. In January 1973 Waylon was booked into Max's Kansas City, at the time the mecca of New York rock clubs. The Velvet Underground recorded a live album in the stronghold of Gotham City's punk rock palace.

Susan Weiner of *Penthouse* mused, "Waylon Jennings at Max's Kansas City? You'd have thought Conan the Barbarian would have been more at home in the androgynous combat zone. The soporpsychic vibes are so heavy when the Dolls perform that the staff gets a special bonus—'combat pay'—as Sam Hood, who books Max's acts, describes it."[2] Earlier, Hood had the Nitty Gritty Dirt Band, which was "a sensational draw." They were, however, a *Los Angeles* bluegrass band, and they didn't claim to be country.

Sam Hood signed Waylon for a week. On opening night RCA staged a press party. Press parties on both coasts are tradition; these parties show company support for the artist and get media

coverage for the act. Many publicists feel that the first consideration frequently overshadows the second. RCA in light on its
difficulties with Waylon went all out that night, under the watchful eye of Neil Reshen.

The dingy club was packed with writers, record executives, a
Metromedia television crew, and some WHN radio listeners.
(WHN, which started broadcasting in 1972, was New York's
pioneer country station.)

Waylon opened his set saying, "I hope you all like what we do.
If you don't—don't ever come to Nashville. We'll kick the hell
out of you!" A female patron responded, "and who in the hell are
you?" "Waylon—Goddamn—Jennings, lady!"

The evening was labeled a success. Peter McCabe of *Country
Music* told a writer, "It's a major breakthrough for country
music." *Penthouse* reported, "Waylon Jennings 'stomped the shit'
out of Max's." The *New Music Express* noted, "Yep, country
meets rock, and everybody wins." Another writer commented,
"This must be a warm-up for his Atlanta pen concert."[3] Waylon
was to give a free concert for the inmates at the federal peniten-
tiary in Georgia.

The New York stay, though taxing, was a success. *After Dark,
Country Music, Penthouse,* and other publications ran stories. In
fact, Waylon by the end of the week had once again contracted
laryngitis and canceled many press appointments. While not a
household name and a poor candidate for a name recognition on
a Q-Profile, Waylon in 1973 got more press ink than in his entire
career. When questioned about "crossing over," Waylon denied
it. Reshen was a bit more candid. He told *Cash Box,* "What you
might call cross over, I call expanding the audience."[4] In record
industry jargon, "crossing over" and "audience expansion" mean
the same thing. In a week Waylon was to fly to Los Angeles to
establish himself with the Topanga Canyon "hillbillies."

Moeller returned Waylon to the Palamino Club in Los
Angeles. On February 8, RCA's West Coast publicity director,
Grelun Landon, staged a gala industry-media opening. Most of
the Los Angeles press people attended, and many record company executives and artists such as Lee Clayton joined them.

The first set confirmed Bob Hilburn's criticism of Waylon's
"inconsistency." Todd Everett in the *Hollywood Reporter* wrote,
"The first set found Jennings uneasy before his press and record
company-laden audience; he fumbled and stumbled through
some good material . . . for the second set, Jennings seemed

more at ease with himself and his audience."[5] Part of the problem was nerves. Many established artists choke at a Hollywood press opening; big stars frequently forget the words to their own songs, and others have gotten sick backstage prior to the opening. Waylon was not feeling well. He was still experiencing the effects of his hepatitis and other medical difficulties. The New York whirlwind gig had also taken its toll.

The opening did generate considerable media coverage. Even the *UCLA Daily Bruin* ran a story, saying, "if the excitement generated by his recent performance at the Palomino is any indication of public sentiment, it may at last be time for a long deserved recognition of that talent."[6] The writer must have been at the second show in the Palomino. RCA took Waylon over to the Troubadour, a night club frequented by industry people. At the Troub', once again he was "ill at ease." He sang four songs—minus the Waylors—including "Good Hearted Woman." A correspondent who was present during the guest appearance noted that Waylon "was a man to be reckoned with" and "the only problem with Jennings' appearance was that some unlucky act had to follow him."[7] Grelun Landon and Neil Reshen were more than pleased with the reception given Waylon in America's two media centers.

Jennings's success in New York impressed many observers, including Bob Hilburn. He suggested, "it may finally be time . . . to break through to a wider popularity that has so long been predicted for him."[8] Los Angeles was not a difficult nut to crack. Gram Parsons, Poco, and the Dirt Band had sown the seeds for country music in Glittertown. Hollywood was the self-proclaimed capital of "country-rock," much to the consternation of Music City.

A month after the media blitz, RCA released *Lonesome, On'ry and Mean.* For the first time a bearded Waylon Jennings appeared on the album cover. The record was presented as the "best he's ever done." Johnna Yursic told a reporter, "it's Waylon's conception of Waylon. It's the first time Waylon has had complete creative control over his work."[9] *Lonesome, On'ry and Mean* was reviewed and generally acclaimed in periodicals that customarily avoided anything made in Nashville. Mike Jahn's piece in *Cue* typical: "Jennings does country music without the bathos and clichés that mar so much commercial Nashville. . . . Jennings gives a clear indication of trying for an audience wider than the country market. He deserves it."[10] Sol Shapiro of the Morris Agency observed, "I think the public today is really groping for a new sound, which we haven't had since rock 'n' roll. This could be it."[11] Neil Reshen's "audience expansion" program was off to a good start. Waylon still wanted a new Silver Eagle.

Custom-designed diesel touring buses originally were little more than redecorated Greyhounds. Reportedly, Bill Anderson was the first to give up his Cadillac for a tour bus. "It's more practical than traveling by plane and more comfortable than a car," he says. It is also safer. What started off as a practical matter quickly became something of a Nashville status game. Who had the biggest, most luxurious, *and* expensive bus? The "keeping up with the Andersons" match shifted from artist to artist. Bunks were converted to queen-sized beds. Stereo and color televisions became essentials for the road. Portable toilets were replaced by dressing rooms. As the opulence grew, Waylon's Black Maria was pointed to as the worst bus in Nashville, "a rolling slum."

Waylon had purchased the Bluebird bus in 1969. The band painted it all black; it looked like a homemade job. The Black Maria, Tennessee plates MUS-025, sported a weatherbeaten luggage rack and two worn spare tires. Inside hung yellowed white curtains. The entrance was converted from a cabin door. The left side showed a prominent dent. The bus looked sinister and run-down. Over a four-year period the group had put over a million miles on its speedometer and replaced the motor six times. Now it was time for a change.

After the break with RCA, WGJ productions ordered a $130,000 Belgian-made Silver Eagle, the "in" bus in Nashville. The advance would make partial payment. Bank financing, however, remained a problem; given Waylon's economic troubles, few bankers were eager to grant him a loan. One day Neil received a call from Jackson, Mississippi, announcing that the bus shell had arrived without tires. Reshen dispatched an assistant to Jackson with orders to buy seven used tires and to transport the vehicle to the Dallas distributor, but the main obstacle was to get the bus financed. Neil located a bank in Norwalk, Ohio, whose president was a Waylon Jennings "freak" who owned all his records. The officer told Neil he would be "honored" to put up $50,000 and sent a bank draft to Eagle Bus Sales in Dallas. Waylon flew to the Cleveland suburb to sign the papers. The bus was his.

When the diesel arrived in Nashville, it was discovered that six of the tires were the wrong size. The problem was easily corrected, and Waylon owned one of the top converted intercity travel vans in Nashville. Economically, it was a wise move in that the entire cost of the bus would be depreciated in a matter of five years.

Terry Guerin in *Penthouse* described the interior of the vehicle:

> The eight-by-twelve galley is the first room behind the driver's cabin. It contains a mounted color television set and eight thousand dollars' worth of stereo equipment. There is also an eating area with a small refrigerator, table space for four and seating space for twelve, and a private waiting room to use before shows when outside facilities aren't available. . . .
>
> The high-backed, double-width booth seats dominate this forward room. The four booths are of uniform construction and design, seamless and sectionless. Frames are of oak plywood with solid braces inside. The sides and tops of the booths are covered with a heavy-grade Formica-like black surfacing called Shellrock, with a hard, durable veneer. The rest is Uniroyal's "English Pub" ebony Naugahyde. Touted as looking like candlelit leather, it is a vinyl-coated fabric that can be made to look like anything—wood, wool, silk brocade, or a batik cotton print. The Naugahyde seat backs are button-tufted and piped in gold velvet. Because of these ersatz country-Spanish pieces, the galley is ink dark and cement-heavy. It is a fine room for an outlaw band from the experiential badlands.

Turning to the sleeping area, he continued his description:

> This room has a big walk-in closet, two mounted ten-inch speakers, a reel-to-reel tape player, and an amplifier mounted in a vertical console finished in Shellrock. It has a bed covered in Indian-print cut velvet against one side wall. Opposite it is a small collapsible table fronted by handmade, high-backed, swivel-wing, black velvet chair. . . .
>
> Above the driver's head hangs a mural, expressed in oils of forest green, sky blue, yellow, russet, and peat brown, portraying a conventionalized form of old-time rural life. For the rustic sum of $500, a young Ohio artist named Paul Ascherl sold Waylon a cure his eyes can turn to from practically anywhere in the bus, a place to instruct all who see it within this ultra-here machine how far Waylon and the Waylors have come, or where he's heading back to, or where he can never go, or where none of us have ever been.[12]

On the heels of his successes at Max's and the Troubadour, Magna booked Waylon with the New Riders and the Grateful Dead. The all-day show was to be held in the former home of the San Francisco 49ers, Kezar Stadium, just blocks away for the

Haight-Ashbury. It was here that the Dead established their career with Sunday afternoon park concerts. It was also the staging area for the 1967 Summer of Love. "When you're goin' to San Francisco be sure to wear a flower in your hair," the song went. Promoter Bill Graham hyped the Dead concert as a celebration of the old Haight-Ashbury period.

Backstage, Graham reproduced an outdoor cafe. Tables were set up with various foods alfresco for the performers. Trailers were hauled in for each performer, Waylon couldn't believe it. Country performers are accustomed to a little dressing room the size of a closet, with a light bulb hanging down from the paint-chipped ceiling. Frequently a storeroom serves as a dressing area. Usually only an uncomfortable hardback chair is provided until the performer goes on stage. "They don't do anything to comfort the artist," says Johnna. "When he played Kezar, we went back-stage and they had T-bone steaks, ham, corn on the cob, and anything you could mention . . . anything to drink, eat . . . one individual trailer for each artist as a dressing area and a lounge area, and the umbrellas and that patio . . . just fantastic man."[13]

At 11:00 A.M., 20,000 people crowded into the stadium to hear the New Riders open the show. Waylon followed. Before going on the makeshift stage, Waylon told the band, "Let's just go up and do our thing like we know how to do it. Cause we gotta live with what we are, you know, we gotta live with whatever we do."

Waylon did have some trouble with the Dead's massive sound system. He and the band didn't play loud enough. When he finished his set, he was uneasy. Coming off the stage, he asked Johnna, "How did it sound? How'd it go? Was it really cool?" "Don't ask me. Look out there, man." He was receiving a stand-ing ovation. "You better go encore or they'll tear this place down." He returned to the stage, did one more song. The rock crowd rooted for another encore. Johnna: "He wasn't sure he'd done a good job. He didn't know how they would react. That was a strange crowd to him at that point. He didn't know what their reactions would be, or how to judge, what this audience really dug and how they showed him." In his trailer, Waylon found a big bouquet of flowers. "That's fancy. You don't suppose they think I'm gonna die, do they?" Waylon's first rock concert was a critical success. On the following day, the *Chronicle* review appeared, "Jennings has long been recognized in the country field. His deep husky voice, cooking band (with steel guitarist Ralph

Mooney) and bent for performing pop songs makes him a perfect candidate for a cross over to the rock audience. He deserved— and made good use of—the major exposure he was getting."[14]

Several weeks before the widely publicized Texas concert, Waylon went back into the apparently insane world of network television. He signed to do the "Dean Martin Summer Replacement Show" on NBC. Neil committed him for the program but could not be there for the taping. Waylon was not eager to do the show. Memories of the Bishop fiasco lingered. Joey Bishop and Dean Martin were members of Sinatra's well-publicized "rat-pack."

Waylon and Captain Midnite went to see Doug Gilmore, the coproducer of the show. Gilmore asked Waylon for some sixteen-track tapes "so they could do it right." He said he wanted to give country singers "the class they deserve." Waylon was not reassured.

The day of the taping was another story. Midnite came along for moral support. It was total confusion. "We had a hell of a time getting anybody's attention," the Nashville disc jockey said. Midnite encountered a buddy from WSM, who provided directions. Waylon was to sing the haunting ballad "We Had It All." The production people insisted he sing the love song sitting on a horse. Waylon told them what they could do with the horse. They changed concepts. Waylon was to stand by a wooden country fence. But the first two lines of the ballad had to go. To compound the situation, the set manager called a break. She was going to the hairdresser. Waylon asked Midnite, "See if you can find out what in the hell is goin' on?" "Hey Chief," retorted the Captain, "she's going to the beauty shop." Enraged, Waylon said, "Get the car." Crew members asked, "Where're you goin'?" "See you in a while, Hoss, be right back." He did not return.

The producers wrote a letter of apology, but in typical Jennings fashion, Waylon did not relent. His negative view of television was firmly established. Later, his experience on the "Cheryl Ladd Special" in 1979 would convince him he was right.

WILLIE'S JULY FOURTH PICNIC: THE COUNTRY WOODSTOCK?

Despite the original Dripping Springs disaster, the consequence of a confrontation of diverse lifestyles, poor attendance, and financial loss, Willie Nelson was determined to try again. All he needed was $25,000 and a place to hold his fourth of July bash. Willie approached some of his powerful friends. His lure was the production of a film of the proposed one-day outdoor festival a la Woodstock. Hitting on local and New York promoters and filmmakers, Nelson was able to secure the front money. He found a location on Route 290 at Dripping Springs. Eddie Wilson of the Armadillo World Headquarters was brought in to stage the event. As things developed, this choice may not have been ideal, for the Armadillo herd was not well organized. "They're too laid back . . . stoned!" said one participant. What developed was total confusion. Who had film rights? Who was coming? Rumors abounded. "Bob Dylan and Leon Russell were gonna' come." One prediction was correct: advertising for the event contained the names of artists not yet signed. Charlie Rich threatened to sue Willie for including him on a poster. Tom T. Hall announced he was coming. Willie hadn't asked him. Everything seemed tentative and chaotic. Many of the performers were not confirmed until Independence Day.

The eve of the Fourth found a group of performers' hangers-on and journalists blindly wandering around the dusty festival site in search of a press party and some food. John Prine bitterly complained, "I'm still expecting a barbecue." There *was* beer. As the sun set, the performers began to appear. Leon Russell was there to try his hand at being country—"Hank Wilson." Kris Kristofferson and Willie joined the new country convert for a night of roarin' and singing at a local ranch house. One journalist described the so-called press party as featuring "the best music of the festival before an audience of friends." Waylon did not attend the all-night party. He and the band were at the Holiday Inn South, a mile away.[15]

The concert began at the crack of dawn. Willie opened the program at 6:00 A.M. First, veterans of the Austin scene appeared. Things backstage were totally hectic, as journalists and people with press credentials milled around. The Armadillos, used to dealing with barroom drunks, could not cope with the situation. Tempers flared. Artists refused to play. Some could not get on to the stage area. Armadillo bullies started to repeat the excesses of the year before; journalists were being physically restrained. This was not the kind of publicity Willie (or Neil) had in mind. Chet Flippo of *Rolling Stone* approached Eddie Wilson. "You can't do this. These people have a job to do. Somebody's

Country Woodstock: Willie's July 4 picnics in Texas, 1974.

going to burn you." Chet was a friend of Wilson and had written a laudatory article about his World Headquarters in the *Stone.* Wilson agreed to "try" to help Chet but cautioned, "I don't know if *I* can get you in." The hot, dry Texas 110-degree sun only made matters worse.

As the day passed into the evening, people mellowed out. Willie's demonic drummer Paul English, wearing a black Dracula Cape, was married on the stage to Dianne Shaw. Local evangelist Bill Cooper performed the rite. Waylon was the best man, aided by Sammi Smith. He didn't look happy and merely glared at the crowd. A roar rose from the audience as the nuptials came to a close. Kris and Rita Coolidge started a set. The power failed. Tom T. Hall finally came on stage. He played until a string on his guitar broke and then, in the best rock 'n' roll fashion, casually threw the expensive instrument into the crowd. A fight broke out. As the dawn finally came, all that remained were cases of empty beer cans and refuse. Pat Carr, writing in the *New York Times,* proclaimed, "The event at Dripping Springs was a party— but not just for Willie Nelson: It was also for Texas, Austin, and peaceful co-existence."[16] The venture was financially a success except for Willie Nelson. Waylon did get paid this time. He received $2,000 and star billing as did Tom T. and Charlie Rich. More significantly, the event garnered a tremendous amount of publicity. Pat Carr coined a phrase, "progressive country," to describe Willie Nelson and his friends. The concept was scoffed at in Nashville, but their scorn would return to haunt the residents of Music City Square.

Willie's picnic was widely publicized. It was described as a "Country Woodstock." Stories and photographs of naked beer totin' Texans made their way into the pages of the underground and rock press. Willie and Waylon, especially, were hailed as the leaders of a new music movement, with its Vatican located in Texas. Much of the coverage was like that of the Woodstock conclave. The skirmishes with security guards were forgotten, the extreme heat and dry dust were played down, the frustrations and tempers were minimized. Memories of the poor organization and economic mismanagement lingered only for a few days. Bad feelings died out after most of the artists, promoters, and investers were paid.

RCA released *Honky Tonk Heroes* in July. All but one song, "We Had It All," was written by Billy Joe Shaver. Shaver, like most of the outlaws, was from Texas. In a Waco high school he began

Willie's July 4th "picnic" filmed for NBC movie theatre distribution, copyright 1975.

writing poetry under the guidance of his English teacher. Billy
Joe dropped out of high school and joined the Navy, a southern
tradition. After "seeing the world," he returned to Texas and
tried his hand at music. The song writing did not put food on the
table, so he wound up working in a saw mill. A serious accident
cut short his career in lumber; he lost two fingers on the right
hand. Willie finally convinced Shaver to try his luck in Nashville.
His adventures in Nashville were typical. He got nowhere until
Bobby Bare signed him as a contract writer for the princely sum
for $50 per week. For years Billy Joe struggled in Music City.
Waylon Jennings, with a reputation as a tunesmith, was one of the
first artists Shaver contacted "Waylon is the first guy I ever
pitched a song to. I pitched several, he didn't record none of
them then. He held them and rocked on for years. I knew he was
digging my songs 'cause they were good songs."[17] With that
thought in mind, Billy was growing impatient. One day outside
of the RCA studios, Billy Joe ran into Waylon. "Hey, Waylon,"
shouted the intoxicated songwriter, "I got a hit for you. If you
don't listen to it, I'm gonna whip you right here." People stared,
waiting for the fight. There was none.

In 1971 Waylon recorded "Low Down Freedom"; "Black
Rose" was cut in May 1972. Both stayed in the corporate can.
"Black Rose," which dealt with an interracial love affair, was
considered a bit strong for the country market by RCA. A superstar like Merle Haggard experienced considerable trouble with a
similar tune. Capitol had had Haggard's song in the vaults for
years prior to its release. Only press coverage and public curiosity sprung the tune.

After watching the reception Billy Joe had received at the first
Nelson reunion, Waylon suggested to Shaver that if "you write
me some of those gutsy songs, I'll cut them." He did. The result
was *Honky Tonk Heroes*.

The production of *Honky Tonk Heroes* was fraught with some
old but all-too-familiar difficulties. Waylon did use the Waylors
on a majority of songs. But Ronnie Light's production touch was
on the first two Shaver songs recorded. Shaver managed to get in
Waylon's bad graces—something that is very easy to do—by
giving "Willy the Wandering Gypsy and Me" to Tom T. Hall as a
single. Waylon vowed never to do any of Billy Joe's songs again.
Waylon's version of the Willie Nelson tribute is far superior to
Tom T.'s, according to most critics; still, he felt betrayed. RCA
released "Willy" as the B-side to "You Asked Me To," which was

a country and western hit. This did not sit well with Waylon, as this was yet another two-sided hit. Mick Brady of the Waylon Jennings Appreciation Society (wjas) in England editorialized, "I can't condone rca's policy of releasing two tracks already available on an album. Not only does it cut down eventual sales of the record thereby spoiling the chances of high chart placings, but also shows disconcern towards the artist's fans anxious for new material to be released. Perhaps next time we'll see the release of some of the tracks recorded with the Crickets."[18]

The critics liked the album. *Billboard* said, "It's as good as anything he's done, which says a great deal." *Country Music* magazine, now firmly establilshed as *the* publication in the field, concluded, "This is probably Waylon's best album."[19] Reaction to the album was mixed. The highest ranking the LP got on the *Billboard* country and western album charts was number 14. Some citizens were more upset with the "hippie-lookin" cover than with what was inside. *Honky Tonk Heroes* is now generally viewed as one of Waylon's outstanding albums.

Dripping Springs had been a media event. Neil Reshen would try for another during the annual Disc Jockey Convention in Nashville. Every year a growing number of broadcasters would descend upon Music City to be wined, dined, and entertained. Record companies dutifully would herd their artists into hospitality suites and present interview and photo opportunities with the media people. The more prominent artists would stage gala cocktail parties in their suburban mansion Neil took advantage of this nonstop promotion effort to present his top country clients. At the plush Sheraton Hotel, he put on "An Appreciation Concert" featuring writer Troy Seals, Sammi Smith, Willie Nelson, and Waylon Jennings.

Posters for the concert dotted the convention. Neil and Sam Utretsky deluged the media with invitations. A ballroom which accommodated 2,500 was jammed. It was a mass of humanity. At 10:00 p.m. the lights dimmed and Troy Seals opened the show. He sang several of his compositions, including "We Had It All." People fidgeted in their crowded environment. When the set was completed, participants rushed to the free refreshments. Some wandered out of the room only to find they could not get back in. The master of ceremonies repeatedly told the audience of deejays and fans how much the artists appreciated their help and support. This was a theme echoed throughout the convention.

Sammi Smith appeared on stage in tight black slacks and

T-shirt. She did songs popularized by Steve Goodman, Jerry Jeff
Walker, and other contemporary writers. She closed with her
award-winning rendition of "Help Me Make It Through the
Night." Another break followed.

Willie Nelson appropriately sang "Mr. Record Man." Selections from his first Atlantic album followed, then some material
from *Phases and Stages*. The response was tremendous. The
audience shouted for an encore, but time would not permit one.

After more refreshments, the master of ceremonies
approached the microphone. "The hip lip of Country Music . . .
Mr. Waylon Jennings." He opened with "Lonesome, On'ry, and
Mean." This was to be one of Waylon's better nights. "Here's a
song written by Willie what's his name." "Good Hearted
Woman" sounded great. "I wish I'd written and recorded this
song before Don Williams. . . ." That night "Amanda" was his.
Several songs from *Honky Tonk Heroes* came next. "That no-good
Billy Joe," he shouted. "I can call him that 'cause I can whip 'em."
He performed some oldies such as "The House of the Rising
Sun." He hit all of the notes. After three encores, Waylon closed
the show with "T for Texas." It was 3:00 A.M. As the crowd
thinned, people were saying, "Wow, man." One British fan
called it "The Greatest Show On Earth."[20] Media people,
perhaps more objective, thought it was a good show. It was the
highlight of the convention, much to the dismay of some Nashville entertainers. Impressing the people who play records is the
name of the game.

Crossing over is tricky business. The artist, especially in country music where fan loyalty borders on devil worship, has to make
a choice. The country music market is dedicated but small. Even
in the mid-1970s, the number of gold records earned by country
and western artists could be counted on the fingers of one hand.
This had nothing to do with the quality of the music; rather, it was
merely the quantity of the audience. A Number One country
album would sell about 400,000 copies, which is still 100,000
copies short of the magic 502,000 to get the esteemed gold disc.
Ideally, a country artist can expand into the pop or middle-of-
the-road category without losing much of his or her original
constituency. Charlie Rich, Glen Campbell, and Tammy Wynette had done this with a measure of success. Johnny Cash did
once, with the *Folsom Prison* album.

Waylon's appearance bothered some of his most ardent admirers, particularly those in the southern and western states. They

could not understand "what had happened to *our* Waylon?" Countless letters to the editor arrived at *Country Music* or *Music City News* to protest the changes. Some deejays refuse to play the album because of the cover. Probably the most vicious and outspoken commentary appeared in the *Las Vegas Panorama*; columnist Hal Blu wrote:

> Waylon Jennings show at the underground nightclub Troubador (in Los Angeles) and all Danny McPhail (former Nevada representative of Waylon's now defunct fan club) can say is "Lotsa luck Waylon" . . . seems Waylon has outgrown country . . . or so, says the high powered New York talent agency now booking him . . . Waylon's being booked into and promoted as an acid rock artist now, playing clubs like Max's in New York and later this month at an all day acid rock festival with the likes of Grateful Dead (dead is right). Danny reports being shocked and bitterly disappointed in Waylon. . . . That his filthy clothing, raunchy manner, physical dissipation and slovenly appearance shook him up so bad he couldn't believe it was really W A Y L O N Jennings . . . . Funny . . . Jennings had the entire country (and much of the pop) music world at his feet . . . but he or his manager think acid rock is more commercial, I guess . . . . Lotsa luck Waylon. Rock audiences are TWICE as fickle as any other, and even if they accept you, you'll have alienated ALL the country fans in the process . . . . Besides which, the method by which Waylon's promoters are keeping him in line is despicable, but all too familiar in the rock music industry . . . . Waylon ditch your filthy clothes, take a bath, get a shave, act like an entertainer, and come back to the country fold, where your roots are and with the people who gave you your start . . . . (Remember Ray Price, Waylon?).[21]

In response to this and other criticisms, Waylon told *Cashbox* that he thought *Honky Tonk Heroes* was really "the *countriest* thing I've done in a long time."[22] Waylon's point was well taken, but *that* cover! "Deviance is in the eye of the beholder," wrote sociologist Howard Becker.

Waylon's return to Los Angeles in August was greeted by the *Los Angeles Weekly News* with the lead "Here come the shitkickers!" The headline was misleading. Bill Yaryan, music company publicist, recited his recent conversion to country music—due to "MacArthur Park"—and his assessment of *Honky Tonk Heroes*.

> Waylon—whose career is now guided by Miles Davis' manager is the major guinea pig at the moment. And he's a good one. The title song of his current LP, "Honky Tonk Heroes," starts off slow and lazy and switches into shitkicking rock overdrive in the middle. Two worlds

joined together in perfect time. It's also the first record of his that faithfully duplicates his onstage sound without the traditional "Nashville sound" welded on. It moves, just like it did at the Palomino and at Marine World in San Francisco and in Austin and at Max's in Manhattan. Waylon Jennings is so good it hurts to see him traveling around shooting flies off horses' asses. Put your make-up kits away, trade you high heeled platform boots for dusty stompers, and give a listen to Waylon's music.[23]

The crossover road proved to be a rocky one. Scores of diehard fans were unhappy, but Reshen was "expanding the audience." In many respects Waylon Jennings and his manager were caught in a historical whirlpool that was not of their making. Once again, the bugaboo of the big city versus middle America was emerging an antagonism represented by the contrast of decadent rock 'n' roll and patriotic country and western music.

Nashville's reaction to the revitalization of rock 'n' roll by the Beatles in 1964 was originally one of indifference. The English groups seemed to provide no obvious threat to Music City. Country music wasn't depressed. Fundamentalist ravings against the "moptops" may have struck a sympathetic chord, but it was believed that the British invasion would not reach Nashville. After the "more popular than Christ" misquote, it was reported that Beatle records were burned in Nashville.[24] It appears that only Chet Atkins took the Beatles' music halfway seriously; he recorded an album of Lennon-McCartney compositions: *Chet Atkins Picks on the Beatles.* The cover provacatively showed Atkins in an ill-fitting wig; George Harrison wrote the liner notes. Atkins did encourage Waylon to cover "Norwegian Wood" on a "folk-country" album.

The advent of the "hippie scene" in San Francisco provided material for hundreds of one-liners at country and western concerts about stoned-out, unwashed, homosexual, radical, long-haired hippies. Texas, following its traditions, did not dismiss the strange goings-on in the Haight-Ashbury. Psychedelic bands began appearing in Austin and Dallas. Some bands tried their economic luck in San Francisco; only the Sir Douglas Quartet succeeded.

Ironically, the Beatles and other so-called hippie bands did not ignore the influence of Nashville. The English quartet recorded several country and western tunes, including Buck Owens's "Act Naturally." West Coast bands, notably the Buffalo Springfield and Moby Grape, did country-style songs; however, it was the Byrds who introduced "country-rock."

"Country-rock" was a natural blend of rock, three-or two-part harmonies, Dylan songs, and a steel pedal guitar, all mixed in the canyons of Hollywood, California. *Sweetheart of the Rodeo* was the first of many country-rock albums by Los Angeles–based bands. *Sweetheart* was originally recorded in Nashville amidst consider-able controversy and contained some ten-to twenty-year-old tunes along with two Dylan tracks. The critical response to the album was mixed. Barry Gifford in *Rolling Stone* wrote: "The new Byrds do not sound like Buck Owens and his Buckaroos. They aren't that good. The material they've chosen to record, or rather, the way they perform the material, is simple, relaxed and folky. It's not pretentious, it's pretty. The musicianship is excel-lent. (They had to practice before playing the Grand Old [sic] Opry)."[25] Without question, the Byrds had added another hyphen to rock and introduced a legion of longhairs to the country genre. This introduction, at the time, was not especially appreciated. Bud Scoppa, a *Rolling Stone* critic, suggested one response from the counter culturites: "The Byrds' underground following was aghast. Those staunch champions of justice whose songs had been the rallying cry of the New Left had turned their backs on their convictions to play songs for rednecks?"[26]

Music City residents were not overjoyed by this merger either. Many tales abounded on Sixteenth Avenue. Reports of orgies, drug abuse, broken equipment, and other horrors were told repeatedly. The appearance of the Byrds at the "Opry" was equally shocking to some traditionalists. Ralph Emery, the powerful all-night disc jockey at WSM, openly refused to air any songs by the Los Angeles group. Gram Parsons retaliated by writing "Drug Store Truck Driving Man," which included the line, "I'm an all night musician in a rock 'n' roll band—why he don't like me I can't understand . . . [spoken] This one's for you Ralph . . . ." Parsons, upon departing the Byrds, further out-raged Emery with his new group, The Flying Burrito Brothers. The Burritos wore Nudie costumes with marijuana plants in sequined green on white. Some of their songs like "Hippie Boy" were outlandish parodies of "Opry" sincerity. "My Uncle" was an openly antidraft song. Not even the controversial hippie country and western artist Johnny Darrell in his wilder moments would dare sing, "So I'm headin' for the nearest foreign border / Vancouver may be just my kind of town." The Burritos were given a Rolling Stone song, "Wild Horses." It was an accident—Jagger wanted Sneeky Pete to do the steel guitar—but the studio rough went into the Burrito's repertoire. It was an FM hit for the ill-fated group. When Gram later died of an overdose, murder or suicide, it was announced that "the father of country-rock was dead."

The failure of Parsons's group was a musical injustice; followers fared much better. Rocker Linda Ronstadt cracked the country and western market. Eagles, a spinoff group, reached the top of the charts. Emmylou Harris, Gram's duet partner, is now a star in her own right. The intense dislike between the two camps was temporary. As with rock-a-billy, the original culture shock would pass and both strains would never be the same again.

Trends in popular music generally last for three or four years, as one generation of teens is replaced by another. By the late 1960s the English invasion was in its death throes. The Beatles were on the verge of splitting up; the Stones had drastically changed their hard bluesy sound; and many other super groups were gone from the scene: Cream, Yardbirds, Zombies, Jerry and the Pacemakers. Acid rock no longer sold outside of California. Rock critics and fans were becoming increasingly disenchanted with the likes of Led Zeppelin and Grand Funk and a host of dreary overproduced attempts to copy *Sgt. Pepper*. Ex-rockers and folkies seemed to have followed Dylan to Nashville, but on a highly selective basis. The new converts were not ready for Buck Owens or Roy Acuff or Loretta Lynn—at least, not yet.

In 1968 only the soft-spoken Chet Atkins openly supported Hubert Humphrey for the presidency. Most of Music City Row was in the Wallace camp. Johnny Darrell was effectively stigmatized for recording an anti-Vietnam war song. Merle Haggard's "Okie from Muskogee" typified the Row's attitude toward Vietniks, pot smokers, and the strange Con III lifestyle. (Ironically, "Okie" was a Con III hit sung by Arlo Guthrie, Phil Ochs, and several rock artists. Most noncountry people thought it was a parody.)

If a detente between Nashville and Los Angeles was created, the main architect was local outcast Earl Scruggs. Scruggs, the banjo virtuoso, enjoyed a successful career in bluegrass music. Starting with Bill Monroe, he pioneered his unique three-finger pickin' style. He co-founded Flatt and Scruggs. The group enjoyed considerable popularity during the folk music revival and had several minor hit records. The theme for *Bonnie and Clyde*, "Foggy Mountain Breakdown," was the best-known bluegrass song in United States prior to "Duelin' Banjos." Earl gained more attention in "The Beverly Hillbillies." Much to the surprise of Nashvillians, Scruggs, the father of three sons, joined in the march on Washington to protest the Viet͟ ͟: War. He was Music City's only participant. With his sons, he formed a country-rockish family review. At the time, he sa͟ ͟ ͟ Music can't stand still. I've always been for progress and ͟ ͟ ͟ping up with the times."

On the road, Earl ran into the then Los Angeles-based Nitty Gritty Dirt Band. The band, having gone through numerous personnel changes, still had a strong bluegrass/folky oriented sound. Their best-remembered hit was Jerry Jeff Walker's "Mr. Bojangles." The *Uncle Charlie* album was quite popular with country rockers. The Scruggs boys like it. Randy, who was to be a sideman on *Honky Tonk Heroes,* and Gary urged their father to go and see the Nitty Gritty Dirt Band at Vanderbilt University. Earl was particularly impressed with banjoist, John McEuen. After the show, Earl complimented John on his pickin'. John "felt great." Scruggs and the Dirt Band spoke of recording together. Jimmy Ibbotson of the Dirt Band recalls: "So Earl starts spreadin' this rumor around that we were going to do this thing *{Can the Circle Be Unbroken?}* and he said, 'well, let's get Vassar Clement to he lp out because he's really good. Let's get Junior Husky . . . .' And then people like Jimmy Martin heard about us and said, 'Earl, let me help out.' Then he went to Maybelle [Carter] and said, 'This is startin' to grow.' Then he went to Merle Travis— Johnny ran into Doc Watson in Los Angeles and the next thing you know this thing is cannonballing."[27] John McEuen returned to complete working out the details in Nashville. In a matter of months, a joint venture between Los Angeles and Nashville was scheduled.

Through Earl, Wesley Rose—no stranger to popular music— heard of the session and suggested that his partner, Roy Acuff, be included. This was a surprise. Acuff was the model of country music conservativism. He came to the studio expecting to find wah-wah pedals. Listening to the out-takes of a previous session, he smiled and said, 'Ah, that's nothin' but mountain music— that's fine—I can do that." Acuff had a good time. *Can the Circle Be Unbroken* was a major hit, outselling nearly all of the country albums that year. Cries of exploitation were heard once again.

"Everyone is really uptight now that it's sold almost a million units," said one Nitty Gritty Dirt Band member. "There's a lot of people down there who would like to sell a lot more records than they do. And they are very angry that we can come down and make a country record and are able to draw on a popular market where they feel they can't. They feel it's unfair. They're doing all they can right now to slur us and to slander us. You know, Acuff talks about these long-haired boys smokin' hash and stuff . . . ." Pausing, he added, "Waylon Jennings is certainly a country musician . . . we're a lot less radical than he is. We're probably conservative in his book."

Despite all the protests, *Circle* did sell over a million copies. At the time, 1972, Waylon did not even come close to that figure. He told one interviewer, "I usually sell 100,000 to 200,000 on country charts. That's a big hit."[28] Neil Reshen was planning to change all that.

PUT ANOTHER LOG ON THE FIRE: TOMPALL AND THE GLASER BROTHERS

The major promoter and catalyst for the so-called outlaw movement was Tompall Glaser. Tompall and his brothers, Chuck and Jim, came from Spaulding, Nebraska. Like Waylon, they did not have the standard country credentials. They rose to fame by way of the televised "Arthur Godfrey Talent Scouts." They won and became regulars on his weekly television show. In the late 1950s they worked with Marty Robbins as his backup vocalists, earning $100 per show. They signed with Marty's label, and on Robbins Records they issued three singles. All but one song, "Yakety Yak," was written by Tompall. When the record label failed, the Glasers were picked up by Owen Bradley, whom Chuck describes as "The Lord and Master of Nashville." "What Owen wanted, Owen got."

Decca did not promote the Glasers as a country act. Instead, to capitalize on the "folk music" revival, the brothers were to emulate the Kingston Trio. Their first single, "Lay Down the Gun Charlie," was a carbon copy of "Tom Dooley." Only the manner of death was changed from hanging to shooting. The group was placed in the "pop/folk catalog." The experience was totally frustrating. Chuck recalls, "We could never get a record going country. They'd never work it. Something else we didn't figure out till later was that all the material that we would be taking to Owen Bradley that was country—that we would want to record—but he was always looking for pop material for us." Their biggest hit for the label was "She Loves the Love I Give Her." It was in the pop market and sold 65,000 copies.

From the beginning, the Glasers were considered outsiders. They were not southerners. They were not Baptist. Several "Opry" executives thought they were Jewish. They were checked out, and it was discovered the Glasers' religious affiliation was Catholic. One Nashville talent agent hated Catholics. He booked the Glasers, but never came to see the group except when they played the "Opry".

In 1962 the brothers set up their own publishing company. This was unheard of. Most publishing in Nashville was firmly controlled by Jim Denny's Cedarwood Company, Acuff-Rose and Hill-Range.

The Glasers' problems with Decca continued. "He'd never let me use steel until the last two years I recorded there," Tompall told an interviewer. "We were pop in those days because they already had country locked into the three chord change."[29] In 1965 the Glasers signed with Jack "The Cowboy" Clement.

Clement had a reputation as a "badass." He had moved to Nashville from Sun Records, where he produced some of John Cash's biggest hits, like "Ballad of a Teenage Queen." He joined RCA as a staff producer until caught with an open bottle of Scotch at a recording session. RCA, given his string of hits, did not dismiss him entirely. He occasionally produced for the straitlaced Atkins.

Clement opened his own studio in 1965, in violation of Nashville norms. Nearly all of the major labels—CBS, Decca, Dot, and RCA—had stipulations in their artists' contracts that a performer must use their recording facilities. Engineers must be company staff people, the unions insisted. For the engineers and the labels, it was a very secure and comfortable arrangement.

Clement began Nashville's first independent studio. Recording the Glasers, he took their material to MGM. For the label, the brothers cut a series of minor hits such as "California Girl" and "Gone Girl." Their major source of income during the 1960s was not from recording but through the publishing company. John Hartford's "Gentle on My Mind" was their song. Since its composition, nearly 250 artists have recorded it. One cigarette company offered the Glasers nearly a quarter of a million dollars to use it in a television spot. They turned down the offer. As the years passed, Tompall was becoming increasingly disillusioned. But at least he was not part of the "Dear Artist" Victor crowd. He knew Bare, Nelson, and Jennings but had little to do with their careers. The Glasers' contact with Chet Atkins was primarily in representing John Hartford.

The Glasers' original contact with Waylon took place in Arizona. Their first recollection of him, like that of many other artists, was as a disc jockey in Phoenix. They pitched some records to him. "Lover's Farewell" especially impressed him. Chuck Glaser claims, "Waylon got his style from Tompall and the Glaser Brothers. His original style. The one he started with. Waylon got a hold of some of those records and dug them. They had a sort of calypso type beat to them and would copy the rhythms of those songs in things he was doing."[30] Whether Chuck is correct in this assessment is hard to tell. Waylon's early style did come from the Tex-Mex influence of the Southwest. The Glasers as Marty Robbins' backup vocal group in the early 1960s were equally affected by the western flavor. The trio at that time had some of the same identity crisis that Waylon had experienced. Herb Alpert was packaging Waylon as a folk artist just as Owen Bradley was doing with the Glasers.

In the early 1970s the Glasers opened their own booking agency and went into independent production. A studio was built on Nineteenth Avenue, two blocks away from Music City Row. Jim Glaser described the operation as "a complete complex to help artists who might otherwise be victimized." Tompall's rationale was simple: "Well, them fuckers deal with me like a company. Some guy standing there and looking at me like I was a company and I have my New York lawyers to whittle them down. I just tore the contracts up into little bitty pieces . . . made me feel good."[31] In creating Glaser Productions, Tompall established the organizational base—"Hillbilly Central"—for the outlaws.

The history of Waylon's actual collaboration with Tompall is difficult to trace. Numerous stories exist as to what actually happened. The current strained relations between the two only make efforts to trace the chronology more difficult. Smith and Captain Midnite recall that Tompall and Waylon originally did not like each other. An encounter at Burger Boy's in Nashville brought them together. Hazel Smith told a writer, "They were playing pinball one night, and they were discussing how to record

TOMPALL   JIM   CHUCK

TOMPALL & THE GLASER BROTHERS

PHOTO CREDIT: JACKI SALLOW/1981

"The original outlaws."

a certain song. It was, like 10:00 P.M. and on the spur of the moment, they quit playing pinball, got pickers in, had them there by midnight and Waylon started recording. Tompall helped him produce that album, I believe, *Honky Tonk Heroes*."[32] Other accounts have Tompall encouraging Waylon to produce "Loving Her Was Easier" for RCA, but this is wrong. Waylon's version of the song was cut December 7, 1970, in Hollywood. Tompall told *Melody Maker* what did happen. "I asked him to come up— produce 'Loving Her Was Easier' from our *Greatest Hits From Two Decades* album, and he co-produced with me. He'd never [sic] produced a record before."[33]

Tompall's assertion that "Lovin' Her" was to be Waylon's first attempt at producing was incorrect. During his days at J.D.'s, he had worked with the downstairs band, Phil and the Frantics, on "I Must Run," a Beatles-type rocker. He also produced Buddy Long's "More Around" and "Louisiana" at Audio Recorders. On August 11, 1967, he took Gene, Ray, and Wes Lyle, then part of the Waylors, and did five "folkie" songs. Ironically, the first song he produced with the Lyles was "Lay Down the Gun Charlie," which appeared on the Glaser's first "folk revival" album with Decca. For the Twin Town label, Waylon cut Billy Cole, now a Des Moines deejay. Cole sang "You'll Drive Me Back into Her Arms Again" backed by "Denver." At Tommy Jennings's request, Waylon did Lawrence Reynolds's "Life Goes On." Waylon, of course, collaborated with Chet Atkins on Jessi Colter's first RCA album, *A Country Star Is Born*. In other words, Waylon was not a total stranger to the world "behind the glass."

Tompall did help Waylon with several songs on *Honky Tonk Heroes*. They were recorded on February 19, 20, and 21, 1973, and included "Ride Me Down Easy," "Ain't No God in Mexico," "Old Five and Dimers (Like Me)," and the title song. Presumably, Tompall was also involved in the Ian Tyson composition of "Summer Wages," which has not been released.[34]

The success of *Honky Tonk Heroes* and Glaser's invitation to "hang around" the Nineteenth Avenue headquarters affected Waylon. He found the scene much more to his liking. It was informal and possessed few, if any, of the formal trappings of RCA Victor. Tompall urged him to use the upstairs studio, and Waylon found the idea appealing. Technically, the board was above average; Tompall bragged that it had the lowest noise level in town. In mid-October, Waylon, the Waylors, and Willie Nelson gathered at Glasers' to record several of Shotgun Willie's songs. "Pick Up The Tempo," "Walkin'," "It's Not Supposed To Be That Way" were cut on Ocober 16, 17, and 18, 1973. Waylon also recorded "Mona," written by Jessi Colter.

RCA was not very happy about the change in recording sites. However, Waylon's new contract called for him to deliver finished masters of his songs. RCA could no longer hold his production company to requirement that "when within 200 miles distance of a Victor studio the artist must use that studio." Or so it appeared.

While Waylon was recording, Tompall was attacking The System. He told a British journalist, "I'm just sick of the whole damn prostituted mess and I'm tired of being quiet about it. People should know what goes on in Nashville. If nobody else'll say it, I will . . . believe you me, if Nashville doesn't re-think its ideas in the near future, it's going to be too late. It'll cease to exist as Music City USA."[35] A prominent songwriter in Nashville retorted, "Tompall talks too much." Such statements were viewed as treasonous and heretical. On the surface, the Row is a close knit community of "just plain folks." Nobody is supposed to badmouth colleagues or competitors—especially not to outside journalists. One important music publisher lectured me for over an hour, insisting that "nothing, but nothing was wrong in Nashville."

What Tompall was telling the press was not without truth. Privately, a number of Music City people were worried. Austin was increasingly being touted as the "alternative Nashville." Chet Flippo's article in the December 1972 issue of *Rolling Stone* created a stir. The mild-mannered contributing editor argued, "Tammy and Loretta and Dolly and Merle and Buck and Charley are still undisputed rulers, but there are indications that things will never again be so secure for them."[36] Flippo, then a resident of Austin, went on to document the forces working against Music City Row. He pointed to country-rock and progressive country as the elements undermining the supremacy of Nashville. Flippo received a considerable amount of hate mail with Tennessee postmarks. His controversial analysis dealt primarily with the schisms within the country field. However, another assault, perhaps more significant, was being mounted in Los Angeles. The new invaders were neatly packaged, middle-of-the-road artists like the petite Olivia Newton-John and the seemingly innocent John Denver. They were beginning to zero in on the country market. Within a year they would bring the entire issue into the pages of the *New York Times* and even *Music City News*. Several people indicated that Flippo's story was inspired by the outlaws. But they had little to do with Chet's article. Waylon rarely makes criticisms to journalists. Even Norman Petty, whom Waylon blames for Buddy Holly's death, was spared in the *Stone*: "The only reason Buddy went on that tour was because he was broke—flat broke. He didn't want to go but he had to make some money. I ain't sayin' the person's name that was the reason he was broke."[37] On the record, he has not put down Lucky Moeller, Chet Atkins, or most of the RCA producers, at least most of the time.

12

THIS TIME

Nearly all of *This Time* was recorded in the Glasers' studio. The title song would be Waylon's first top-ranked *Billboard* country single. February 8, 1974, found him back in the RCA studios minus the Waylors. He recorded "Ramblin' Man" and several other songs. Ray Pennington, the composer, co-produced. In July, Waylon returned to Glasers' studio to finish work on a new album. RCA had accepted the material for *This Time* that had not been cut in their studios, but there was still some doubts about using another recording facility. Waylon checked with Reshen. Neil told him, "Do what you want." *Ramblin' Man* was finished on Nineteenth Avenue, South.

The masters were taken to RCA. The company refused the master tape, arguing that the electrical technicians would balk. The National Academy of Recording Arts and Sciences is a very powerful union. RCA claimed that if *Ramblin' Man* were released, NARAS could shut down the record company as well as NBC radio and television. Reshen petitioned Ken Lansey, president of RCA. Neil knew Lansey from previous dealings. Lansey urged Reshen to talk directly with the union. Neil did reach a tentative agreement with the labor organization.

Jerry Bradley once again raised the question of the RCA studio. He argued that the unions wanted to protect their people. According to their contract, members receive a percentage of every album sold. Neil told RCA that this was their problem, not

Waylon's, and that they should rectify it with NARAS. Fortunately for Waylon, RCA and NARAS were then in negotiations so a settlement was made possible. (In two years, RCA would close its Nashville studio operation.) Waylon was now free to record at Glasers'.

Waylon received more good news when a Phoenix jury returned a ruling in his favor, clearing him of any responsibility in the bridge accident that resulted in the death of Chuck Allen. Stew "Allen" Punsky's claim was not upheld.[1]

Waylon's problems with the law were not yet over. A Tucson promoter, Moshen Farhand, had won a damage suit against him; Waylon allegedly had failed to appear for a scheduled concert. Farhang received a default judgment of $3,192.50 in real damages and $10,000 in punitive damages. In July 1973, Waylon was ordered to pay the amount. The singer appealed. A year later, Superior Court Commissioner Lawrence K. Bret Harte denied the motion and ordered that the judgment be paid with an annual interest rate of 6 percent.[2]

In June, just as "This Time" was climbing to the Number One country and western chart position, Waylon signed with a new booking agency, Nova Productions. Nova was based in Nashville and operated by Chuck Glaser. Chuck is unlike his brother, Tompall; he is soft-spoken with a sly twinkle in his eye. He is, however, an outsider in the Glaser tradition. He had managed John Hartford, Nashville's first hippie writer. He booked the irrepressible Jerry Lee Lewis, whose escapades have easily filled the pages of a book. He introduced Kinky Friedman and the Texas Jewboys into the Music City scene. His agency also booked Ray Charles, David Allen Coe, musical satirist Gamble Rogers, and now Waylon Jennings. Chuck's philosophy was quite simple—to sell performers to anyone who wanted them. "They are entertainers," he said, "even though I sell a lot of country dates I don't sell dates as country performers." Because of this practice, many traditional talent buyers did not care to deal with Glaser. "The old line promoters don't want to deal with me for several reasons . . . . I'm dealing with what they call the "outlaws" . . . . I'm selling them not at their prices but at my prices or my artists' prices."

Veteran concert promoters shrugged off Nova. A major criticism was that Glaser's artists were "no shows." "How do I know that he is going to be there?" they asked. Jerry Lee Lewis, especially, has suffered a reputation of avoiding concert appearances or getting there in no shape to perform. Waylon had acquired a similar reputation, but his concerts had been canceled primarily because of illness or fatigue. Most of the missed dates had been made up.

In a matter of months, Glaser doubled Waylon's price to $3,500. He was working halls that sat 3,000 paying customers. Waylon stipulated that he would work only in certain types of clubs. The Crab Orchards were out. He refused to do dances. "Waylon does a show which means," explains Chuck, "it is an hour or an hour and 15 minutes, but he is not going in to play for 45 minutes of dancing and 15 minutes off and 45 minutes of dancing and 15 minutes off again all night long . . . when a club owner calls you and says I want Waylon Jennings to work from nine to two, then immediately I tell them that they have the wrong guy."[3]

Glaser's strategy was to move an artist "from honky-tonks to showrooms." The battle plan worked. Waylon was earning $50,000 to $60,000 a month from his concert dates. This was a universe away from the Moeller days.

In 1975, for the third successive year, Waylon returned to Willie Nelson's Fourth of July picnic. This year the event was moved from Dripping Springs to the Texas World Speedway at College Station. Willie anticipated 50,000 people. Only half that number showed up. The atmosphere this time was more in the Woodstock tradition than that of Dripping Springs. Leon Russell with the ever-present Lone Star beer can in hand introduced the performers. The crowd frequently became restless because of delays caused by a "Midnight Special" camera crew. Waylon's set went well, but many journalists and fans complained that the entire affair wasn't "country."[4]

On September 18, Waylon had a second Number One country hit in *Billboard*. "Ramblin' Man" followed "This Time" to the top spot. It had taken Waylon ten years with RCA Victor to accomplish that feat. It was only when he wrestled away production control that he succeeded.

Waylon returned to Texas, flying to Dallas. At the Western Palace he was to do his first "live" album. He was scheduled the next day for the Opry House in Austin. An RCA recording crew would tape both shows. The results were to appear as a two-record set for release in late 1975. Only the material from the Western Palace would see the inside of the record store. Most of the 33 selections recorded in Austin are still in the RCA vaults.

The success of "This Time" and "Ramblin' Man" prompted the members of the CMA to nominate Waylon for the award as Male Vocalist of 1974. The other four nominees were Merle Haggard, Ronnie Milsap, Carl Smith, and Charlie Rich. The eighth annual CMA show was scheduled for October 14 at the "Grand Ole Opry." This was to be the last such ceremony staged at the venerated Ryman Auditorium. John R. Cash was the host. Listed to perform were some of the superstars of Nashville. Waylon was to sing "Ramblin' Man." The day of the awards, Waylon, Tompall, and the ever-present Midnite conferred with executive producer Joe Cates. Cates explained to Waylon that because of time limitations each artist would be given only two minutes to do a song. This meant "Ramblin' Man" would be cut almost in half. Recollections of the TV shows with Joey Bishop and Dean Martin flashed. He was not going to do the song or the show.

Midnite ran into Tompall and Waylon in the hall. "Hey Chief, you got a dressing room down here?"

"I had a dressing room. Let's get the hell out of here!"

"It sure don't take you long to do a TV show does it," mused the Captain.

John R. attempted to intervene, offering to give Waylon some of his time. He refused the offer.

At 9:00 P.M. Milton DeLugg's orchestra played the fanfare. A roster of artists was read by the network announcer. Waylon's name was deleted. The Man in Black opened the show. Lynn Anderson presented the candidates for Male Vocalist of the Year. She nearly spit out "Waylon Jennings." Ronnie Milsap won. A strange thing happened that night. Australian pop singer, Olivia Newton-John was named Female Vocalist of the Year. Cash closed the show saying, "It's been a grand night for the country music awards." Few in the audience thought so. Waylon's refusal to play caused a stir; reporters called. Waylon explained his actions to *Record World*:

> I guess it looks like I'm a troublemaker, but really I want to get along with people and have everything run smooth . . . . I left because I thought it would make for a better show. I thought they expressed an attitude that did not show respect for me as an individual or for country music. I felt I had to take a stand. I really hated to leave and do all that but I couldn't let them walk over me . . . They only care for the money and they don't really care for the music.[5]

Waylon told other writers, "Yeah, 60 million people lookin' there and I was at home."[6] Waylon and friends felt they were right.

This Time, 1975. Courtesy of RCA.

Normally, Waylon's refusal would have dominated Music City's Tuesday-morning quarterbacking. Telephone lines buzzed. But conversations focused on Olivia Newton-John. How did she get the award? By her own admission, "I like country music, but I don't know much about it." Many country artists were unhappy. At first, Music City Row attempted to maintain the "one-big-happy-family" facade. On the record, Newton-John's award was shrugged off. Privately, a number of charges and countercharges circulated. One artist claimed, "The CMA does not represent us. There are no entertainers on their board."[7] This was true. The sixteen-member board was composed solely of publishers and record company people.

One insider said, "Out of 3,500 voting CMA members, 1,900 or so are disc jockeys. Most of 'em don't come out of country music. They don't like George Jones or any of the greats. They just go for likes of Olivia or John Denver. That *they can understand*, and they are in a majority."[8] His point was well taken, and it was echoed in *Billboard*. Radio stations broadcasting country sounds had experienced a phenomenal ten-year growth. They were no longer tied to one geographical area or market. In 1972, a New York City radio station, WHN, went full time to country and western. Austin had a "progressive country" station. In major markets outlets, like these competed for listeners with middle-of-the-road and rock stations. The formats were geared toward the more "acceptable" products of Nashville *and* Los Angeles. Bluegrass and honky-tonk music was *too* country for many of these stations.

In the late 1960s broadcasters were no longer interested in attracting an older, rurally based audience. CBS television dropped "The Beverly Hillbillies," "Green Acres," "Petticoat Junction," and the highly rated "Hee Haw" because the "demographics weren't right." Radio programmers were very much aware of this trend and aimed for people in the eighteen to thirty-five category.

Many urban disc jockeys had backgrounds in other formats and musical genres. They did not appreciate ole-timey or traditional music. They often chose as "golden oldies" Earl Scruggs, "Foggy Mountain Breakdown," or "Duelin' Banjos." Their tastes did run to John Denver and Newton-John. These jocks were a contributing factor in the success of "countripolitan" artists exhibiting a pop or rock influence. They would help artists like Linda Ronstadt, John Denver, and Kenny Rogers break into country and western charts.

In the midst of the CMA controversy, Waylon wheeled his yellow-and-white Cadillac to suburban Hendersonville, the home of the House of Cash. This was to be the first professional collaboration with John R. since the March 15, 1970, appearance on the network Cash program. On the show, Waylon sang "Only Daddy That'll Walk the Line," "Brown Eyed Handsom Man," and a duet with John, "Waylon's Back in Town." The last song was originally recorded as "John's Back in Town." During the taping, June Carter Cash kept a close watch on Waylon. She and some of the Cash people blamed Waylon for John R.'s former drug problem. Waylon had been on the yellow-and-green Phoenix Flashes during their apartment-sharing days, but John R. had gotten the pill habit long before Jennings came into the picture. At best, Waylon was an accessory after the fact.

None of the Waylors were excited about recording at the House of Cash. Rumors about dress codes and abstinence abounded. There were no dress codes, but drinking and "smoking" were prohibited.

Cash, whose recording career at the time was not going well, recruited his old Sun producer, Jack Clement, to cut four songs. The Waylors and "the Chief" would do the instrumentals with the Tennessee Three. The trio was less than pleased with the arrangement. Carl Perkins mused to a *Washington Post* writer that John was asking for trouble. "He's started hanging around with Waylon Jennings. That Waylon, he'll take a doorknob down if he thought it would taste good."[9]

The session began with the Tennessee Three and Waylon working out a guitar lead. The Waylors huddled around the drum gazebo, just watching. Cash wanted to do four songs: "So Doggone Lonesome," "My Ship Will Sail," "No Earthly Good," and "Moses Rankin." The bass player Duke Goff and Richie were uncomfortable. June Carter made them nervous. "June just sat there and stared," recalled one participant.[10] They did only one three-hour session and left. At the end, Cash had four tracks on tape; they needed work but were "pretty good."

Three weeks after the CMA television extravaganza, some artists went public with their complaints. Gathering at the palatial estate of Tammy Wynette, approximately fifty performers founded the Association of Country Entertainers (ACE)."[11] Bill Anderson was chosen chair and spokesman for the group. A long statement was issued on November 14, 1974. In essence, ACE declared that "country music awards should be limited to those persons who *consider* themselves as country music artists, and whose *primary* endeavors are to perform on records that will be considered in the various country music charts." This, despite the disclaimers, was addressed to the intruders from Los Angeles. Waylon, with his now-famous "I can't go pop with a mouthful of fire crackers" seemed to be exempt from ACE criticism. One person confided, "that damn meeting at the ACE things was just ridiculous but it was inspired by Waylon's actions." But the little girl from Australia was seen as more of a villian than the "outlaw" from Texas.

Producers, songwriters, and music publishers were not sympathetic. Frank Jones at Capitol remarked, "I feel it's a communications gap."[12] Harlan Howard said, "I'll tell ya what, the world is coming to country music. Now what's wrong with that?"[13] "I think it is a bunch of crap," suggested a well-known producer with a string of pop hits under his belt. "I think the people that are involved should cut better records . . . . Everything has to progress. If it doesn't, then it's dying . . . . Everybody bitches and moans and whines about Olivia Newton-John or Denver and that's a self-defeating thing, because all they are doing is broadening the horizon of country music." Another executive said, "They named it wrong. It should have been called the 'Under Fifty Thousand Record Sales Club.'"[14]

Roy Acuff, Billy Walker, Porter Wagoner, Conway Twitty, and others obviously did not agree with these criticisms, but they were all suffering from the changes taking place. Johnny Paycheck, who in several years' time would join the outlaws, told the *New York Times*: "We don't want somebody out of another field coming in and taking away what we've worked so hard for all year."[15]

The resentment that spilled forth after the CMA affair was justified. The Acuffs, Jones, and Monroes had logged millions of highway miles. They had paid their dues in hundreds of Crab Orchards and endured the tyrannies of Nashville producers. Now that doors to the lucrative urban markets were beginning to open, they wanted a piece of the action. Few of them would be able to capitalize on these new trends. Bill Monroe, originally shocked by long-haired hippie pot smokers, learned to accept his new fans.[16] Others were either unwilling or were unable to reach the new market. Ernest Tubb, no matter how talented, could not go beyond the confines of the "nostalgic" Grand Ole Opry. In Toledo he tried to sing a Kristofferson song; it was a disaster.

The singers and writers who were charged with "not being

country" were the very ones about to crossover. Waylon said, "I'd be a babbling musical idiot if I didn't change." Willie went off to Texas to sing the same songs that bombed in Nashville. It was the audience that changed, not the artists.

The ACE outburst was short-lived. Two of their members, Wagoner and Wynette, were elected to the CMA board. Bill Anderson cooled out the situation. "It boiled down to a lack of understanding," said Anderson. "In the future, we can all work together and that's the important thing."[17] Willie Nelson, when asked how he and Waylon fit into the debate, replied, "We don't fit in anywhere."

Willie did not know of a Nashville television appearance by Waylon. On the program, Jennings criticized the CMA, the awards show, and repeated his opinion of the "Opry." *Billboard* dismissed the comments, labeling him a "cosmic cowboy" who features "his own style of country music."

Although the debate died down, the objective situation had not changed. Structural conditions were such that only the strong would survive. The country market had fragmented. A new breed of disc jockey was putting together playlists. Producers, publishers, and writers, who received a percentage of every record sold and aired, were all too happy to service an expanded market at the cost of mandolins and nasal twangs.

Even in Nashville, ACE artists were having their difficulties. WSM, for years the dominant country station, was being successfully challenged by WKDA. The station program director, Charlie Potter, commented, "We've raised quite a fuss down here." According to Potter, he was receiving considerable opposition from the CMA. The organization was protesting the lack of traditional music on the tightly formated station. In a press release WKDA replied:

> The CMA has also become top heavy in it monopolistic control of the music and has gone out of its way to stiffle [sic] and suffocate the work of new innovative artists that do not conform to the Nashville sound and this is even true of many of your traditional and basic country artists. People will eat just so much schlock and the CMA has been feeding us with it for such a long time. Of course, they are trying to cover up this whole Progressive Country Movement. They have a lot to lose—mostly money—but their entertainment monopoly is being disfused [sic] and its [sic] happening right at their home base in Nashville and in other disparate places like Austin, San Francisco . . . and Los Angeles. So the question arises: Which side of

the fence are we going to be standing on? The answer: The Progressive Country side—that's where.

ACE, in a widely publicized two-year campaign, rallied against this attitude. Despite their protestations, most country stations did give more airplay to country rock and the progressives.[18]

Adding to Nashville's difficulties was its press coverage. Music City has enjoyed for years a form of sweetheart arrangement with the print medium. Faron Young's *Music City News* was more of a public relations device than a newspaper. Articles about performers were nearly always full of praise. Some of the contributors were local publicity people. Lesser known country publications frequently had fan club members writing articles about their heroes. None of these essays were designed to offend the subject.

The national media was not much better. The news magazines *Time* and *Newsweek* would send reporters to Nashville for a quick three-to-four-day stay. Their tour usually included a trip to the "Opry," the Country Music Hall of Fame, a recording session, and finally lunch with Chet Atkins. What they came away with was a rustic, unrealistic picture of the country music industry.

With the advent of the progressive sound, some rock journalists began to explore the world of country and western. Given their lifestyles and backgrounds (many were ex-*Rolling Stone* contributors), they viewed the outlaw and Austin scenes as the liberation of the South. They were not shocked by long hair, dope smoking, or any of the other excesses attributed to these renegades.

The advocates of "new journalism" possessed attitudes that their predecessors had not. They were not in awe of Nashville's superstars, nor where they totally ignorant of the ways of the music industry. In some instances, their knowledge prompted uncomfortable questions. How come road bands are not used in studios? Rock groups do it all the time. Why do Nashville producers have all that power? Many rock musicians produce themselves. These not-so-subtle comparisons allied many urban writers with the progressives. From journalists, Waylon, Willie, and Tompall received further exposure and in some cases psychological support.

Nashvillians claimed that these outsiders were biased. In some cases, the charge was valid. Contributors to *Rolling Stone* and sometimes *Country Music* magazine were as intolerant of the traditional country sound as the old-timers were of the progressives. Opryland was described as a Tennessee branch of Dis-neyworld. Gospel music, as *Country Music* illustrated, was writ-ten about with irreverence.[19] Despite the bias of the newcomers, most Music City people were fairly open and accessible to the press. The questions were getting touchier to answer, in some cases. The days of easy questions like "what's your new album?" were slowly disappearing.

Wittingly, many new converts to country music promoted the outlaw image. A few were all too eager to present the progres-sives as liberators or revolutionaries fighting an old and corrupt system. The outlaw press handouts were, in some instances, treated less critically than usual. It was easy, too easy, to believe that the good guys wore the black hats and Indian jewelry while the bad guys wore the white leisure suits and ran the commerce of Music City. A Los Angeles *Free Press* writer commented, "All good liberal and (i.e.) outer culture unestablishment sorts grew up thinking or learned to think that they should hate the south, Red Necks and, of course, their music, country music."[20] This was a gross overstatement, but it did make good copy. Outlaws were accepted in the large metropolitan markets. "Redneck shitkickers" were rejected as vestiges of a racist Confederacy. Somehow, the realities of the situation got lost in the gallons of ink devoted to the CMA controversy.

In the aftermath of the ACE controversy, Waylon returned in 1974 and 1975 to the West Coast. He appeared at San Francis-co's Boarding House, a rock club. He sold out three shows. A local critic, Joel Selvin, wrote, "The audiences—supposedly sophisticated urbanites—were howling and shrieking like the Louisiana Hayride. No small wonder, either because Waylon Jennings not only gave—pound for pound—as fine a musical performance as has appeared at the Boarding House all year, but clearly demonstrated an almost overwhelming personal magne-tism on the crowd." Waylon did not miss the opportunity to snipe at Nashville. Opening a set, he asked the audience, "How many of you were at Kezar Stadium?" Fans recalling his appearance with the Grateful Dead applauded. "That changed a lot of things right there." He said, *"Now we don't have to do nothing in Nash-ville."* Waylon characteristically mumbled something like, "I didn't mean that" or "I just made that up." In print Selvin remarked, "He seems determined to break loose."[21]

The next night Waylon was in Los Angeles at the Santa Monica Civic Auditorium, the site of his poor performance some years

Promo photo for Don Bowman's syndicated radio show, 1974.

back. He opened for country-rockers Commander Cody and His Lost Planet Airmen. Along with the Byrds and the Flying Burrito Brothers, Cody did much to popularize the country sound with rock fans. Waylon surprised the Los Angeles rockers. Running through his repertoire of current album cuts—"Ramblin' Man," "Midnight Rider," and "Amanda"—he captivated the audience. Bob Kirsch in *Billboard* noted, "Watching the artist get the same frenzied response from the rock crowd as he does from the country ones without changing his own standards, one gets the distinct impression that this is indeed one of the across-the-board superstars of the future."[22]

After the show, Waylon and Johnna discussed the "perks" Commander Cody had received. The Commander had a rider with his contract that stated that the concert promoter must provide certain foods, beverages, and other comforts. Country acts never got these. "We almost had to beg to get a bottle of beer." Upon their return to Nashville, Johnna and Chuck Glaser would add a similar rider to Waylon's Nova contracts.

During his Los Angeles stay, Waylon was persuaded to appear on the syndicated *Dinah Shore Show*. Waylon was not anxious to do it. He had been burned by television hosts, even friends, in the past, and memories of CMA were fresh. Record companies at the time viewed talk-show hosts Merv, Mike, Dinah, and Johnny as prime vehicles for artist exposure. The artist would appear on these shows for union scale, $320. They would usually sing one or two songs from their current single or album, with the host, and then depart. Theoretically, there were tens of millions watching these shows.

Waylon was booked to appear with Doc Severenson of the "Tonight Show" and Richardo Montalban. Arriving at the studio, Waylon was very uptight; he wanted to get in and out quickly. Talk shows are a game. Johnna Yursic: "They care about getting what they need on tape and the hell with everything else. They don't give a shit whether its complimentary to you or detrimental or whatever. They don't care. They're flesh peddlers, man. And the TV market is worse—it's terrible." Waylon, Johnna, and Chuck Glaser devised a plan. Waylon would come on second, not last, as had occurred with the "Joey Bishop Show." Chuck Glaser would be in the control booth to monitor taping. All of these precautions would give him some control. He was more comfortable. Waylon didn't like the idea of make-up. Johnna talked him into it, explaining that it was necessary for color television.

Reluctantly he went to the make-up room. He sat in the chair for an hour and fifteen minutes. "He looked like a guy sitting crouched behind a bush waitin' for the stagecoach to come by. He was uncomfortable and fidgety . . . ." He was made more nervous by the overtly effeminate make-up man. Johnna describes what happened. "This little short heavy set guy . . . had kind of feminine movements . . . he started putting make-up on Waylon. Waylon had a cigarette in his hand pretty uncomfortable and he put the cigarette up to his mouth and burned this guy's hand. Waylon felt bad about it. He said, 'Hey hoss, I'm sorry.' The make-up man leaned over to Waylon, just real close in his face and said, 'Man, don't feel sorry, I kind of dug it.' Waylon turned to me—his head snapped around and he looked like that coyote as he goes off the edge of a cliff and looks back over his shoulder just where he drops into the canyon." Johnna broke up and left the room. Waylon came out of the room mumbling, "Goddamn it . . ."[23]

Waylon appeared on the set and sang Jack Clements's "Cowboys Sing the Blues." Dinah greeted him with the comment, "Waylon, that's a great song. You didn't write that?"

"No. Jack Clement wrote that . . . ."

"And he is a real cowboy . . . ."

"No, only when he is drunk . . . ," Waylon grinned.

Dinah smiled and politely changed the subject. "Thats funny. I want to talk to you more about country and western, rock and pop because . . . ." She maneuvered into an introduction for Montalban. The Latin actor dominated the conversation while Waylon nervously chain smoked his Winstons.

Again changing guests and subjects, Ms. Shore requested another song from Waylon. As he finished "Amanda," the hostess asked, "Waylon, is that a country song? What do you call that."

"What a stupid question," thought Johnna.

WJ: I think it's a country song, it is now—I just did it. I think most anybody can relate to that song because I think that is what most people are trying to say anyway, in their life. They're tired of all the hard times, you know.

DS: You have had a running battle with Nashville over the country sound and I didn't quite understand it when they were telling me about it. Explain to me why you are at odds with them about the sound.

WJ: I think Nashville is afraid of change. I think they think that maybe the change and to try and bring something new to the music and throw off some of the shackles is going to destroy the old country, what they call the true country . . . they can't do that. I've always wanted to expand it, I think we have just as much right to use any instrument in our music as anybody else because it is an art, really. It's a soul music and it's in the soul of the singer. Ancient folksingers used the most modern instruments they could and Jimmie Rogers, one of the original country singers used Dixieland all the time, you know. He's a hillbilly [meaning Doc Severenson].

DOC: Oh, I don't know how you can tell, Waylon.

WJ: You look like a psychedelic cowboy singer.

DOC: There seems to be a certain kind of misunderstanding. I would like to see less suspicion between the different areas of musicians. Like I know Waylon, Ray Price, and Charlie Pride and a lot of those guys and on the other hand I know my horn-blowin' friends that play in the rock bands and there seems to be a divide there and I mean, why can't they just accept each other for what they are and not worry about it.

WJ: I think that is comin' around.

DS: The crossover, you mean?

WJ: Yea, like the Memphis Horns, I'm going to work with them some.

DOC: I don't like them.

WJ: Danny Davis, he listened to one of my records one time and he sent it back.

DOC: That's what I mean. Underneath it all, we are people and we all are essentially trying to say something.

DS: Well, I think it's all to soul. I mean if you feel it, I don't care for soul music or country music or blues music, there are certain people who will read a melody and not even know what they are saying in it.

RM: Isn't it wrong for everything, don't you think that the place that is the purest has the right to preserve the tradition of that and then somebody comes and innovates that and this thing flourishes but you cannot forget the purest because then I am afraid that without tradition the very essence could disappear.

WJ: Really, I love the music of Roy Acuff. That's the roots of our country music.

DS: That's for sure. Roy Acuff and all the boys who really started with the Opry but then it developed and you realized that Johnny Cash, who was pure country moved over into the pop field and is accepted now.

WJ: He didn't move. I think *they* moved.

DS: Ok. Now for instance, Glen Campbell is someone who has bridged the gap. I think, to a large degree, Loretta Lynn, Lynn Anderson—they are all people who are beginning to be accepted by the pop world and for instance, Ray Charles singing country music is the essence of soul, it's what the lyrics are trying to say. Isn't that what you mean?

WJ: He did as much for country music, Ray Charles did because he did it great. He did it his way. Country music comes from the Black Man's Blues and it's the same man singing the same song about the same good times and bad times and a woman he can't hang on to. I think people are reaching for that because it's real. I think they're reachin' back and finding simplicity.

DS: It's basics. Go back to basics.

DOC: That's true with every artist and that's simplicity. The greatest art is always simple.

Then the nonsense began. Dinah brought out "folk" instruments like a comb, a set of spoons, and a kazoo.

DS: We have some little instruments there that we thought some of us could perform on to prove your point.

WJ: I ain't never played one.

DOC: First of all, let's see if it is authentic.

WJ: One of the very best.

DS: Grab that tissue paper and comb.

WJ: No, I'd rather have a pair of spoons. Because that's where I do my business.

DOC: Waylon, Waylon you got the wrong end, man.

DS: All right.

WJ: We've got them in Nashville.

DOC: Hey, right in tune.

DS: OK country boys, let's go.

DOC: Well, I think what Waylon was just trying to say that even with a kazoo country is country and jazz is jazz—so let's let the country lead on.

DS: All right. Lead off with a little country.

DOC: Give us a Waylon Jennings . . . .

Waylon's next television spot was with Merv Griffin. He got the unenviable task of following Zsa Zsa Gabor, a limited actress who specializes in rich husbands and talk shows.

MG: . . . His current hit single is "Ramblin' Man." We're delighted to welcome RCA Victor record star—Waylon Jennings. He gets more standing ovations wherever he performs. So the pressure is on folks. He has a Grammy, he has a long list of million selling record hits behind him and nothing but more success ahead. Here's Waylon Jennings . . . . Waylon sings "Cowboys Sing the Blues."

MG: That's great. Waylon Jennings! We're going to put you right over there.

WJ: All right.

MG: Right next to the "pink lady."

WJ: Like this better than Littlefield.

MG: Than who?

WJ: Littlefield.

ZG: Where's Littlefield?

WJ: That's in the suburbs of the cotton patch in West Texas.

ZG: Cotton Patch? Do you know where that is? It's in Texas, I guess.

MG: Where they raise cotton?

WJ: Yeah, and I picked a whole lot of it. You know I picked cotton?

ZG: Yes, of course I do and I know Texas very well too.

WJ: You do?

ZG: Yes, I do.

WJ: Well, I can't help it because I'm from there. Can't hold it against me.

ZG: I wouldn't hold it against you.

WJ: I bet I'm the only Texan you ever did see.

ZG: Nothing is wrong with Texas.

WJ: No, there's a lot of right about Texas. I was hungry all the time there, really.

ZG: Were you?

WJ: Really. I had a hard time in Texas.

MG: Good statement. You are more close to the rock artists than other country artists. You work with the Grateful Dead—there's really a mixture for those audiences isn't there?

WJ: Yeah, I have a lot of friends in rock 'n' roll music and things but actually country music and rock 'n' roll music basically come from the same things. From the black man's blues—they're just about a foot apart.

MG: But the approach is different.

WJ: The country music and the black man's blues is just about the same man singin' the same song about the same problems and the same women that get him into trouble that he can't hang on to.

MG: But the orchestra does a different approach to the backgrounds.

WJ: Yeah, but if I sing it, it's still country. With the orchestra, you know.

ZG: You write your own material, do you?

WJ: Some of it. I'm more into other writer's stuff. I have a tendency to put mine away for somebody else's songs. I like to try and interpret a song to a point to where it's mine, you know.

MG: But Waylon, most artists today are singing just their own things, aren't they?

WJ: Not really.

MG: We hear that a lot on the show.

ZG: I thought that. I thought they all sang . . . it's a whole new form of music, isn't it?

WJ: I think Kristofferson gave that impression and Mac Davis writes a whole lot, and I used to write a lot too, but when you spend 250 days on the road . . . .

MG: You don't feel like writing?

WJ: Not in a green and yellow room, you know. [Snickers.] No offense, Mr. Holiday.

MG: We'll take a break, we'll be right back.

ZG: At Holiday Inn, right?

WJ: Right.

MG: America's art form . . . .

WJ: That's right. I think people are reaching back to the things that are real. Country music, now I say country the type of music I've seen of Willie Nelson, Mac Davis and some of our groups from around there so many bring people together that the so-called rednecks and the blacks and everything like that that never came together before because of the long hairs, you know. And religion and politics haven't been able to get together and I think music can.

ZG: Wouldn't that be just beautiful if it would?

WJ: I think—all the politicians coming with their guitars.

ZG: Actually, darling, most of the Presidents play something.

MG: Well all the politicians *use* famous singers to come and sing on the bandstand to get the crowds around and then they get up and bore everybody to death—right?

WJ: Well, Andrew Jackson, his wife Rachel had . . . .

MG: *How do you know her name?*

WJ: Well a lot of people did, you know . . . .

ZG: Did what, you never got to the point.

MG: Rachel was in the top 10.

WJ: I think he was because he's got a guitar for a driveway.

ZG: Guitar (gee-tar), you have an accent.

MG: You're one to talk. Do you know that a Vice President of the United States wrote, I love trivia, one of the most familiar melodies—we sing it all the time and it was written by a Vice President Daws—known as "Daws Melody," plus it has become popular—"Many a Tear Has To Fall, But It's All In The Game." Now if Rockefeller heard that . . . "I Almost Didn't Make It, I Almost Didn't Make It."

WJ: Jimmy Davis—Governor of Louisiana, wrote one that most people have heard. "You Are My Sunshine."

ZG: Why, that's a very famous one.

MG: Did he write that—I didn't know that.

WJ: He wrote a lot of songs. He's a great cowboy singer, I mean country singer. And he would go back and be Governor of Louisiana for awhile and the Longs would take it back over.

MG: It's a heck of a deal—if you can get into it.

ZG: Merv, we have a Governor who was in show business, right?

MG: Ronald Reagan, right?

ZG: He was pretty good in show business.

MG: He'll be here the day after tomorrow, he and Nancy.

ZG: They are lovely people.

MG: Tell me Waylon—you almost had a very bad problem, you had a brush with . . . you came very close to death, didn't you—with Buddy Holly and the Crickets. What was that story?

WJ: I was Buddy Holly's protégé. Actually, everybody thought I was one of the Crickets and everything or one of his band but I was just . . . I played bass for him for about two or three months and we were on this tour, the last tour, and he chartered a plane for himself and myself and Tommy Allsup, the guitar player and we had been riding on the bus—a school bus which had been converted, so the Big Bopper asked me to take my place and go on the plane—so I told him yes and he did and of course, everybody knows what happened.

ZG: Isn't that amazing—how the Lord chose the way to decide who goes where. Seriously—truly.

WJ: That still seems . . . I think of that a lot.

ZG: Of course.

MG: Look how we lost Jim Croce. That is really sad . . . Jim Croce.

WJ: Still, that's more less forced flying. You know, like when you miss a plane and try to charter one.

ZG: Don't ever do that.

WJ: I did it once. One where all the lights went out—we landed it and then got another one and it run out of gas.

ZG: Oh my, if you run out of gas in the air—what happens?

MG: Looks a little suspicious.

WJ: Well, I told him if you can get this one down—let's cool it and just get a motel somewhere, 'cause I don't think we are going to make it. That was right outside of Longview, Texas, and he found an airport that there ain't nobody could find . . . .

MG: Waylon Jennings! We'll be back after this word with Orson Bean.

While on the coast Waylon also taped a segment for the Don Kirshner "Rock Concert." His songs were aired May 16, 1975, with the Rolling Stones headlining the bill.

In the closing days of April, the "Mike Douglas Show" arrived in Nashville for three days of taping. Loretta Lynn and Mel Tillis would cohost the broadcasts from Opryland. Waylon and Jessi were booked for the Tillis program. Waylon would not use his band; instead, Johnna was asked to pick up a good Martin D-28 guitar for the show. The day of the taping, confusion reigned backstage. Acquaintances were renewed. Following Tillis and the two veteran "Opry" regulars, Waylon appeared.

MD: The gentleman about to come out now has had an interest in music ever since he was a little boy. He became one of the youngest disc jockeys in America at age 14. And today, he's one of the most unique artists in the country music field. Would you welcome with us, please, Mr. Waylon Jennings! How can a guy be a disc jockey at age 14? Had your voice changed Waylon, at that point?

WJ: I was changin' in the process. I think, you know, they had that at 12–14. Actually what I did, on this local radio station in my home-town—nobody liked country music but me. And so what I did . . . .

MD: In Texas?

WJ: If you're gonna talk, I want ya . . . .

MD: Can you . . . . We gotta move along here.

WJ: In Littlefield, Texas. That's a suburb of a cotton patch.

MD: Oh yeah—nobody liked country music except you?

WJ: That's just about the way it was. In them days, you know, what the deal was, if you listened to country music, you rolled up the windows in your car, you know, whether you had an air conditioner or not, because it wasn't it, you know. And, I think people liked it, but nowadays it's just kind of hip to be country—but in them days, it wasn't, you know.

MD: You started out as a bass player with the late Buddy Holly—what made you switch to country music? Because Buddy Holly was not playing country music. He was just rock 'n' roll.

WJ: He was playin' what they basically called . . . when I first really met Buddy, see he was a country singer and then the rock 'n' roll thing came in and actually, it was called rock-a-billy music. And I probably was the world's worst rock 'n'roll bass player. I was playin' country bass behind a rock 'n' roll singer. How does that go?

MD: Not too well. They like to hear a very heavy beat. Were you with Buddy at the time of his death?

WJ: Yeah. We played in Clear Lake that night, and of course, he thought of a plane—he chartered a plane and he chartered it for himself and myself and the guitar player, Tommy Allsup and the Big Bopper, J.P. Richardson, who was on the plane with him, came and asked me if he could take my place on the plane and the same thing happened to Richie—Tommy Allsup agreed to give his place.

MD: If it wouldn't have been for that incident—you would have been on that plane.

WJ: I just seemed like it took the best guys out of the whole tour, you know. It makes you stop and think about it.

MD: Did you fly after that?

WJ: For a long time I wouldn't you know. And actually before that, I'd never had any thoughts about flyin' because Buddy's flyin', you know he had several hours to be a pilot, you know. And he was gettin' me into that too, you know. And we'd fly up and go on up to Odessa and here and there and everywhere.

MD: You lost your interest after that, huh?

WJ: Really—to this day I still, you know, like if I'm force flying. What I call force flying is like when, if you miss a plane or something like that and you have to get on a charter. And really, I'll tell you, I'll say, "How old is your airplane and how many pilots you got?" And the last time I think I flew, they didn't know it but I was serious, you know. He said to me, he said, you know, I asked him that very question, I said, "Well, do you two pilots have faith in each other?" And they said, "Yeah." And I said, "Well, you can have faith in me—if you start fallin', I think I can whip both of ya before we get to the ground."

MD: Waylon, there's a lovely lady backstage who is quite a performer in her own . . . and why don't you introduce her to us.

WJ: Well, this is Jessi Colter—the poor little ugly thing that barely can sing . . . this is my wife.

MD: Ok, Jessi Colter. You have a great new song—it's called, "I'm Not Lisa." I heard it on the radio last night—it's a haunting thing. There's got to be a story behind that. I want you to do it for us and then maybe you can tell us the story. Maybe the story won't need telling after you do it.

JC: I hope not.

MD: Let's hear Jessi Colter sing that hit record—"I'm Not Lisa."

"I'm Not Lisa," written some four years prior to its chart appearance, was a major crossover hit. Jessi composed it in five minutes while doing an old music theory exercise. It was first performed on "Hee Haw" but not recorded. People remembered it, however. "For years, people came up to me while I was on the road and ask about it—even little girls. I thought it was unusual for people to remember a song that way—just from hearing it one time . . . ." "Lisa is very much a female song," she told an interviewer.[24] The lyrics tell the story of a woman whose husband mistakenly calls her by a previous wife's name: "I'm not Lisa, my name is Julie . . . ."

The reason that "I'm Not Lisa" was delayed was Waylon's career. In *Texas Country Western Magazine*, she explained: "And then Waylon came down with hepatitis. He was sick, real sick. And that's when it flashed to me that all my energy needed to be—not that I had spent all that much energy on my career—but I knew that Waylon really needed something to happen in his career. And besides, his child had come to us during those years—three children—so I really aimed all my efforts at our family and our marriage and to Waylon's energy as much as possible."[25]

After making the rounds of the talk shows, Waylon was still unhappy with television. "The people in the production end of it don't understand what we're doing and where we're coming from or anything. And it's hard, really, to communicate with people who don't understand us as people. Talking with Merv Griffin or talking with Mike Douglas automatically they lower their communication level about a foot—if you want to go by inches—when they're talking to you and anything you say that's above that shoots right over their heads. And you wind up, consequently, with no communication. Basically, they consider country people—or anybody from that—to be in a lower mental bracket and they don't understand it. They don't know what it is, you know, the old image of country music is hayseed, and some of the

ESSI COLTER

Promo photo for "I'm not Lisa"; Jessi and Waylon were married for six years. Jessi Colter, 1976.

smartest people I know of are country."[26] Jessi concurred: "I
hate TV," she said. "Unless we do our own special or set up
something with very talented people. I don't like it because it is
far too structured."[27] Waylon did not return to the green-room
circuit.

Waylon's relationship with some of his pre-outlaw fans was
obviously souring. Some disapproved of his appearance and
alleged lifestyle. A truck driver complained, "I can't believe
Waylon Jennings (my favorite tape, *Jewels* by Waylon Jennings).
What has happened to this man? He looked like a pig (and I don't
mean policeman) and sounded worse. Can it be that pot has crept
into country music?"[28] Waylon didn't smoke pot; the drug just
makes him sleepy.

His interactions with the press in 1975 were going badly. He
was tired of the "seat change" questions. His increased popularity made press demands more frequent. Waylon, Neil, and
Johnna attempted to control the media by requiring that journalists sign a statement allowing Waylon to censor anything they
might print. Most writers will not abide this system. Consequently, they stayed away, a reaction that pleased Waylon.

Waylon's attitude toward the press was curious. His media
coverage generally was quite good. The questions may have
become tiresome, but very few writers put him down. Only
occasional concert reviews called him inconsistent. None of the
national music magazines attacked the singer. Dan McPhail's
comments printed in the *Las Vegas Panorama* reached only a
handful of people. Tim Patterson's charge that Waylon's "lyrics
revolve around a cruder and explicit male chauvinism that can be
found in most American popular music" were addressed to the
faithful *Guardian* subscribers.[29]

The only comment Waylon has made about his relations with
the press was to Bob Campbell of *Country Music*:[30]

> I had a lot of problems with me saying one thing and somebody
> printing another. It's things like *People Magazine*. This guy [Bob
> Windeler] chased us halfway across the country trying to get us to do
> that interview. So we did it. Then here he comes along, saying Jessi
> wanted me to get a vasectomy. And he said 'Waylon answered him
> no in his male chauvinistic way saying my next wife might want
> children.' Now that was a lie. That was never even discussed and it
> wouldn't have been in front of that snaggle-toothed S.O.B. anyway. I
> had to have somebody tell me what a vasectomy was. And when I
> found out what it was—I didn't ever want it mentioned to me again.

W.J. and Johnny Rodriquez on "Soundstage." Courtesy of Mercury
Records, 1975.

It's things like this. If people would just tell the truth—what was really said . . . .[31]

Despite these developments, Waylon's concert fees and record sales soared. The outlaw image was paying off. Waylon was developing a new audience outside the traditional country music sphere. The "six-gun mystique" and his opposition to the "Hee Haw" stereotype suited urban dwellers in San Francisco, Los Angeles, New York, and Austin.

Waylon had always preferred songs that reflect his feelings and attitudes. "The Stage" was a tribute to Buddy Holly. "Anita, You're Dreaming," "This Time," and the outrageous "Poor Ole' Ugly Gladys Jones" were all about ex-wives. "John's Back in Town," "Good Time Charlie's Got the Blues," "Low Down Freedom," "Slow Moving Outlaw," and "Amanda" reflected his life and times on the road.

In February 1975 after a Jamaican holiday with Jessi, Waylon began a series of autobiographic songs dealing with Nashville. The day of his return he began work on "Music City Blues," later to be retitled "Are You Sure Hank Done It This A' Way." The four-verse song was an autobiographical indictment of the Music City Establishment as he saw it. The opening stanza hits at "Opry" policies of preserving only the old and refusing to change. The song goes on to the rigors of ten years on the road doing club dates in different cities while "speedin' my young life away." The closing states, "I don't think Hank done it this way . . ." (Baron Music Publishing: 1975). This is one of Waylon's best solo compositions.

Another composition, "Bob Wills Is Still the King," was a commentary on the Austin scene. He introduced the song rhetorically, asking, "Is it true that people in Austin think when they die they're goin' to Willie's house? They aint." In the lyric, Waylon discounts the "Grand Ole Opry" and, to some extent, Willie Nelson: "Don't matter whose in Austin, Bob Wills is still the king." Both tunes, released as singles, were big country hits.

The night prior to the 1975 CMA show, Waylon gave the keynote address before the Nashville Songwriters Association. It was the Hall of Fame presentation. "I don't know much about speeches," he opened. "In fact, I don't ever recall giving one." "I'm not sure how I got talked into this," he continued, "but I think it had something to do with Johnny Cash. He called from Chicago a little while ago and said he was on his way to Dallas for a last minute booking—but that sounds like a mighty weak excuse to me. Especially since he's not the one with the reputation for blowing dates . . . Jessi got me dressed up in this zoot suit to come down here and talk to you songwriters. And all I can say is that Willie hasn't quit laughing since he hit the door."

Waylon appealed to the 700 people in the audience for greater autonomy and support for composers:

> Songwriters should get more involved with their business. More involved with their publishing and the recording session. Today, country songs are getting locked in. They are following the same pattern. If you are a songwriter, you ought to be yourself. Don't be afraid to write what you want.
>
> Someone or some organization needs to establish a place for the young writer. Nashville is an awfully rough town. There should be a place where a young songwriter can go—someplace he could feel at home when he gets there . . . . Every songwriter needs to remember how important he is to this industry. It's pretty easy to find a good singer to do the song, but it's pretty damned hard to find a *good* song today.[32]

The audience totally agreed. The next night, Waylon would once again wear the "zoot suit" to the CMA presentations because he was sure Jessi would win an award. His attendance would surprise the media and invited guests. Dressed in a black tuxedo and white open shirt collar, he stared at the brightly lit stage. Glen Campbell was the host of the show. Waylon was nominated in four categories: Entertainer of the Year, Song of the Year— "Ramblin' Man", Album of the Year, and Male Vocalist of the Year. He lost in the first three categories. John Denver, much to the dismay of ACE, Freddie Fender, and Ronnie Milsap captured these divisions. Then came time for the Male Vocalist of the Year award. Tammy Wynette and Tanya Tucker opened the envelope and announced "Waylon Jennings . . . ." The outlaw strolled on stage.

"They told me to be nice. I want to sincerely thank everyone who voted for me as Male Vocalist of the Year. I really do appreciate everybody's support." With those brief comments, he left.

Glen Campbell, returning to the podium, editorialized, "All I can say Waylon is—it's about *damn* time."

After the show, Waylon posed with the other winners for the obligatory photo session. A reporter asked "Why are you here?"

"I went to the Awards Show because of my wife Jessi Colter." Jessi was nominated in several classifications—primarily for her hit, "I'm Not Lisa." "I really thought she'd win something there and I wanted to be with her. I never expected to win anything

JOHN HARTFORD

Flying Fish

P.O. Box 638   Indian Hills, CO. 8045-
303 697-5110

Nashville's first "hippie" who changed the song writing thrust in Music City.

myself." He continued. "If I thought it would have done any good, I'd have not accepted the award, but that isn't the way to solve what is wrong. There are problems within this industry just like any other business. In order for country music to grow, we who are in the business have to solve our own problems. We will work them out but that just takes time."[33]

On that note, Waylon and Jessi left the premises. Waylon still thought Jessi should have won.

The 1975 awards rekindled the controversy of the previous year. Country music fans almost unanimously condemned John Denver's selection as Entertainer of the Year. Letters poured into *Country Music* magazine. "Last night we watched the CMA Awards and were sorely disappointed in some of the winners. Naming John Denver as Entertainer of the Year, for instance . . . . To us, John Denver does not embody country music." Another reader commented: "The selection of John Denver . . . was ridiculous. He's not even a country singer." Or:

> The Country Music Association is sick. Last year it was Olivia Newton-John, who sounds like a sophisticated restroom. During the awards show, she left the country and they felt it was necessary to cram her down our throats.
>
> This year it's John Denver who sounds like a club sandwich served in the restroom. How, in good conscience, can he be the Entertainer of the Year? We get to see Denver in front of the TV cameras, grinning like a skunk chasing a bumble bee across a plowed field on a frosty morning . . . .

Readers had mixed reactions to Waylon's award. "Waylon Jennings, Male Vocalist of the Year, they should have given him a bath instead of an award." Another fan did not care for Glen Campbell's "expletive" on the show. Waylon did get some support. "It's about time! We Waylon fans have waited too long." A Pine Bluff couple objected to the manner in which Jennings was treated on the program. "Just because he chooses to keep some privacy in his life, be a nonconformist, and have a rough-looking appearance, plus a rough-looking band, it seems that Nashville has a tendency to turn its back on him. We were really irritated with Tanya's remark about Waylon's 'song from the underground.' We think Waylon is great and is long past due an award. Hurray for last night—he deserves it. We'd like to know who told him to 'be nice' and why?"

January 12, 1976, found RCA joining the outlaws. Jerry Bradley issued a press bulletin announcing the release of *Outlaws*, featuring Waylon Jennings, Jessi Colter, Willie Nelson, and

Tompall Glaser. He said, "The gathering of this great talent on one album assures us of a most exciting recording event which we expect to be one of the most important releases of 1976."[34] Chet Flippo, again, did the liner notes. The notes were designed to introduce the four singers to a noncountry audience. The comments acknowledged that the battle had been won.

> They *are* musical rebels, in one sense, in that they challenged the accepted ways of doing things. Like all pioneers, they were criticized for that but time has vindicated them . . . They've been waiting in the wings for years, too many years, to assume their proper places in the structure of American Music. . . . Call them *Outlaws*, call them innovators, call them revolutionaries, call them what you will, they're just some damned fine people who are also some of the most gifted songwriters and singers anywhere.[35]

Outlaws was a sampler album containing a number of songs taken from the RCA vaults and remixed. Jessi and Willie at one time had both been with the label. Victor rented two of Tompall's songs from MGM, a company he was soon to leave for ABC. Nearly all of the songs were familiar both to country fans and to the outlaw cult following in the big cities. To sell the album RCA mounted an extensive promotional campaign that paid off handsomely.

Country Music People observed "the real importance of this album is that it could easily be another Country-Pop-Rock crossover. Sure enough, the artists are well known to the country followers, but now's the chance for these entertainers—spearheaded by Waylon Jennings, who is already making inroads in these directions—to breakthrough to the rock devotees, already getting to know country through the work of Emmylou Harris, Linda Ronstadt and the numerous country-rock bands."[36] *Melody Maker*, the influential English music magazine, reported, "The *Outlaws* album is a perfect example of the new commercialism. It recently made the Top 20 Pop Chart in the United States . . . in other words, the album appealed to more than simply the limited country market and captured a significant rock audience."[37]

On April 5, RCA announced, "Waylon Jennings' band of outlaws this week raided the vaults of the Recording Industry Association of America (RIAA) and rode out of town with a huge haul of gold bullion. Worried officials of the RIAA certified the job was extremely well planned—so well, that suspicion immediately was focused on RCA Records for complicity. And, although the platinum vaults immediately were given extra protection, a harried spokesman threw up his hands and exclaimed: 'The way they're operating—how can we really feel the platinum is safe?' "[38] It wasn't.

Outlaws certainly achieved its goals, but once again, the more dedicated followers were growing restless. Several critics complained, "some new material would be welcomed." Waylon especially took some printed flak for following his live concert with a sampler. Many industry insiders see live albums as nothing more than a free ride for the artist—singing their hits in a concert situation. Mick Brady, president for the wjas, in obviously guarded terms voiced some reservations about the album. Diplomatically, he termed *Outlaws* as a "superb release . . . having said that, I must add that I'm not entirely convinced that the album a whole is as good as it might have been—perhaps I was expecting *TOO* much."[39] Brady praised "Honky Tonk Heroes" but then added, "But did we need another version?" He made similar comments about "Good Hearted Woman"—probably the best cut on the album. On "Heaven or Hell," Mick pointed out that Willie contributed only one line. Discussing Nelson's individual tracks, he noted that both had come from the *Yesterday's Wine* album. Moreover, "How I wish they'd left them [the two cuts] alone." One person in the Jennings organization commented, "I don't understand why he doesn't want to release some of the stuff in the can." In an interview with Mike Bane, Bradley explained, "it definitely helped everybody. But to the diehard Willie or Jessi fan, I think they might have been a little bit offended. But if it was a good album. *It served a purpose.*"[40]

On December 6, 1976, *Outlaws* was certified platinum. It was the first country and western album in history to sell over a million copies.

The quality of Waylon's releases could no longer be blamed on Chet Atkins or faceless executives in rca's Nashville or New York offices. Off the record, a critic said, "He was better on offense than defense. But, you know, most of his new fans will never know the difference." In the music industry, especially, success has its price. Fans and artists are both affected. This is particularly true for a "cult hero" such as Waylon Jennings. Prior to *Outlaws*, Waylon was known in the country field and to a loyal group of devotees in the country-rock sphere. His crossover hit pleased some and offended others. Cultists frequently object to any performer's deserting their tiny righteous band for the "chords of fame." It has happened to Bob Dylan and a few jazz and country artists. In 1976 Waylon was treading on thin ice with the media gatekeepers and his growing, but divided, audience.

To readers of music magazines, Waylon's future musical directions were muddied. Reports of an "Outlaw Express" tour were rumored. *Rolling Stone*'s widely read "Random Notes" had Waylon pulling out of Austin in June for a ten-day midwestern tour featuring Leon Russell, Marshall Tucker Band, Rusty Weir, and "guests Bob Dylan and Joan Baez."[41] In the next issue the Bicentennial train tour was called off. Pat Bullock, once Waylon's road manager, told the magazine, "It was a case of too many irons. in the fire. Things were going smoothly enough but we just didn't have enough time to pull it off."[42] Instead, Waylon and Jessi spent their June appearing in Lafayette and Downsville, Louisiana; at Pine Knob in Michigan; and playing in Columbia, Maryland, followed by Richmond, Virginia.

Are You Ready for the Country, released in 1978 was the first album in over a year that contained original material. Except for "MacArthur Park (Revisited)," the songs were new. Waylon included three of his own tunes: "I'll Go Back to Her," "So Good Woman," and "Old Friend." "So Good Woman" was obviously for Jessi. "Old Friend" was a tribute to Buddy Holly: "Ole Buddy we sure have missed you, but you ain't missed a thing." This was Waylon's second or third Holly commemorative. "The Stage" on Trend 61 had been the first; he destroyed the master because of the poor production quality. Some people claim that Waylon wrote "Buddy's Song," recorded by Bobby Vee in 1963 at the Norman Petty Studios. However, writer's credits go to E.H. Holley, Buddy's mother.[43]

Are You Ready a surprise, a gospel tune, "Precious Memories." This classic may well have been to satisfy Waylon's mother Lorene Gilbert, who had been after Waylon to do spirituals for years.

March 24, 1977, found *Dreaming My Dreams* certified gold. It sold over the magic number of 502,000 copies. This was Waylon's first solo gold album, a feat partly generated by the strength of *Outlaws*. Platinum albums cause catalogue sales. *Outlaws* had helped everyone but Tompall, who was changing record companies.

In September the CMA posted its 1977 nominees. Waylon received nominations in six categories; Willie Nelson garnered five. Waylon was selected for Entertainer of the Year, Male Vocalist, Vocal Duo of the Year, and Duo of the Year for "Good

Hearted Woman," and Album of the Year for *Outlaws*. Not since the Jesse James era had outlawing done so well.

A week before the October 11, presentations, Waylon attempted to withdraw his name for "personal reasons," but officials of the CMA refused. They argued that the request was too late and the balloting had been completed. Several years later Waylon explained his action. "I don't want to compete with anybody. That's what I told the Country Music Association. I'm not into competing with any of the other singers. I am a fan of this business. Let's put it this way—Willie and I were up for the same award. Now, there is no way I am going to sit there beside him if he had won—and I didn't. I just don't want that type of stuff. It affects your music. The best thing to do would be to give it to new artists to help them along."[44]

Waylon and Willie won the Duo of the Year award. Willie accepted. Paul Cohen, the man who told Buddy Holly to quit the business, was elected to the Country Music Hall of Fame. Jennings missed that event. Predictably complaints were voiced over the awards. The selection of Mel Tillis as the top performer was questioned. "Mel is a talent but he hasn't had a big hit in some time." The critic continued, "Waylon may be a #*%¢ in Nashville, you know, but look at his hits."

Stardom impacts on the artist. Growing numbers of agents, promoters, talent sellers, journalists, and hangers-on gravitate to the performer. Various economic and psychological games are played. "Star fucking" is what the process is called. The game is played with all the intrigue of Renaissance Florence or the French court. Advisers accuse each other of disloyalty or, worse yet, dishonesty. Managers and record companies promise enormous sums of money "if only the artist will sign with them."

Hillbilly Central rapidly became Hillbilly Hell. Charges and countercharges filled the air. Johnna was accused of robbing Waylon blind by making bootleg tapes of his concerts. Tompall found himself being tabbed as a rip-off artist with Baron Publishing. Ken Mansfield, the producer, was blamed for "recording failures and excessive points—percentage of royalties. By 1977, Johnna was back in New Mexico. Mansfield was banished. Waylon moved out of the Glasers' office suite. Nearly all of the accused deny the charges, vaguely pointing to New York as the cause of the difficulties.

Waylon's latent suspicions, given his past difficulties, merely needed to be tapped. He'd been taken enough times; he was determined "it wouldn't happen again." In retrospect, it appears that the "stealing scare" was more a power play than case of actual theft. Neither Yursic nor Mansfield has ever been charged with breaking any civil or criminal codes. Waylon reportedly sued Tompall for $300,000; Glaser filed a countersuit.

With the exception of Reshen and Willie, the main architects of the outlaw movement were no longer in the Jennings camp in 1977. And Reshen's days with the singer were numbered. Moreover, Willie's career has moved into the area of motion pictures, although Willie and Waylon still do appear on the other's albums.

Journalists, all asking essentially the same questions, became a nuisance. This is the price of stardom. Waylon enjoyed his success, but people's demands were growing. He was not comfortable in this new role, and he responded by withdrawing. Press interviews became virtually nonexistent. Security provisions at concerts were tightened. Just getting an autograph was becoming a Herculean task: rent-a-cops and outlaw bikers provided formidable obstacles.

13

ARE YOU SURE HANK DONE IT THIS A' WAY?

Waylon's new-found stardom did not deter him from resuming the long-standing feud with RCA. Once again, he was protesting and threatening to desert the label. At a Minneapolis concert in 1977 a "new Waylon" appeared minus his beard and with shortened hair. He explained to the audience, "the reason I got a haircut was—I got to meet with RCA tomorrow and I want to look like John Denver and David Bowie. They've [RCA] been givin' them all the money."[1]

Upon his returning to Nashville, Waylon was named an "Honorary Police Chief"—badge and all.[2] In August the police department would have cause to question the award.

In the beginning of April 1977, RCA released "Luckenbach, Texas," which skyrocketed up the trade charts. Jerry Bradley announced, "This record obviously is going to be a giant. Country stations throughout the country have responded overwhelmingly and it has been added to the playlists of over 120 of the stations we track. Crossover to MOR, Top 40 and progressive stations already has begun and we have sold more than 100,000 copies of the record in the first week."[3]

Luckenbach, Texas (official population,3), isn't listed in the *Rand McNally Road Atlas*. Yet, a year later, swarms of media people and tourists were invading the privately owned town. The networks sent film crews in and wire service reporters appeared. *Rolling Stone* and other writers stood in line—waiting to inter-

GRAM PARSONS

The "father" of country-rock. Courtesy of Reprise Records.

Los Angeles meets Nashville or vice-virtue! Doc Watson and the Nitty Gritty Dirt Band. Courtesy of United Artists.

The Dirt Band
Management Aspen Artists, Inc.

William D. Roberts
8800 Hollywood Hills Road
Hollywood, California 90046
(213) 654-0938

William E. McEuen
P.O. Box 1915
Aspen, Colorado 81611
(303) 925-1645

UNITED ARTISTS R

How come they sold a million records when Nashville artists could not until *Outlaws?* 1972. Courtesy of United Artists.

HE NITTY GRITTY DIRT BAND

How come they sold a million records when Nashville artists could not until *Outlaws?* 1972. Courtesy of United Artists.

OLIVIA NEWTON-JOHN

In 1974 Olivia Newton-John won the CMA award, and shook Nashville. Courtesy of MCA.

Waylon in the platinum days. Courtesy of RCA, 1979.

view a local storekeeper. *Newsweek* described the town—dominated by a huge shade tree and consisting of a house, a run-down blacksmith's shop, a dance hall, and a honky-tonk also serving as the post office—as a community that "belongs on an MGM back lot."[4]

All the commotion was caused by the duet. "Let's go to Luckenbach, Texas; Waylon and Willie and the boys . . . maybe it's time we got back to the basic of love." The fastest climbing single in country music history extolled the glories of giving up keeping up with the urbanized Jones' and of returning to a more laid-back, pastoral lifestyle.

Few artists were taken with the place. Waylon had never been there. Jerry Jeff Walker recorded *Viva Terlingua* in Luckenbach as a tribute to Hondo Crouch, a local personality and character. Hondo had purchased most of the town so he could keep the bar open. The impact of the song was tremendous. The Associated Press noted: "people in the Texas hill country hamlet are getting the idea they need more than one parking meter . . . vacationers by the hundreds now brave back roads—seeking the place with the funny name."[5] There were no road signs, as souvenir hunters had carried them off.

The tune about a sleepy hamlet some 65 miles north of Austin was a national sensation; it became a front runner for the CMA Song of the Year award. It generated a great amount of media coverage benefiting the so-called outlaws. *Ol' Waylon*, containing "Luckenbach," was rushed into production. Its urban response was summed up by *Rolling Stone*'s David Marsh: "An unfortunate title, given the recycled implication. In fact, this is the best Jennings album these Yankee ears have ever heard."[6] On June 20, 1977, *Ol' Waylon*, after six weeks in the record stores, was certified gold. RCA release said, "Any way you read the gauges, that's hot! The album currently is Number One on the country charts and is racing up the pop charts. At the same time, Waylon's single 'Luckenbach, Texas' also is Number One on the country charts and in the top 40 on the pop charts."[7]

Nonetheless, the Texas scene was rapidly deteriorating. The previous year Willie had attempted a fourth annual picnic. The elements (it rained) and the unruly crowd marred the event. Fences were torn down and only half of the 50,000 people paid for admission. Violence was rampant; some fifteen stabbings, a drowning, and several rapes were reported to the police. Waylon didn't appear on the stage. Willie, Doug Sahm, and Leon Russell did brief sets. According to *Rolling Stone*, the promoters lost in the neighborhood of $100,000. Neil Reshen and Willie Nelson acknowledge it was a failure but vowed to try again, "til we get it down perfect."[8]

DON'T YOU THINK THIS OUTLAW BIT DONE GOT OUT OF HAND?

A stern-faced Roger Mudd on CBS, substituting for Walter Cronkite, on the August 24, 1977, "Nightly News" read: "Country singer Waylon Jennings has been arrested for possession of cocaine. . . ." Waylon's picture briefly flashed on the green background. Mudd then quickly moved on to the next 30-second news item.

On the preceding Monday, Mark Rothbaum, an aide of Neil Reshen's, allegedly called World Courier, Inc., to pick up a package at his Danbury, Connecticut, home. The parcel was taken to John F. Kennedy International Airport. That night, Danny Bryiter became suspicious of the package; he had been instructed by his employer to open anything that appeared not to be paper documents. (Private parcel carriers are allowed by law to open packages in their custody. The Postal Service does not have this right.) When Byriter unraveled the manila parcel and unfolded the newspaper inside, he found a smaller envelope addressed "personal and confidential—Waylon Jennings only." Inside the second envelope were three plastic packets of white powder protected by lined yellow legal paper. Byriter split a plastic bag and sniffed the powder. He assumed it was some kind of drug. He then notified Bill Berger, the president of the company.

Berger called the Drug Enforcement Agency (DEA) office in New York. Agent Bill Rosenberger was assigned to the case at 10:00 A.M. the following day. He arrived at the World Courier offices an hour later. He performed the usual field tests for cocaine and read a positive reaction. Weighing the substance on a balance beam scale, he discovered a total of 27 grams—one gram less than an ounce. The cocaine had a Nashville street value of $2,500 to $3,000. Rosenberger confiscated all but two grams of the illegal substance and repackaged the rest for shipment to Nashville.

Rothbaum, according to the DEA, was becoming impatient. He

placed several calls to the transport company. Rosenberger provided World Courier with a cover story. Rothbaum was told the
package had been misplaced by American Airlines. Speaking to
Helena Cazjkowski, a secretary, Rothbaum protested that "the
package contained very important contracts that had to be in
Nashville by 3:00 P.M. to close a real estate deal."[9] Later he
phoned Fred Zimmer at World Courier and stressed the importance of the package and its delivery. "The package contains very
important music recordings."[10] Finally, Ms. Cazjkowski informed the agitated caller that the package was en route and
would arrive at Nashville Metro Airport on Braniff Airlines at
7:40 in the evening.

Rothbaum called Waylon's secretary, Lorri Evans, and informed her of the arrival time. He contacted World Couriers
once again and said that Lorri would pick up the material.
Rosenberger phoned his colleague Bill Tucker in Nashville and
made the arrangements.

Under the watchful eye of federal and state agents, a Checker
cab driver retrieved the package at the airline counter and handed it to the secretary. Ms. Evans took the package to her red-and-
white Ford Bronco with another woman and drove to American
Studios, 1117 Seventeenth Avenue, South. The studio was located next to Waylon's business office.

All seemed peaceful that night. In the elegant Victorian recording studio, Waylon was overdubbing a "Storms Never Last"
for *New South*, a Hank Williams, Jr., album. Ms. Evans entered
the studio. The narcotics agents followed in a matter of minutes.
The package was not in sight. Everybody denied knowledge of
the "hot item." "When we went in, she pointed to someone later
identified as Richard Albright and said she gave the package to
him," recalled agent Tucker. "There followed an exchange between them so I took her outside. She said she put it in the blue
chair and Albright was leaning over the chair at the console."

Waylon was recording. "I mean, when we were cutting the
New South album, the DEA came into the studio and bust
Waylon," says Hank, "but everybody kept on playin'."[11] Waylon
called out of his recording booth. Tucker told him they had a
warrant for his arrest. "I think I ought to call my attorney." the
singer said.

The musicians went back to overdubbing "Storms Never
Last." One participant said, "They were very nice but they held
everybody while they went to get a search warrant . . . ." The

"And the room filled up with law," the drug bust session.

warrant was obtained from U.S. Magistrate Kent Sandidge III at his home.

A few minutes after midnight, State Agent Taylor Bettis called Tucker into the studio bathroom. He had found two soaking-wet plastic bags in a trash container on the floor to the left of the toilet. The bags matched the description provided by Rosenberger. Field tests, again, disclosed the presence of cocaine. The agents also found small portions of marijuana and "coke" in the possession of some of the people in the studio. Waylon was "clean." Waylon and his secretary were arrested. The charges were "conspiracy and possession of cocaine with intent to distribute." The maximum penalty upon conviction is fifteen years' imprisonment and a fine up to $15,000.

A hearing was set for 9:00 that morning. "They weren't taken into custody and put in the lock-up," said the assistant U.S. attorney, Ray Whitley. A nonsecurity bond of $7,500 was posted and they were released on their own recognizance.

At the hearing, Waylon arrived with attorneys John Archer, who had been brought in the night before, and Tom Binkley. Newspaper people crowded around the singer.

"How're you doing," asked a *Banner* correspondent.

"I'm hanging in there."[12]

The hearing before Sandidge lasted twenty minutes. Waylon, dressed in his usual jeans and a denim vest, sat silently. Waylon's lawyers requested that he be able to travel throughout the United States in order to fulfill his previous bookings. Whitley did not object. The magistrate approved but asked if Waylon had a passport. The singer responded, saying it had expired. After some haggling, a preliminary hearing date was set for the next Wednesday. After five minutes, the judge interrupted, "It's just a probable cause hearing. It's not the end of the world." Waylon and Lorri were then taken from the courtroom by a federal deputy marshall to be photographed and fingerprinted.

Following the legal session, Waylon and his entourage went to his lawyer's offices for a consultation. The press followed. When Waylon emerged from the Parkway Towers, television lights went on. Reporters stuck microphones into the singer's face. Richie Albright attempted to shield Waylon. In the process, local camraman Harold Lowe was struck in the face with a flying Coca-Cola can. Lowe said, "I was trying to get in front of the group when a man told me not to get any closer."[13] Lowe ignored the warning. Richie tried to pour the soft drink on the camera. Lowe pushed the drummer. Richie tossed the can at him. Lowe required minor hospital treatment. wTVF announced the station would file assault-and-battery charges against the drummer. Things were getting out of hand.

News of the arrests spread like wildfire through Music City Square. Knowing glances were exchanged. A number of "I told you so's" were expressed. One artist said, "It's about time." A good deal of hostility that usually surfaced only at CMA award balloting erupted.

Other reactions were more favorable. Utopia Productions publicist Bill Conrad observed, "Waylon Jennings has never been an outlaw. Actually he leads a sedate sort of life. The whole idea of his being a dope dealer is ridiculous. He makes $15,000 a show. The man does not have to distribute or deal dope."[14] Another person close to Waylon called it a "frame-up." "This is definitely a set-up. All we have to do is find out who did it. Waylon's been doing real good lately. He's been keeping pretty straight." Another insider told columnist Bill Hance that the drug bust would have positive benefits. "Oh, hell yes. It can't help, but help," replied the unidentified person. "Waylon will have a whole new following now. I'll bet he does another million dollars worth of business next year. He may lose some of the hard core country fans but not many. A lot of his songs have crossed over in the past from country to pop. But since this has happened, he's got a pop music identity. There's no stopping him now."[15] Hance's source appeared prophetic.

The only resident of Music City Square openly upset for a time was the owner of American Sound Studio, Chips Moman. Moman was stopped the night of the raid, searched, and informed of the impending search warrant. He told the *Tennessean*, "I could just see them tearing this place apart with a crowbar after all the work we've done to restore it. They had a search warrant but I told them they didn't need a search warrant. I would show them around." He did, but they did not find anything outside of the bathroom.

"I'm one of the last of the independent producers," he continued. "I own this studio and rent it out to different people. I lost $1,000 last night and $1,000 today when people canceled their sessions."

He wasn't too happy with Waylon. "They just happened to be

over here when the drug agents came. He could have been down the street in a phone booth or somewhere else. If they had waited awhile, he would have been next door in his own office."[16]

Waylon and Willie announced they would not participate in the CMA awards. The day prior to the arrest the CMA had nominated Waylon as a finalist in five categories. "Luckenbach" was one of the top five singles. Once again, he was chosen one of the candidates for Entertainer of the Year as well as Male Vocalist. He and Willie were in the best Duo classification. The winners would be announced on October 10 at the nationally televised program held in Opryland.

Twelve hours after the hearing, Waylon appeared at Willie's concert at the Municipal Auditorium. A crowd of 8,000 gave him a standing ovation. During Willie's "Pick Up the Tempo," Waylon changed the line "He don't give a damn" to "*I* don't give a damn."

Mark Rothbaum was charged in New York and ordered to appear in Nashville for the upcoming hearing. He surrrendered to the U.S. attorney's office in New Haven.

For the preliminary hearing the tiny courtroom was jammed with media people and spectators. Judge Sandidge ruled people would not be allowed to stand. "I will allow people, as we do down here in the South, to 'hunker down' if they want to." Some did.

Waylon was represented by a battery of lawyers. Elliott Sagor and Jay Goldberg joined Nashville attorneys Archer and Binkley. Sagor and Goldberg were from New York. The defense opened with a series of motions. The Nashville attorneys wanted the hearing closed to the press, but they were overruled. Sagor argued that the charges be dismissed on the grounds "popular entertainers . . . receive package after package from people." This, too was dismissed by the magistrate. "We're not talking about just anyone who sent the package. Mr. Rothbaum was an agent of Mr. Jennings."

The government opened its case with Rosenberger reciting the events leading up to the time "the room filled up with law." Agent Tucker recounted the search of American Sound Studios, concluding that only two wet plastic bags contained a small dosage of cocaine.

In cross-examination Sagor made some significant points:

Sagor: Do you have any proof that Waylon Jennings ever received the package?

Tucker: No.

Sagor: Do you have any proof that he asked that it be sent to him in any way?

Tucker: No.[17]

After the prosecution presented its case, Judge Sandidge commented, "They don't have enough to convict. I don't think, but there's probable cause . . . ." Waylon and Mark Rothbaum were bound over to the federal grand jury. Charges against Lorri Evans were dropped.

After the ruling, Sagor asserted: "There is no proof that Mr. Jennings ever received it—that it was put in his hands. There he was in the sound room singing away. If he had been anxious to get the package, it would be found on him. There is no doubt that somebody has committed a crime. There is no difference between her case and his case except that he is Waylon Jennings." Sagor did not yet know, apparently, that Lorri had agreed to turn "state's witness." Ray Whitley, a veteran drug prosecutor, presented a familar theme. "We resent Mr. Sagor's coming down here from New York City and saying we are prosecuting Mr. Jennings because he is a public figure. It's not right and your Honor knows it's not right."

A week prior to the CMA show, the grand jury convened. Gary Halsey, Jack Ruth (a songwriter), Lorrie Evans, Neil Reshen, Richie Albright, and Hugh Cherry (one of the most respected deejays in country music), were called. Cherry was present during the raid, collecting interviews for a New Year's Day program to commemorate the twenty-fifth anniversary of the death of Hank Williams. U.S. District Court Judge L. Clure Morton had ordered that the tape be provided to the grand jury.

Press accounts as to the importance of the tape varied. The *Tennessean* headlined "Waylon's 'Damaging' Tape Ordered In." Kathleen Gallagher, who had covered the case from the beginning, argued that Waylon's new attorney, Dale Quillen, attempted to have it suppressed because it would be "very detrimental to Mr. Jennings to give up the tape."[18] The rival *Banner* took a completely different approach. "Tape Will Clear Jennings of Cocaine, Charges Lawyer." The paper quoted Quillen as retracting his previous statement and saying, "I did say it was a vital piece of evidence, but I meant that in its entirety it is strong evidence in his [Jennings] favor." Quillen went on to contend that Waylon's voice was not on the controversial cassette. The tape would turn out to be a red herring.[19]

On the evening of the tape story, Quillen called Waylon, now back at American Sound Studios, and informed him that the charges against him had been dismissed "without prejudice." In legalese, "without prejudice" means that the singer could be indicted at a later date. Waylon was elated. Quillen explained the verdict. "You look after it for me," he told the lawyer.

The reasons for the dismissal are not clear, as is the case with most grand jury actions. Quillen speculated, "I think it was an attempt to circumvent the Speedy Trial Act [suspect must be indicted within 45 days] so they may continue the investigation in hopes of coming up with additional evidence . . . to again seek an indictment. It would be pure speculation on my part what they have in mind." He added, "As far as this case is concerned, they don't have a case against Waylon Jennings. As far as Rothbaum is concerned, one man can't conspire with himself . . . if the evidence is not there, he [the government attorney] can't go out and manufacture it. He didn't personally handle the investigation."[20]

One of those "unidentifiable sources" so frequently found in court cases gave a different version for the *Banner*. Nashville's "Deep Throat" alleged that the government had crippled the case in New York. "They should have let the entire package go through and then maybe they would have come up with more evidence." They also may have waited too long to enter the studio. There was just not enough evidence to convict.

Little if any mention of the dismissal appeared in the national media. The arrest has garnered space in over one hundred newspapers, frequently with accompanying photographs. Only the two daily Nashville papers gave the dismissal front-page coverage. Interestingly, the country music press almost totally ignored the entire case. Many people still don't know the charges were dropped.

As the CMA presentations drew near, Waylon reasserted his intention not to participate in any way, as "he objected to musicians competing for awards." Again, the CMA refused to withdraw his name. There was little doubt before or during the presentations that Waylon would win. Insult was added to injury by fellow RCA artist Jerry Reed. Reed, in presenting an award, chided Waylon's lack of participation and alluded to the drug arrest. He suggested, "Waylon is parking cars at Opryland but he refused to come in." He also joked about a potential jail sentence. The audience appeared to support Jerry's remarks. The next day, an RCA executive cautiously stated, "You know how

Jerry is!" and refused to discuss the incident. Others openly questioned the selection of pop singer Kenny Rogers's "Lucille" over the highly successful and well-publicized "Luckenbach, Texas." The vote was dismissed as just another example of CMA politics. Another added, "the drug bust didn't really hurt. It merely justified the already existing animosity." "Waylon's his worst enemy," said another Music City mainstay.

Unlike the 1969 Canadian border incident, which created a furor in *Music City News*, the "coke" bust did not hurt Waylon's career. In fact, the event generated a Number One country and western song about how "singin' through my nose got me busted by the man." Only the *Monroe News Star* in Louisiana complained in an editorial, "Waylon and Drugs." The writer warned, "If Jennings is convicted and thus gains further notoriety of a negative sort, interest in cocaine will doubtless increase among the impressionable who like his music."[21]

The case was not closed. The government had five years to pursue the charges. In April 1978, Mark Steven Rothbaum pleaded guilty in Bridgeport to a single count of distributing cocaine.[22] He had been indicted in Nashville. Technically, Waylon is still open to indictment, but few think this is likely to happen.

The outlaw image was now reinforced to the hilt. By 1977 the outlaw thing had accomplished its goals. Waylon and Willie were acclaimed as superstars. Waylon became the first country artist in history to "ship gold." Willie reached the cover of *Newsweek*. Cracks, however, were beginning to show in the outlaw movement.

Waylon's problems with law and the CMA were compounded by troubles from an unlikely source. In September 1977 *Rolling Stone* magazine declared in its "Random Notes" section and the nationally syndicated "Pop Scene" column: "Waylon Jennings and his wife Jessi Colter are refusing to grant interviews these days unless the interviewers agree to the terms of a contract which gives the subject the right to approve the manuscript before it is submitted for publication. The pair also demand the right to approve or reject any photographs which are taken of them for publication."[23] The unidentified writer went on to discuss the problems *Country Music*'s Mike Bane encountered in receiving clearances for a chapter. "According to Bane, when he returned the chapter to Jennings for approval, Waylon first demanded that the chapter on Tompall Glaser, his former business partner, be removed and that a chapter on Jessi Colter be substituted." Bane reportedly refused—but later compromised. He agreed to alterations, including three more paragraphs on Jessi and the deletion of the references to his touring schedule and the removal of a quote dealing with Chet Atkins. According to the *Stone*, the missing quote was "Chet, it wasn't you I was against personally, it was the corporation."[24]

The *Stone* went on to complain about the treatment of fans. "Even members of Waylon's fan club are getting the cold shoulder." The article pointed to the August edition of Gary and Ella Mae Kessell's monthly newsletter. In the mimeographed sheet the Kessells warned that Waylon doesn't send out autographed pictures. "Those who want an autographed picture real bad, usually find a way to get it in person. Admittedly, it's not easy— but then, what worth having is?"[25]

This kind of publicity is harmful to any country music artist. Country fans have a mixed relationship with their entertainment idols. They are awed by them. However, they expect their idols to be accessible. Country music is unlike the world of popular music. A mere glance of an artist speeding away in a limo after the show just won't do. Country artists normally stand around after a show signing autographs on pieces of paper, photos, and record jackets. This practice, although taxing, is highly profitable in good will and income. Records and glossy 8 x 10 photographs are frequently sold at high prices. Band members and the road manager pass through the audience selling albums at list price. The same records could easily be purchased at a local store for several dollars less. But Waylon does not care to "play the game." He dislikes fan contact. He told Bob Campbell, "See, *I'm an introvert in an extroverted business.* And I'm not the great conversationalist. I make people nervous when they first come around me because of all the things they have heard about me. Then I react to that reaction."[26]

An early fan club newsletter stated: "He's a man who loves children and life but finds it very hard to talk to people—I guess you could say he is really shy, especially in crowds. Sometimes this shyness is mistaken for snobbishness by some fans but anyone who has met and talked with him know right away what a wonderful person he is." Waylon's mother reportedly said: "Waylon has a heart as big as a mountain—full of love for people but the *only way* he can truly show it is through his singing and playing the guitar."[27] Many fans misunderstand Waylon's feelings and write him off. One disgruntled old-time Jennings enthusiast in Michigan said, "He's forgotten his roots—his people. He's trying to be a rock star." Many other loyalists agree at least with the opening part of the sentence.

Waylon's shyness is a factor in this dilemma, but there is more. The main contradiction is Waylon's status as a crossover artist. Up until 1973, Waylon did abide by the rules of the game, remaining available to fans. In some cases, he had little choice, as dressing rooms were either absent or uninhabitable. There was no place to hide. In lounges he did sign autographs and pose for Kodak snapshots. He and his fans played the game. "I don't like doin' it, you know," he told a reporter, but he did cooperate. Crossing over did change the picture. Pop and rock audiences are different from those on the Moeller tours. They are larger, younger, and less manageable. Signing autographs for a few devotees is one thing, but accommodating hundreds of people is entirely another matter. Many country rock concerts, as the Dripping Springs bash indicated, are oversized skull orchards. There is an element of danger, not to mention inconvenience, in these situations. Talent agents, record companies, and others concerned with the safety of their valuable artists tend to err on the side of caution. Many fans have complained about the security around Waylon; the bikers evoke images of Altamont and "Wild One" films.

Waylon's country fans ignore the realities of the present situation in some cases and grumble. Their perceptions should not be discounted as short-sighted; right or wrong, fans' expectations have to be dealt with. Public relations—not just the media—has been a problem plaguing Waylon's career for years. Chet Flippo warns: "Country music fans would be forever loyal to their stars unless their stars committed the one total and unredeemable sin: turning on their followers, refusing to sign autographs. If they, in short, quit being just a singing representative of their peers and started putting on airs, then by God, they would be dropped so fast their pants'd be sucking wind before they hit the ground."[28]

Talent agents and record companies promote artists *within* the music industry. They get artistic exposure in nightclubs, concert halls, and the broadcast and print media. Nightclub owners, radio stations, and the press then bring public attention to the artist. Ideally, that is. Many country lounge owners barely advertise their "coming attraction." Advertising is an added expense and they frequently assume—quite incorrectly—that the "name" of the act will fill the room. During Waylon's Moeller days, this happened repeatedly, especially outside of the Southwest. In Phoenix and Las Vegas he was a "name draw," but in other parts of the country, it was "Waylon who?" RCA did get Waylon air play and some limited print coverage. The problem was, at the time, that there were fewer country music radio stations and even fewer country and western magazines. Most of Waylon's press coverage during the 1960s appeared in a few local newspapers and the trade publications. A handful of fans read *Billboard* or *Cashbox*. Consequently, a country artist was personally responsible for his or her own public relations. This included everything from announcements like "Here's a song off our new album. Hope you like it" to visiting radio stations while on tour and supporting fan clubs.

In country music, fan clubs are an important asset. They can also be a "pain." Fan clubs, in most instances, are little more than unpaid publicity departments for the artist. Fans write or telephone radio stations requesting their "favorite new song." They send out newsletters that are chatty and full of praise, poems and songs dedicated to their idol. Waylon got his share—such as "Ode to Waylon's Love" or "W A Y L O N J E N N I N G S."

WAYLON JENNINGS

W- is for "Waylon," a "Brown Eyed Handsome Man"
    A sexy eyed guy who's tops in Country Music Land.

A- is for "Anxious," his fans are always that way
    To see and hear him each and every day.

Y- is for "You," his supporter and fan
    Always ready to uphold this special man.

L- is for "Label," RCA is the name
    Where he records his way to fame.

O- is for "Ontario," where he often appears
    This is when "Camilla" is sure to be near

N- is for "Nifty," his show is really "Neat"
    A country fellow that's hard to beat.

J- is for "Jet," he travels fast and far
    With his group, "The Waylors" and his guitar

E-   is for "Entertain," this he does with ease
   For his aim is to give his best and to please.

N-   is for "Nashville," country music's home
   From where all country stars roam.

N-   is for "National," his fame is spread all around
   for so many people love his country sound.

I-   is for "Irresistable," this he is to his fans
   They're always chasing after this No. 1 man.

N-   is a "Number" that goes with every new song
   It's Number 1 to prove that he just can't go wrong.

G-   is for "Grammie," [sic] an award he can claim
   To add to his trophys on his road to fame.

S-   is for "Star," he shines so warm and bright
   He's sure to brighten up the darkest night.

Each month the letters contain birthday greetings for members. Donations of postage stamps are duly acknowledged. The members are alerted as to where their idol will be appearing. Such support is all to the good until the officers of an organization begin to make excessive demands on the artist. Waylon's past relations with fan clubs can only be described as grim.

Waylon's fans are a mixed breed. They range from laid-back street people in San Francisco to a seventy-four-year-old Ted Brincefield in Van Wert, Ohio. Most of the fan club members, however, are teenagers, middle-aged couples, or women. There are a few notable exceptions, but females are the heart of the fan clubs. Jan George, from Columbus, Ohio, is a case in point. A middle-aged housewife started the first Waylon Jennings fan club in June 1969. Mrs. George devoted most of her free time to the group, when she was not caring for a bedridden mother. She sent out the usual newsletters with a picture of her and the singer prominently displayed. The newsletter frequently spent as much ink on Jan as Waylon: "As this goes to the printers, my son John just broke his collar bone as a result of being thrown from his bike. He will be in a brace for six to eight weeks. So, I can see how I'll have my hands full, taking care of him and my mother who still isn't doing too well." Waylon, who reluctantly consented to the club, wasn't too happy with it. "I think she bugged him to death," said a member. "She called him and went to his motel room and that sort of thing . . . followed him all over. I think she was just a big bore. I don't think she ever really had the ability nor the wish to really promote Waylon. I think for her it was just a way to follow Waylon and see his show. Waylon tried to help her out financially with the club—but rather than put it into the club, she had spent it on personal traveling to his shows." The Waylon Jennings National Fan Club was short-lived.

In 1971 Jackie Siljander was promoting a "Waylon Jennings Fan Club." It appears to have folded within a year.

Two years later Bill and Marge Damron of East Peoria wrote former fan club members and officers, promising the formation of yet another "authorized" International Fan Club. The Damrons' first encounter with Waylon was at a concert in 1969. At that meeting they told him about their invalid son, Elvis, who was a big admirer of Jennings. Waylon was very kind to the child. In return, the Damrons, in their son's name, purchased a block in the "Walkway of Stars" at the entrance to the Country Music Hall of Fame. The concrete slab cost $1,000. Waylon reportedly offered to pay for part of it. The Damrons refused.

The Damrons were quite different from Jan George. Referring to the club, they wrote one member, "We're family friends (personal) of Waylon and can't be 'bugging' him so often as to when he is going to get it started."[29] This characterized their view of Waylon. Even when the club did get started, they stayed away from the singer. At Illinois appearances, the Damrons attended his concerts but did not visit with the singer backstage, as is the custom with most fan club officers. Nevertheless, the relations between the Damrons and WGJ Productions were strained. By 1974 the club had disbanded. Waylon was totally disillusioned with the concept. Several fans approached Johnna, urging him to authorize Mick Brady to head an international fan club. Johnna said that might be possible because "he did want a *good* club." Waylon apparently refused.

In England Mick Brady had begun "The Waylon Jennings Appreciation Society." Brady had been a Buddy Holly fan who discovered Waylon's RCA albums in 1966; he was a musician and songwriter in Hickory Wind, a British country band. Conway Twitty had recorded Brady's "Friars Point, Mississippi," but the song has not been released. In August 1972 Mick wrote, "Welcome to the first newsletter of the Waylon Jennings Appreciation Society. The Society has been formed to keep Waylon's fans on this side of the world up to date with record releases and activities and to promote the name and music of Waylon Jennings in this country. I hope that all members will find the Society invaluable. Future plans include a quarterly magazine with exclusive features, import of Waylon's records as they are released, an annual meeting of members and special services for all fans."[30] Although Brady's hopes were not realized completely, his *Waylonews* was much superior to anything produced by the United States clubs. Poems, odes, and songs written by fans were excluded from his newsletter, members' birthdays and contributions were absent, and there were infrequent appeals for postage stamps. Instead, Brady reprinted articles about Jennings, record reviews, and occasional interviews with visiting country artists. Mick's limitations were financial and geographic. The newsletter was dependent upon the dedication of American members who mailed in clippings of articles and reviews. These arrived in starts and stops. Despite the problems, Brady maintained his journal for seven years.

By mid-summer of 1979 *Waylonews* was no more. Pleading economic difficulties, Mick Brady ceased publication of the mimeographed newsletter, opting for a joint venture with a Sheffield record store. A new publication, *Outlaws*, appeared with a similar format, but it was primarily devoted to advertising records available by mail order. Waylon International was posted in the credits, but *Outlaw* is a poor successor to the twenty-eight issues of *Waylonews*. Mick Brady, a loyal advocate, appears to have become one more casualty in the Jennings success story.

Gary and Ella Mae Kessell in November 1974 introduced themselves to American and Canadian WJAS members. In their newsletter they stated: "Now we are acting only as United States and Canadian Representatives for Mick!" In some respects, the Kessells were a combination of Jan George and the Damrons. They enjoyed visiting with Waylon after concerts and had their pictures taken with him and Johnna. Ella Mae wrote, "I really admire and care for this GUY Waylon, so very much and if, unintentionally, and it would be unintentionally, say I would do some little thing or something stupid for I do this sometimes and don't mean no harm, but maybe he would take it wrong! You know what I'm trying to say? I love people and I love good clean fun, but I always have this fear of just doing something and I would make him angry at me!"[31]

The Kessells' monthly newsletter lacked the quality of *Waylonews*. It quickly became a just another fan club publication. Little homilies about members appeared; birthdays and stamp donors again became important; cards were requested to celebrate Waylon's June birthday. In each issue, a monthly itinerary appeared, always with the disclaimer that fans planning to travel long distances should first confirm the scheduled concert. The Kessells obviously knew about Waylon's "no shows." The Kessells' operation outlived all of the preceding American newsletters. The Gaithersburg, Maryland, letter was discontinued in 1978. One state representative said, "The main problem with the fan club was that Waylon *doesn't* want one . . . ."[32]

Encouraged by the success of *Outlaws*, Jerry Bradley began thinking of a follow-up. This was not simple; "creative problems" kept cropping up. The difficulties were that the four outlaws were on different labels and critical reaction to *Outlaws* was weak. Bradley was nervous about pulling more material out of the Victor vaults for another package. Getting three labels— Capitol, ABC, and Columbia—to release their artists for another record would be nearly impossible. Moreover, Waylon refused to include Tompall in the venture. "After the *Outlaws* album, I told Waylon, 'look, we are going to put out a Waylon and Willie album,'" Bradley noted. "It can be five old songs of you and five old songs of Willie. We can do that. We don't have to talk to anybody. But what do you think about going in and recording on Willie's tracks and putting your voice on it and let's make some duets?" Waylon said he would try. "He talked to Willie and we decided we would try because that would make a better album than five old tracks of Waylon and five old tracks of Willie."

Bradley phoned Rick Blackburn at CBS. After some negotiations, the CBS vice president agreed. "It was an opportunity for Willie to do a thing with Waylon and we worked it out with RCA," Blackburn explained to *Billboard*.[33] In exchange for Willie's services, Bradley agreed to let Waylon appear on three forthcoming albums, one with John R. Cash, Earl Scruggs, and George Jones. Waylon's collaboration with John R. found "Ain't No Good Chain Gang" on the top of the country and western charts. Waylon and John introduced the song on Cash's May 7, 1978, "Spring Fever" special (CBS).

"After a duel between the presidents of our record companies, . . ." started Cash.

". . . that's why it's a duet," chimed in Jennings.

Jessi appeared as a special guest and sang Cash's "Cowboy's Last Ride." Waylon soloed with "Looking for a Feeling." The couple helped close the program with a chorus of "The Saints Go Marchin' In." This was perhaps Waylon's most successful television appearance up to this time, but it was not without mishap. At the opening of the show, the announcer mumbled, "Waylom Jemmings . . . ."

Waylon was touring a week or ten days a month. The troupe included Jessi, the ever-changing Waylors, and occasionally Willie—the addition of the other outlaw depended on the market. In New York, Willie was a co-headliner; in Des Moines, Waylon was the star.

The splendid isolation of stardom was beginning to take its toll. Rumors of feuds between Waylon and his fellow outlaws raged like wildfire. If all of the tales were to be believed, Waylon's would be a classic case of paranoia.

"One of the hardest things for me to do is to go out amongst people who are in a club and that gets me uptight a little bit because I'm not really outgoing not that much as a person."[34] In fact, Waylon Jennings—macho image and all—is a somewhat bashful and shy person. Manifestations of these feelings frequently are misinterpreted as signs of rudeness or insensitivity. Waylon is just not comfortable around people. He was not ready for the fame that was thrust upon him. There are no books or courses for coping with fame and fortune.

By 1978 only Richie Albright and Neil Reshen appeared to be close to the singer. Johnna reportedly was thinking of going to court for back wages. Waylon and Tompall were suing each other to the tune of some $300,000. They weren't speaking. Success does have its price.

Following the 1978 Super Bowl, Waylon appeared at an all-night celebration party staged by the victorious Dallas Cowboys. "Y'all do play some damn good football around here," commented the former high school placekicker. The party raged into the wee hours of the morning. Bob Breunig, a middle linebacker, borrowed Waylon's leather-covered guitar and sang "Jailhouse Rock," along with three other Presley tunes. He told a reporter, "We had this little thing at training camp where Elvis was going to come back if we won the Super Bowl . . . so here he is."[35]

After the Cowboys' bash, Waylon and Willie flew to New York for a joint press party to promote their new album, *Waylon and Willie*. It was already certified gold. For Waylon, the event

Courtesy of RCA, 1979.

was a disaster. It only heightened his dislike of being a superstar. RCA staged the gala party at the Rainbow Room high atop the Rockefeller Center. Duck à l'orange and cold salmon were served. Guests were given promotional copies of the album pressed in gold-colored vinyl.

Waylon and Willie sat in the darkest corner of the room. Occasionally, an RCA press person would allow photographers a "photo opportunity." Waylon reluctantly did a brief interview with Jane Pauley of the "Today" show. It was the gregarious Nelson, however, who did most of the talking. Martha Hume of *Rolling Stone* asked Willie if the "outlaw thing" wasn't over. He denied it. Waylon, according to Hume, looked like a convicted criminal. "Oh baby," he said, "I feel like I'm all tied up." Hume noted, "Waylon is obviously uncomfortable with the constant public exposure. Contrary to his image, Jennings is a shy, gentle man who does not mix well with the public. As the evening wore on, he edged farther and farther back into the darkest corner of the room, speaking only when spoken to . . . ." A participant said, "Poor Waylon, he is trapped at the star table to which RCA and Neil have guided him like show biz sheepdogs, his back to the windows and his face to the flashbulbs . . . he's twisting, turning, fidgeting and fretting, longing for an escape." Willie wasn't happy, either. Sensing Waylon's discomfort, he called the party an example of "managerial mismanagement."[36]

After the Rainbow Room gala, Waylon and Jessi flew to London to work on Paul Kennerley's *White Mansions* album. Kennerley, a former rock-group manager, fashioned the album for Waylon. "Two and a half years ago I was listening to Tim Rice on Capitol Radio and he played a track called 'That's Why the Cowboy Sings the Blues' by a fellow called Waylon Jennings whom I'd never heard of because I'd never listened to country music at all. But I was knocked out by this guy's voice. It was so ballsy and not like Jim Reeves at all. So I went out and bought one of his albums and was staggered by this guy who had a tremendous clout to his style." Kennerley continued, "*White Mansions* was way off in the future and songwriting then was just a hobby for me . . . hearing Waylon set me off and I developed all these Southern images. Bit by bit, I developed ideas and now I'm devoted to the idea of using records to tell stories . . . ."[37]

The story Kennerley told was the southern side of the American Civil War as seen through the eyes of several characters. The tale centers on Matthew J. Fuller, a *Gone With The Wind* type of

WHITE MANSION

L to R: JOHN DILLON, STEVE CASH, PAUL KENNERLEY

Session from the *White Mansions* album, 1979. Courtesy A & M Records.

Confederate captain; Polly Ann Stafford, his plantation sweet-heart; Caleb Stone, a redneck; and the Drifter, a commentator on the doom to befall the South. Waylon was the Drifter and Polly was portrayed by Jessi Colter. Waylon cut five songs for the concept album: "Dixie, Hold On," "The Southland's Bleeding," "Dixie, Now You're Done," "They Laid Waste to Our Land," all with John Dillon of the Ozark Mountain Daredevils, and he dueted with Jessi on "The Union Mare and the Confederate Grey."

The album, despite Kennerley's objections, was billed as a meeting of superstars. Also appearing in the saga were Bernie Leadon of the Eagles and Eric Clapton. The album was outstanding, but it did not get much attention, as is usually the case with "concept" products. In fact, some critics objected to the content of the album. Mike Oakfield of *Melody Maker* bitterly wrote, "What next? A rock musical about Auschwitz told from the point of view of the guards?"[38] The so-called country rock opera was generally ignored in the press and by most record buyers.

In mid-1978 the outlaws were invited to the White House. Willie and his wife Connie, Jessi Colter, Buddy Jennings, and several Waylors went. Waylon refused. He rented a car and went sightseeing; a presidential aide said, "He's loose on the town." Willie, dressed in blue jeans, a red checkered shirt, and canvas hat strolled through the hallways of the White House. A reporter asked, "Isn't this just about the classiest honky-tonk you've ever seen?" "Yup, big beer joint." After a lunch of steak and fruit cocktail, the entertainers met with Jimmy Carter.

Willie chided the president for not joining in the night before. "We missed your voice in the choir last night," he said. "I know all the words," replied Carter. Willie was referring to the "Amazing Grace" sing-a-long. The president commended Willie on his gospel album, *Troublemaker*. "I play it whenever I've got troubles. Which means I listen to it a lot." When they departed the mansion, Waylon was still driving around.[39]

Waylon and Willie, although an economic success, did not garner especially favorable press attention. Said Greg Oatis in the *Toledo Blade*: "While Jennings and Nelson are compatible, sharing the same vinyl, *Waylon and Willie* lacks the distinction of some of each's solo work."[40] Nick Tosches in the *Rolling Stone* aptly summed up most reviewers' sentiments, writing, "When will there be another *Honky Tonk Heroes* from Jennings, another *Red Headed Stranger* from Nelson? How long can people who own the bank pretend to be outlaws?"[41]

With *I've Always Been Crazy* (1978), Waylon broke the bank again. The album was first in country music history to ship "gold." RCA mounted a massive promotional campaign, including Sunset Strip billboards usually reserved for rock artists. The album was his most autobiographical effort. Three of the songs, written by Waylon and Shel Silverstein, discuss his career, relations with the press, and the cocaine bust. It also included the long-awaited Buddy Holly medley recorded in 1974. Some of the other material was not as strong. Waylon's cover of Cash's standard "I Walk the Line" was disappointing, even to Mick Brady and to other critics. (Some felt the song had been released as a *quid pro quo* for the *Waylon and Willie* album.) Terry Atkinson called the interpretation "an unnecessarily lugubrious version."[42] Most critics felt the overall effort was his best in years.

In repetitive fashion, Waylon and Willie were renominated in 1978. The CMA Single of the Year ballot listed "Mammas Don't Let Your Babies Grow Up to Be Cowboys." Waylon and Willie were in the running for Album of the Year and the Top-Ranked Duo. Once again, Waylon boycotted the October 9 telecast. He didn't win, either. Again, complaints were aired by CMA members. "Why wasn't Loretta Lynn in the Top Female Vocalist category?" Some suggested that Willie Nelson's hit "Stardust" should not have been on the ballot. Others objected to the inclusion of Linda Ronstadt's "Blue Bayou." Waylon's fans wanted to know why he was not in the running for Top Male Vocalist.

A Music City insider commented, "The drug bust didn't help . . . but Willie's hotter than Waylon and you don't need two of *them* up there. That would be like admitting that the 'progressives' had won. So who's the best compromise candidate—Ronnie Milsap. Everybody likes him and he is *kinda* country."

WAYLON AND VISUALS

Amidst all the production activity, Waylon found himself narrating a TV show. He was no stranger to narratives or film scores. Narration was no problem, considering his early years as a deejay. "He thinks well on his feet," says Midnite. "And he may not be that much of an orator or anything, but when he does radio stuff, he always comes off good. Lots smarter than a lot of people probably give him credit for."[43]

Waylon's first film track, of course, had been *Nashville Rebel.* Waylon had done six songs written by Shel Silverstein for Mick Jagger's ill-fated film debut in *Ned Kelly,* a mediocre film about a famous Australian outlaw. A reviewer observed, "Sound track album it is with all the music and lyrics (some pretty raunchy) of Shel Silverstein of "Boy Named Sue' fame—but there's precious little of Mick Jagger involved. He's got one song—a simple little penny-whistle throw-away of a number. The rest is mostly tribute to Waylon Jennings, who sings six of the eleven tracks in a harshly guttural folk style. Like the movie . . . the album leaves a great deal to be desired where Jagger is concerned."[44]

In 1973 Duane Eddy had called Waylon, asking him to do a song for Richard Boone's projected new television series, "Hec Ramsey." Recalling the success his Phoenix sidekick Johnny Western had had with "Paladin," Waylon had agreed to do it. The song, written by Red Stargall, was cut in Los Angeles with the top session people, including Jim Burton. "Dick heard him sing," recalled Eddy, "and flipped over him. Boone said, 'Boy if I was a singer I'd want to sing like him' and they just got on great." But Universal Pictures didn't like the song. The company wanted one of its own tunes, which could then be released on MCA Records. NBC did not care for any of the songs offered, especially in the country music genre. A dispute arose, but the network prevailed. The "Hec Ramsey" theme has never seen the light of day, and Waylon took a loss on the venture. Boone said he would pay for Waylon's transportation and lodgings "but never got around to it." Boone did pick up the session costs.

A year after the "Ramsey" fiasco, Waylon was approached about writing a soundtrack for *Moonrunners.* The film was a sequel to the highly successful drive-in saga *Thunder Road.* Robert Mitchum's son Jim was chosen to repeat his father's role. "It's funny, you know," Waylon said. "He looks just like Robert Mitchum until he opens his mouth and that squeaky voice just don't quite fit that big ol' boy."[45] Waylon and Ralph Mooney wrote fourteen songs for the movie. Unfortunately, the soundtrack has never been released on record.

Penland Productions commissioned Waylon to do part of the music for their *MacIntosh and T. J.* film, which was to be the first movie in a decade for Roy Rogers. Waylon recut several standards, "Ride Me Down Easy" and "Bob Wills Is Still the King." The title song, "All Around Cowboy," was new. The Waylors recorded a number of instrumentals, including Ralph Mooney's classic "Crazy Arms." RCA did release an album. Neither the movie nor the soundtrack were a success. Mick Brady, in his newsletter, lamented: "It must offer the poorest value ever for a full-price album—just nine tracks including two versions of the same song, two re-cuts of previously issued tracks, four in-strumentals and one re-release of a track by Willie Nelson—this together with poor sleeve design are all RCA has to offer the record buyer for his $6.98. Whatever happened to 'bonus' tracks, I wonder?" He concluded, "in all, a very disappointing release."[46] This kind of criticism was unusual for the head of the Waylon Jennings Appreciation Society.

Then, in January 1979, CBS—hoping to boost its ratings—premiered "The Dukes of Hazzard," a show loosely based on the *Moonrunners* feature film. The program, according to Bill Kaufman, was "an action-packed combination of 'The Beverly Hillbillies' and 'Green Acres' and even down-home 'Starsky and Hutch' with a little of Burt Reynolds" movie epics tossed in . . . the show would seem to prove that good taste is relative." The show's producer, Paul Picard noted, "the reviews we got were 98.9 percent really dreadful—awful."[47] The show went on to become one of CBS's hottest properties. Each program opens with Waylon singing "Just two good ol' boys / Never meanin' no harm / Beats all you ever saw / Been in trouble with the law / Since the day they were born." The musical background is done by the Waylors under the direction of Richie Albright. In one episode, a Jessi Colter song is the focus of the story. Waylon was asked by *TV Guide* why the Colter song is the focus of the story and why he did the show. "Listening to the TV series," he replied, "may help people to decide for themselves what country-western music is about . . . A lot of folks who haven't heard us think we play something with kazoos."

Waylon provides more to "Dukes" than just music. He is the narrator of the show. He also fills dead air with homilies and folksy observations about the action. "Ain't this fun" or "Y'all stay with me while I unwind this yarn" were typical comments on the opening show. Waylon refuses to appear on the program. His participation is confined to recording his remarks in Nashville and sending them to the producer. "I don't want a lot of things that come with being recognized as a star. I like to run loose—just go out and play pinball or whatever." Waylon's reasoning is interesting, as he creates a mob scene everywhere he goes.

On February 15, 1979, NARAS staged its annual nationally televised Grammy Awards show in Los Angeles. Waylon was nominated in two categories: Best Country Male Singer and Best Vocal Performance of a Country Group. The later he shared with Willie Nelson. Neither attended the presentation. Willie won the country and western male award for "Georgia on My Mind." Glen Campbell and Tanya Tucker sang the nominations for the country group award: "Waylon and Willie are liable to start to roar if they don't win for 'Mammas, Don't Let Your Babies Grow Up to be Cowboys." Campbell opened the envelope and announced, "Waylon JENNINGS and Willie NELSON . . . ." Then he commented, "Waylon and Willie won't walk a mile to watch a pissant eat a bale of hay . . . ." John Denver, the host, hurried on stage and admonished, "It's live folks." Waylon had captured his second Grammy for Best Performance by a Group. The Grammy for "MacArthur Park" would now have company.

The night was not a memorable one. Grammy choices tend to be highly conservative. Willie's version of "Georgia" was good, but it has never been considered a country song. It did appeal to the NARAS membership, which refused to acknowledge the existence of the Beatles until 1969. The highlight of the evening was comedian Steve Martin, who made his entrance dressed in a tux and only his undershorts.

Cheryl Ladd, a star of "Charlie's Angels," added another chapter to Waylon's misadventures in videoland. In hopes of beefing up its Oscar night audience ABC scheduled a "Cheryl Ladd Special." The program was billed as "Charlie's Angel Goes Country as Cheryl Ladd sings with Waylon Jennings and Montana's Mission Mountain Wood Band; and dances in an outdoor sequence among farm animals." Waylon was scheduled to perform "Mammas Don't Let Your Babies Grow Up to Be Cowboys," "Don't You Think This Outlaw Bit's Done Got Out of Hand?" and "I've Always Been Crazy," and a duet with Cheryl on "Luckenbach."

Ms. Ladd, with a brand-new Capitol album, used the hour to showcase her very limited vocal abilities. Toward the end of the first half-hour, the camera sequed into the middle of "Don't You Think." The setting was a truckstop, which had little, if any, connection with the theme of the show. Waylon, supported by the Waylors, did "I've Always." After the song, Ms. Ladd appeared on the platform. "How do you get to be a Waylor?" sparkled Cheryl.

"Walk around and say 'Chief' . . .," replied Waylon.

"Hi Chief!"

After several similarly profound exchanges, Cheryl took Willie Nelson's part on their Grammy Award warning to cowboys' mothers. "It was awful" seemed a common reaction; the segment was out of place on the show. Waylon's indictment "get the cowboy singer" seemed all the more appropriate. Television prior to the 1980s did not seem to know how to deal with country artists.

After months of speculation and threats, Waylon renewed a contract with RCA Victor in March 1979 under what were called "generous terms." Rumors had been rampant for years that he wanted his own label, like Willie Nelson's Lone Star Company. He didn't get it. Instead, RCA did allow Waylon to use a new Indian design logo in the shape of flying "W". The negotiations of 1979 were a far cry from the tension-filled encounters of the past. Waylon was now one of RCA's hottest acts.

In the fall of 1978, Liz Smith, the syndicated gossip columnist, reported that Jessi Colter was expecting, after eight years of marriage. The couple refused to confirm the story. Waylon Albright Jennings was born on May 19, 1979. The Jennings family tradition of using the initials W.A. would continue. The middle name, of course, came from Waylon's long-time friend and drummer, Richie.

Waylon's career was progressing, but not at the frantic pace of his fellow cowboy Willie Nelson. Besides touring and recording, Willie was entering the world of motion pictures. He was scheduled to do *Electric Horseman* with Robert Redford and Jane Fonda. Rumors abounded that Waylon would follow. Waylon was content with his role as a proud father, a few concerts, selected television appearances, and a *Greatest Hits* album. Johnny Cash explained to a writer: "Waylon is more free inside and free from the business world of the music business . . . he demands his privacy, demands exclusiveness to be not involved in everything going around . . . ain't nobody in the world gonna be able to find him because he's going to be hiding out resting somewhere."[48]

Waylon's attitude offended more fans and writers. Mick Brady, increasingly critical, objected: "Waylon's next studio album has been postponed until the autumn . . . its place RCA has issued a *Greatest Hits* collection with a baffling selection of tracks—"Honky Tonk Heroes," "Ladies Love Outlaws," "Amanda," and "Lonesome On'ry and Mean" have no right to be there and there's a criminal omission of several hits such as "This Time," "You Asked Me To," "Can't You See" and "The Wurlitzer Prize." Brady tempered his remarks in the next sentence by praising the album cover design.[49] Record critics seemed to agree. Many questioned the timing of the album and the selections included. "Amanda," a Don Williams hit, was frequently cited as being out of place on the album. Only Dave Marsh in *Rolling Stone* applauded its inclusion. He was correct. Waylon's version of "Amanda" became the Number One country song in a matter of weeks, and the album went platinum. Waylon's musical instincts appeared vindicated, at least by the record-buying public.

What Goes Around Comes Around appeared in the record stalls in time for the 1979 holiday season. *Newsweek* recommended the album as an ideal musical holiday gift. Critics were somewhat baffled by the direction of the "long-awaited" work. Ken Emerson in the *New York Times* observed: "[These are] ballads full of vulnerability and self-doubt that Mr. Jennings has seldom shown before. This gruff voice has softened and his macho bluster has turned tender, creating an effect that is quite touching and also rather brave, since it is not the kind of manner or music that most of Mr. Jennings' fans will accept. That Waylon Jennings should attempt such a change of style—at a time when many other country artists are fiddling with their formulas in order to 'crossover' and win the mass popularity Mr. Jennings already enjoys—is an act of consideration and commendable courage."[50] Others weren't too sure about his being a *mellower* singer. Mick Brady in *Outlaws* suggested: "The album has far more depth than I originally gave it credit for, not a great release, granted, but by no means a bad one."[51] The album did require some getting used to, especially for long-standing fans. The *Toledo Blade* writer Jeff Bush summed up their feelings. "This album has to rate as somewhat a disappointment, basically because it contains too many soft country love ballads that are impossible to take seriously because of his voice and too few of the good ol' country rockers that Jennings is usually known for . . . the general mood of the LP is too slow paced and very close to boring."[52] The *Blade* writer's assessment did reflect the attitude of certain fans. However, the main difference between *What Goes Round* and previous albums was the concentration on ballads; Jennings usually mixed up-tempo material with love songs. The album was gold, and "Come with Me" reached the top of the country charts. Even an album that was admittedly a departure from the usual Jennings formula was a success in 1980.

Waylon appeared to be softening in areas other than music. On January 31, 1980, he joined John R. Cash at the "Grand Ole Opry" in a special benefit concert for the widows of Nashville policemen and firemen killed in the line of duty. This was a far cry from the man who told *Genesis*, "I don't like the way law enforcement is becoming; Protect and serve—I think they've forgotten that a little bit. I really believe that they spend too much time protecting us from ourselves and arresting people who are victims."[53]

The year 1980 was a good one for awards. Waylon won the fourth annual *Rolling Stone* readers' poll as "the country male vocalist of 1979." He also placed first in the *Stone's* critic's poll—a clean sweep. *Billboard's* annual country rating placed him second only to the "red hot" Kenny Rogers. Some fans grumbled that Rogers wasn't "country."

These successes had little impact on the CMA. In 1980, despite a string of single hits and successful gold albums, Waylon was not nominated in any category. One writer commented, "They're going to need him more in the future than the other way around." Recent nominations and award shows seem to indicate that he may well have been right.

Waylon's attitude toward politics seems to have changed during the election year. Perhaps Jessi's and Buddy's going to the White House and Willie Nelson had something to do with it. Waylon did a few benefits for Jimmy Carter. Reportedly Waylon added some $70,000—before matching funds—to the presidential campaign chest.[54] Even Waylon's attitude toward television was evolving. The change had begun in 1979.

Although leery of Hollywood network specials and daytime variety talk show, Waylon did consent to appear in Nashville television presentations, especially when they were hosted by close friends like Johnny Cash or Hank Williams, Jr. Opryland was rapidly becoming a major television showcase and was convenient for local artists. Waylon felt little hesitation about repeating his appearance on what was becoming an annual event— "The Johnny Cash Spring Special." Aired May 9, 1979, the one-hour program featured Hank Williams, Jr., Earl Scruggs, and Waylon's singing idol, George Jones. Waylon did "Amanda," then high on the charts. He changed several lines in autobiographical fashion: "Finally made 40 still wearing jeans" and "a Gemini's wife." Waylon joined several of the other guests for duets. John R. and Waylon did "Even Cowgirls Get the Blues," written by Cash's son-in-law Rodney Crowell. Jessi would later record the song. George Jones helped them with "Keep on the Sunny Side" in a salute to the Carter Family. Sadly, this tribute would be done later in the year after the passing of Maybelle Carter.

"The Unbroken Circle: A Tribute to Mother Maybelle Carter" was described by a newspaper columnist as "one of the best hours of country music ever presented on television."[55] The program was headlined by the biggest names in and around Nashville. John R. opened with his hit "Ghost Riders in the Sky." After thunderous applause, Cash commented, "She cared for me at a time I needed help." Willie Nelson followed. Waylon was introduced by Ray Charles. He sang "Black Jack David" accompanied only by an acoustical Martin guitar. Ray Charles and Waylon sang one verse of "Can the Circle Be Unbroken" at the close. It indeed was one of country music's television high points.

Between these two shows Waylon finally appeared on NBC's "Today" program. Jane Pauley asked a few nondescript questions and Waylon sang "Don't You Think the Outlaw Bit is Gettin' Out of Hand."

Much of "Buddy Holly: Reminiscing" (1980) was taped on a Jennings tour, which now included the Crickets Jerry Allison and Joe B. Mauldin. Doug Brooker filmed them, with Sonny Curtis, doing soundchecks and in hotel rooms. Waylon appeared briefly in the tribute joining the trio in "Peggy Sue." Waylon was characterized as "the personification of what Buddy Holly was and could be." He made a few perfunctory remarks, none of which offered any new information: "Buddy was the first person to have faith in me as a singer . . . . he said you're not a hillbilly . . . . you'll see eventually you'll be accepted in most fields . . . . in times I was down I could look back at what Buddy Holly told me. The encouragement he gave me. He was my friend first and foremost . . . last and not least." A knowledgeable viewer could only wonder once more about the ghost of Buddy Holly in Waylon's career. He hasn't really said much about the subject for years, yet he has recorded medlies of Holly songs, has used the Crickets on tour, and he even lends his voice to "Peggy Sue." This is but one more unexplained complexity of the man.

For a time, Waylon's television career seemed destined to be tied to the praise of fallen stars. Jim Owen and Hank Williams, Jr., asked Waylon to participate in "Hank Williams: A Tribute to a Man and His Music" (1980). He did a tape with Hank, Jr. The song appeared in the middle of the show; it contained the line, "most wanted outlaw in the land." It was a motif Waylon had established in the few interviews he was doing at the time. The song, however, was overshadowed by Jim Owens's dramatization of Hank Williams, which was the meat of the syndicated 90-minute Multi-Media production.

Announced by full-page ads in the trades, *Rolling Stone*, and *Country Music,* the album *Music Man* was released in the summer of 1980. It was an immediate commercial success featuring several hits, including the innocuous "Theme from the Dukes of Hazzard." Most critics were unkind. Bob Allen of *Country Music*, a long-standing Jennings partisan, wrote:

> All in all, there's something rather listless about this entire LP. The choice of material is fine, as are the singing and the arrangements. Unfortunately, the energy level is dangerously low. It's as if there's a sheet of glass between Waylon Jennings and to whoever he's singing.
>
> MUSIC MAN is a good album by anyone's standards but Waylon Jennings; but when you compare it to great Jennings LP's of the past like DREAMIN' MY DREAMS, and ARE YOU READY FOR THE COUNTRY, it is but a faint whisper.[56]

Waylon was able to break away from musical eulogizing by appearing on ABC's "Country Gold," a program hosted by Dennis Weaver. Waylon merely lip-synched two songs from *Music Man*. His performance *was* listless.

Nearly a year following the taping of "Reminiscing," Jack Thompson approached Waylon about doing an hour TV special. Waylon had known Thompson from his early days in Phoenix. The producer suggested taping a concert and a segment at the Manizanita Speedway in Phoenix. James Garner of the "Rockford Files" would be the guest. The idea did not seem too farfetched. Waylon controlled his public appearances (some fans complain, "too well"). Much of the Holly documentary had been done on the road, and Waylon was fond of stock car racing. He had been grand marshall at the 420 Grand National in Nashville. The show would underline his "Dukes of Hazzard" image. RCA had just released the "Dukes" theme as a single. The footage was shot in the American Studios in Nashville, Phoenix, and the awe-inspiring Red Rock Amphitheatre outside Denver. In the final editing the raceway material finished up on the cutting-room floor.

One week after "Country Gold," the "Waylon" program aired nationally on the ABC. This was Waylon's first commercial network special. (He had done a "Soundstage" for PBS some years before.) The broadcast was presented in semi-documentary fashion. It opened with a convoy of three vehicles led by a chrome-plated eighteen-wheeler with the flying "W" logo. Two buses followed with Waylon, Jessi, and Garner in the Silver Eagle playing poker. "Are You Sure Hank Done It This Way" provided musical background. The convoy was a vast improvement over the white Cadillac of old, the ill-fated Dodge camper, or even the mechanically temperamental Black Maria. Many country artists have elaborate Silver Eagles, but *two* buses and an equipment-packed Mack truck are another matter. Mr. Luckey's was the first stop. The compact nightclub was *the* country music bar in Phoenix during the 1970s. Aspiring local talent such as Virgil Warner played there. Waylon's appearance there was probably more for the camera effect than for profit.

Waylon opened his set with a few obscure remarks about ex-wives and "I used to get in a lot of trouble [here] a long time ago," which was an understatement. Before his financial settlement with Lynne, Waylon rarely appeared in the area because Lynne would send the sheriff out with a lien for back alimony and child support. Waylon had to grab his money and run whenever he did play Phoenix. The management of Mr. Luckey's at one point had been leery of him and the Waylors. But now the times obviously had changed.

Waylon's choice of songs was autobiographical. Rodney Crowell's "Ain't Living Long Like This" alluded to his experiences with the law. "Good Hearted Woman" was directed to Jessi, sitting in the audience, with new allusions to "world's largest dirty ole man" and "my Mickey Mouse ways she don't understand." "This Time" was thrown in for good measure—another song with a personal history.

After the show, the "documentary" moved to a simulated pool game with Garner. Waylon again raised the Holly issue, telling the actor about his first bus trip with his friend. The Crickets would appear in the show later.

The caravan moved north to Red Rock. Following an obligatory but uninspired duet with Garner, segments of the performance were filmed before 8,500 screaming fans who had paid from $9.50 to $10.50 to see the singer, Jessi, and the Crickets. The concert grossed $88,424. Five years earlier, Waylon had been earning $2,000 a night. As always, Waylon joined the Crickets in "Peggy Sue." This was the usual seque from the old

Holly group to Waylon's show. Waylon ran through a string of hits like "I've Always Been Crazy," "Mammas Don't Let Your Babies . . . . ," "Luckenbach," and "Honky Tonk Heroes." Back on the bus, the card game with Garner as Maverick resumed. The show ended with the convoy rolling toward Nashville, some 1,190 miles away. The program was nominated for an Emmy.

On October 23, 1980, Waylon joined a small country elite. Only a handful of Nashville performers such as Cash, Crystal Gayle, Barbara Mandrell, and Kenny Rogers were considered viable as network draws. Shows like "Nashville Palace" or "Country Gold" showcased five to seven artists and were aimed at the largest possible audience. Now "Waylon who?" seemed past history.

Reportedly, ABC was satisfied with the show despite its marginal audience share. Waylon was next to appear in a television film, *The Oklahoma City Dolls,* with Susan Blakely. Waylon should be able to handle the role after his experience at Littlefield High School; if not, he could always consult his friends on the Dallas Cowboys, someone maintained. *Dolls* was a blue-collar version of *9 to 5* with a little *Norma Rae* mixed in. The film's story line was described in the promotional literature: "The guys say their girls belong in the kitchens and the bedroom—not on the football field. The women say they're wrong. But to prove it . . . they've got to win!" Waylon is one of the macho guys, Wayne Doak, Sally Jo's [played by Susan Blakely] boyfriend. When Sally Jo decides to start a female gridion unit, Wayne suggests that she "go back to being a lady." Needless to say, Sally Jo and company overcome all odds and prevail. The film closes with Wayne's telling the heroine, "I have to say somethin' not easy to admit—I love a quarterback!" They walk off the empty football field: fade out and credits. Waylon's performance was undemanding, and he did well in a familiar story line. Otherwise, the 1980s for the "last of the outlaws" marked yet another "new beginning."

Since *This Time* Waylon had enjoyed ten gold albums, that is 5,020,000 units sold, and three platinums, or 3,000,000 units. (Criteria for gold and platinum records are set by the R.I.A.A.) At 87 cents (which assumes a "superstar" point contract) per record sold at 7.98 list, he would have grossed $6,977,400 over the six-year period.[57] The "Dukes" single also went gold. Add to that mechanicals (or publishing fees) and royalties, and the figure increases. Waylon receives $.0275 for each song he has written for an album. An equal amount comes from airplay of his material.[58] His concert income, as he admitted to *Genesis*, was between $15,000 and $25,000 an appearance. A Nashville UPI correspondent confirmed this claim.[59] Waylon also received larger residuals for showing his hands and doing the theme for "Dukes." Nevertheless, by late 1980 Waylon was in deep financial trouble. Don Davis, a former employee, observed: "He had a million coming in and two million going out."[60] Too many employees, flunkies, Silver Eagle buses, eighteen wheelers, and the excessive perks of superstardom. His first reaction—a typical one—was to fire people. The entire staff of Waylon's renamed Utopia Productions was dismissed. Waylon severed his relationship with manager Neil Reshen. Many considered this a grievous mistake. Rumors abounded that even Richie Albright's position was in jeopardy. Richie, of course was an original Waylor. In eary 1981, Waylon exhibited a scaled-down organization and increased his touring schedule. Don Wocjik of the Lavender Talent agency, now booking Waylon, told *Billboard* "he doesn't ask for limos or fancy 12-course French dinners. He does require a hot meal for his band and road crew (about 30 people), but this is because otherwise they won't have time to go out and eat before setting up the show."[61]

He would now agree to do state fairs and amusement parks when the price was right. A forty-eight-day, thirty-concert tour began in May. Tony Joe White was added to the roster. The basic structure of the two-and-a-half-hour show remained the same. Tony Joe would open, followed by the Crickets. Waylon would join in on "Peggy Sue." Jessi would do her usual numbers as well as duets on "Storms Never Last" and another cut from the *Leather & Lace* album.[62] The closing hour would be Waylon's. He still would say little except "Thank you very much. Good night." An encore traditionally would follow. Touring seemed the cure to Waylon's cash flow problems, as *Leather & Lace* fared poorly in contrast to previous albums. Another partial cure for Waylon's economic ills was to release *Black on Black,* which reached the racks in the opening months of 1982 minus Richie Albright.

Waylon joined Jerry Weintraub Management Three in Los Angeles in 1982. Weintraub also manages Bob Dylan, John Denver, and Gordon Lightfoot. He is considered to be one—if not the best—of the top "sharks" in the music business. Waylon was in good company.[63]

It is impossible to predict what the future holds. But in the still of the Tennessee night, a lyric from his duet with John R. may flash by:

> She keeps me off the streets
> And she keeps me out of trouble.
> Sometimes at night, Lord, when I hear the wind
> I wish I was crazy again. (©Hall-Clement Publications BMI.)

But, on the flip side there is his other line:

> I ain't cut out to be no Jesse James.

14

EPILOGUE

Waylon Arnold Jennings has come a long way from the cotton
fields of West Texas. In his travels, Waylon may well have saved
Nashville from becoming what Bill C. Malone once called "com-
mercialized folk music." "Waylon won," wrote Hank Williams,
Jr., "he read the audience better than the music moguls in Nashville." Charlie Rich said, "Waylon and Cash have helped their
fellow man in the same business."[1] Now he's a superstar who has
sold over 16 million albums since the outlaw campaign began. It
may be a mistake to present Jennings as a romantic hero or a
radical crossing swords with the power structure of Music City
and its value system. Waylon's sense of musical identity was a
factor in shaping his choices. More significantly, many of his
actions were those of desperation, not rebellion. The time for
change had finally reached Sixteenth Avenue, South. What next?
In this case, history is not a good teacher. Waylon still looks like a
contemporary Jesse James, but as he told a Nashville writer,
"What I want to know, do daddys make good outlaws?"[2] He
could easily have changed that to "do granddaddys in Lear jets
make good outlaws?"

As late as 1982 the paradox of the outlaw image continued. A
60-second television spot on a Detroit station to advertise
another of his greatest hit albums began, "the last of the outlaws . . . ." On the screen a black-and-white leather holster
appeared. A six-gun was quick drawn and six rounds were

pumped into the gold record on the jacket cover. Waylon has artistic control over his advertising and jacket covers.

The contradictions of the ad and his apparent desires fit the pattern. Waylon doesn't like talking about the "seat change" or Buddy Holly, yet his road act includes the Crickets and in concert he always joins in on at least one Holly song. "He's a Gemini!" one astrologically oriented fan said, which is true. However, there may be more earthly explanations.

Waylon, like "the man in black" and his friend Hank, Jr., may need the anchor of a successful formula. A less charitable view is that the artistic well may be temporarily dry. In 1981 Waylon was absent from *Billboard*'s annual top fifty singles list. Ironically, the reunited Glaser Brothers did place, with "Loving Her Was Easier." Waylon's standing on the LP rankings reflected the strength of the *Greatest Hits* album, now platinum. *Leather and Lace* was politely received by the critics, but the album was a commercial also-ran.

As Joe Galante, RCA's vice president of marketing observed, "Nashville today isn't the same Nashville of five years ago . . . it's a whole new ball game with a new set of players."[3] In 1981 another generation characterized by a "Sun Belt Pop" sound and led by Kenny Rogers seemed to be taking over. (The term was coined by Steve Holden to describe the soundtrack of *Urban Cowboy*, a film Waylon was scheduled to appear in but didn't.) Since "Lucille," Rogers all but lived on the top of the country singles and albums charts. His crossover ability matched and frequently surpassed that of Willie Nelson and Waylon. In a candid statement, Rogers admitted is folk/pop career had run its course. Country seemed the road to rejuvenation: "In the pop market," said Rogers, "you're as good as your last hit. But in country music, I've seen people without a hit for years who still are big favorites."[4]

Rogers's phenomenal crossover ability, unlike Waylon's or Willie's, had little to do with his singing or songwriting abilities. Kenny and his ex-producer, Larry Butler, found pearls as "The Gambler," "Coward of the County," or "She Believes in Me." The producer screens over two hundred songs for each album: "Larry Butler usually finds all the material and he and I jointly will pick all the final songs . . . ."[5]

Following *Outlaws*, Waylon has not been quite as adventurous. Partly this is because he is his own producer and he trusts a small coterie of writers and songsmiths like Rodney Crowell. *Black on*

A gambler who won big, very big. Courtesy of United Artists.

LARRY BUTLER

The man behind Kenny Rogers' success. He picked the songs. Courtesy of United Artists.

Black, released in the early part of 1982, aptly demonstrates this career pattern. The album photo is captioned "Waylon, friends, kin and then some." The selections on the record more than verify his dependence on an inner circle. Two of the ten songs were retooled previous recordings—"Just to Satisfy You" and "Folsom Prison Blues." Waylon wrote three of the tunes. The remainder were by Paul Kennerley (*White Mansions*), Rodney Crowell, and the others by producer and studio owner Chips Moman and super session man Buddy Emmons. Some critics were unimpressed by the Emmons and Moman compositions. *Billboard,* which rarely criticizes any artist, noted: "the one weak spot on the album is that not all of the material lives up to the high caliber of the performer and producer."[6] *Black* sold fairly well, reaching the sixth ranking on the *Billboard* country album chart on July 24. "Just To Satisfy You," with Willie Nelson, was a single's hit. Since the formula had worked, Willie and Waylon put out *WW II,* which reached the third spot on the chart the following year.

Hank Williams was one of the major nonconformists in Music City. He was the first to use his own band in a Nashville studio, and he made few attempts to hide his personal foibles. He's in the Hall of Fame. Barring CMA politics, Waylon just may get there someday.

The verdict on Waylon as an individual is still out. He likes children and puppies, but there are legions of musicians, fans, employees, and others who in some real or imagined way "crossed" him and paid for it heavily. On Waylon's Lear jet, Chet Flippo asked him about this. His reply is revealing: "You ain't got enough tape for me to tell you what I've done that I regret. I've made a lot of mistakes. Most of the things I did, I thought I was doing right. I felt right, or I did them when I was stupid; so if I had to do them over and I didn't know what I know now, I guess I'd probably do them again."[7]

Waylon might well be the Bob Dylan of country music, an "introvert in an extroverted business." Or, as one former associate put it, "except for that giant talent, as a person he's the Richard Nixon of country. Not politics as people." "Any artist that's too big to be accessible," cautioned Bobby Bare, "is not going to be a big artist very long."[8]

There's another totally different view. Hazel Smith, then at "Hillbilly Central," repeatedly told stories of Waylon's generosity to her and to the office staff. George Jones relates the follow-

ing anecdote. He received a phone call from Waylon, whose
intention was to forgive a $50,000 loan. "We're behind you. You
don't owe us nothing. We owe you." That was it. He [Waylon]
was at Johnny's [Cash] house when he called. I was never able to
figure that out."[9] George immediately checked into a detoxifica-
tion unit with hope, feeling that "somebody cared." At times,
Waylon and John R. expressed considerable dissatisfaction with
George's "backsliding" but rejoiced when he appeared sober and
straight.

It remains difficult to ignore the bitterness, disappointment
and even the downright fear that ordinary people, especially
fans, experience around Waylon. A fan wrote, "I feel a little
afraid around Waylon when I do get the opportunity for so many
people have told me that once you make him angry at you, he
never forgets it!!"[10] Many others have echoed this sentiment,
including those in the ever-changing inner circle. The problem
appears to be that very few people have any inkling of what
"crosses the Chief." A seemingly harmless action, comment, or
association can lead to banishment and exile. Can it be a case of
Robert Louis Stevenson's Dr. Jekyll and Mr. Hyde? One may
recall that Dr. Jekyll was presented as one of the foremost
medical innovators of his time. Waylon enjoys the same status in
country music.

NOTES

PREFACE

1. See Julian Smith, "Pale Horse, Pale Rider; Pale Car, Pale Driver: On the Road to Nashville with *Pay Day*," *Journal of Popular Film and Television* 7 (1979): 190–201.

INTRODUCTION

1. *Popular Music and Society*, 3(1974), 137.
2. Roberta Plunkett interviews, 1974–1975.
3. Johnny Western, "Waylon Jennings—Future Unlimited," liner notes, *Waylon*, RCA Victor Records, LSP–4260.
4. John L. Smith, "Waylon Jennings: Free Spirit," liner notes, *This Time*, RCA Victor, APL 1–0539.
5. Robert Hilburn, "Kristofferson, Jennings in Mainstream," *Los Angeles Times*, February 5, 1972, sect. 2, p. 6.
6. Robert Hilburn interview.
7. Jay Elher, "Waylon Jennings: Rocking the Country Soul," *Country Sky*, May 1972, p. 6.
8. Clipping from West Coast RCA Victor publicity file.
9. Maureen Orth, "Outlaw Breed," *Newsweek*, Aug. 26, 1974, pp. 84–85. John Grissom, *Country Music: White Man's Blues* (New York, 1970), Paperback Library 69.

10. Howard Husock, "Waylon Jennings' Honky Tonk Heroism," *Boston Phoenix*, April 2, 1974, sec. 2, p. 6.

11. Peter Yarrow interview.

12. Letter, Waylon Jennings to Mrs. Virgie Risenger, n.d. (1969).

13. Teddy Bart, *Inside Music City U.S.A.* (Nashville: Aurora Publishers, 1970), 47.

14. Interviews with Paris, Kristofferson, Tucker's musicians.

15. Denisoff, "Waylon Jennings Interview," *Popular Music and Society*, 3(1974), Interviews with Waylon Jennings, March 1974.

16. Dan McPhail quoted in Hal Blu, "Who's Around," *Las Vegas Panorama* (1974), p. 12. Also, "Waylon At the Golden Nugget [sic] Las Vegas," *Waylonews* (March 1974)

17. John S. Wilson "You Can't Take the Country Out of Chet," *New York Times*, April 7, 1974, p. 32-D.

18. Chet Flippo, "Waylon Jennings Gets Off the Grind," *Rolling Stone*, Dec. 6, 1972, p. 28.

19. John T. Pugh, "Waylon Jennings: 'Country Music Is Soul,'" *Music City News*, June 1970, p. 13. Interview with Bob Luman.

20. Waylon Jennings interview.

21. Roy Silver interview.

CHAPTER 1

1. See Norm Cohen, "Scopes and Evolution in Hillbilly Songs," *John Edwards Memorial Foundation Quarterly* 6 (Winter 1971): 177; Jens Lund, "Fundamentalism, Racism and Political Reaction in Country Music," in R. Serge Denisoff and R.A. Peterson, eds., *Sounds of Social Change* (Chicago: Rand McNally, 1972): 79–90. Also Ray Ginger, *Six Days or Forever? Tennessee vs. John Thomas Scopes* (New York: Quadrangle, 1969).

2. Walter D. Haden, "Vernon Delhart" in Bill C. Malone and Judith McCulloh, eds., *Stars of Country Music* (Urbana: Univ. of Illinois Press, 1975), 64–85.

3. Paul Hemphill, *Nashville Sound: Bright Lights and Country Music* (New York: Simon & Schuster, 1970), 12.

4. Nolan Porterfield, *Jimmie Rodgers: The Life and Times of America's Blue Yodeler* (Urbana: Univ. of Illinois Press, 1979).

5. Bill C. Malone, "Bob Wills: He Put the West in Country & Western," *Rolling Stone*, Oct. 10, 1974, p. 15.

6. J. Fred MacDonald, "'Hot Jazz'—The Jitterbug and Misunderstanding: The Generation Gap in Swing 1935—1945," *Popular Music and Society* 2:1 (Fall 1972): 43–55.

7. Willie Nelson, "A Tribute to Bob Wills," *Country Music*, Aug.

1974, p. 73; and Charles R. Townsend, *San Antonio Rose* (Urbana: Univ. of Illinois Press, 1976).

8. Lewis Killian, "The Adjustment of Southern White Migrants to Northern Urban Norms," *Social Forces* 32 (Oct. 1953), 68.

9. Bob Shelton and Burt Goldblatt, *The Country Music Story* (New Rochelle: Arlington House, 1971), 91.

10. Roger Williams, *Sing a Sad Song: The Life of Hank Williams* (Garden City, N.Y.: Doubleday, 1970), 213.

11. Chet Flippo, *Your Cheatin' Heart: A Biography of Hank Williams* (New York: Simon & Schuster, 1981).

12. Chet Atkins, *Country Gentleman* (Chicago: Henry Regnery, 1974), 192–93. John S. Wilson, "You Can't Take the Country Out of Chet," *New York Times*, April 7, 1974, sec. D, pp. 17, 32.

13. Jerry Hopkins, *Elvis: a Biography* (New York: Simon & Schuster, 1971), 66.

14. David Dalton, "Interview with Steve Sholes," in Albert Goldman, *Elvis* (New York: McGraw-Hill, 1981), 163.

15. Chet Atkins quoted in Wilson, "You Can't Take the Country," 32.

16. Bob Luman interview.

17. Bobby Bridger quoted in Jan Reid, *The Improbable Rise of Redneck Rock* (Austin: Heidelberg Press, 1976), 190.

18. Bob Kirsch, "Tompall Glaser Goes Out on His Own: Still a Stubborn Renegade," *Billboard* (Aug. 31, 1974).

19. Tompall Glaser interview.

20. David Rensin, "Kris Kristofferson," *Country Music*, Sept. 1974, pp. 28–29.

21. Kirsch, "Tompall Glaser"; Kip Kirby "Opry Facing a Crucial Period," *Billboard* (Jan 8, 1983), 61, 63.

CHAPTER 2

1. Texas Dept. of Health, Bureau of Vital Statistics, Standard Certificate of Birth #2554 filed July 5, 1937, Lamb County, Texas.

2. "Johnny Cash Interviews Waylon," *Country Music*, April 1, 1981, p. 27. When Wayland became Waylon is hard to pin down. Tommy Jennings told Mick Brady in an unpublished interview, "I think there was a kid down the street called Waylon . . . ." He also claims that Lorene's first name choice was Tommy.

3. Paula Lovell Hooker, "Jessie [sic] Colter and Waylon Jennings," *Country Music*, Dec. 1979, p. 38.

4. Tony Byworth, "Last of the Cosmic Cowboys," *Record Mirror*, Feb. 16, 1974.

5. Tommy Jennings interview.

6. Ibid.; *Music City News*, May 1966, p. 14.

7. Chet Flippo, "Penthouse Interview: Waylon Jennings," *Penthouse*, Sept. 1981, p. 142.

8. Tommy Jennings interview.

9. Ibid.

10. 20/20 interview, ABC-TV, March 25, 1982.

11. Tommy Jennings interview.

12. Waylon Jennings interview.

13. See Chet Flippo, "The Texas Rock and Roll Spectacular," *Phonograph Record*, Mar. 1974, pp. 20–29.

14. Denisoff, "Waylon Jennings Interview," 118.

15. W.J. Duncan interview.

16. Tommy Jennings interview.

17. "Nashville Welcomes Waylon Jennings," *Music City News*, May 1966, p. 14.

18. "Cash Interviews Waylon," 22, 24.

19. Tommy Jennings interview.

20. "Nashville Welcomes Waylon Jennings," 14.

21. Letter from Lorene Jennings Gilbert to fan. Courtesy Mrs. V. Rissenger.

22. Tommy Jennings interview.

23. Ibid.

24. Ibid.

25. John Grissom, *Country Music: White Man's Blues* (New York: Paperback Library 1970), 60.

26. Waylon Jennings interview.

27. An artist recorded it for the Dart label. Waylon refers to him as a "ding-a-ling." Quoted in Jay Ehler, "Waylon Jennings," *Door*, Dec. 1971.

28. Chet Flippo, "Near to the Maddening Crowd," *Texas Monthly*, Feb. 1975, p. 54.

29. Tommy Jennings interview.

30. Pat Salvo and Barbara Salvo, "Hustler Interview: Waylon Jennings," *Hustler*, June 1975, p. 73.

31. Susan Toepfer, "'I'm Not Gonna Put Up with Anything from Anybody," *Photoplay*, Feb. 1974, p. 100.

32. Robert Windeler, "Couples," *People*, Sept. 29, 1975, p.46. Also Norma M. Stoop, "Waylon Jennings: Big Country Singer Hits the Big City," *After Dark* (April, 1973): 51.

33. Tommy Jennings interview.

34. Mrs. Gilbert correspondence to Mrs. Rissenger.

35. Hi-Pockets Duncan interview.

36. "Nashville Welcomes," 14.

37. Flippo, "Penthouse," ibid., 108.

38. Tommy Jennings interview.

39. Waylon Jennings interview.

CHAPTER 3

1. See John Goldrosen, *Buddy Holly: His Life and Music* (Bowling Green, Ohio: Popular Press, 1975), 35–39; also Claude and Barbara Hall, *This Business of Radio Programming* (New York: Billboard Publications, 1977, 34; and Richard P. Stockdell, "The Evolution of a Format: Putting Country Music in the Mainstream," *Journal of Popular Culture* (in press).
2. Bob Montgomery interview.
3. Sonny Curtis interview.
4. Transcript of Mick Brady interview with Tommy Jennings.
5. Sonny Curtis interview.
6. Anonymous interview.
7. Hi-Pockets Duncan interview.
8. Sonny Curtis interview.
9. Dan Pietromonaco, "Interview with Waylon Jennings," *Billboard's* TWA Airline Audio Service (1976).
10. Sonny Curtis interview.
11. Mary Lou Fairbairn, "Lubbock Now Has Its Answer to Elvis," *Lubbock Evening Journal,* Oct. 23, 1956, pp. 1, 5.
12. Jack Hurst, *Nashville's Grand Ole Opry* (New York: Harry N. Abrams, 1975, 226.
13. Don Helms, "Ballad of Hank Williams" recorded by Hank Williams, Jr., *The Pressure Is On* (Elektra 5E–535).
14. *Buddy Holly,* 45–46.
15. Buddy chose the title from John Wayne's film *The Searchers.*
16. Ray Odum interview.
17. Hi-Pockets Duncan interview.
18. Sonny Curtis interview.
19. Anonymous interview; Tommy Allsup interview; Don Bowman interview.
20. Waylon Jennings interview.
21. Sonny Curtis interview.
22. Hi-Pockets Duncan interview.
23. Mick Brady interview.
24. Sonny Curtis interview.
25. Tommy Jennings interview.
26. Goldrosen, *Buddy Holly,* 143.
27. Waylon Jennings interview.
28. Ibid.
29. Bob Montgomery interview.

CHAPTER 4

1. Tommy Jennings interview.
2. "Leaves for New York Monday," *Littlefield Register,* n.d.

3. Waylon Jennings interview.
4. Goldrosen, *Buddy Holly*, 183.
5. Ibid, 184. Because of contractual obligations to the producers of the film "The Buddy Holly Story," Maria Diaz, now remarried, is unavailable for interviews.
6. Transcription of the Snuff Garrett radio show "Salute to Buddy Holly" (Feb. 4, 1959), KSYD—Wichita Falls, Tex.
7. Tommy Allsup interview.
8. Waylon Jennings interview.
9. Ibid.
10. This conversaton has been reported in numerous accounts. "Interview with Waylon Jennings by Sky Corbin," Feb. 3, 1969, KLLL Lubbock, Tex., is probably the best description.
11. "Interview with Waylon Jennings," 1970, KRIZ Phoenix, Ariz. Transcript provided by John Goldrosen.
12. Tommy Allsup interview. Also Goldrosen, *Buddy Holly,* 189; John Firminger, "Buddy Holly—Last Tour," *Outlaws,* Mar. 1980, p. 46; and "The Waylon and Buddy Holly Story," *Country Style,* Apr. 1979, pp. 13, 40.
13. Goldrosen, *Buddy Holly*, 191.
14. Tommy Jennings interview.
15. Bob Montgomery interview.
16. Greil Marcus, liner notes from *Legendary Master's Series: Bobby Vee* (United Artists—UA LA025 (Available only in United Kingdom) (G-3, G-4).
17. Tommy Allsup interview.
18. Waylon Jennings interview.
19. Ron Gavatt, *Billboard*, Feb. 9, 1959.
20. "Album Covers of the Week," *Billboard*, Mar. 9, 1959, p. 27.
21. Tommy Allsup interview.
22. Anonymous interview.
23. Tommy Allsup interview.
24. Waylon Jennings interview.
25. Hi-Pockets Duncan interview.
26. Waylon Jennings interview.

CHAPTER 5

1. "Nashville Welcomes Waylon Jennings, "*Music City News*, May 1966, p. 14.
2. Chet Atkins, *Country Gentlemen* (Chicago: Regnery, 1974).
3. Don Bowman interview.
4. Waylon Jennings interview.
5. Hi-Pockets Duncan interview.

6. Bob Garbutt, "The Road to Nashville: Waylon Jennings," *Goldmine*, Dec. 1979, p. 20.

7. Tommy Jennings interview.

8. Duane Eddy interview.

9. Mae Boren Axton, *Country Singers As I Know 'Em* (Austin: Sweet Publishing Co., 1973), 126. The story about the raise should be taken with caution. Perrin, like most rural radio station owners, paid substandard salaries.

10. Duane Eddy interview.

11. Ray Odum interview.

12. Salvo and Salvo, "Hustler Interview," 24.

13. *Urban Cowboy* seems to have defused the "orchard" atmosphere in some places. See Jean Williams, "Jennings Opening Act At Big Fort Worth Spot," *Billboard*, Feb. 28, 1981, pp. 29, 47.

14. Grissom, *Country Music*, 76.

15. Toepfer, "I'm Not Gonna Put Up With Anything," 71ff.

16. Howard Turner interview.

17. Ray Odom interview.

18. Waylon has ordered that the master be destroyed and warned those with a tape of the tune not to reproduce it.

CHAPTER 6

1. *Nashville Sound*, 257.

2. Don Bowman interview. Also Nat Freedland, "Moss Traces A & M Rise to Eminence," *Billboard*, August 26, 1972, pp. 1, 84. Judith Sims, "Two Lonely Bulls and How They Grew," *Rolling Stone*, Oct. 12, 1972, 14.

3. Don Bowman interview.

4. Jerry Moss interview.

5. Herb Alpert, Jerry Moss, Bob Garcia interviews.

6. Herb Alpert, Jerry Moss interviews.

7. Letter to author from A & M.

8. Don Bowman interview.

9. RCA tear sheet (n.d.).

10. Jerry Moss interview.

11. Bo Powel, "Waylon Jennings: Interview," *Country Music People*, July 1971, p. 18. In my interviews Waylon contrasted Flatt and Scruggs to Martino.

12. Herb Alpert interview.

13. Bob Bare interview.

14. Don Bowman interview.

15. Letter from Topper Morris, Phoenix, Ariz.

16. Ray Odom interview.

17. Richie Albright interview.

18. "Wailers" was a term used in West Texas to describe up-tempo rockers such as "Rave On." Waylon used the name for the J.D.'s band.

19. Arizona Republic (1964), n.p.

20. Liner notes from *Johnny Rivers At the Whisky 'A Go-Go* (Imperial Records LP-12264).

21. Waylon Jennings interview.

22. Tape of Waylon Jennings and Don Bowman performance at J.D.'s in 1964. Courtesy of Don Bowman.

23. Don Bowman interview.

24. Richie Albright interview.

25. Tommy Jennings interview.

26. Anonymous interview.

27. Roberta Plunkett interview.

28. Mrs. Betty Rood interview.

29. Roberta Plunkett interview.

30. Bobby Bare interview.

31. Duane Eddy interview.

32. Grissom, *Country Music*, 77.

33. Two of the songs, "Going Home to Stay" and "I Wonder Where I Went Wrong," were recorded by Joe Seay on the BJB label.

34. Duane Eddy interview.

35. Charlie Williams radio interview with Waylon Jennings. AFRS, Mar. 5, 1971 (courtesy of the Country Music Foundation Library).

36. Bob Luman interview.

37. Bob Montgomery interview.

38. Atkins denies this, but most Nashville observers credit Chet with the "folk country" concept.

39. Anonymous interview.

40. Herb Alpert interview.

41. Don Bowman interview.

42. Jerky Moss interview.

43. Herb Alpert interview.

44. Don Bowman interview.

45. Anonymous interview.

46. Jack Miller interview.

47. Richie Albright interview.

48. Nelson Allen, "Willie Nelson Talks," *Picking Up the Tempo* 7 (May 1975): n.p.

CHAPTER 7

1. Hemphill, *Nashville Sound*, 37.

2. Roger Schutt interview.

3. Waylon Jennings interview.

4. Anonymous interview.

5. Don Bowman interview.

6. Waylon Jennings interview.

7. Chuck Glaser interview. Also see Richard A. Peterson and Howard G. White, "Simplex: The Form of Informal Organization" (paper presented at American Sociological Association meeting, Chicago, Ill., Sept. 9, 1977).

8. Statement made on Phil Donahue Show, 1978.

9. Grissom, *Country Music*, 208. Also Frank Jones interview.

10. Anonymous interview.

11. Chuck Glaser interview.

12. Felton Jarvis quoted in Maggie Wilson, "Waylon Jennings—The New Nashville Sound," *Arizona Days and Ways Magazine*, Apr. 3, 1966, p. 11. Folk-style artists rarely made the singles charts. They were album artists. Even stars like Joan Baez relied on LP movement, and FM radio in 1966 was an infant industry.

13. Chuck Glaser interview.

14. Letter to author.

15. Betty Rood interview.

16. Tommy Jennings interview.

17. Christopher Wren, *Winners Got Scars Too: The Life and Legends of Johnny Cash* (New York: Ballantine, 1974), 146.

18. Anonymous interview.

19. John R. Cash, *Man In Black* (Grand Rapids, Mich.: Zondervan, 1975): 122.

20. Anonymous interview.

21. Anonymous interview.

22. Cash, *Man in Black*, 122. Also, "Johnny Cash Interviews Waylon," *Country Music*, April 1, 1981, pp. 22–30, and anonymous interview. In his autobiography, Cash denies this story; claiming, "Waylon never mentioned that busted glove compartment to me and the fact he didn't was another thing that brought me to a sobering awakening period."

23. Wren, *Winners Got Scars*, 188.

24. Michael Watts, "You Gotta Be A Man First, 'Fore You Can Be Anything . . . ," *Melody Maker*, Aug. 11, 1973, p. 25.

25. Wren, *Winners Got Scars,* 199.

26. Ibid, 197. How Wren managed to overlook the "legendary" lifestyle at Madison is hard to understand.

CHAPTER 8

1. Jay Ehler, "Waylon Jennings," *Door*, Dec. 9–23, 1971, pp. 2–3.

2. Powell, "Waylon Jennings, 18.

3. Watts, "You Gotta Be a Man First . . .,"25.

4. "Nashville Welcomes Waylon Jennings," *Music City News*, May 1966, pp. 14, 18.

5. Merle Haggard with Peggy Russell, *Sing Me Back Home: My Life* (New York: Times Books, 1981), 191–197.

6. Tommy Jennings interview.

7. Salvo and Salvo, "Hustler Interview, 77. Also Norma McLain Stoop, "Waylon Jennings: Big Country Singer Hits the Big City," *After Dark*, April 1973, p. 52.

8. Denisoff, "Waylon Jennings Intervew," 127.

9. Ibid., 126.

10. Ibid., 127.

11. Waylon Jennings interview.

12. Anonymous interview.

13. Grissom, *Country Music*, 67.

14. Harlan Howard interview.

15. Bobby Bare, Don Bowman interviews.

16. Letter to author, Mar. 12, 1975.

17. "An Interview with Waylon Jennings," *Country Song Round-Up* (1966), 42–43.

18. Waylon Jennings interview.

19. Nick Tosches, "Waylon Jennings," *Zoo World* Aug. 1, 1974, p. 22.

20. Remarks presented at Popular Culture Association meeting, Indianapolis, 1973. Industrial insurance was geared to the poor people of the south. It was much more expensive than regular life or disability insurance. Agents came by twice a month to collect on the policy. In most cases, the payments, overall, were much greater than the value of the policy. Tenant farmers would have been better off putting the money in the bank and collecting interest.

21. Bill C. Malone, comments at "The Country Music" panel at the Popular Culture Association meetings, Indianapolis, 1973. Also see Richard Peterson and Paul DiMaggio, "The Early Opry: Its Hillbilly Image in Fact and Fancy," *Journal of Country Music* 4 (Summer 1973): 39–51. For a more recent view see Jerry Flowers and Pat Carr, "The Opry Now," *Country Music*, Oct. 1975, pp. 43–44, 55.

22. Bill Ivey, remarks presented at Popular Culture Association meeting, Indianapolis, 1973.

23. Peterson and DiMaggio, "The Early Opry." Also see his "Single-Industry Firm to Conglomerate Synergistics: Alternative Strategies for Selling Insurance and Country Music" in *Growing Metropolis: Aspects of Development in Nashville* (Nashville: Vanderbilt Univ. Press, 1975), 341–57.

24. Ivey, at Popular Culture Association meeting, 1973.

25. Jay Ehler, "Waylon Jennings: 'Diamond In a Laid-Back Rough,'" *Country Life*, Mar./Apr. 1973, p.4

26. Haggard, *Sing Me Back Home*, 243–44.

27. Tanya Tucker interview.

28. Denisoff, "Waylon Jennings interview," 125.

29. John L. Smith, transcript of an interview with Waylon Jennings Aug. 2, 1968—unpublilshed paper. Excerpts appear in "Waylon Jennings," *Town & Country World*, Nov. 1972, p. 15.

30. P.J. Russell, "Some People Say I'm Not Country," *Country Song Round-Up*, Mar. 1975, p. 48.

CHAPTER 9

1. "Downs Crash Kills Musician," *The Daily Pantagraph*, Feb. 10, 1969, p. 2. Other details provided by Richie Albright.

2. "Crash Blame Fixed," ibid., Feb. 11, 969, p. 1.

3. Quoted in Jay Ehler, "Waylon Jennings: Rockin the Country Soul," *Country Sky*, May 1972, p. 4.

4. Chet Flippo, "Waylon Jennings: 'If I Was Everything People Make Me Out To Be, I'da Been Dead Long Ago,'" *Creem*, July 1973, pp. 35–37, 75. Also, Mike McQuade, "Letter to Mick Brady," n.d.

5. Mike McQuade interview.

6. Johnna Yursic interview.

7. Mike McQuade interview.

8. Johnna would later become Waylon's aid-de-cap and road manager, from 1972–1976.

9. Johnna Yursic interview.

10. Mike McQuade interview.

11. Denisoff, "Waylon Jennings Interview," 128.

12. Letter to author, 1975.

13. Richie Albright interview.

14. Waylon Jennings interview. "Musicians Face Trial for Pot" (AP wire, June 10, 1969).

15. Billy Ray Reynolds interview.

16. Richie, too, would leave the tour. Crab Orchard, Ky., was more than he could stand. "It was just one of those days that I remember. I had been riding in the back of the camper on the instruments. I had been laying back there on the instruments sleeping cause I had just driven 20 hours from someplace and we got there late and pulled up in front of the place and I climbed out and there was a line of people and a condemned show building and it was one of the most dismal sights that I can remember in my life and that's when I came to a decision." He quit several months later when they returned to Phoenix. Eddie Fox, Marty Robbin's ex-drummer, replaced him.

17. John T. Pugh, "Waylon Jennings: Country Music is Soul," *Music City News*, June 1970, p. 13.

18. Floyd Ramsey interview.

19. "How Waylon Jennings Escaped Death" (1970), RCA West Coast Publicity file), 36.

20. John Goff, "Television Review: 'Love of the Common People' KTTV, October 5, 9–10 p.m.," *Hollywood Reporter*, Oct. 7, 1969.

21. Quoted in Guida Jackson, "Jessi Colter," *Texas Country Western Magazine* (Nov./Dec. 1976), n.p. An excellent unpublished interview is "A Conversation with Jessi Colter, Capitol Records Recording Artist," Capitol Records press release (Feb. 1975), 1/6.

22. Duane Eddy interview.

23. Ibid.

24. Ibid.

25. Anonymous interview.

26. "Musician Shot Dead at Party," *Atlanta Journal-Constitution*, Apr. 4, 1968, p. 14.

27. Richie Albright interview.

28. Ibid., A brief account is found in the *Arizona Gazette*, Dec. 26, 1968. n.p.

29. "Jessi Colter: Country Star of the Month," *Song Hits Magazine* (Feb. 1977) n.p. Also, Hazel Smith, "Jessi's the One Star Who's Got It Altogether," *Music City News* (June, 1975): 25.

30. Grissom, *Country Music*, 23.

31. "Suit Names Owner of Tempe Club," *Arizona Republic*, Dec. 12, 1969: n.p.

32. Waylon Jennings interview.

33. Clipping from RCA Victor West Coast files. No citation attributed.

34. See Bill McAllister, "Guitarist Combines Many Country Music Facets," *Fort Worth Star-Telegram*, Feb. 9, 1975, pp. 2, 11. Also Ken Stambaugh, "The Moon Shines Bright," *Country Music*, July 1976, pp. 41–45.

35. Concert, Toledo, 1974.

36. Powel, "Waylon Jennings: Inteview," 16–18.

37. J.R. Young, "The Monstor Voice of Waylon Jennings," *Rolling Stone*, Dec. 9, 1971, p. 58.

38. Ehler reprinted the original *Door* interview in several publications, including *Country Sky*.

39. J.R. Young interview.

40. Robert Hilburn interview.

41. Bob Hilburn, "Country Music Show at Shrine Auditorium," *Los Angeles Times*, Jan. 28, 1969.

42. Bob Hilburn, "Waylon Jennings Will Open Stand," *Los Angeles Times*, Dec. 1, 1970, sec. 5, p. 15.

43. Elher, "Waylon Jennings."

44. Bob Hilburn, "Waylon Jennings: Hero of Own Story," *Los Angeles Times*, reprinted in *Waylonews* 27 (Winter 1979): n.p.

45. Richie Albright interview.

CHAPTER 10

1. Maureen Orth, "Outlaw Breed." *Newsweek* (Aug. 26, 1974: 84).
2. Bo Powell, "Swarmin'," *Country Music Reporter,*(Sept. 1972): n.p.
3. Johnna Yursic interview.
4. Waylon has claimed that his debts ranged in the $700,000 figure. According to Reshen and other sources, it was closer to a quarter of a million.
5. Neil Reshen Interview.
6. Reshen quoted in Terry Guerin, "Country Buses," *Penthouse*, June 1975, p. 84.
7. Michael Bane, *The Outlaws: Revolution in Country Music* (New York: Country Music Press/Doubleday, 1978), 71.
8. Bob Campbell, "Waylon," *Country Music*, Jan./Feb. 1979, p. 53.
9. Neil Reshen interview.
10. Clive Davis interview.
11. Neil Reshen interview.
12. Waylon Jennings interview.
13. Flippo, "Waylon Jennings: 'If I Was Everything People Make Me Out To Be, I'da Been Dead Long Ago,'" 37.
14. Neil Reshen interview.
15. Jeff Thomas, "Sound Track," *Hollywood Reporter*, Oct. 25, 1972, n.p.
16. Chet Flippo, "Willie Nelson's New York Country Sessions," *Rolling Stone*, Apr. 12, 1973, p. 14.
17. Jan Reid, *Incredible Rise of Redneck Rock* (Austin: Heidelberg Publishers, 1974), 284.
18. Anonymous interview.
19. Neil Reshen interview.
20. Quotes from "Nashville Managers Vow to Reverse Flight of Talent," *Billboard*, Nov. 5, 1978, p. 77.
21. Neil Reshen interview.
22. Ibid.
23. Ibid.
24. Gail Thomas, "Lee Clayton: He's Gone More Than a Couple of Rounds With His Dreams," *Country Music,* Nov./Dec. 1978, p. 17–18.
25. Neil Reshen interview.
26. Johnna Yursic interview.
27. Chet Flippo, "Country Music: The R & R Influence,"*Rolling Stone*, Dec. 20, 1972, p. 16.
28. Anonymous interview.
29. Harlan Howard interview.
30. See Paula Hyun, "What Happened at Willie's Picnic?" *Los Angeles Free Press*, July 13, 1973, pp. 27–29. Also Pat Carr, "It's So Progressive in Texas," *New York Times*, July 22, 1973, pp. 2–9.
31. Reid, *Incredible Rise*, 311–12.

32. Dave Hickey, "In Defense of the Telecaster Cowboy Outlaws," *Country Music*, Jan. 1974, pp. 90–95.

33. Thomas, "Lee Clayton."

CHAPTER 11

1. Neil Reshen interview.

2. Susan Weiner, "Country Comes to Town," *Penthouse*, May 1973.

3. Linda Solomon, "Country Star Jennings Invades One of the Homes of Rock," *New Music Express* (Jan. 27, 1973), p. 1.

4. "Waylon Jennings: Caught in the Crossover Crossfire," *Cashbox* (1973). Rpt. in *Waylonews* 6 (Oct. 1973). n.p.

5. Todd Everett, "Waylon Jennings: Palomino February 8–9," *Hollywood Reporter*, (Feb. 12, 1973, p. 10).

6. Jean Eklund, "Waylon Along," *UCLA Daily Bruin*, Feb. 22, 1973, p. 14.

7. Michael G. Davis, "The Troubadour Gives a Hoot—Every Monday," *The Staff*, Feb. 18, 1973, p. 35.

8. Robert Hilburn, "Time for a Jennings Break Through?" *Los Angeles Times*, Feb. 10, 1973, sec. 2, p. 6.

9. Eklund, "Waylon Along."

10. Mike Jahn review of *Lonesome On'ry and Mean*, *Cue*, Mar. 24, 1973.

11. McCandlish Phillips, "Leaders in Country Music See Chance to Win the City," *New York Times*, Apr. 16, 1973, p. 50.

12. Guerin, "Country Buses," 83–85.

13. Johnna Yursic interview.

14. Joel Selvin, "Superb Sound at Kezar," *San Francisco Chronicle*, May 31, 1973. n.p.

15. Reid, *Improbable Rise*.

16. Carr, "It's So Progressive in Texas" 9.

17. Darrell Rowlett, "Country Music Chronolog," *Country Song Round-Up* (n.d.): 35, 48; and Townsend Miller, "Country Music: The Birth of 'Honky Tonk Heros'," *American Statesman*, Feb. 1, 1974.

18. Mick Brady, "Review of You Ask Me To/Willy the Wandering Gypsy and Me," *Waylonews* 6 (Oct. 1973): 2.

19. John Gabree review of *Honky Tonk Heroes*, *Country Music* (1973).

20. Robin Williams, "Greatest Show on Earth," *Waylonews* 7 (Dec. 1973): 3–4. Also Dave Hickey, "In Defense of the Telecaster Cowboy Outlaws," *Country Music*, Jan. 1974, pp. 90–95. Jim Smith, "Nasal Week in Nashville," *New Musical Express*, Nov. 10, 1973, p. 53.

21. Hal Blu, "Who's Where in Country Music," *Las Vegas Panorama*

(n.d.), p. 12. McPhail's biased comments did not go unnoticed. Johnna spilled—accidently or intentionally—a glass of wine on the deejay at the Golden Nugget. Reportedly, he then threatened Johnna with a gun. Yursic's and McPhail's versions of the incident greatly vary. Whose story is correct has been impossible to verify.

22. "Waylon Jennings," *Cashbox.*

23. Bill Yaryan, "Here Come the Shitkickers!" *Los Angeles Weekly News*, Aug. 24, 1973, p. 13.

24. Hunter Davies, *The Beatles* (New York: Dell Book 1968), 236.

25. Barry Gifford, *"Sweetheart of the Rodeo," Rolling Stone,* Sept. 14, 1968, p. 20.

26. Bud Scoppa, *The Byrds* (New York: Scholastic Books, 1971), 80.

27. Jimmy Ibbotson interview.

28. Elher, "Waylon Jennings," *Country Life*, 4–5.

29. Bryan Chalker, "Nashville Sickness," *Melody Maker*, Dec. 8, 1973, p. 48.

30. Chuck Glaser interview.

31. Tompall Glaser interview.

32. *Outlaws*, 44, 46.

33. Chalker, "Nashville Sickness," 48.

34. In 1975 Waylon was talking about putting out "Summer Wages" exclusively for the Canadian market. He did not. In light of the feud with Glaser and the lawsuits between them, it is doubtful that song will be made available.

35. Chalker, "Nashville Sickness," 48.

36. Flippo, "Country Music: The R & R Influence," 16.

37. Chet Flippo, "Waylon Jennings Get Off the Grind," *Rolling Stone*, Dec. 6, 1972, p. 28.

CHAPTER 12

1. "Country Singer Cleared in Suit," *Arizona Republic*, Apr. 18, 1974. n.p.

2. "Singer Told Again to Pay," *Tucson Daily Citizen*, Oct. 10, 1974. Also, Case #140230, Arizona Superior Court.

3. Chuck Glaser interview.

4. Johnny Yursic interview.

5. Don Cusic, "TV Troubles Tail Jennings," *Record World,* Oct. 26, 1974, p. 54.

6. Roger Schutt interview.

7. Everett J. Corbin, *Storm Over Nashville: A Case Against Modern Country Music* (Nashville: Ashlar Press, 1980).

8. Anonymous interview.

9. Paul Hendrickson, "Little Known Man of Rock Now Rolling," *Toledo Magazine,* Jan. 7, 1979, p. 15.

10. Pat Carr, "Waylon and Johnny in the House of Cash," *Village Voice,* Nov. 14, 1974, pp. 66, 80.

11. "Our Association: What WE THINK IT IS: How We View Ourselves and Our Industry and What We're NOT" (mimeographed press release).

12. Frank Jones interview.

13. Harlan Howard interview.

14. Richard A. Peterson, "The Production of Cultural Change: The Case of Contemporary Music," *Social Research* 45 (Summer 1978): 293.

15. B. Drummond Ayres, Jr., "'Crossovers' to Country Music Rouse Nashville," *New York Times,* Dec. 1, 1974, p. 75.

16. Jens Lund and R. Serge Denisoff, "The Folk Music Revival and the Counterculture: Contributions and Contradictions," *Journal of American Folklore* 84 (1971): 395–405.

17. Drummond, "'Crossovers'" 75.

18. "Opposition to Extensive Utilization in Country Radio of the Short Playlist, Tight Format, Top-Forty Approach," A.C.E. (mimeographed press release).

19. John Pugh, "Gospel Now," *Country Music,* Jan. 1975, pp. 24–31.

20. Hyun, "What Happened at Willie's Picnic?" 27–29.

21. Joel Selvin, "Waylon Jennings: Rocking at the Boarding House," *San Francisco Chronicle,* Dec. 13, 1974, p. 70.

22. Bob Kirsch, "Commander Cody and His Lost Plant Airmen: Waylon Jennings," *Billboard,* Jan. 4, 1975, p. 12.

23. Johnna Yursic interview.

24. "Jessi Colter," *Capitol Records Biography* (July 1976): 4.

25. Jackson, "Jessi Colter."

26. Stacy Harris, "The Nashville People," *Country Side,* rpt. in *Waylonews* 19 (June, 1976): 6.

27. Nancy Hadler, "Colter's New Album 'Spiritual Thing,' " *The Champaign-Urbana News Gazette,* Apr. 11, 1977, n.p.

28. "Letters," *Country Music,* Dec. 1974, p. 4. In a subsequent issue the editors noted that mail opposing Mr. Barnes's condemnation was at a 3:2 ratio. *Country Music,* Feb. 1975, p. 4.

29. Tim Patterson, "Critique of Country Music," *Guardian,* June 18, 1975, p. 19.

30. *Country Music* has been more than kind to Waylon and Jessi. It has printed letters to the editor critical of the singer but negative comments are almost never voiced in the feature sections. Jessi's press introduction for the Capitol album is a classic example. Her Capitol media bio was written by Captain Midnite, Hazel Smith did a follow-up for *Music City News,* and Dave Hickey wrote a story for *Country Music.*

While Jessi's album was both a commercial and aesthetic success, none of the above writers could, in any sense, be labeled objective or unbiased. The few writers allowed near Waylon in the last eight years have been with *Country Music*.

31. Campbell, "Waylon," 50–53, 55).

32. "Waylon Speaks Out," *Country Hotline News*, reprinted in *Waylonews* 17 (Dec. 1975): 4.

33. Martha Hume, "Denver, Parton, Jennings Take CMA Awards," *Country Music*, Jan. 1976, p. 13.

34. "Waylon Gathers the Outlaws Together for Special New RCA Album," *RCA News* (press release, Jan. 12, 1976).

35. Liner notes to *Wanted: Outlaws* (RCA-Victor Apl1–1321).

36. Review of *Wanted: Outlaws*, in *Country Music People*, Apr. 1976, p. 20.

37. "Outlaws In Redneck Land," *Melody Maker*, Apr. 17, 1976, p. 21.

38. "Outlaws Get the Gold," *RCA News* (press release Apr. 5, 1976).

39. Mick Brady, review of *Outlaws*, *Waylonews* (Mar. 1976), 1.

40. Bane, *Outlaws*, 114–15.

41. "Random Notes," *Rolling Stone*, June 3, 1976, p. 24.

42. Ibid., June 17, 1976, p. 23.

43. I have not been able to verify this contention. The structure of the song does seem to reflect the material Waylon did for Trend 61.

44. Campbell, "Waylon."

CHAPTER 13

1. "Random Notes," *Rolling Stone*, Jan. 13, 1977, p. 22.

2. In 1971 Waylon was made an "Honorary Sheriff" in Butler County in Ohio. Waylon Jennings Fan Club newsletter, Jan. 1971 (mimeographed.)

3. "Waylon Jennings' New Single Hits Country Charts at Highest Position Ever for New Entry," *RCA News* (Apr. 11, 1977).

4. "In the Heart of Honky-Tonk Rock," *Newsweek*, Sept. 19, 1977, p. 86.

5. "Good Old Luckenbach," *Toledo Blade Magazine*, Oct. 22, 1977, p. 26.

6. Dave Marsh, "Ol' Waylon," *Toledo Blade*, May 22 , 1977, p. 2.

7. "Waylon Jennings' Newest RCA Album Certified Gold by R.I.A.A.," *RCA News* (June 20, 1977).

8. "Random Notes," *Rolling Stone*, Aug. 1976, p. 30. Also see Chet Flippo, "The Austin Scene and Willie Nelson: A Reconsideration," *Popular Music and Society* 6 (1979): 280–83

9. Kathleen Gallagher, "Jennings Bound On Drug Counts," *Tennessean,* Sept. 1, 1977, p. 10.

10. Ibid.

11. Chet Flippo, "Hank Williams Jr.'s Hard Road," *Rolling Stone,* June 1, 1978, p. 18.

12. Larry Brinton, "Waylon Faces Federal Cocaine Charge," *Nashville Banner,* Aug. 24, 1977, p. 6.

13. Ibid.

14. Kathleen Gallagher, "Waylon Back On Stage After Drug Charge Arrest," *Tennessean,* Aug. 25, 1977, p. 10.

15. Bill Hance, "Singer May Profit from Arrest," *Commercial News* (Danville, Ill.), Sept. 11, 1977. On the other hand, one study indicates country fans are not supportive of drug use or songs about drugs. See Wendell Rawls, Jr., "Times Are Changing Country & Western Songs," *New York Times,* Feb. 16, 1980, p. 8.

16. Gallagher, "Waylon Back On Stage," 10.

17. Gallagher, "Jennings Bound," 10.

18. Kathleen Gallagher, "Waylon's 'Damaging' Tape Ordered In," *Tennessean,* Oct. 4, 1977, pp. 1, 8.

19. Bruce Honik, "Tape Will Clear Jennings of Cocaine Charge: Lawyer," *Nashville Banner,* Oct. 4, 1977, p. 1.

20. Bruce Honik, "Waylon Case Said 'Botched' in New York City," *Nashville Banner,* Oct. 5, 1977, p. 1.

21. "Waylon and Drugs," *Monroe News Star,* Sept. 5, 1977; n.p.

22. Kirk Loggins, "Waylon Manager Aide Pleads Guilty," *Tennessean,* Apr. 26, 1978, p. 1; "Jennings Aide Faces Sentence," *Nashville Banner,* Apr. 27, 1978, n.p.

23. This policy has been rescinded in recent years. However, only a handful of journalists have been allowed interviews. "He's about as accessible," one said "as Elvis." (Colonel Parker refused to grant interviews.) Waylon did break his silence on Sept. 6, 1979, and appeared on the *Today Show* in a taped question and answer with Jane Pauley. This was a unique event, as he still avoids the media like the plague.

24. *Rolling Stone,* Sept. 1977. The quote was historically accurate. Why Waylon wanted it dropped is difficult to explain. Similarly, the number of days he tours per year is a matter of public record. One merely needs to consult back issues of his fan club newsletters or check out *Performance* magazine.

25. "Rolling Stone: Pop Scene," *Toledo Blade,* Sept. 3, 1977, sec. P, p. 5.

26. Campbell, "Waylon," 50–53, 55.

27. Jan George, "Wailin' for Waylon," *Waylon Jennings Official Fan Club Journal* (1969–1970), 5.

28. Chet Flippo, *Your Cheatin' Heart* (New York: Simon & Schuster, 1981), 72.

29. Bill and Marge Damron letter, Mar. 18, 1973.

30. Mick Brady, "Editorial,"*Waylonews* 1 (Aug. 1972): 1.

31. Letter to author, Oct. 10, 1974.

32. Anonymous interview.

33. Bob Campbell, "Jennings Set for Three cbs LP's After 'Waylon and Willie' Deal," *Billboard,* Jan. 28, 1978, p. 102.

34. Waylon Jennings interview.

35. "Random Notes," *Rolling Stone,* Mar. 9, 1978, p. 35.

36. Martha Hume, "Waylon and Willie In New York," *Rolling Stone,* Mar. 23, 1978. Also "Willie and Waylon Invade New York," *Country Music,* Aug. 1978, pp. 18–19.

37. Chris Welch, "Fighting Talk," *Melody Maker,* June 3, 1978, pp. 34, 53.

38. Mike Oakfield, "Whitewash," *Melody Maker,* May 27, 1978, p. 28.

39. Richard Meyer, "Country & Western In Washington," *Toledo Blade,* Apr. 26, 1978, p. 1.

40. Greg Oatis, "Ear Shots," ibid., Jan. 22, 1978, p. 2.

41. Nick Tosches, "Waylon and Willie," *Rolling Stone,* Mar. 23, 1978, p. 66.

42. Terry Atkinson, "Cowboy Jennings Ropes a Top LP," rpt. in *Waylonews* 27 (Winter 1979), n.p.

43. Roger Schutt interview.

44. rca West Coast publicity files.

45. Dave Goodrich and Edana Corbin, "Waylon: This Renegade Makes Sense," *Country Music News,* Oct. 1975, n.p.

46. Mick Brady, "Reviews . . . .MacIntosch and T.J.," *Waylonews* 19 (June 1976): 4.

47. Bill Kaufman, " 'The Dukes' Are Foolin' 'Em," *Toledo Blade,* Mar. 18, 1979, sec. G, pp. 1, 5.

48. Pat Carr, "Johnny Cash's Freedom," *Country Music,* Apr. 1979, p. 27.

49. Mick Brady, "Waylon News and Comment," *Waylonews* (Summer 1979): 1.

50. Ken Emerson, "Country Music—Confusion in Profusion," *New York Times,* Nov. 18, 1979, sec. D, p. 24.

51. Brady, "What Goes Around Come Around," *Outlaws* 1.

52. Jeff Bush, "Ear Shots," *Toledo Blade,* Dec. 16, 1979, sec. E, p. 4.

53. "Waylon Jennings Interview" in *Genesis,* reprinted in *Waylonews* 28 (Summer 1979): n.p.

54. See Roman Kozak, "Musicians Omnipresent in Presidential Race," *Billboard,* Aug. 2, 1980, p. 6.

55. Lee Winfrey, "Country Music's Best Pays Tribute to Maybelle Carter," *Toledo Blade,* Nov. 29, 1979, sec. P, p. 4.

56. Bob Allen, "Music Man," review, *Country Music,* Sept. 1980, p. 56.

57. The figure is the artist's gross, excluding record company ad-

vances, agent's percentage, and other costs, which vary on the basis of the artist's contract.

58. Mark Mehler, "Where Does Your Money Go?" *Country Music*, Mar. 1980, pp. 22–23. Also Kenny Rogers with Lenny Epand, *Making It with Music* (New York: Harper & Row, 1978), 115–16.

59. Mark Schwed, "Country Superstars Demand and Get Concert Megabucks," *Daily Sentinel Tribune*, Apr. 22, 1981, p. 4.

60. "Miscellaneous Notes," *Country Music*, Apr. 1981, pp. 18, 20.

61. Kip Kirby and Robyn Wells, "Country Acts Curtail Demands in Riders to Help Cut Costs," *Billboard*, Nov. 14, 1981, p. 84.

62. The title of the LP came from a song, excluded from the album, by Fleetwood Mac star Stevie Nicks. Ironically, her single with Eagle Don Henley made the top 10 on the *"Billboard* Hot 100."

63. Kip Kirby, "Nashville Artists Seeking Local Managers, Agents," *Billboard*, Jan. 16, 1982, p. 27.

CHAPTER 14

1. Hank Williams, Jr., *Living Proof* (New York: Putnam's, 1979), 58; and Bob Allen, "Charlie Rich: Just Rollin' With the Flow," *Country Music*, Apr. 1979, p. 42.

2. Quoted in Bane, *Outlaws*, 85.

3. Kip Kirby, "Platinum, Gold Gild RCA Nashville," *Billboard*, July 4, 1981, p. 57.

4. Bob Allen. "And the Winner Is . . . Kenny Rogers," *Country Music*, Dec. 1979, pp. 25–31. Also, Rogers and Epand, *Making It with Music*.

5. Allen, "And the Winner Is," 28.

6. "Billboard's Recommended LPs," *Billboard*, Feb. 27, 1982, p. 57.

7. Flippo, "Penthouse Interview, 140.

8. *Billboard*, Oct. 24, 1981, p. 56. David Dudley recorded "Wave at 'Em Billy Boy," echoing this sentiment.

9. Mark Rose, "George Jones: Last Exit Off a Dark Highway," *Village Voice*, Sept. 23–29, 1981, p. 32.

10. Letter to author, Oct. 10, 1974.

WAY
LON

SELECTED BIBLIOGRAPHY

The best beginning source of information dealing with Waylon Jennings is published in the United Kingdom. Mick Brady's *Waylonews* (126 Oaksfold Road, Sheffield S5 OTH, England) was a fairly evenhanded magazine—unlike most "fanzines"— which reprinted reviews and articles about the artist with occasional interviews. A full set of the twenty-eight issues or even *The Best of Waylonews* will probably tell average readers more than they want to know about the singer.

There exists no systematic bibliography dealing with Jennings. The reason is simply that, with the exception of the Country Music Association Hall of Fame Library and the Jonathan Edwards Memorial Foundation, there are no depositories of any consequence for country music material. Even these invaluable institutions have their limitations. Much of the material appearing in this book has come from record companies, musicians, talent agents, fans, and other sources. Many of the articles and clippings do not contain dates, names of publications, or any of the other niceties writers and academics are accustomed to. What follows is a bibliographical listing of articles and books with as much information as possible; most should not be hard to locate.

Journalistic interviews tended to be repetitive. The better stories usually emerge in the early stages of an artist's career, assuming the reporters know their subject. This was the case with Waylon. "Nashville Welcomes Waylon Jennings" (*Music*

City News, May 1966) is the best published account of his early
years in Littlefield and Phoenix. John Grissom's *Country Music:
White Man's Soul* (Paperback Library, 1970) runs a very close, if
not even, second. Waylon's candor in both places is remarkable.
As the dates indicate, these works are old. Grissom's work,
unfortunately, is out of print. Other interviews of interest appear
in two very unlikely places. Pat Salvo's interview in *Hustler* and
Susan Toepfer's "I'm Not Gonna Put Up with Anything from
Anybody!" (*Photoplay*, 1974) are somewhat redundant but do
contain a great deal of new information. Most Jennings interviews and new biographies are carbon copies of what has come
before. Waylon has good reason to resent "seat change" questions. After 1974, there were few good "Question and Answer"
or biographical articles in circulation. Mike Bane's *Outlaws*
(Country Music Press/Doubleday, 1978) has some state-of-the-
art information (c. 1977). *Willie and Waylon* (1979) is a picture
book. Bob Campbell's "Waylon" (*Country Music*, 1979) is significant as it is one of the few interviews allowed by Utopia Productions for several years. *Country Style*'s (1979) "The Waylon and
Buddy Holly Story" was a gross disappointment—except for the
"rare photo"—as it was little more than a rehash of John Goldrosen's *Buddy Holly* (Popular Press, 1975) and several often-
repeated discussions of the "last tour."

Unfortunately, there exist very few accurate pieces on Jessi
Colter. The best of the lot is Guida Jackson's "Jessi" (*Texas
Country Western Magazine*, 1976). Hazel Smith's "Jessi's the One
Star Who's Got It Altogether" (*Music City News*, June 1975) is
better than most. Ironically, a number of country music maga-
zines ran the Capitol "bio" as gospel.

The Austin scene has been fairly well covered by Chet Flippo
in a series of *Rolling Stone* articles (1971–1974) and in *Popular
Music and Society*. Jan Reid's *The Improbable Rise of Redneck Rock*
(Heidelberg Press, 1974) is a controversial, in places painfully
detailed, and occasionally inaccurate account of the Austin City
Limits and its inhabitants. For the roots of the Texas country
music scene see Professor Townsend's brilliant biography of Bob
Wills: *San Antonio Rose* (University of Illinois Press, 1975).

Johnny Cash's autobiographical sermonette, *Man in Black*
(Zondervan, 1975), briefly deals with Waylon, although his rec-
ollections of that period do not jibe with other accounts. On Chet
Atkins, see his *Country Gentleman* (Regnery, 1976) and Bill

Ivey's chapter in *Stars of Country Music* (University of Illinois Press, 1976). Unfortunately, neither work tells the reader much about the 1965–1975 period at RCA.

The list of articles below includes all items from my files that carry some type of indentification such as the name of the publication and the date. Frequently, page numbers are not available. This is by no means an exhaustive bibliography; my files are jammed with clippings and articles that carry no citations. These are omitted.

BOOKS

Allen, Bob. *Waylon and Willie.* New York: Quick Fox, 1979.

Atkins, Chet. *Country Gentleman.* Chicago: Regnery, 1974.

Axton, Mae Boren. *Country Singers As I Know 'Em.* Austin: Sweet Publishing Co., 1973.

Bane, Michael. *The Outlaws: Revolution In Country Music.* New York: Country Music Press/Doubleday, 1978.

Bart, Teddy. *Inside Music City U.S.A.* Nashville: Aurora, 1970.

Cash, John R. *Man In Black.* Grand Rapids: Zondervan, 1975.

Flippo, Chet. *Your Cheatin' Heart.* New York: Simon & Schuster, 1981.

Gaillard, Faye. *Watermellon Wine: The Spirit of Country.* New York: St. Martin's Press, 1977.

Goldrosen, John. *Buddy Holly: His Life and Music.* Bowling Green, Ohio: Popular Press, 1975.

Grissom, John. *Country Music: White Man's Blues.* New York: Paperback Library, 1970.

Guralnick, Peter. *Lost Highway: Journeys & Arrivals of American Musicians.* Boston: Godine, 1979.

Hemphill, Paul. *Nashville Sound: Bright Lights and Country Music.* New York: Simon & Schuster, 1970.

Malone, Bill C., and Judith McCulloh, eds. *Stars of Country Music.* Urbana: Univ. of Illinois Press, 1975.

Shestack, Melvin. *The Country Music Encyclopedia.* New York: Thomas Y. Crowell, 1974.

Townsend, Charles R. *San Antonio Rose.* Urbana: Univ. of Illinois Press, 1976.

Wren, Chris. *Winners Got Scars Too: The Life and Legends of Johnny Cash.* New York: Ballantine Books, 1974.

ARTICLES

Allen, Nelson. "Willie Nelson Talks." *Picking Up the Tempo* (May 1975).

Alterman, Loraine. "Sing On, Country Soul." *New York Times,* May 19, 1974, sec. D.

Anderson, Bill. "Country Music." *Argosy,* Jan. 1975, pp. 40–43.

Anderson, Patrick. "The Real Nashville." *New York Times Magazine,* Aug. 31, 1975, pp. 10ff.

Ayres, B. Drummond, Jr. " 'Crossovers' to Country Music Rouse Nashville." *New York Times,* Dec. 1, 1974, p. 75.

Ayres, Tom. "Ralph Mooney Shadows the Outlaws." *Rambler,* Dec. 2, 1976.

Axthelm, Pete. "Songs of Outlaw Country." *Newsweek,* Apr. 12, 1976, p. 79.

———."Willie Nelson: King of Country Music." *Newsweek,* Aug. 14, 1978, pp. 50–58.

"Ballad of a Nashville Rebel: Waylon Jennings." *Country Music Review,* Mar. 1975, pp. 16–17.

Bane, Michael. "The Waylon Tapes." *Country Music,* May 1978, pp. 38–41.

Basham, Tom. "The Jessi & Waylon Life-Style: Honkin', Tonkin', Holdin' On." *Baltimore Sun,* Feb. 12, 1982, sec. B, p. 2.

Battle, Bob. "Waylon Tired of Image." *Country Style,* Sept. 1978.

Beck, David L. "Waylon Jennings Belted Out Best-of-West Songs Despite Blare." *Salt Lake Tribune,* Feb. 23, 1974.

Brady, Mick. "Editorial." *Waylonews* 1 (Aug. 1972): 1.

———. "Originality and Perfection." *The Star Top Stars,* July 1970, p. 18.

———. "Waylon News & Comment." *Waylonews,* 28 (Summer 1979): 1.

Brinton, Larry. "Figure in Waylon's Drug Case Gives Up." *Nashville Banner,* Aug. 26, 1977, pp. 1, 8.

———. "Waylon Faces Federal Cocaine Charge." *Nashville Banner,* Aug. 24, 1977, pp. 1, 6.

Bush, Jeff. "Ear Shots." *Toledo Blade,* Dec. 16, 1979, sec. E, p. 4.

Byworth, Tony. "Last of the Cosmic Cowboys." *Record Mirror,* Feb. 16, 1974.

———. "Waylon's Latest: A Cert for the Crossover Market." *Country Music People,* June 1977.

Campbell, Bob. "Jennings Set for Three CBS LPs After 'Waylon and Willie' Deal." *Billboard,* Jan. 28, 1978.

————. "People." *Country Music,* Oct. 1980.

————. "Waylon." *Country Music,* Jan./Feb. 1979, pp. 50–53, 55.

Carr, Patrick. "Cow-hip Proper: A Letter from Nashville." *Village Voice,* Nov. 19, 1980, pp. 80–81.

————. " 'I Couldn't Go Pop With a Mouthful of Firecrackers.' ' *Country Music,* Apr. 1973, pp. 42–46.

————. "I Left My Yo-Yo in Nashville." *Village Voice,* Mar. 28, 1974, pp. 1, 22, 26.

————. "It's So Progressive in Texas." *New York Times,* July 22, 1973, sec. 2, p. 9.

————. "Johnny Cash's Freedom." *Country Music,* Apr. 1979, p. 27.

————. "Waylon and Johnny in the House of Cash." *Village Voice,* Nov. 14, 1974, pp. 66–80.

"Caught in the Act." *Melody Maker,* Aug. 2, 1975, p. 23.

Chalker, Bryan. "Nashville Sickness." *Melody Maker,* Dec. 8, 1973, p. 48.

"Concert Reviews." *Variety,* July 6, 1977, p. 59.

————. *Variety,* Apr. 26, 1978, p. 70; Dec. 4, 1974, p. 56.

————. *Variety,* Dec. 6, 1978, p. 76; Dec. 4, 1974, p. 56.

————. *Variety,* Dec. 12, 1979, p. 70.

Coppage, N. "Crossing Over With Waylon Jennings." *Stereo Review,* Oct. 1976, pp. 104–6.

————. "Tom T. Wants to Reform Outlaws." *Stereo Review,* May 1978, p. 128.

————. "Waylon Jennings: Suddenly a Low-pitched Baritone is the Voice to Have." *Stereo Review,* Oct. 1975, p. 74.

————. "Waylon Jennings: About as Unbuttoned as It's Wise for Anyone to Get." *Stereo Review,* Feb. 1979, p. 104.

"Country Award Nominees Led by Waylon Jennings." *Toledo Blade,* Aug. 23, 1977, p. 2.

"Country Western Crossovers Brush Radio." *Variety,* Mar. 29, 1978, p. 75.

"Crash Blame Fixed." *Daily Pantagraph,* Feb. 11, 1969, p 1.

"Current Swamp Opera Trail Blazers." *Hi Fi Musical America,* June 1974, pp. 38–41.

Cusic, Don. "Jennings' Appeal Attracts All Ages." *Record World,* Aug. 9, 1975.

————. "TV Troubles Tail Jennings." *Record World,* Oct. 26, 1974.

Davies, Tom. " 'The Outlaw' Is Coming to Toledo." *Toledo Blade,* June 14, 1981, sec. F, p. 1.

Davis, Michael G. "The Troubadour Gives A Hoot—Every Monday." *The Staff*, Feb. 18, 1973, p. 35.

Denisoff, R. Serge. "Country Music Goes Uptown." *Exit*, Sept. 4, 1974, pp. 8–9.

———. "Nashville Rebels: Myth or Reality." *Popular Music and Society* 5 (1976), 79–88.

———. "Waylon Jennings Interview." *Popular Music and Society* 3 (1974): 118–37.

———. "Waylon Jennings and the 'Last Tour.' " *Journal of Popular Culture* 14 (1980): 663–71.

"Downs Crash Kills Musician." *Daily Pantagraph*, Feb. 10, 1969, p. 2.

Edwards, Joe. "Will Dolly, Waylon Be Upset?" *Toledo Blade*, Aug. 21, 1977, sec. F, p. 2.

Ehler, Jay. "Waylon Jennings: 'Diamond in a Laid-Back Rough.' " *Country Life*, Mar./Apr. 1973, pp. 4–5.

———. "Waylon Jennings: Rocking the Country Soul." *Country Sky*, May 1972, pp. 1, 3–6. Reprinted from *Door*, December 1971.

Eklund, Jean. "Waylon Along." *UCLA Bruin*, Feb. 22, 1973, pp. 14–15.

Emerson, Ken. "Country Music—Confusion in Profusion." *New York Times*, Nov. 18, 1979, sec. D, pp. 24, 31.

Everett, Todd. "From Buddy Holly Sideman to Troubadour Headliner." *Los Angeles Press*, May 4, 1973, p. 26.

———. "Waylon Jennings: Palomino February 8–9." *Hollywood Reporter*, Feb. 12, 1973, p. 10.

Firmington, John. "Buddy Holly—Last Tour." *Outlaws*, Mar. 1980, pp. 4–6.

———. "Country Scene." *Melody Maker*, Jan. 9, 1971, p. 2.

———. "Waylon Jennings." *Country*, July 1972.

"Five Gatherings (Musical & Otherwise)." *New Yorker*, Dec. 23, 1975, pp. 25–26.

Flippo, Chet. "The Austin Scene and Willie Nelson: A Reconsideration." *Popular Music and Society* 6 (1979): 280–83.

———. "Country and Western: Some New Fangled Ideas." *American Libraries*, Apr. 1974, pp. 185–89.

———. "Country Music: The R & R influence." *Rolling Stone*, Dec. 20, 1972, p. 16.

———. "Hank Williams Jr.'s Hard Road." *Rolling Stone*, June 1, 1978, p. 18.

————. "Near to the Maddening Crowd." *Texas Monthly*, Feb. 1975, pp. 48, 51–53.

————. "Penthouse Interview: Waylon Jennings." *Penthouse*, Sept. 1981, pp. 108–12, 142–43.

————. "The Texas Rock and Roll Spectacular!" *Phonograph Record*, Mar. 1974, pp. 22–29.

————. "Waylon Jennings Gets Off the Grind." *Rolling Stone*, Dec. 6, 1972, p. 28.

————. "Waylon Jennings: 'If I Was Everything People Make Me Out to Be, I'da Been Dead Long Ago.' " *Creem*, July 1973, pp. 35–37, 75.

————. "Willie Nelson's New York Country Sessions." *Rolling Stone* Apr. 12, 1973, p. 14.

Gallagher, Kathleen. "Jennings Bound on Drug Counts." *Nashville Tennessean,* Sept. 1, 1977, pp. 1, 10.

————. "Waylon Back on Stage after Drug Charge Arrest." *Nashville Tennessean*, Aug. 25, 1977, pp. 1, 10.

————. "Waylon's Damaging Tape Ordered In." *Nashville Tennessean*, Sept. 4, 1977, pp. 1, 8.

Garbutt, Bob. "The Road to Nashville: Waylon Jennings." *Goldmine*, Dec. 1979, pp 20–23.

Goff, John. "Television Review: 'Love of the Common People' KTTV, October 5, 9–10 p.m." *Hollywood Reporter*, Oct. 7, 1969.

"Good Old Luckenbach." *Toledo Magazine*, Oct. 2, 1977, p 26.

Goodrich, David. "Waylon: This 'Renegade' Makes Sense." *Country Music News*, Oct. 1975, p. 8.

"Grateful Dead, Jennings to Star in Area Concerts." *Baltimore Sun*, Aug. 28, 1980, sec. B, p. 6.

Guerin, Terry. "Country Buses." *Penthouse*, June 1975, pp. 83–85.

"Guitars of the Stars." *Rolling Stone*, Feb. 13, 1975, p. 36.

Hadler, Nancy. "Colter's New Album 'Spiritual Thing.' " *Champaign-Urbana News Gazette*, Apr. 11, 1977.

Hall, Claude. "Jennings Mixes Country With Rock in Solid Act." *Billboard*, June 15, 1968, p. 12.

Hanauer, Joan. "New Shows Termed Mediocre." *Daily Sentinel Tribune*, Jan. 26, 1979, p. 4.

Hance, Bill. "Singer May Profit From Arrest." *Commercial News*, Sept. 11, 1977.

Hickey, Dave. "In Defense of the Telecaster Cowboys Outlaws." *Country Music*, Jan. 1974, pp. 90–95.

————. "Jessi Colter." *Country Music*, Sept. 1975.

————. "Outlaw Blues." *Country Music*, Feb. 1977.

————. "Waylon & Dolly: Nashville Rebels." *Circus*, Nov. 1975, pp. 20–21.

————. "Waylon: More and Better, Faster and Stronger." *Country Music*, Dec. 1974, pp. 24–31.

Hilburn, Robert. "Bill Graham Going All Out For Rock." *Los Angeles Times*, May 5, 1973, sec. II, p. 5.

————. "Country Show at Shrine Auditorium." *Los Angeles Times*, Jan. 28, 1969.

————. "Jennings Will Open Stand." *Los Angeles Times*, Dec. 1, 1970, sec. 5, p. 15.

————. "Kristofferson, Jennings in Mainstream." *Los Angeles Times*, Feb. 5, 1973, sec. 2, p. 6.

————. "Time for a Jennings Break Through?" *Los Angeles Times*, Feb. 10, 1973, sec. 2, p. 6.

Honick, Bruce. "Tape Will Clear Jennings of Cocaine Charge: Lawyer." *Nashville Banner*, Oct. 4, 1977, p. 1.

————. "Waylon Case Said 'Botched' in New York City." *Nashville Banner*, Oct. 5, 1977, p. 1.

"Honky Tonk Heroes." *Melody Maker*, Nov. 1, 1975, pp. 30–31.

Hooke, Lois, "Waylon Jennings: The Outlaw." *Music Gig*, Oct. 1975, p. 37.

Hooker, Paula L. "Christmas and Other Love Stories." *Country Music*, Dec. 1979, pp. 37–38.

————. "Jessie [sic] Colter and Waylon Jennings." *Country Music*, Dec. 1979, p. 38.

Hume, Martha. "Waylon and Willie in New York." *Rolling Stone*, Mar. 23, 1978.

Husock, Howard. "Waylon Jennings' Honky Tonk Heroism." *Boston Phoenix*, Apr. 2, 1974, sec. 2, p. 6.

Hyun, Paula. "What Happened at Willie's Picnic?" *Los Angeles Free Press*, July 13, 1973, pp. 27–29.

"In the Heart of Honky Tonk Rock." *Time*, Sept. 19, 1977, pp. 86–88.

Ives, Mike. "Waylon Jennings: Still Just Good Ole Boy," *Melody Maker* Sept. 25, 1974, pp. 21, 23.

Jackson, Guida. "Jessi Colter." *Texas Country Western Magazine*, Nov.–Dec. 1976.

"Jennings' Wife Wants an Out." *Arizona Republic*, Jan. 12, 1967.

Jensen, E. "Creativity & Its Sources." *Journal of Music Education* 55 (March 1969): 34–36.

"John Cash Interviews WAYLON." *Country Music*, Apr. 1981, pp. 22–30.

Kaufman, Bill. "'The Dukes' Are Foolin' 'Em." *Toledo Blade*, Mar. 18, 1979, sec. G, pp. 1, 5.

Kirby, Kip. "Nashville Artists Seeking Local Managers, Agents." *Billboard*, Jan. 16, 1982, p. 27.

Kirby, Kip, and Robyn Wells. "Country Acts Curtail Demands in Riders to Help Cut Costs." *Billboard*, Nov. 14, 1981, p. 84.

Kirsch, Bob. "Commander Cody and His Lost Plant Airmen: Waylon Jennings." *Billboard*, Jan. 4, 1975.

———. "The Country 'Outlaws.'" *Billboard*, Oct. 18, 1975, p. 36.

———. "Waylon Jennings: Free Thinker Sings His Own Kind of Music." *Billboard*, June 1, 1974, p. 14.

Langham, Barbara. "Late Train to Nashville." *Texas Parade*, Apr. 1973, pp. 42–45.

Leviton, Mark. "Waylon Jennings and Ronnie Milsap: New Nashville." *Daily Bruin*, May 23, 1974.

———. "Waylon Jennings: New Nashville." *Pop Top*, May 1975, p. 13.

Loggins, Kirk. "New Arrest Seen in Jennings Case." *Nashville Tennessean*, Aug. 26, 1977, pp. 1, 8.

———. "Waylon's Manager Aide Pleads Guilty." *Nashville Tennessean* May 26, 1978, p. 1.

Lund, Jens, and R. Serge Denisoff. "The Folk Music Revival and the Counter Culture: Contributions and Contradictions," *Journal of American Folklore* 84 (1971): 395–405.

McAllister, Bill. "Guitarist Combines Many Country Music Facets." *Fort Worth Star-Telegram*, Feb. 9, 1975, sec. H, p. 2.

McNelly, Dave. "Recording: Waylon Wails On For Album." *Dallas Morning News*, Sept. 28, 1974.

Mehler, Mark. "Where Does Your Money Go." *Country Music*, Mar. 1980, pp. 22–23.

Meltzer, Richard. "Topical Bozo." *Voice*, Aug. 8, 1974, p. 50.

Meyer, Richard. "Country and Western in Washington." *Toledo Blade*, Apr. 26, 1978, p. 1.

Mouldner, John. "Waylon & Willie." *Country Rambler*, Nov. 4, 1976, pp. 3–4.

"Musician Shot Dead At Party." *Atlanta Journal-Constitution*, Apr. 4, 1968, p. 14.

"Nashville Welcomes Waylon Jennings." *Music City News*, May 1966, pp. 14, 18.

Nelson, Willie. "A Tribune to Bob Wills." *Country Music*, Aug. 1974, pp. 68–73.

"New Acts." *Variety*, Jan. 24, 1973, p. 56.

Newcombe, Jim. "A Waylon Jennings Recording Session." *Country Music Review*, June 1976, pp. 24–25.

Ochs, Michael. "Slippin' Around." *Melody Maker*, July 13, 1974, p. 46.

———. "Waylon the Texan Rebel." *Melody Maker*, Sept. 7, 1974, p. 49.

"The Odd Couple." *Country Style*, May 1978.

Offen, Carl. "Seven Lonely Cowboys Try To Warm Up Central Park." *Country Music*, Oct. 1973, pp. 19–20.

"Ol' Waylon Endorses Sex." *Country Style*, May 1978, p. 8.

Orth, Maureen. "Outlaw Breed." *Newsweek*, Aug. 26, 1974, pp. 84–85.

"Outlaws Blues." *Rolling Stone*, Oct. 6, 1977, p. 16.

Parachini, A. "Waylon Jennings." *Stereo Review*, Feb. 1974, pp. 63–65.

"Part Of Me." *Billboard*, Oct. 18, 1967.

Patterson, Tim. "Critique of Country Music." *Guardian*, June 18, 1975, p. 19.

Petromonaco, Don. "An Interview with Waylon Jennings." *Country Style*, Dec. 1976, pp. 31–34.

"Pinch Us on Federal Drug Rap." *Variety*, Aug. 31, 1977, p. 62.

Powel, Bo. "A Detailed Study of the Chart Career of Waylon Jennings." *Country Music People*, Nov. 1976, pp. 22–27.

———. "Swarmin'." *Country Music Reporter*, Sept. 1972.

———. "Waylon Jennings: Interview." *Country Music People*, July 1971, pp. 16–18.

Powers, Charles T. "A Nashville Renegade Reins Up." *Los Angeles Times*, May 16, 1974, sec. 4, p. 10.

Pugh, John T. "Waylon Jennings: 'Country Music Is Soul.'" *Music City News*, June 1970, pp. 1, 13.

Pyke, Jackie. "The Waylor—Waylon Jennings." *Country Round-Up*, Mar. 19, 1971, pp. 7–12.

Redshaw, Davis. "Waylon on the New Frontier." *New Music Express*, Apr. 27, 1974.

Reinert, Al. "King of Country." *New York Times Magazine*, Mar. 26, 1978, pp. 20ff.

"Renegades." *Country Hotline*, Aug. 1974.

Rose, Bob. "Wailing Waylon Wows 'Em with First-Rate Country Tunes." *Toledo Blade*, June 18, 1981. p. 2.

Russell, P.J. "Some People Say I'm Not Country." *Country Song Round-Up*, March 1975, pp. 14–15, 48.

Salvo, Pat, and Barbara Salvo. "Hustler Interview: Waylon Jennings." *Hustler*, June 1975, pp. 22ff.

Satterfield, LaWayne. "A Star Discusses 'How It Really Is.'" *Music City News*, Jan. 1975, pp. 4, 23.

Schneider, Lynn. "Waylon Jennings & the Speeding Pompadour." *Crawdaddy*, Apr. 1973, pp. 26–27.

Schutt, Roger. "Road Manager Is Star's 'Right Hand' Man." *Music City News*, Jan. 1975, p. 10.

———. "Waylon Jennings & John Cash." *Country Style* Aug. 1976, p. 11.

Schwed, Mark. "Country Superstars Demand and Get Megabucks." *Daily Sentinel Tribune*, Apr. 22, 1981, p. 4.

Selvin, Joel. "Waylon Jennings: Rocking at the Boarding House," *San Francisco Chronicle*, Dec. 13, 1974, p. 70.

Siegel, Eric. "Jennings & Kristofferson: Outlaws Are Coming to Town." *Baltimore Sun*, Feb. 12, 1982, sec. B, p. 2.

"Singer Told Again to Pay." *Tucson Daily Citizen*, Oct. 10, 1974.

Smith, Hazel. "Jessi's the One Star Who's Got It Altogether." *Music City News*, June 1975, p. 25.

Smith, John L. "Waylon Jennings." *Town and Country World*, Nov. 1972, p. 10.

Smith, Julian. "Pale Horse, Pale Rider; Pale Car, Pale Driver: On the Road to Nashville with *Pay Day*." *Journal of Popular Film and Television* 7 (1979): 190–201.

Solomon, Linda. "Country Star Jennings Invades One of the Homes of Rock." *New Music Express*, Jan. 27, 1973.

Stafford, John. "The Rebel: Waylon Jennings." *Country Music People*, Apr. 1974, pp. 16–17.

Stoop, Norma M. "Waylon Jennings: Big Country Singer Hits the Big City," *After Dark*, April 1973, p. 51

Stuklane, Ellen. "Waylon Jennings." *Rock*, Oct. 22, 1973, p. 8.

"Texas Town Up for Sale." *Daily Sentinel Tribune*, Aug. 21, 1981, p. 2.

Thomas, Gail. "Lee Clayton: He's Gone More Than a Couple of Rounds with His Dreams." *Country Music*, Nov./Dec. 1978.

Thomas, Jeff. "Sound Track." *Hollywood Reporter*, Oct. 25, 1972.

Toepfer, Susan. "I'm Not Gonna Put Up with Anything from Anybody." *Photoplay*, Feb. 1974, pp. 71ff.

Tosches, Nick. "Waylon Jennings." *Zoo World*, Aug. 1, 1974, p. 22.

Tudor, Mary. "Waylon Jennings: Straight from the Soul." *Country Song Round-Up*.
"Waning Waylon." *Melody Maker*, July 9, 1977.
Watts, Michael. "You Gotta be a Man First, 'Fore You Can Be Anything . . . . " *Melody Maker*, Aug. 11, 1973, pp. 24–25.
"Waylon and Buddy." *Country Style*, May 1979, pp. 13, 42.
"Waylon and Drugs." *Monroe News Star*, Sept. 5, 1977.
"Waylon & Jessi Get Tough With Writers." *Rolling Stone*, Sept. 22, 1977, p. 26.
"Waylon & Willie Sing in New Year." *Billboard*, Jan. 24, 1976, p. 50.
"Waylon Jennings." *Billboard*, June 15, 1968.
"Waylon Jennings." *Billboard*, Aug. 7, 1976, p. 16.
"Waylon Jennings . . . Best Foot Forward." *K-Tuf Country*, Dec. 1968.
"Waylon Jennings LP Debuts at #1." *Record World*, May 21, 1977.
"Waylon Jennings Part of Me." *Billboard*, Oct. 28, 1967, p. 92.
"Waylon Jennings—Superstar Looking for a Place to Happen." *Country Song Round-Up*. (1971), 26–27.
"Waylon Reflects on His Outlaw Ways." *Country Style*, June, 1976, p. 48.
"Waylon Speaks Out." *Country Hotline News*, Nov. 1975.
"Waylon's Outlaw Blues." *Rolling Stone*, Oct. 6, 1977.
"Waylon Voice of TV Series."*Country Style*, May 1979, p. 20.
Weiner, Susan. "Country Comes to Town." *Penthouse*, May 1973.
Welch, Chris. "Fighting Talk." *Melody Maker*, June 3, 1978, pp. 34, 53.
Williams, Jean. "Jennings Opening Act at Big Ft. Worth Spot." *Billboard*, Feb. 28, 1981, pp. 29, 47.
"Willie and Waylon Invade New York." *Country Music*, Aug. 1978, pp. 18–19.
Wilson, Alan. "Jennings Plays 'Get It-On' Country Music." *Arizona Republic,* July 13, 1973.
Wilson, Maggie. "Waylon Jennings—The New Nashville Sound." *Arizona Days and Ways Magazine*, Apr. 3, 1966, pp. 11–13.
Windeler, Robert. "Couples." *People*, Sept. 29, 1975, pp. 45–47.
Widner, Ellis. "Jessi Raps About Music and Ole Waylon." *Country Rambler,* Dec. 30, 1976.
Wood, Gary. "Close-up." *Billboard*, Jan. 28, 1978, p. 102.

Wren, Christopher. "Country Music." *Look*, July 13, 1971, pp. 11–42.

Yaryan, Bill. "Here Come the Shitkickers." *Los Angeles Weekly News*, Aug. 24, 1973, p. 13.

Young, J.R. "The Monster Voice of Waylon Jennings." *Rolling Stone*, Dec. 9, 1971, p. 58.

Young, Martin. "Waylon Live!" *Outlaws*, Feb. 1980, pp. 4–5.

DISCOGRAPHIES

John L. Smith, compiler

WAYLON JENNINGS ALPHABETICAL TITLE LISTING—
1959 THROUGH 1981

Title	Master Number	Recording Date	Release Number
"Abilene" (Paul Foster)		12/64	BAT-1001
			VL-73873
"About That Woman"	BWA-1958	12/18/72	
"A Couple More Years"	FWA5-0834	3/24/76	APL1-1816
"A Couple More Years"	GWA5-2894	11/77	AFL1-2686
"Ain't No God in Mexico"	CWA4-1165	2/20/73	APL1-0240
"Ain't No God in Mexico" (live)	DWA5-1284	9/26/74	
"All Around Cowboy"	EWA4-1073	10/14/75	APL1-1520
"All Around Cowboy"	EWA4-1075	10/21/75	APL1-1520
"All of Me Belongs to You" (w/Anita Carter)	UWA4-2928	11/9/67	LSP-4260
"Alone"	WWA4-7423	12/3/68	LSP-4137
"A Long Time Ago"	HWA5-5166	4-5/78	AFL1-2979
"Amanda"	DWA5-1114	7/15/74	APL1-0734
			AHL1-3378
			CPL1-3406
"Amanda"	DWA5-1114	4/9/79	PB-11596

Title	Master Number	Recording Date	Release Number
"Amanda" (live)	DWA5-1209	9/25/74	
"Anita, You're Dreaming"	SWA4-2649	7/28/65	47-8729
			LPM/S-3620
			447—0797
			LSP-4341
"Anita, You're Dreaming" (live)	DWA-1315	9/26/74	
"Another Blue Day"		1960/1961	TREND-102
		1963	RAMCO-1997
"Another Bridge to Burn"	SWA4-2321	3/16/65	LPM/S-3523
			ACL1-0306
"Another Man's Fool"	JWA5-7802	1/17/79	AHL1-3493
"Are You Ready for the Country"	FWA5-0827	3/22/76	APL1-1816
			PB-10842
"Are You Sure Hank Done It This Way"	EWA4-0767	9/2/74	PB-10379
			APL1-1062
			AHL1-3378
			CPL1-3406
"As the 'Billy World Turns"	HWA5-5161	4-5/78	AFL1-2979
"Atlanta's Burning Down"	AWA4-1420	4/26/71	
"A Whiter Shade of Pale" (w/W. Nelson)			
"A World of Our Own" (w/The Kimberlys)	XWA4-1422	4/8/69	LSP-4180
"Baby Don't Be Looking in My Mind"	SWA4-2653	7/28/65	LPM/S-3620
"Back in the Saddle Again" (instrumental)	EWA4-1080	10/20/75	APL1-1520
"Beautiful Annabel Lee"	TWA4-0896	5/24/66	LPM/S-3660
"Belle of the Ball"	FWA5-1194	12/19/76	APL1-2317
			PB-10924
"Big Ball in Cowtown" (live)	DWA5-1282	9/26/74	
"Big, Big Love"	DWA4-1019	1/11/72	
"Big, Big Love" (live)	BWA5-1312	9/26/74	
"Big Boss Man" (live)	DWA5-1320	9/26/74	
"Big D"	ZWA4-1321	4/22/70	LSP-4567
"Big Mamou"		12/64	BAT-1001
			VL-73873
"Billy"	HWA5-5165	4-5/78	AFL1-2979
"Black Rose"	BWA4-1426	5/16/72	APL1-0240
"Blame It on the Kellys"	6355	4/70	UAS-5213
"Bob Wills Is Still the King"	DWA5-1121	7/16/74	
"Bob Wills Is Still the King" (live)	DWA5-1205	9/25/74	APL1-1062
			PB-10379
			APL1-1108
"Bob Wills Is Still the King"	EWA4-1083	10/21/75	APL1-1520
"Born to Love You"	TWA4-1315	9/8/66	47-9146
			CAL/S-2183
			ACL1-7019

Title	Master Number	Recording Date	Release Number
"Brand New Goodbye Song"	FWA5-1196	12/18/76	APL1-2317
"Breakdown" (live)	DWA5-1206	9/25/74	
"Bridge Over Troubled Water" (w/Jessi Colter)	ZWA4-1383	4/22/70	47-9992 LSP-4567
"Brown Eyed Handsome Man"	WWA4-7422	12/3/68	74-0281 LSP-4260 447-0836 SPS-33-570
"Burning Memories"		12/64	BAT-1001 VL-73873
"Busted"	TWA4-0904	6/1/66	LPM/S-3660 CAS-2556
"But That's Alright"	TWA4-0616	2/17/66	LPM/S-3620
"But You Know I Love You" (w/The Kimberlys)	XWA4-1429	4/10/69	74-0210 LSP-4180
"California Sunshine"	UWA4-2189	2/14/67	LPM/S-4023 ACL1-0306
"Can't You See"	FWA5-0829	3/22/76	APL1-1816 PB-10721 GB-10927
"Casey's Last Ride"	ZWA4-9187	12/8/70	LSP-4487 SPS-33-570
"Cedartown Georgia"	WWA4-7420	12/3/68	
"Cedartown Georgia"	XWA4-1361	3/20/69	48-1003 LSP-4567
"Change My Mind"	WWA4-7430	12/5/68	
"Change My Mind"	WWA4-7478	12/16/68	LSP-4137
"Chet's Tune" (w/various RCA artists)			47-9229
"Christina"	UWA4-2790	9/20/67	LPM/S-4023
"Cindy of New Orleans"	SWA4-2340	3/19/65	LPM/S-3523
"Cindy, Oh Cindy" (w/ The Kimberlys)	XWA4-1427	4/9/69	LSP-4180
"Cloudy Days"	DWA5-1116	7/15/74	APL1-0734
"Clyde"	KWA5-8338		AHL1-3602 PB-12007
"Come and Stay with Me" (w/The Kimberlys)	XWA4-1423	4/8/69	LSP-4180
"Come Early Mornin"	BWA4-1189	3/9/72	
"Come with Me"	JWA5-7761	7/26/79	PB-11723 AHL1-3493
"Cowhouse Campout" (instrumental)	EWA4-1076	10/20/75	
"Crazy Arms"	AWA4-1779	8/31/71	LSP-4751
"Crazy Arms" (instrumental)	EWA4-1086	10/21/75	APL1-1520
"Crying"		12/64	BAT-121639 BAT-1001 VL-73873

Title	Master Number	Recording Date	Release Number
"Dark Side of Fame"	swa4-2338	3/19/65	47-8652
			cal/s-2183
			acl1-7019
"Days Gone By" (instrumental)	ewa4-1084	10/21/76	
"Days of Sand and Shovels"	wwa4-7425	12/4/68	
"Days of Sand and Shovels"	xwa4-1358	3/20/69	74-0157
			lsp-4341
"Delia's Gone"	xwa4-1304	2/24/69	74-0157
			lsp-4341
"Delta Dawn"	bwa4-1428	5/16/72	lsp-4751
"Destiny's Child"	uwa4-2193	2/15/67	lpm/s-3825
"Dixie Hold On"		1/78	a&m sp-6004
"Dixie, Now You're Done"		1/78	a&m sp-6004
"Doesn't Anybody Know My Name"	twa4-0617	2/17/66	lpm/s-3620
"Do It Again"	kwa5-8342		ahl1-3602
"Donna on My Mind"	xpa3-0812	12/17/69	lsp-4418
"Donna on My Mind" (live)	dwa5-1285	9/26/74	
"Do No Good Woman"	awa4-1780	9/1/71	lsp-4647
			sps-33-570
			74-0961
"Don't Cuss the Fiddle" (w/Willie Nelson)	gwa5-2892	11/77	afl1-2686
"Don't Let the Deal Go Down" (instrumental)	ewa4-1077	10/20/75	
"Don't Play the Game"	xwa4-1302	2/24/69	
"Don't Play the Game"	xwa4-1360	3/20/69	lsp-4260
"Don't Think Twice"		12/64	bat-1001
			vl-73873
"Don't Think Twice"		12/64	a&m sp-4238
"Don't Waste Your Time"	uwa4-2195	2/15/67	lpm/s-3825
"Don't You Think This Outlaw Bit's Done Got Out of Hand"	hwa5-5164	4-5/78	afl1-2979
			pb-11390
"Down Came the World"	swa4-2333	3/18/65	lpm/s-3523
			cal/s-2183
			acl1-7019
"Dream Baby"		12/64	bat-121639
			bat-1001
			vl-73873
"Dream Baby"	swa4-2335	3/18/65	cal/s-2183
"Dream Baby" (live)	dwa5-1319	9/26/74	
"Dreaming My Dreams"	ewa4-0736	9/3/74	pb-10270
			apl1-1062
			gb-10927
"Driving Nails in the Wall" (w/The Kimberlys)	xwa4-1430	4/10/69	lsp-4180
			47-9782
"East Virginia Blues" (w/Don Bowman and Willie Nelson)		1979	l-4605

Title	Master Number	Recording Date	Release Number
"Even Cowgirls Get the Blues" (w/Johnny Cash)	NCO-127490	8/1/78	
"Falling for You"	TWA4-0613	2/16/66	LPM/S-3620
"Farewell Party"	WWA4-7428	12/4/68	74-0105
			LSP-4137
"Folsom Prison Blues"	WWA4-4740	8/6/68	LSP-4085
			CAS-2556
"Folsom Prison Blues"	LWA5-6620	9/8/81	AHL1-4247
"Foolin' 'Round"	TWA4-0907	6/1/66	LPM/S-3660
			CAS-2556
"For the Kids"	WWA4-7427	12/4/68	
"For the Kids"	WWA4-7479	12/16/68	LSP-4137
"Four Strong Winds"	1073RE		A&M 739
			A&M SP-4238
"Freedom to Stay"	BWA4-1955	12/18/72	LSP-4854
"Freedom to Stay" (live)	DWA5-1280	9/26/74	
"Frisco Depot"	BWA4-1192	3/9/72	LSP-4751
"Games People Play" (w/The Kimberlys)	XWA4-1432	4/10/69	LSP-4180
"Gardenia Waltz" (instrumental) (w/Johnny Gimble)	EWA4-1081	10/20/75	APL1-1520
"Gentle on My Mind"	UWA4-2709	8/29/67	LPM/S-3918
			CAS-2608
"Get Naked with Me"	LWA5-6624	9/21/81	AHL1-4247
"Ghost of General Lee"	AWA4-1421	4/26/71	
"Girl I Can Tell (You're Trying to Work It Out)"	HWA5-5169	4-5/78	AFL1-2979
			PB-11390
"Goddamn You Charlie, What a Man"	CWA1-1089	1/22/73	
"Gold Dust Woman"	GWA5-2893	11/77	AFL1-2686
"Gone to Denver"	ZWA4-1361	4/22/70	74-0886
			LSP-4854
"Gonna Write a Letter"	LWA5-6625	9/11/81	AHL1-4247
"Goodhearted Woman"	AWA4-1782	9/1/71	74-0615
			LSP-4647
			SPS-33570
"Goodhearted Woman" (live) (w/Willie Nelson on APL1-1321)	DWA5-1200	9/25/74	PB-10529
			APL1-1108
			APL1-1321
			GB-10928
			AHL1-3378
			CPL1-3406
"Good Time Charlie's Got the Blues"	BWA4-1431	12/14/72	LSP-4854
"Good Time Charlie's Got the Blues" (live)	DWA5-1306	9/26/74	
"Got a Lot Going for Me"	DWA4-0794	2/8/74	PB-10020

Title	Master Number	Recording Date	Release Number
"Greasy Grit Gravy" (w/Bobby Bare)		1978	KC-35314
"Greatest Cowboy of Them All" (w/Johnny Cash)	NCO-12789	8/1/78	
"Green River"	TWA4-1420	7/5/66	47-9025 LPM/S-3736
"Grey Eyes You Know"	XWA4-1631	6/12/69	LSP-4487
"Hangin' On"	UWA4-2715	8/30/67	LPM/S-3918 CAS-2608
"Heartaches by the Number"	TWA4-0903	6/1/66	LPM/S-3660 CAS-2556
"Heartaches for a Dime"	TWA4-0906	6/1/66	LPM/S-3660
"Heaven or Hell" (w/Willie Nelson)	DWA4-0804	10/30/73	APL1-0539 APL1-1321 PB-10529
"Heaven or Hell" (live)	DWA5-1283	9/26/74	
"He Went to Paris"	EWA4-1023	11/24/75	
"He Went to Paris"	KWA5-8345		AHL1-3602
"High Time (You Quit Your Low Down Ways)"	EWA4-0771	10/30/74	APL1-1062
"Honky Tonk Blues"	LWA5-6617	9/23/81	AHL1-4247
"Honky Tonk Heroes"	CWA4-1168	2/21/73	APL1-0240 APL1-1321 AHL1-3378 CPL-3406
"Honky Tonk Heroes" (live)	DWA5-1300	9/26/74	
"Honky Tonk Woman"	XPA3-0813	12/17/69	LSP-4418 SPS-33-570
"Hoodlum" (instrumental)	TWA4-1422	8/30/66	LPM/S-3736
"Hot Blooded Woman" (w/Willie Nelson and Don Bowman)			L-4605
"House of the Rising Sun" (live) (see also: The Real House of the Rising Sun)	DWA5-1311	9/26/74	APL1-1108
"House Song"	XWA4-1303	2/24/69	
"House Song"	XWA4-1359	3/20/69	LSP-4567
"How Long Have You Been There"	UWA4-2786	9/19/67	LPM/S-3918
"How Much Rain Can One Man Stand"	WWA4-1872	2/7/68	LSP-4085
"I Ain't Livin' Long Like This"	JWA5-7800	8/8/79	AHL1-3493 PB-11898
"I Ain't the One" (w/Jessi Colter)	XWA4-2308	8/20/69	74-0280 LSP-4333 47-9920
"I Ain't the One" (w/Jessi Colter)	KWA5-8704		AAL1-3931
"I Believe You Can" (w/Jessi Colter)	KWA5-8701	12/16/80	AAL1-3931

Title	Master Number	Recording Date	Release Number
"I Came Here to Party"		6/12/78	PB-12007
"I Can Get Off on You" (w/Willie Nelson)	GWA5-2891	11/77	AFL1-2686 PB-11198
"I Can't Keep My Hands Off of You"	DWA5-1118	7/15/74	APL1-0734
"(I'd Be) A Legend in My Time"	XWA4-2305	8/19/69	
"(I'd Be) A Legend in My Time"	XWA4-2517	10/29/69	LSP-4487
"I Don't Believe You"	1119		A&M SP-4238 A&M 762
"I Don't Mind"	SWA4-2651	7/28/65	LPM/S-3523
"I Fall in Love So Easily"	UWA4-2384	4/26/67	LPM/S-3918
"If I Were a Carpenter"	XPA3-0816	12/18/69	LSP-4418 SPS-33-570
"If the Shoe Fits"	TWA4-1318	9/9/66	LPM/S-3825
"If You Could Touch Her at All"	DWA4-0809	10/29/73	APL1-0539
"If You Could Touch Her at All" (live)	DWA5-1313	9/26/74	
"If You Could Touch Her at All" (w/Willie Nelson)	GWA5-2889	11/77	AFL1-2686
"If You Really Want Me to I'll Go"	TWA4-0614	2/16/66	LPM/S-3620
"If You're Going Girl"	DPA3-1610	5/17/74	
"If You See Her"	JWA5-7807	7/5/79	AHL1-3493
"If You See Me Getting Smaller"	FWA5-1197	12/18/76	APL1-2317
"If You Were Mine to Lose"	WWA4-4742	8/6/68	LSP-4085
"I Got the Train Sittin' Waitin' "	JWA5-7803	1/8/79	AHL1-3493
"I Got You" (w/Anita Carter)	WWA4-1878	2/9/68	47-9480 LSP-4137 LSP-4341
"I Knew You'd Be Leaving"	ZWA4-1852	10/12/70	LSP-4647
"I'll Be Alright"	KWA5-8698	12/15/80	AAL1-3931
"I'll Fly Away" (w/Johnny Cash, George Jones, and Hank Williams, Jr.)	NCO-130217	1/24/79	
"I'll Go Back to Her"	FWA5-0830	3/23/76	APL1-1816 PB-10721
"I Lost Me"	WWA4-7421	12/3/68	LSP-4137
"I'm a Long Way from Home"	TWA4-1421	7/5/66	LPM/S-3736
"I'm a Man of Constant Sorrow"	SWA4-2334	3/18/65	LPM/S-3523
"I'm a Ramblin' Man"	DWA4-0793	2/8/74	APL1-0734 PB-10020 AHL1-3378 CPL1-3406
"I'm a Ramblin' Man" (live)	DWA5-1213	9/25/74	APL1-1108
"I May Never Pass This Way Again"	XWA4-1632	6/12/69	LSP-4260
"I'm Doing This for You"	UWA4-2787	9/19/67	LSP-4085
"I'm Gonna Leave (While I Still Love You)"	XWA4-1629	6/12/69	LSP-4567

Title	Master Number	Recording Date	Release Number
"I Never Said It Would Be Easy"	HWA5-5149	4/78	PB-11344
"In This Very Same Room"	TWA4-0898	5/24/66	LPM/S-3660
"I Recall a Gypsy Woman"	EWA4-0765	9/2/74	APL1-1062
"It Ain't Easy"	ZWA4-1012	2/27/70	
"It Doesn't Matter Anymore"	CPA3-2831	5/5/73	
"I Think I'm Gonna Kill Myself"	GWA5-2537	1/5/77	APL1-2317
"I Think It's Time She Learned"	AWA4-1423	5/12/71	48-1003
			LSP-4751
"It'll Be Her"	DWA5-1115	7/15/74	APL1-0734
"I Tremble for You"	TWA4-0625	2/18/66	LPM/S-3825
"It's All Over Now"	UWA4-2381	4/26/67	CAL/S-2183
			ACL1-7019
"It's All Over Now"	XWA4-1627	6/12/69	74-0615
			LSP-4567
"It's Alright"	KWA5-8339		AHL1-3602
			PB-2067
"It Should Be Easier Now"	AWA4-1778	8/31/71	LSP-4647
"It's Not Supposed to Be That Way"	DWA4-0305	10/17/73	APL1-0539
"It's Not Supposed to Be That Way" (live)	GDWA5-1296	9/26/74	
"It's Not Supposed to Be That Way" (w/Willie Nelson)	DWA5-2890	11/77	AFL1-2686
"It's So Easy"		12/64	BAT-1001
"It's So Easy" (Buddy Holly medley)	DPA3-1611	5/17/74	AFL1-2979
"It's Sure Been Fun"	XWA4-2518	10/29/69	
"It's the World's Gone Crazy" (Cotillion)	JWA5-7804	1/17/79	AHL1-3493
			PB-11898
"It Wasn't God Who Made Honky Tonk Angels" (w/Jessi Colter)	KWA5-8699	12/12/80	AAL1-3931
"I've Always Been Crazy" (long)	HWA5-5147	4/11 & 4/14/78	PB-11344
			AFL1-2979
			AHL1-3378
			CPL1-3406
"I've Always Been Crazy" (short)	HWA5-5148	4/11 & 4/14/78	
"I've Been Along Time Leaving (But I'll Be a Long Time Gone)"	EWA4-0769	9/5/74	APL1-1062
"I've Been Needing Someone Like You"	UWA4-2788	9/19/67	LSP-4137
"I've Got Eyes for You"	AWA4-1141	1/29/71	LSP-4567
"Ivory Tower"	JWA5-7805	6/26/79	AHL1-3493
"I Walk the Line"	CWA4-1264	3/13/73	AFL-2979
"I Wish I Was Crazy Again" (w/Johnny Cash)	NCO-120870	7/6/76	KC-35313
			3-10742
			KC-35637
"I Wonder Just Where I Went Wrong"	SWA4-2320	3/16/65	47-8572
			LPM/S-3620

Title	Master Number	Recording Date	Release Number
"Jack of Diamonds"	FWA5-0833	3/24/76	APL1-1816
"John's Back in Town"	TWA4-1320	9/9/66	CAL/S-2183
			ACL1-7019
"Jole Blon"		10/1958	BR9-55130
"Julie"	UWA4-2717	8/30/67	47-9414
			LPM/S-3918
"Just Across the Way"	UWA4-2389	4/27/67	LSP-4260
"Just for You"	SWA4-2652	7/28/65	LPM/S-3523
"Just to Satisfy You"	1074		A&M 739
			A&M SP-4238
"Just to Satisfy You"	WWA4-7426	12/4/68	
"Just to Satisfy You"	WWA4-7480	12/16/68	LSP-4137
			LSP-4341
			CAS-2608
"Just to Satisfy You" (live)	DWA5-1318	9/26/74	
"Just to Satisfy You" (w/Willie Nelson)	LWA5-6618	9/21/81	AHL1-4247
"Kentucky Woman"	WWA4-2078	4/16/68	LSP-4023
"Kisses Sweeter Than Wine"			A&M SP-4238
"Ladies Love Outlaws"	BWA4-1020	1/11/72	LSP-4751
			AHL1-3378
			CPL-3406
"Ladies Love Outlaws" (live)	DWA5-1281	9/26/74	
"Lady in the Harbor"	CPA3-2832	5/5/73	
"Laid Back Country Picker"	BWA4-1430	12/14/72	
"Laid Back Country Picker" (live)	DWA5-1298	9/26/74	
"Lang's Mansion" (instrumental)	TWA4-1424	8/30/66	LPM/S-3736
"Lang's Theme" (instrumental)	TWA4-1423	8/30/66	LPM/S-3736
"Last Letter"	BWA4-1035	1/12/72	
"Last Letter" (live)	DWA5-1299	9/26/74	APL1-1108
"Lay It Down"	BWA4-1033	1/12/72	LSP-4854
"Leavin' Town"	TWA4-0626	2/18/66	LPM/S-3620
			CAS-2556
			CAS-2608
"Let Me Stay Awhile"	XWA4-2515	10/29/69	LSP-4567
"Let Me Talk to You"	UWA4-2386	4/26/67	LPM/S-3918
			ACL1-0306
"Let Me Tell You My Mind" (w/The Kimberlys)	XWA4-1431	4/10/69	LSP-4180
"Let's All Help the Cowboys" (Sing the Blues)	DWA4-1268	1/30/75	APL1-1062
			PB-10142
"Let's Turn Back the Years"	EWA4-0768	9/5/74	APL-1062
"Life Goes On"	XWA4-2522	10/30/69	47-9967
"Lila"	XWA4-2306	8/19/69	47-9819
"Lisa's Only Seven"	BWA4-1956	12/12/72	
"Listen, They're Playing My Song"	UWA4-2390	4/27/67	CAL/S-2183
			ACL1-7019

Title	Master Number	Recording Date	Release Number
"Lock, Stock and Teardrops"	UWA4-2382	4/26/67	LPM/S-3918
"Lonely Weekends"	WWA4-7431	12/5/68	LSP-4137
"Lonesome, On'ry and Mean"	BWA4-1954	12/18/72	LSP-4854
			AHL1-3378
			PB-11596
			CPL1-3406
"Lonesome, On'ry and Mean" (live)	DWA5-1304	9/26/74	
"Long Gone"	UWA4-2387	4/26/67	LPM/S-4023
"Long Way Back Home" (w/The Kimberlys)	XWA4-1425	4/19/69	LSP/S-4180
"Lonigan's Widow"	6351	4/70	UAS-5213
"Looking at a Heart That Needs a Home"	UWA4-2714	8/30/67	LPM/S-3918
"Looking for a Feeling"	GWA5-2703	8/14/77	PB-1118
			AFL1-2686
"Look Into My Teardrops"	SWA4-2648	7/28/65	47-8729
			LPM/S-3523
"Look Into My Teardrops" (live)	DWA5-1316	9/26/74	
"Lorena" (Paul Foster)		12/64	BAT-1001
			VL-73873
"Louisiana" Women	DWA4-0801	10/16/73	APL1-0539
"Louisiana" Women (live)	DWA5-1198	9/25/74	
"Love Denied"	1041		A&M 722
"Love in the Hot Afternoon"	AWA4-1140	1/29/71	
"Love of the Common People"	UWA4-2190	2/15/67	47-9259
			LPM/S-3825
			447-0797
			SPS-33-570
"Love of the Common People" (live)	DWA5-1321	9/26/74	
"Love's Gonna Live Here"		12/64	BAT-1001
			VL-73873
"Lovin' Her Was Easier"	ZWA3-9184	12/7/70	LSP-4487
			SPS-33-570
"Lovin' Her Was Easier" (live)	DWA5-1214	9/26/74	
"Low Down Freedom"	AWA4-1776	8/31/71	APL1-0240
"Lucille"	GWA5-2539	1/8/77	APL1-2317
"Luckenbach, Texas" (w/Willie Nelson)	GWA5-2534	1/7/77	PB-10924
			APL1-2317
			AHL1-3378
			CPL1-3406
"MacArthur Park" (w/The Kimberlys)	XWA4-1424	4/8/69	74-0210
			LSP-4180
			LSP-4341
			SPS-33-570
"MacArthur Park (Revisited)"	FWA5-0836	3/26/76	APL1-1816
"Mama I'll Sing One Song for You"	ZWA3-9186	12/8/70	
"Mammas Don't Let Your Babies	GWA5-2886	11/77	PB-11198

Title	Master Number	Recording Date	Release Number
Grow Up To Be Cowboys" (w/Willie Nelson)			AFL1-2686 AHL1-3378 CPL1-3406
"Many Rivers"	DWA5-1122	7/16/74	
"Marriage on the Rocks"	ZWA4-1014	2/27/70	
"Mary Ann Regrets" (w/The Kimberlys)	XWA4-1428	4/10/69	LSP-4180
"Maybe Baby" (Buddy Holly medley)	DPA3-1611	5/17/74	AFL1-2979
"May I Borrow Some Sugar From You"	LWA5-6622	9/23/81	AHL1-4247
"Me and Bobby McGee"	BWA4-1193	3/9/72	LSP-4854
"Me and Bobby McGee" (live)	DWA5-1201	9/25/74	APL1-1108
"Me and Paul" (live)	DWA5-1204	9/25/74	APL1-1108
"Memories of You and I"	DWA5-1117	7/15/74	APL1-0734
"Mental Revenge"	UWA4-2186	2/14/67	47-9146 LSP-4085
"Mental Revenge" (live)	DWA5-1297	9/26/74	
"Mes'kin" (instrumental)			PB-11723
"Midnight Rider"	CWA4-1266	3/13/73	
"Midnight Rider"	DWA5-1123	7/16/74	APL1-0734
"Midnight Rider" (live)	DWA5-1301	9/26/74	
"Mississippi Woman"	ZWA4-1016	2/27/70	LSP-4487 47-9967
"Mississippi Woman" (live)	DWA5-1307	9/26/74	
"Mobile Blues"	ZWA3-9185	12/7/70	
"Mona"	DWA4-0807	10/17/73	APL1-0539 APB0-0251
"Mona" (live)	DWA5-1314	9/26/74	
"Money Cannot Make the Man"	TWA4-1316	9/9/66	LPM/S-3825 ACL1-0306
"Money (That's What I Want)" (Jerry Gropp)		12/64	BAT-1001 VL-73873
"Must You Throw Dirt in My Face"	XPA3-0817	12/18/69	LSP-4418
"My Baby Left Me" (Elvis medley)	GWA5-2540	1/8/77	APL1-2317
"My Baby Walks All Over Me"		1960/1961 1963	TREND-106 RAMCO-1989
"My God and I"	BWA4-1191	3/9/72	
"My Heroes Have Always Been Cowboys"	EWA4-0979	11/24/75	APL1-1321
"My Ramona"	WWA4-1873	2/7/68	LSP-4085
"My World"		1963	RAMCO-1997
"Nadine"		6/20/78	PL-43166
"Nashville Bum"	TWA4-1416	7/5/66	LPM/S-3736 ACL1-0306
"Nashville Rebel"	TWA4-1418	7/5/66	LPM/S-3736
"Nashville Wimmin"	KWA5-8341		AHL1-3602

Title	Master Number	Recording Date	Release Number
"Ned Kelly"	6347	4/70	UAS-5213
"Never Again"		1960/1961	TREND-102
		1963	RAMCO-1989
"Never Been to Spain"	BWA4-1429	5/16/72	LSP-4751
"Never Been to Spain" (live)	DWA5-1309	9/26/74	
"New York City R.F.D."	WWA4-1874	2/7/68	LSP-4085
			CAS-2608
"Night Life" (w/George Jones)		4/6/78	EPIC-35544
"No One's Gonna Miss Me" (w/Anita Carter)	UWA4-2929	11/11/67	47-9480
"No Regrets"	XPA3-0819	12/19/69	LSP-4418
"Norwegian Wood"	TWA4-0624	2/18/66	47-8822
			LPM/S-3736
			SPS-33-570
"Nothin' Worth Takin' or Leavin'"	BWA4-1022	1/12/72	74-0808
"Now Everybody Knows"	SWA4-2322	3/16/65	LPM/S-3523
"Oklahoma Sunshine"	DWA4-0792	2/8/74	APL1-0734
"Old Five and Dimers Like Me"	CWA 4-1167	2/20/73	APL1-0240
"Old Friend"	FWA5-0835	3/25/76	APL1-1816
"Old Love, New Eyes"	JWA5-7808	7/19/79	AHL1-3493
"Omaha"	CWA4-1170	2/23/73	APL1-0240
"One of My Bad Habits"	ZWA4-1702	7/14/70	LSP-4647
"Only Daddy That'll Walk the Line"	WWA4-2076	4/16/68	47-9561
			LPM/S-4023
			SPS-33-570
			447-0836
			ACL1-0306
			AHL1-3378
			CPL1-3406
"Only Daddy That'll Walk the Line" (live)	DWA5-1197	9/25/74	
"Out Among the Stars"	JWA5-7806	8/8/79	AHL1-3493
"Pastels and Harmony"	KWA5-8700	12/9/80	AAL1-3931
"Peeping Tom" (instrumental)	EWA4-1085	10/21/75	
"Peggy Sue" (Buddy Holly medley)	DPA3-1611	5/17/74	AFL1-2979
"People in Dallas Got Hair"	XWA4-2523	10/30/69	
"Pickin' White Gold"	XWA4-2549	10/30/69	LSP-4567
"Pick Up the Tempo"	DWA4-0802	10/16/73	APL1-0539
"Pick Up the Tempo" (live)	DWA5-1210	9/25/74	APL1-1108
"Pick Up the Tempo" (w/Willie Nelson)	GWA5-2888	11/77	AFL1-2686
"Pleasures of a Sunday Afternoon"	6356	4/70	UAS-5213
"Poor Old Ugly Gladys Jones" (w/Don Bowman)	WWA4-3171	6/68	74-0133
			LSP-4230
"Precious Memories"	FWA5-0828	3/22/76	APL1-1816
"Pretend I Never Happened"	BWA4-1427	5/16/72	74-0808
			LSP-4854

Title	Master Number	Recording Date	Release Number
"Ragged But Right"	XPA3-0815	12/18/69	LSP-4418
"Rainy Day Woman"	DWA5-1119	7/15/74	APL1-0734
			PB-10142
"Rainy Day Woman" (live)	DWA5-1305	9/26/74	APL1-1108
"Rainy Day Woman" (from "Moonrunners" soundtrack)		1974	
"Rainy Season" (w/Jessi Colter)	KWA5-8697	12/15/80	AAL1-3931
"Ranchin' in the Evening"	6354	4/70	UAS-5213
"Rave On"	1042		A&M 722
"Revelation"	AWA4-1783	9/1/71	LSP-4751
"Ride Me Down Easy"	CWA4-1162	2/19/73	APL1-0240
"Ride Me Down Easy"	EWA4-1079	10/20/75	APL1-1520
"Right Before My Eyes"	UWA4-2713	8/29/67	LPM/S-3918
			47-9561
"Rings of Gold" (w/Anita Carter)	UWA4-2930	11/9/67	LSP-4137
			ACL1-0306
"River Boy"			A&M SP-4238
"Rock Salt and Nails" (w/Lee Hazlewood)	XPA3-0820	12/19/69	LSP-4418
"Ruby, Don't Take Your Love to Town"	TWA4-1314	9/8/66	LPM/S-3825
			LSP-4341
			CAS-2608
"Rush Street Blues" (instrumental)	TWA4-1426	8/30/66	LPM/S-3736
"Sally Was a Good Old Girl"		12/64	BAT-1001
"Same Old Lover Man"	AWA4-1424	5/12/71	LSP-4647
"Sandy Sends Her Best"	BWA4-1034	1/12/72	LSP-4854
"San Francisco Depot"	BWA4-1192	3/9/72	LSP-4751
"San Francisco Mabel Joy"	BWA4-1433	12/14/72	LSP-4854
"Satin Sheets"	GWA5-2535	1/4/77	APL1-2317
"See You Around (On Your Way Down)"	WWA4-2079	4/16/68	LSP-4085
			ACL1-0306
"Seven Bridges Road"	CWA4-1164	2/19/73	
"Shadow of the Gallows"	6350	4/70	UAS-5213
"Shadow of the Gallows"	ZWA4-1456	7/9/70	47-9885
"She Called Me Baby"	TWA4-0899	5/24/66	LPM/S-3660
"She Comes Running"	XPA3-0818	12/19/69	LSP-4418
"She Loves Me (She Don't Love You)"	UWA4-2385	4/26/67	CAL/S-2183
			APL1-7019
"She's Gone, Gone, Gone"	TWA4-0902	6/1/66	LPM/S-3660
"She's Looking Good"	EWA4-0770	10/30/74	APL1-1062
"Shopping" (instrumental)	EWA4-1082	10/20/75	APL1-1520
"Shutting Out the Light"	UWA4-2194	2/15/67	LSP-4260
"Sick and Tired"	XPA3-0821	12/19/69	LSP-4418
"Sick and Tired" (live)	DWA-1302	9/26/74	
"Silver Ribbons"	TWA4-1419	7/15/66	47-9025
			LPM/S-3736
"Singer of Sad Songs"	XWA4-2514	10/29/69	47-9819
			LSP-4418
			SPS-33570

Title	Master Number	Recording Date	Release Number
"Shine"	LWA5-6605	9/14/81	PD-1-6344
			PB-12367
			AHL1-4247
"Shine" (Bluegrass version)		1981	PD-1-6344
"Sing the Blues to Daddy"	WWA4-7429	12/5/68	
"Sing the Blues to Daddy" (w/Bobby Bare)	WWA4-7477	12/16/68	LSP-4137
"Sing the Girls a Song Bill"	1101		A&M 753
"Six Strings Away"	WWA4-4743	8/6/68	47-9642
			LSP-4085
"Six White Horses"	XWA4-2524	10/30/69	LSP-4487
"Slow Movin' Outlaw"	DWA4-0806	10/29/73	APL1-0539
"Slow Rollin' Low"	DWA4-0803	10/17/73	APL1-0539
"Slow Rollin' Low" (live)	DWA5-1208	9/25/74	
"Slow Rollin' Low" (from "Moonrunners" film soundtrack)		1974	
"So Good Woman"	FWA5-0831	3/23/76	APL1-1816
			PB-10842
"Some Kind of Fool"	AWA4-1422	5/12/71	
"Something's Wrong in California"	WWA4-7424	12/4/68	74-0105
			LSP-4341
"Song for the Life"	LWA5-6623	9/17/81	AHL1-4247
"Sorrow (Breaks a Good Man Down)"	UWA4-2711	8/29/67	LPM/S-4023
			74-0281
"Sortin' Things Out" (instrumental)	EWA4-1074	10/14/75	
"Spanish Penthouse" (instrumental)	TWA4-1425	8/30/66	LPM/S-3736
"Stars in Heaven" (see: The Stage)			
"Stay All Night" (w/Willie Nelson)		1973	SD-7262
			APL1-1520
"Stepping Stone"			A&M SP-4238
"Stop the World and Let Me Off"	SWA4-2337	3/18/65	47-8652
			LPM/S-3523
			ACL1-0306
"Stop the World and Let Me Off" (live)	DWA5-1207	9/25/74	
"Storms Never Last" (w/Jessi Colter)	KWA5-8344		AHL1-3602
"Storms Never Last" (w/Jessi Colter)	KWA5-8703	12/8/80	AAL1-3931
"Straighten My Mind"	UWA4-2789	9/20/67	LSP-4137
"Such a Waste of Love"	WWA4-1879	2/9/68	LPM/S-4023
"Summer Wages"	CWA4-1166	2/20/73	
"Sunday Morning Coming Down"	XWA4-2516	10/29/69	LSP-4487
"Sunset and Vine"	TWA4-0901	5/24/66	LPM/S-3660
"Sure Didn't Take Him Long"	BWA4-1021	1/11/72	74-0716
			LSP-4751
"Sure Didn't Take Him Long" (live)	DWA5-1317	9/26/74	
"Suspicious Minds" (w/Jessi Colter)	ZWA4-1732	8/18/70	47-9920
			APL1-1321
			GB-10928
"Sweet Caroline"	GWA5-2536	1/5/77	APL1-2317

Title	Master Number	Recording Date	Release Number
"Sweet Dream Woman"	AWA4-1781	9/1/71	LSP-4647
			74-0716
"Sweetheart" (w/Jessi Colter)	ZWA4-1735	8/19/70	
"Sweet Music Man"	KWA5-8343		AHL1-3602
"Taos, New Mexico"	TWA4-0618	2/17/66	LPM/S-3825
"Tennessee"	TWA4-1417	7/5/66	LPM/S-3736
"T for Texas"	CWA1-1090	1/22/73	
"T for Texas" (live)	DWA5-1203	9/25/74	APL1-1108
"Thanks"	ZWA4-1699	7/14/70	LSP-4751
"That'll Be the Day"		5/5/73	
"That's All Right" (Elvis medley)	GWA5-2540	1/8/77	APL1-2317
"That's the Chance I'll Have to Take"	SWA4-2339	3/19/65	47-8572
			LPM/S-3523
"(That's What You Get) For Lovin' Me"	TWA4-0615	2/17/66	47-8917
			LPM/S-3620
			CAS-2556
"The Bite" (instrumental)	EWA4-1087	10/21/75	
"The Cabin" (w/The Earl Scruggs Revue)		1978	JC-35319
"The Chokin' Kind"	UWA4-2383	4/26/67	
"The Chokin' Kind"	UWA4-2388	4/27/67	47-9259
			LPM/S-3918
			SPS-33-570
"The Crowd"	UWA4-2710	8/29/67	LPM/S-3918
"The Door Is Always Open"	EWA4-0766	9/2/74	APL1-1062
"The Everglades"	TWA4-0900	5/24/66	LPM/S-3660
"The Hunger"	DWA5-1120	7/16/74	APL1-0734
"The Last Letter"	DWA5-1125	7/16/74	
"The Last One to Leave Seattle"	BWA4-1957	12/18/72	
"The Leaving Coming On"	CWA4-1169	2/21/73	
"Theme From The Dukes of Hazzard"	KWA5-8340		AHL1-3602
			PB-12067
"Them Old Love Songs"	FWA5-0832	3/23/76	APL1-1816
"The One I Sing My Love Songs To"	DWA5-1124	7/16/74	
"The Race Is On"	1102		A&M 753
			A&M SP-4238
"There Ain't No Good Chain Gang" (w/Johnny Cash)	NCO-120871	7/6/76	KC-35313
			3-10742
			KC-35637
"The Real House of the Rising Sun"	1120		A&M SP-4238
			A&M 762
"The Road"	UWA4-2187	2/14/67	LPM/S-3825
"These New Changing Times" (w/The Kimberlys)	XWA4-1426	4/19/69	LSP-4180
			47-9782
"The Southland's Bleeding"		1/78	A&M SP-6004
"The Stage" (also titled: "Stars in Heaven")		1960/1961	TREND-106

Title	Master Number	Recording Date	Release Number
"The Taker"	zwa4-1364	4/22/70	47-9885
			lsp-4487
			sps-33-570
"The Taker" (live)	dwa5-1212	9/25/74	
"The Thirty-Third of August"	xwa4-1628	6/12/69	lsp-4260
			sps-33-570
"The Union Mare and the Confederate Gray"		1/78	a&m sp-6004
"The Year 2003 Minus 25" (w/Willie Nelson)	gwa5-2887	11/77	afl1-2686
"They Laid Waste to Our Land"		1/78	a&m sp-6004
"This Is Getting Funny"	fwa5-1195	12/17/76	apl1-2317
"This Time"	dwa4-0800	10/29/73	apl1-0539
			apb0-0251
"This Time" (live)	dwa5-1211	9/25/74	apl1-1108
"This Time Tomorrow (I'll Be Gone)"	xwa4-2521	10/30/69	lsp-4260
"Tiger by the Tail"	twa4-0905	6/1/66	lpm/s-3660
"Till I Gain Control Again"	gwa5-2538	1/7/77	apl1-2317
"Time Between Bottles of Wine"	xpa3-0814	12/17/69	lsp-4418
"Time to Bum Again"	twa4-0612	2/16/66	47-8822
			lpm/s-3620
			cas-2556
			cas-2608
"Time Will Tell the Story"	swa4-2336	3/18/65	47-8917
			lpm/s-3620
"To Beat the Devil"	zwa4-1015	2/27/70	lsp-4647
"Today Is Mine" (from "Moonrunners" soundtrack)		1974	
"Today I Started Loving You Again"	wwa4-4741	8/6/68	lsp-4085
			cas-2608
"Tomorrow Night in Baltimore"	zwa4-1701	7/14/70	lsp-4567
			sps-33-570
"Tonight the Bottle Let Me Down"	hwa5-5168	4-5/78	afl1-2979
"Too Far Gone"	wwa4-2080	4/16/68	lpm/s-4023
"Tulsa"	zwa4-1855	10/12/70	47-9925
			lsp-4487
"Twelfth of Never"			a&m sp-4238
"Two Streaks of Steel"	uwa4-2192	2/15/67	lpm/s-3825
"Unchained Melody"			a&m sp-4238
"Under Your Spell Again" (w/Jessi Colter)	awa4-1130	3/11/71	47-9992
			lsp-4751
"Unsatisfied"	awa4-1777	8/31/72	lsp-4647
"Walking"	dwa4-0808	10/16/73	apl1-0539
"Walking" (live)	dwa5-1308	9/26/74	
"Walk on Out of My Mind"	uwa4-2716	8/30/67	
"Walk on Out of My Mind"	uwa4-2792	11/9/67	47-9414
			lpm/s-4023
			lsp-4341

Title	Master Number	Recording Date	Release Number
"Waltz Across Texas"	KWA5-8347		AHL1-3602
"Wave Goodbye to Me"	UWA4-2712	8/29/67	LPM/S-4023
"Waylon and Willie" (w/Willie Nelson and Don Bowman)		1979	L-4605
"Waymore's Blues"	EWA4-0737	9/3/74	APL1-1062
			PB-10270
"Weakness in a Man"	WWA4-2081	4/16/68	LPM/S-4023
"We Had It All"	CWA4-1265	3/13/73	74-0961
			APL1-0240
"We Had It All" (live)	DWA5-1310	9/26/74	
"Well All Right" (Buddy Holly medley)	DPA3-1611	5/17/74	AFL1-2979
"We Made It As Lovers (We Just Couldn't Make It As Friends)"	LWA5-6619	9/18/81	AHL1-4247
"What About You"	ZWA4-1698	7/14/70	
"What About You"	KWA5-8346		AHL1-3602
"What Goes Around Comes Around"	JWA5-7801	7/26/79	AHL1-3493
"What Makes a Man Wander"	SWA4-2650	7/28/65	LPM/S-3523
"What's Happened to Blue Eyes"	KWA5-8702	12/8/80	AAL1-3931
"What's Left of Me"	SWA4-2341	3/19/65	LPM/S-3523
"When She Cries"	CWA4-1267	3/13/73	
"When Sin Stops"		1958	BR9-55130
"When the World Has Turned You Down" (w/Ernest Tubb)		1978	FGLP-0002
"Where Love Has Died"	XWA4-2519	10/29/69	LSP-4260
"Whiskey Man" (from "Moonrunners" film soundtrack)		1974	
"Whistlers and Jugglers"	HWA5-5170	4-5/78	AFL1-2979
"White Lightning"		12/64	BAT-1001
			VL-73873
"Wild Side of Life" (w/Jessi Colter)	KWA5-8699	12/15/80	AAL1-3931
"Willie, Ain't You Ever Comin' Home"	XWA4-1630	6/12/69	
"Willie and Laura Mae Jones"	XWA4-2307	8/19/69	LSP-4647
"Willy, the Wandering Gypsy and Me"	BWA4-1432	12/14/72	
"Willy, the Wandering Gypsy and Me"	CWA4-1163	2/19/73	APL1-0240
			APB0-0086
"Willy, the Wandering Gypsy and Me" (live)	DWA5-1201	9/25/74	
"Woman, Don't You Ever Laugh at Me"	UWA4-2188	2/14/67	LPM/S-3918
"Woman Let Me Sing You a Song"	TWA4-0897	5/24/66	LPM/S-3660
"Woman You Need a Man"	ZWA4-1013	2/27/70	
"Women Do Know How to Carry On"	LWA5-6616	9/21/81	AHL1-4247

Title	Master Number	Recording Date	Release Number
"Wurlitzer Prize"	GWA5-2702	8/14/77	PB-1118
			AFL1-2686
"Yellow Haired Woman"	XWA4-2530	10/30/69	LSP-4260
"Yes, Virginia"	TWA4-1317	9/9/66	CAL/S-2183
			ACL1-7019
"Yes, Virginia"	UWA4-2391	4/27/67	LSP-4260
"You Are My Sunshine" (w/Duane Eddy)			EPIC-45359
"You Ask Me To"	CWA4-1302	4/10/73	APL1-0240
"You Ask Me To"	CWA4-1517	8/3/73	APB0-0086
"You Ask Me To" (live)	DWA5-1199	9/25/74	
"You Beat All I Ever Saw"	TWA4-1596	8/30/66	CAL/S-2183
			APL1-7019
"You Can Have Her"	BWA4-1190	3/9/72	74-9886
			LSP-4854
"You Can Have Her" (live)	DWA5-1303	9/26/74	
"You'll Look for Me"	ZWA4-1700	7/14/70	47-9925
			LSP-4487
"You'll Think of Me"	WWA4-1877	2/9/68	LSP-4023
"You Love the Ground I Walk On"	UWA4-2791	9/20/67	LSP-4085
"You Nearly Lose Your Mind" (w/Ernest Tubb)		1978	FGLP-0002
"You Never Can Tell (C'est la Vie)" (w/Jessi Colter)	KWA5-8696	12/15/80	AAL1-3931
"Young Widow Brown"	TWA4-1319	9/9/66	LPM/S-3825
"You're Gonna Wonder About Me"	TWA4-0623	2/18/66	LPM/S-3620
"You're Not My Same Sweet Baby"	KWA5-8705		AAL1-3931
"Yours Love"	WWA4-2077	4/16/68	47-9642
			LSP-4085
			CAS-2608
"You've Got to Hide Your Love Away"	UWA4-2191	2/15/67	LPM/S-3825
"You Were Never There" (w/Jessi Colter)			PD-1-6344

WAYLON JENNINGS SINGLE RELEASE LISTING

BR9-55130	"Jole Blon"	3/59
	"When Sin Stops"	
TREND-102	"Another Blue Day"	1961
	"Never Again"	
TREND-106	"My Baby Walks All Over Me"	4/63
	"The Stage"	
A&M 722	"Love Denied"	4/64
	"Rave On"	

A&M 739	"Four Strong Winds"	8/64
	"Just to Satisfy You"	
A&M 753	"Sing the Girls a Song Bill"	10/64
	The Race Is On"	
A&M 762	"I Don't Believe You"	1965
	"The Real House of the Rising Sun"	
BAT-121639	"Crying"	
	"Dream Baby"	
47-8572	"I Wonder Just Where I Went Wrong"	5/65
	"That's the Chance I'll Have to Take"	
47-8652	"Stop the World and Let Me Off"	8/65
	"Dark Side of Fame"	
47-8729	"Look into My Teardrops"	12/65
	"Anita, You're Dreaming"	
47-8822	"Time to Bum Again"	4/66
	"Norwegian Wood"	
47-8917	"Time Will Tell the Story"	8/66
	"That's What You Get for Loving Me"	
47-9025	"Silver Ribbons"	11/66
	"Green River"	
47-9146	"Born to Love You"	3/67
	"Mental Revenge"	
47-9229	"Chet's Tune"	6/67
RAMCO-1989	"Never Again"	7/67
	"My Baby Walks All Over Me"	
47-9259	"Love of the Common People"	7/67
	"The Chokin' Kind"	
RAMCO-1997	"My World"	12/67
	"Another Blue Day"	
47-9414	"Julie"	12/67
	"Walk on Out of My Mind"	
47-9480	"No One's Gonna Miss Me" (w/Anita Carter)	3/68
	"I Got You" (w/Anita Carter)	
47-9561	"Right Before My Eyes"	6/68
	"Only Daddy That'll Walk the Line"	
447-0797	"Anita, You're Dreaming"	9/68
	"Love of the Common People"	
47-9642	"Yours Love"	10/68
	"Six Strings Away"	
74-0105	"Something's Wrong in California"	2/69
	"Farewell Party"	
74-0133	"Poor Old Ugly Gladys Jones" (w/Don Bowman)	4/69
74-0157	"Delia's Gone"	4/69
	"Days of Sand and Shovels"	
74-0210	"MacArthur Park" (w/Kimberlys)	7/69
	"But You Know I Love You" (w/Kimberlys)	
74-0280	"I Ain't the One" (w/Jessi Colter)	10/69

74-0281	"Sorrow Breaks a Good Man Down"	10/69
	"Brown Eyed Handsome Man"	
47-9782	"These New Changing Times"	11/69
	(w/Kimberlys)	
	"Driving Nails in the Wall" (w/Kimberlys)	
47-9819	"Lila"	3/70
	"Singer of Sad Songs"	
47-9885	"The Taker"	7/70
	"Shadow of the Gallows"	
47-9920	"I Ain't the One" (w/Jessi Colter)	10/70
	"Suspicious Minds" (w/Jessi Colter)	
47-9925	"You'll Look for Me"	10/70
	"Tulsa"	
447-0836	"Only Daddy That'll Walk the Line"	12/70
	"Brown Eyed Handsome Man"	
47-9967	"Life Goes On"	3/71
	"Mississippi Woman"	
47-9992	"Bridge Over Troubled Water" (w/Jessi	5/71
	Colter)	
	"Under Your Spell Again" (w/Jessi Colter)	
48-1003	"Cedartown, Georgia"	7/71
	"I Think It's Time She Learned"	
74-0615	"It's All Over Now"	12/71
	"Good Hearted Woman"	
74-0716	"Sweet Dream Woman"	5/72
	"Sure Didn't Take Him Long"	
74-0808	"Nothin' Worth Takin' or Leavin' "	9/72
	"Pretend I Never Happened"	
74-0886	"Gone to Denver"	1/73
	"You Can Have Her"	
74-0961	"Do No Good Woman"	5/73
	"We Had It All"	
APB0-0086	"You Asked Me To"	9/73
	"Willy; the Wandering Gypsy and Me"	
APB0-0251	"This Time"	3/74
	"Mona"	
PB-10020	"I'm a Ramblin' Man"	7/74
	"Got a Lot Going for Me"	
PB-10142	"Rainy Day Woman"	12/74
	"Let's All Help the Cowboys Sing the	
	Blues"	
PB-10270	"Dreaming My Dreams"	4/75
	"Waymore's Blues"	
PB-10379	"Bob Wills Is Still the King"	8/75
	"Are You Sure Hank Done It This Way"	
PB-10529	"Good Hearted Woman" (w/Willie	12/75
	Nelson)	
	"Heaven or Hell" (w/Willie Nelson)	
PB-10653	"Suspicious Minds" (w/Jessi Colter)	4/76
	"I Ain't the One" (w/Jessi Colter)	

PB-10721	"Can't You See"	7/76
	"I'll Go Back to Her"	
PB-10842	"Are You Ready for the Country"	12/76
	"So Good Woman"	
PB-10924	"Luckenbach, Texas" (w/Willie Nelson)	4/77
	"Belle of the Ball"	
GB-10927	"Dreaming My Dreams"	9/77
	"Can't You See"	
GB-10928	"Good Hearted Woman" (w/Willie Nelson)	9/77
	"Suspicious Minds" (w/Jessi Colter)	
PB-11118	"The Wurlitzer Prize"	9/77
	"Lookin' for a Feelin' "	
E-45359	"You Are My Sunshine" (Duane Eddy) (w/Waylon and Willie)	
PB-11198	"Mammas Don't Let Your Babies Grow Up to Be Cowboys"	1/78
	"I Can Get Off On You"	
3-10742	"There Ain't No Good Chain Gang" (w/Johnny Cash)	5/78
	"I Wish I Was Crazy Again" (w/Johnny Cash)	
PB-11344	"I've Always Been Crazy"	8/78
	"I Never Said It Would Be Easy"	
PB-11390	"Don't You Think This Outlaw Bit's Done Got Out of Hand"	11/78
	"Girl I Can Tell (You're Trying to Work It Out)"	
PB-11596	"Amanda"	6/79
	"Lonesome, On'ry and Mean"	
PB-11723	"Come with Me"	10/79
	"Mes'kin" (instrumental)	
PB-11898	"Ain't Living Long Like This"	1/80
	"The World's Gone Crazy"	
PB-12007	"Clyde"	6/80
	"I Came Here to Party"	
PB-12067	"Theme From the Dukes of Hazzard"	8/80
	"It's Alright"	
PB-12176	"Storms Never Last" (w/Jessi Colter)	/81
	"I Ain't The One" (w/Jessi Colter)	
PB-12367	"Shine"	2/82
	"White Water" (instrumental)	

WAYLON JENNINGS ALBUM RELEASE LISTING

SOUND LTD 1001	*Waylon Jennings at JD's*	12/64
LPM/S-3523	*Folk-Country*	3/66
LPM/S-3620	*Leavin' Town*	10/66

LPM/S-3736	*Nashville Rebel*	12/66
LPM/S-3660	*Waylon Sings Ol' Harlan*	3/67
LPM/S-3825	*Love of the Common People*	8/67
CAL/S-2183	*The One and Only*	11/67
LPM/S-3918	*Hanging On*	2/68
LPM/S-4023	*Only the Greatest*	7/68
LPM/S-4085	*Jewels*	12/68
LSP-4137	*Just to Satisfy You*	3/69
VL-73873	*Waylon Jennings*	7/69
LSP-4180	*Country Folk (w/The Kimberlys)*	8/69
LSP-4260	*Waylon*	1/70
A&M SP-4238	*Don't Think Twice*	3/70
LSP-4333	*A Country Star Is Born (Jessi Colter)*	
LSP-4341	*The Best of Waylon Jennings*	6/70
UAS-5213	*Ned Kelly*	7/70
LSP-4418	*Singer of Sad Songs*	11/70
LSP-4487	*The Taker/Tulsa*	2/71
LSP-4567	*Cedartown, Georgia*	8/71
LSP-4647	*Good Hearted Woman*	2/72
CAS-2556	*Heartaches by the Numbers*	3/72
SPS-33-570	*Get Into Waylon Jennings*	5/72
LSP-4751	*Ladies Love Outlaws*	9/72
CAS-2608	*Ruby, Don't Take Your Love to Town*	2/73
LSP-4854	*Lonesome, On'ry and Mean*	3/73
APL1-0240	*Honky Tonk Heroes*	7/73
ACL1-0306	*Only Daddy That'll Walk the Line*	1/74
APL1-0539	*This Time*	4/74
APL1-0734	*Ramblin' Man*	9/74
APL1-1062	*Dreaming My Dreams*	6/75
APL1-1321	*Wanted: The Outlaws*	1/76
APL1-1520	*Mackintosh and TJ*	3/76
APL1-1816	*Are You Ready for the Country*	6/76
ACL1-7019	*The Dark Side of Fame* (reissue of CAS-2183)	10/76
APL1-1108	*Waylon - Live*	12/76
APL1-2317	*Ol' Waylon*	4/77
AFL1-2686	*Waylon and Willie*	1/78
KC-35313	*I Would Like to See You Again* (Johnny Cash)	4/78
A&M SP-6004	*White Mansions*	7/78
AFL1-2979	*I've Always Been Crazy*	9/78
KC-35637	*Johnny Cash - Greatest Hits Volume Three*	10/78
AHL1-3378	*Waylon - Greatest Hits*	4/79
FGLP-0002	*Ernest Tubb - The Legend and the Legacy*	5/79
CPL1-3406	*Waylon - Greatest Hits* (picture disc)	8/79
BFX-15029	*Rave On* (Europe)	9/79
CDL-8501	*Early Years* (Europe)	9/79
AHL1-3493	*What Goes Around Comes Around*	11/79
EPIC-35544	*George Jones and Friends*	11/79
AHL1-3602	*Music Man*	5/80
PL-43166	*Waylon Music* (Europe)	1/81

AAL1-3931	*Leather and Lace* (w/Jessi Colter)	1/82
PD1-6344	*The Pursuit of D.B. Cooper* (soundtrack) (w/Jessi Colter)	1/82
AHL1-4247	*Black on Black*	2/82
AHL1-4455	*WW II* (w/Willie Nelson)	9/82

INDEX

WAYLON: A Biography has been set on the Linotron 202N in eleven point Garamond with one point of spacing between lines. Times Roman has also been used as display. The book was designed by Jim Billingsley, composed by Williams of Chattanooga, printed offset by Thomson-Shore, Inc., Dexter, Michigan, and bound by John H. Dekker & Sons, Grand Rapids, Michigan. The paper on which the book is printed bears the watermark of S. D. Warren and is designed for an effective life of at least three hundred years.

THE UNIVERSITY OF TENNESSEE PRESS : KNOXVILLE